The Economics of Feasible Socialism

The Economics
of Feasible Socialism

Alec Nove

Emeritus Professor of Economics, University of Glasgow

London
GEORGE ALLEN & UNWIN
Boston   Sydney

11/27/84

George Allen & Unwin (Publishers) Ltd,
40 Museum Street, London WC1A 1LU, UK

George Allen & Unwin (Publishers) Ltd,
Park Lane, Hemel Hempstead, Herts HP2 4TE, UK

Allen & Unwin, Inc.,
9 Winchester Terrace, Winchester, Mass 01890, USA

George Allen & Unwin Australia Pty Ltd,
8 Napier Street, North Sydney, NSW 2060, Australia

First published in 1983

British Library Cataloguing in Publication Data

Nove, Alec
    The economics of feasible socialism.
1. Marxian economics
I. Title
335.4'08   HB97.5
ISBN 0-04-335048-8
ISBN 0-04-335049-6

Library of Congress Cataloging in Publication Data

Nove, Alec
    The economics of feasible socialism.
    Includes bibliographical references.
1. Socialism. 2. Socialism – History. 3. Marxian economics.
4. Economic history. I. Title.
HX73.N67 1983   338.9'009171'7   82-18169
ISBN 0-04-335048-8
ISBN 0-04-335049-6 (pbk.)

Set in 10 on 11 point Plantin by Typesetters (Birmingham) Ltd
and printed in Great Britain
by Mackays of Chatham

Contents

Une société d'où la justice et la morale seraient bannies ne saurait évidemment subsister.

(V. Pareto)

The political uniqueness of our own era then is this; we have lived and still live through a desperate political and social malaise, while at the same time we have *outlived* the desperate revolutionary remedies that had once been thought to solve them.

Alvin W. Gouldner

Preface

The word 'socialism' is apt to produce strong feelings, of enthusiasm, cynicism, hostility. It is the road to a future just society, or to serfdom. It is the next stage of an ineluctable historical process, or a tragic aberration, a cul-de-sac, into which the deluded masses are drawn by power-hungry agitator-intellectuals. My own attitude will emerge in the pages that follow. Let me make it clear that my object is not propagandist, in either direction. It is to explore what *could be* a workable, feasible sort of socialism, which might be achieved within the lifetime of a child already conceived. I have spent the last quarter-century studying and trying to understand the 'socialist' countries of Eastern Europe. Brought up in a social-democratic environment, son of a Menshevik who was arrested by the Bolsheviks, I inherited a somewhat critical view of Soviet reality: if this really was socialism, I would prefer to be elsewhere. (Luckily, I *was* elsewhere!) Of course the Soviet system did not take the shape it did because of 'betrayal', or the accident of Stalin's personality. I have tried to describe the way in which the system developed, paying particular attention to the economic aspect. I have listened to critics who have contrasted the Soviet variety of socialism with the vision of Marx. That there are differences is obvious, but plainly it is not enough to note them, and then to criticise the reality of the USSR because it does not conform to the vision of Marx, or indeed of Lenin. What if the vision is unrealisable, contradictory? Does it make sense to 'blame' Stalin and his successors for not having achieved what cannot be achieved in the real world? Can the excesses and crimes which they *did* commit in the real world have been due in some part to the doctrines they espoused? (If a loyal Marxist protests that these doctrines were humanist, that they did not envisage a despotic society or mass repression, one can remind him or her of what happened in other countries with a Christian doctrine – and that fellow-Christians were the most numerous victims!) As an economist, I have been struck by the fact that the functional logic of centralised planning 'fits' far too easily into the practice of centralised despotism.

Very well, but what is the alternative? Marx contrasted socialism utopian with socialism scientific. For reasons which will be expounded in the first part of this book, I believe that Marx's socialism was utopian. Can there be a 'socialism scientific'? Not 'scientific' in the sense that it can be proved 'scientifically' that this is the way history marches, nor yet in the form of a blueprint of a perfect society which we would call 'socialist'. Nothing perfect, nothing optimal. Something that can reasonably be expected to function with a reasonable probability of avoiding both despotism and intolerable inefficiency.

I feel increasingly ill-disposed towards those latter-day Marxists who airily ascribe all the world's evils to 'capitalism', dismiss the Soviet experience as

irrelevant, and substitute for hard thinking an image of a post-revolutionary
world in which there would be no economic problems at all (or where any
problems that might arise would be handled smoothly by the 'associated
producers' of a world commonwealth). I feel not too well-disposed either
towards the Chicago school, whose belief in 'free enterprise' seems quite
unaffected by the growth of giant bureaucratic corporations, and whose
remedies for current ills seem to benefit the rich and ignore unemployment.
And even Milton Friedman is preferable to the abstract model-builders whose
works fill the pages of our professional journals, since he at least advocates
action in the real world (even though I believe the action he advocates is
wrong).

Unexpectedly, I find myself quoting an American theologian:

> At least we've got to examine socialism and not let it be a 'scare-word' of the
> generation; at least we've got to challenge capitalism and not let it be the
> sacrosanct word of the generation; at least we've got to investigate some new
> mixes of the two that don't escalate into Stalinism, but also don't escalate
> into the mind-blowing profits that are clutched by the few at the cost of
> hope, and even life, to the many.*

Yes, I know that the profit rate has fallen in recent years. Nor is it by any
means obvious that the poor are poor *because* successful businessmen make a
great deal of money. None the less, I do find the present distribution of wealth
offensive, especially as it seems to bear so little relationship to any real contribution to welfare in any recognisable sense.

So I have put to myself some questions. What species of socialism *could* be
envisaged? Would such a socialism be free of the defects of the Soviet model
and of other 'really existing' variants? Could it operate with reasonable
efficiency, and give satisfaction to the citizens in their capacities as consumers
and producers? Since economic and social problems cannot be assumed out of
existence, a realistically conceived socialist society will have to cope with
them, there will be contradictions, there will be strains, disputes. If human
beings are free to choose, they are also free to choose wrongly, and there
would be conflicts with choices made by others.

The plan of this book is as follows. After a brief examination of why it is
that socialist ideas and aims must be taken seriously, I launch into a critical
review of Marx's ideas on socialism which, to my mind, are very seriously
defective and misleading. This is followed by an examination of the
experience of the USSR and some other countries which have sought to
introduce 'socialism', to see what lessons can be drawn. I also discuss there the
lessons which some existing critics have already drawn, and the alternatives
they propose. This is followed by a discussion of the problems of transition:
how can one move towards an acceptable form of socialism, bearing in mind
the many errors which can be (have been) committed on what was thought to
be the way? Finally, a sketch is attempted of an economic system which would

*Robert McAfee Brown, 'Theological implications of the arms race' (undated, presumably 1961).

have two characteristics: it would be called socialist, and it could work, within a reasonable time scale.

All this may seem vastly ambitious. A German colleague to whom I described my intentions smiled and said: 'All you want is to replace "Das Kapital" with "Das Sozial".' This is not so. Apart from my intellectual limitations, the task would call for a multi-volume treatise. All that is being attempted here is to put forward ideas which could be further discussed, which certainly need further development. I hope readers will not consider the ideas half-baked; but they do not pretend to be complete.

I must particularly thank Wlodimierz Brus, Agota Dezsenyi-Gueullette, Michael Ellmann, Radoslav Selucky and Ljubo Sirc who read several parts and made critical comments. I had the benefit of advice from, and discussions with, Dubravko Matko, Xavier Richet, Louis Baslé, Robert Tartarin, Marie Lavigne, Jan Elster, participants in seminars in Paris, Amsterdam and Oxford, and several Hungarians who should remain anonymous. Thanks, too, to my University of Glasgow, for providing a stimulating environment and giving me time for study and travel. Last but far from least, I am grateful for the work of Elizabeth Hunter in deciphering my writing and typing the text. The remaining sins of omission and commission are all my own work.

A Note on the Notes

The notes are at the end of each part. Where the work cited is in a foreign language, the translations are my own (unless otherwise stated). Titles of articles are only given when they seem relevant to the theme, or are needed for identification. I have provided no bibliography, because the notes contain a great many references to works of importance on this subject, and a full list of books bearing on the economic problems of socialism, or Marxism, would fill a large volume.

Introduction: Socialism – Why?

This book is about 'feasible socialism'. Its author must therefore declare his interest. Why write about this theme? Is the author intending to mount an attack on socialism in the name of efficient allocation of resources, Pareto optimality and the virtues of free enterprise? And what 'socialism' does he have in mind?

Let us leave this last and very important question aside for the present: one reason for writing this book is precisely to help to arrive at a definition of a socialism that is feasible, that could work with reasonable effectiveness (since a socialism that does not function can be of little help to anyone). Let me put a few cards on the table, by explaining my motives and my starting point. In doing so I shall make some very sweeping generalisations. The reader will, I trust, forgive me if I do not write a long essay defending each general statement and modifying it to fit the many exceptions and modifications that it doubtless needs.

First, it appears to me that the basic assumptions of liberal capitalism are ceasing to be true. At one time it really was the case that the pursuit of personal and sectional interest, on balance, was the way to obtain the best available approximation to the general interest. Of course, there were many exceptions – there always are – but the rationality of a free market economy tended to prevail, and appeared superior to any possible alternative arrangement of our society. To Hayek or Friedman it seems still to be the case today. However, several factors are now working against the efficacy, or even the survival, of the liberal-capitalist model. Many of these have to do with the consequences of *scale* and of *specialisation*. The polarisation of society into a small group of super-monopoly-capitalists and impoverished proletarians foreseen by Marx has not come to pass, and there are indeed a multitude of small businesses, while large packets of shares in big business are held by pension funds and insurance companies, representing aggregations of predominantly small savings. But, when all allowance is made for this, the fact remains that enormous business corporations and conglomerates dominate a whole series of vital industries, and many of the small businesses are highly dependent upon being subcontractors to the giants. Some interesting theories about the motivations of managers of large corporations have developed in the last few decades, which put into question some axioms such as profit 'maximisation', but this aspect we will leave aside. The important points in the present context are:

(*a*) monopoly power and its social-economic consequences,
(*b*) vulnerability,
(*c*) alienation.

Monopoly is, of course, almost always relative. There will usually be close substitutes, or some species of monopsony or monopolistic competition. It is not my purpose to enter into controversy on the relative efficiency of the large corporation, its contribution to innovation, and so on. Its decisions affect many thousands of people and could cause grave distress to whole conurbations which rely on it for employment. Its sheer size and the remoteness of its headquarters – in another country in the case of multi-nationals – complicate labour relations, and can lead to damaging disputes. The greater the degree of monopoly power, the more it is possible to increase profits at the expense of the customer or of quality or of choice, for the less is the importance of the customer's goodwill (a point too easily overlooked by those who try to devise criteria for nationalised monopolies in Britain, for instance). The small number of giants and the power they wield has led to a reconsideration of an economic theory based upon an infinite number of competing units, a theory of the 'firm' which, at its worst (in the words of Shubik), sees no difference between General Motors and a corner ice-cream shop. There has been recourse to games theory, and much research on business behaviour and on how prices are actually determined or 'admin-istered'. Joan Robinson's and Chamberlin's insights about imperfect com-petition have been deepened. Side by side with mathematically elegant and abstract general-equilibrium models, we have seen growing concern with the consequences of increasing returns, and their converse, increasing unit costs when production declines, leading to higher (cost-based) prices at a time of falling demand. Monopoly power also has its political aspects: both govern-ment control over monopolies, and the power of large corporations over government.

There is also the monopoly power of trade unions, which has increased *pari passu* with the vulnerability of the economy to attack from sectional interest groups. We all know that a quite small group of key workers in one com-ponent factory can cause enormous damage to industry. Specialisation by plant and by trade has added greatly to this power. Right-wing analysts stress, understandably, the harm trade unions can do to productivity, competitive-ness and, ultimately, to the living standards of the union members them-selves. In so far as this is indeed so, it is another illustration of the thesis advanced above: that the pursuit of sectional interest has ceased to be com-patible with the general interest, including in some cases that of the group pursuing the sectional interest. Lest the words 'general interest' upset the orthodox left ('What about the class struggle?'), let me at once explain that the above statement remains valid even if confined to the working class as a whole. Surely it cannot be seriously disputed that repeated work stoppages, plus a variety of restrictive practices, must adversely affect productivity, and it is a naive socialist indeed who fails to note that there is some connection between productivity and the level of real wages. Yes, I am aware that pro-ductivity is affected also by the quality of management and the level (and nature) of investments. Perhaps it can also be recognised that industrial relations are not a zero-sum game, that when (as in West Germany and Japan) there is industrial peace and efficient management, both managers and workers reap the benefit. All this is not an argument for 'reformism', just a simple statement of fact. Industrial strife could be the deliberate aim of those who wish to 'bash the unions', and certainly *is* the deliberate aim of revolutionary groups who desire to destabilise and overthrow existing society. However, the essential feature of the situation does not relate to plots of ultra-right or ultra-left: groups pressing their demands, their 'just claims', may be of no political colouring, and the disruption of the economy is usually the consequence of what is believed to be self-interest, justified by the fact that the basic ideology of society is the pursuit of self-interest ('Look after Number One', 'I'm all right, Jack', and other modern proverbs).

There is taking place in many Western countries a breakdown in traditional deference, in the willingness to obey the boss because he is the boss, which is due to more than simply a greater sense of security. Income inequalities formerly taken for granted come to be resented – and this can happen in a stratified communist-ruled country such as Poland, as well as in, say, Italy or Sweden. Some forms of inequality or privilege are indeed irrational, or can easily and reasonably seem so.

I find it hard to accept that merely allowing others to use my money, or my land, is a 'productive' activity, on a par with actually working – though naturally management is work, too, and of course it should be efficient. Why should vast riches go to those who have had the luck to own some oil-bearing land, or to have forebears who were given land in exchange for services rendered (sometimes in bed) to some long-dead monarch? This has nothing whatever to do with any contribution to production or welfare in any sense, and makes it seem more than a little silly to urge 'wage restraint' at a time when the very rich do not need to work at all. Industrial leadership, company directorships, too often go to those with the right birth, connections and shareholdings, and they may or may not be the most efficient at their job. In Britain at least the breakdown in deference is accompanied, in some cases deservedly, by lack of respect for the competence of senior management. This is combined with a sense of alienation: large-scale units are run by virtually unknown bosses; the outcome of the work, and its organisation, is none of the business of the workforce. Their lack of interest and commitment can affect not only their job-satisfaction but also efficiency and productivity. Conversely, pride in work, a sense of achievement and identity, has a positive economic effect, too often ignored in textbooks on microeconomics. One has only to study a country in which, for reasons not easily understood by Europeans, this effect seems to have been achieved: Japan.

All this is connected also with inflation. Powerful groups in society ask for more. This leads to *excess demands*. Purely monetarist 'explanations' of inflation seem remarkably superficial. There have always, of course, been people who have wanted more – more wages, more social benefits, more defence spending, or whatever. History provides numerous examples of debasing coinage, printing too much money, and so on. But it is surely significant that worldwide inflation, affecting countries under very different political parties and regimes, or widely differing levels of development, should have become so universal, so difficult to combat. Needless to say, these pressures and demands do lead to an increase in the money supply (so Friedman is not 'wrong', but the real causes remain unanalysed by him).

Inflation has effects on economic behaviour which move it far from the paths of rationality. Ota Sik has argued that society's investments should not be an incidental consequence of the struggle to divide up the national income. It is one of the less satisfactory features of the neo-Ricardian or 'Sraffa' models that, even though they assume that investment is wholly financed from profits, real wages are seen as the result of the class struggle: what labour does not get the capitalists do, and vice versa. This is a sophisticated version of the zero-sum-game approach, and seems to me remarkably undynamic: even in the medium run, real wages can scarcely rise significantly without investments! Imagine a situation in which, by powerful class struggle, the workers reduce net profits to zero. There is then in the model no net investment, therefore no growth, because investment is assumed to be financed out of profits, directly or indirectly; increased production of consumers' goods could scarcely occur under these circumstances. But individuals or groups, understandably, see only their own individual or group interests. Nor is it a matter of stupidity or blinkered vision. It is impossible to demonstrate that any one segment of a complex society which demands more for its own consumption is thereby hindering the process of growth which could be financed by others. (Thus members of the Association of University Teachers quite reasonably ask for higher salaries, and would vote for lower taxes too, although their salaries are paid out of taxes, since there could always be less spent on something else, and their salaries represent a tiny percentage of the state budget.) So, although demanding more for current consumption, people may in fact be acting against their own best interests, but, from where they are situated, this *cannot* be seen. In a world in which each freely takes what he or she can, it is in the interest of any individual or group to pursue its own narrowly defined advantage, because others are doing so. (Perhaps instead of the 'prisoner's dilemma' we should speak of a free man's dilemma!)

But at the same time those who invest seek, understandably enough, a hedge against inflation, shelter from the prevailing uncertainty. This leads to a concentration on the short term, reflected in and reflecting the high rate of interest. It is quite logical, as in the case of the railway union pension fund, to 'invest' in old masters and to keep the paintings in a secret vault. It may pay the individual to keep money in Zurich. So, apart from the question of how much *should* be invested, the choices between investment alternatives are twisted out of shape, with a short time-horizon plus security as dominant aims. Of course, an element of risk-taking, the need to cope with uncertainty and imperfect information, always existed, and mistakes were made, gambles taken. But the decision-maker today is presented with a remarkably unclear and confused set of signals. It is hard enough to guess what the costs of materials, labour, the rate of interest, will be in six months' time, let alone six years' time (and it takes that long to build any large factory). At least all this sets up the presumption that rational investment decisions would represent a remarkable coincidence, rather than being the normal outcome of the institutional and economic circumstances.

Another aspect of 'rational' investments relates to their effects on employment. In the more developed countries there is increasing danger that labour-saving innovations will be introduced at a rate far exceeding the possibility of providing alternative jobs, with serious chronic unemployment as the consequence – and this apart from and in addition to unemployment that arises out of cyclical trends or deflationary policies. There is likely to exist a contradiction between the profitability of labour-saving at microeconomic levels and the macro and/or social consequences. There might have to be organised work-sharing, with much shorter hours, but neither the employers nor the trade unions seem able to focus on the problems of implementing such a strategy. Matters are exacerbated by the possibility – or perhaps even the likelihood – of material shortages which obstruct growth in output. To mention this does not imply the acceptance of a full gloom-and-doom scenario *à la* Club of Rome. But the energy crisis appears to be long-lasting, the troubles and disruptions among Third World producers of materials and fuels are all too likely to persist, and we can face various unpredictable bottlenecks. Some products, say, cocoa and iron ore, could be in ample supply, but demand for them would be constrained by production difficulties and recession occasioned by shortage of, say, oil and non-ferrous metals. Conventional economic analysis and the normal market mechanism are not well attuned to handling physical shortage. This is no doubt one reason why central controls are usually imposed in wartime. Or take another example: fish in the North Sea. Shortage causes higher prices, which stimulates further efforts to catch fish, which makes the shortage worse, and so on, until there are no fish. A higher profit is supposed to act as a stimulus to higher output, on the implied assumption that this does not run into physical limits which make higher output impossible. This is why, in the case of fish, government regulation is necessary. Such instances could become more common in the future, as issues of environmental protection have become already. (NB: I appreciate that in, for example, the USSR, scarce resources have been wastefully exploited, and the rivers and atmosphere polluted. The point is that this mode of behaviour can be quite consistent with private profit-making, whereas at least the *model* of a socialist planning system implies that such things should not happen. Why they *do* happen will be analysed later in this book.)

In general, socialists should be stressing the importance of *externalities*, these being circumstances in which effects external to the given transaction are sufficiently important to be taken into consideration. In a sense, every action has *some* external effects, but they are mostly insignificant, and the cost of taking them into account would be totally prohibitive. However, instances exist, and are recognised by all schools and ideologies, in which externalities matter: diseconomies, such as pollution, ugliness, congestion, noise, the killing of bees by insecticides, and so on; economies, such as the advantage obtained by third parties, or society in general, from efficient urban transportation, reliable postal services, or the planting of attractive flowers in a neighbour's garden. In our modern world the number of instances in which externalities matter seems to be increasing. So, therefore, does the number of occasions in which private or sectional interest can conflict with a more general interest.

Reverting to the earlier example of employment and unemployment, one sees this particularly vividly in the so-called Third World. The reasons are sometimes obscured by rhetoric. Thus the fact that, in many Third World countries, industrial investment is labour-saving when labour is overabundant is blamed on multinational corporations. This question I discussed in an article many years ago, under the heading of 'The explosive model'.[1] The problem is not in fact due to the machinations of multinationals, imperialists, or foreign investors. For a number of reasons which this is not the place to examine, modern labour-saving technology is in fact profitable to use even where wages of unskilled labour are low. Thus a bulldozer saves so much labour that it would be cheaper to use it even if the labourers it replaced were paid at bare subsistence rates. Domestic capitalists also find that it pays to substitute capital for labour, not only in industry but also in agriculture. The 'explosive' nature of this model arises from the fact that, with high population growth, this leads to a growth of underemployed or unemployed *marginados*, a source of social disorder and human misery.

This is but one of the issues that arise in developing countries which incline many of them to opt for what they believe to be a 'socialist' road. That for many this turns into a disastrous blind alley is not in dispute, at least not by me. What does seem clear is that there are powerful reasons why the capitalist road is rejected. Some relate to traditional attitudes of a pre-capitalist kind. These were strong in pre-revolutionary Russia. Among aristocrats, intellectuals (whether conservative, like Dostoevsky, or radical-revolutionary, such as Lenin or Gorky) and peasants, there was a kind of gut reaction against the mercantile spirit of Western capitalism. Thus the peasants had to have the notion of private property in land forced upon them by the Stolypin reforms of 1906–11, and promptly undid the bulk of these reforms in the chaos of revolution, reverting spontaneously to quasi-medieval forms of communal tenure. These attitudes were among the causes which shaped the Russian revolution. More recently we have seen in Iran the militantly conservative-traditionalist rejection of Western-style capitalist development. One sees, in varying degrees, the social-political unacceptability of rapid transformation of societies in the name of private profit, where highly imperfect markets and uneven development enable some individuals to grow very rich indeed while the very poor remain very poor.

Again, this is a huge subject, with (I know) much to be said on both sides. All I wish to do at this point is to note that there exists an ideology of developmental socialism, often confused and naive, but anti-capitalist. Maybe, as Lord Harris would doubtless argue, development would be speeded if these countries all adopted the policies which produced good results in South Korea (though the latest reports on political repression there are not exactly encouraging). But it may be no more meaningful to advise Algeria to adopt the South Korean economic model than to instruct Great Britain to introduce Japanese-style labour relations. In all societies there must be a minimum of consensus, of acceptance of the political and economic basis of society.

Without it there could be chaos, or organised repression, whether of the Stalin or the right-wing militarist variety. Economic development involving rapid structural change not only provides huge opportunities for (often undeserved) private profit, but also stimulates strong opposition.

It is sometimes said that private ownership of the means of production is a necessary condition for political democracy. Maybe. But it most certainly is not a sufficient condition. The experience of many (most?) developing countries suggests a reverse correlation: the capitalist development road requires the maintenance of order by a powerful repressive apparatus, a military or one-party regime. Or one could look at the question another way. Rapid, destabilising structural change hurts many people, upsets traditional modes of life, often involves sacrifice. This must be in the name of something. a principle, an ideology. It is surely no accident that this ideology is so frequently socialist in its language, though nationalism is also a potent force. So we will have to pay some attention to the logic (and dangers too) of 'developmental socialism'.

There is a point of more general application. Contrary to the belief of many economists, 'no social system can work which is based exclusively upon a network of free contracts between (legally) equal contracting parties, and in which everyone is supposed to be guided by nothing except his own short-run utilitarian interest'. The quotation is from Schumpeter;[2] it can be reinforced by a similar one from Joan Robinson, and I have already cited Pareto in a similar vein. Societies concerned *only* with profit will fall to pieces. Corruption, in the literal and the figurative sense, can flourish where the making of money becomes the primary aspiration, the dominant criterion of success.

As will become clear in the course of this book, I am aware that human acquisitiveness is a force which cannot be ignored, which indeed must be harnessed in the search for efficiency. But it hardly requires to be stimulated, by advertising and militant commercialisation. There is something genuinely repulsive in the amount of money to be made by pandering to the lowest common denominator, in the mass communication industry, with some of the highest incomes going to presenters of shows, or disc-jockeys. The very concept of 'show business' can hardly fail to offend anyone seriously concerned about culture. Concern for quality of life frequently collides with the profit motive. Galbraith's 'public squalor' is a consequence of the concentration of attention on commercially meaningful activities, on private wealth. In my own city of Glasgow an excellent parks department has built a splendid walkway along a river, and maintains fine botanic gardens, available to the public free. It is not obvious that expenditure for such purposes generates less human satisfaction than private spending on girlie magazines, or on advertising detergents and deodorants.

'Socialism' is thought of as an alternative to a society still based largely on private ownership and private profit. Generations of reformers and revolutionaries envisaged a world in which there would be no great inequalities of income and wealth, where common ownership would prevail, where economic (and political) power would be more evenly distributed, where ordinary people would have greater control over their lives and over the conditions of their work, in which deliberate planning for the common good of society would replace (at least in part) the elemental forces of the market-place. In the preceding pages I have tried to put forward a *prima facie* case for taking all this seriously, without using familiar (and question-begging) phrases about the contradictions of capitalism, its final crisis, exploitation, misery, and so on. As I stressed at the beginning, I know that there are counter-arguments. The system that now exists in the West differs greatly from the *laissez-faire* capitalism analysed by Marx. The Soviet system generates many of the same deficiencies and distortions, and some specific to itself, for reasons that will be discussed later. Some, at least, of the negative aspects of contemporary society may relate more to large-scale industrialism than to private ownership as such. There is much that is vague, confused, impractical, in socialist economic ideas, whether or not derived from Marx, and it will be the principal task of this book to discuss and analyse these ideas in a critical spirit. Indeed, the very definition of 'socialism' raises serious difficulties. One must recognise that it is a great deal easier to point to blemishes in existing societies than to find effective remedies, to devise an alternative model that actually works. Authors of pedestrian textbooks can confine their analysis to a 'world' of perfect competition, perfect markets and perfect knowledge, in which the initial axioms and definitions eliminate all the problems of real life. Socialists, understandably, have little patience with such models. They, in their turn, cannot substitute for them an equally unreal model of their own, in which all-knowing 'democratic' planners provide all that is needed for the good of society, and in which the (predictable) diffi-culties which these planners will face are assumed not to exist. To use Peter Wiles's phrase, perfect competition and perfect computation are alike in being perfect (and equal in their unreality). Marx has provided a powerful critique of capitalist society. But did he indicate a feasible alternative? It is to this question that the first part of this book will be devoted.

The preceding pages were already written when I came across some relevant thoughts on a related theme by Charles Taylor. He wrote: 'Societies destroy themselves when they violate the conditions of legitimacy which they themselves tend to posit and inculcate.' While denying the validity of 'vulgar-Marxism', he points to

> features of industrial society – the meaninglessness and subordination of work; the mindless lack of control over priorities, above all the fetishisation of commodities . . . (in a non-Marxist sense, endowed magically with the properties of life they subserve) . . . We see ourselves as playthings of mindless impersonal forces, or worse as victims of a fascination for mere things . . . There is a crisis of allegiance in our society.

He does not fail to stress 'the scramble for income and advantage in which powerful forces competed and maintained their position at the expense of the unorganised through inflation', and he sees 'inflation as the visible signs of our disarray'. (Compare these observations with the superficial monetarist platitudes!)

'It is a society', Taylor writes, 'which is sapping the bases of its own legitimacy.' But it does not follow that capitalism is about to destroy itself. He ends his argument by asking: 'Is this a self-destruction of *capitalism?* Is it only the capitalist form of society which drives it towards the kind of hypertrophy which provokes a legitimation crisis?' This is a very important point. Is it large-scale industrial society as such that is at the heart of our perplexities and discontents? Are there perhaps other causes too? Should we not be seeking answers to such questions? Taylor's article ends with the words: 'Only then will socialist thought be in a position to effect the theoretical renewal it so desperately needs.'[3]

Notes: Introduction

1   A. Nove, *Review of Development Studies*, October 1966.
2   Quoted in W. Brus, *Journal of Comparative Economics*, vol. 4, 1980, p. 53.
3   Charles Taylor, 'Growth, legitimacy and the modern identity', *Praxis International*, July 1981, pp. 111–25.

Part 1

The Legacy of Marx

What Did Marx Mean by Socialism?

It is my contention that Marx had little to say about the economics of socialism, and that the little he did say was either irrelevant or directly misleading. The word 'feasible' is in the title of this book as a kind of flank guard against utopian definitions. One can, if one chooses (and, as I shall show, many have so chosen), *define* socialism in such a way that economic problems as we know them would not, indeed *could* not, exist. If one assumes 'abundance', this excludes opportunity-cost, since there would be no mutually exclusive choices to make. If one assumes that the 'new man', unacquisitive, 'brilliant, highly rational, socialised, humane', will require no incentives, problems of discipline and motivation vanish. If it is assumed that all will identify with the clearly visible general good, then the conflict between general and partial interest, and the complex issues of centralisation/decentralisation, can be assumed out of existence. If human beings in society can see *ex ante* what needs to be produced and the correct way of producing and utilising all products, then there is no need for *ex post* verification; the indirect and imperfect link between use-value and exchange-value, via exchange relations and the market, can be replaced by direct conscious human decisions on production for use. Division of labour will have been overcome, by 'brilliant' multipurpose human beings. 'While not everyone may be able to paint as well as Raphael, everyone will be able to paint exceedingly well.' Everyone will govern, there will not be any governed. Since all competing interests will have disappeared, there will be no need to claim rights of any sort, no need for restrictive rules, laws, judges, or a legislature. Of course, there will be no state, no nation-states (and so no foreign trade, or any trade). The wages system will have gone, as well as money.

Bertil Ollman has gathered together Marx's sayings about communist society, and the above represents a summary, with a few quotations, of his article.[1] He points out, correctly, that Marx never offered a systematic account of communist society, that he considered such attempts as 'foolish, ineffective and even reactionary'. One has broad indications, scattered about his works, often in the form of a contrast with the capitalist system that he was criticising.

It is sometimes alleged that no distinction was known to Marx between socialism and communism, or even that such a distinction was an invention attributable to Stalin and Stalinists. This is surely not so. Marx's *Critique of the Gotha Programme* spoke of a first or lower stage. And certainly Bukharin and Preobrazhensky distinguished between socialism and communism on similar lines; see their *ABC of Communism*, which expressed the Marxist-

Leninist orthodoxy of the time. Trotsky, too, spoke of 'the lower stage of communism or socialism', even while denying that Stalin's Russia had reached that stage.[2] The ideologists of Brezhnev's USSR claim that it is a society of 'mature', or 'developed' socialism, and engaged in 'building communism'. Many Marxists sharply criticise the Soviet system, denying its claim to be socialist. It is then relevant to ask: by what *criteria* is one to judge the claim? Clearly no one supposes that the USSR is communist in the 'Ollman' sense. Most people, surely also most Marxists, do not believe that it could have been. Some prefer to regard any society which is not communist, but is on the road towards communism or 'real' socialism, not as 'socialist' but as 'transitional'. Some apply this term to the USSR, others attack it as a new kind of class system. This is not the place for a discussion of this topic.[3] I should like instead to include in my own definition of 'feasible socialism' the notion that *it should be conceivable within the lifespan of one generation* – say, in the next fifty years; conceivable, that is, without making extreme, utopian, or far-fetched assumptions. I would add that for a society to be regarded as socialist one requires the dominance of social ownership in the economy, together with political and economic democracy. My reasons for not at present going beyond this doubtless oversimple definition will become apparent later.

It is surely the case that Marxists saw communism not as a distant dream, but as an attainable reality, 'feasible' in the sense used here. Such men as Lenin, Trotsky, Bukharin, sincerely believed that young party members might see its achievement. The 'socialism' of the *Critique of the Gotha Programme* is already a long way towards communism, the principal difference being that rewards would be in accordance with work and not yet with need, and workers would be issued with vouchers in respect of the time they devoted to social labour. Bettelheim is right in ascribing to Marx and Engels the view that, when socialism wins, when the workers take hold of the means of production, 'even at the beginning there would be neither commodities, nor value, nor money, nor, consequently, prices and wages'.[4] So there is much to support the proposition that classical Marxism saw socialism and communism as, if not exactly interchangeable terms, then as one being the incomplete stage of the other, containing many of its essential elements.

The problem that we must tackle is twofold. First, what view did Marx and his followers take of the political economy of socialism? Secondly, what are we to make of their general image or model of a socialist society?

One answer, supported by a considerable set of precedents, is that *there is not and cannot be a political economy of socialism*. Let me quote Bukharin:

Political economy is a science . . . of the unorganised national economy. Only in a society where production has an anarchistic character, do laws of social life appear 'natural', 'spontaneous' laws, independent of the will of individuals and groups, laws acting with the blind necessity of the law of gravity. Indeed, as soon as we deal with an organised national economy, all the basic 'problems' of political economy, such as price, value, profit, etc., simply disappear. Here the relations between men are no longer expressed as 'relations between things', for here the economy is regulated not by the blind forces of the market and competition, but by the consciously carried out *plan* . . . The end of capitalist and commodity society signifies the end of political economy.[5]

This may seem to follow from the definition of socialism that Bukharin thought he inherited from Marx. If economics is concerned with uncontrolled ('anarchic') phenomena, with purchase-and-sale, exchange, markets, profits, money, exploitation, then what relevance can it have under socialism? The 'law of value', and economic laws generally, relate to capitalism.

Similar opinions were expressed also by Preobrazhensky, in the course of discussions in the 1920s with such Marxist economists as Skvortsov-Stepanov. He wrote that to consider that political economy relates 'to relations of production in general . . . contradicts totally all that Marx has written on the object and methods of political economy . . .'.[6] Bukharin made several times the point that 'in an organised economy . . . a socialised economy of the socialist state, we would not encounter a single problem the solution of which is related to the theory of political economy'. Skvortsov-Stepanov, on the contrary, argued that Marxist economics ought also to relate to pre- and post-capitalist formations. He was in a small minority at the time.

Naturally, they recognised that the law of value survived in the USSR of the New Economic Policy (NEP); but this was because of the survival of private property and of the market-based relationship with the peasantry. Under socialism, by definition, it would be eliminated. There would then be something like 'scientific management', 'the science of socially organised production', but it would not be economics. These were phrases used respectively by Bukharin and Preobrazhensky. A remarkably well-documented survey of the debate on the law of value and other economic laws under socialism has been written by Louis Baslé.[7]

Already in 1920 Lenin was not satisfied with such an answer. In his marginal notes on Bukharin's *Economics of the Transition Period*, he remarked, first, that it is not quite true to describe capitalism as 'unorganised': it too is organised. He also pointed to the survival even under communism of such economic laws as those governing the basic proportions of the economy.[8] He might have agreed with Baslé, who imagined two species or aspects of the law of value: 'LV1' relates to the allocation of labour in various proportions for various purposes, which must exist in any society, and 'LV2' is the form in which this manifests itself in the commodity economy, with exchange, markets, competition, and so on.

Some contemporary Soviet economists adopt a similar posture. Thus Kosolapov quotes in his support the following from Volume III of *Das Kapital*:

After the abolition of capitalism . . . under socially organised production, value determination [*opredeleniye*] remains dominant in the sense that the regulation of labour time and the distribution of social labour between different sectors of production, and the accountancy that encompasses all this, become more important than ever.

Kosolapov draws from this the conclusion that there will be no commodities and no value, as there will be no one to exchange with, *and* that commodities and values *will* exist.[9] Presumably by putting forward this deliberately contradictory view he is trying to argue on the lines of Baslé's 'LV1' and 'LV2'.

This question is discussed in an interesting essay by X. Richet,[10] and also by the Hungarian A. Brody,[11] and by A. Mattick,[12] who in their various ways consider the meaning of Marx's recognition of the fact that *all* societies need to distribute social labour in given proportions to satisfy needs. Richet challenges Mattick's assertion that Marx did not have in mind an 'economic law of universal validity', thereby taking up a position similar to Baslé's 'LV1'. Brody writes: 'For Marx the notion of value becomes significant from the time that there is choice between various activities and various products'; while Marx sees that there can be no exchange-value in the absence of commodity production,

> nevertheless the underlying notion, value, will be present so long as there is division of labour, so long as there are different activities to be compared. So long as it is necessary to economise the labour of society, the notion of value is necessary whether or not there is a market . . .

But in any case the purely negative answer cannot possibly satisfy us, and this for several reasons. First, it amounts to saying that economic problems in socialism would have to be solved without reference to Marx or Marxism, which, unless one so defines socialism as to ensure the absence of economic problems, leaves one in an uncomfortable intellectual void. One *must* discuss what sort of economic problems it is reasonable to expect to encounter in any socialism defined with some reference to real-life possibilities. Secondly, Marx's own view of capitalism, his basic analysis of its features, rests explicitly and implicitly on his picture of an alternative society. Its precise blueprint he left vague, and so should we, but its essential features cannot be simply assumed to be the unanalysed consequences of revolutionary struggle. Thirdly, it is important for Marxists, or for anyone analysing feasible socialism, to face up to the objection that what is proposed is an unrealisable utopia. As long ago as 1908 Barone, commenting on the failure of the Marxists of his time to reply to his arguments, wrote that 'their attitude in this respect is reminiscent of the reluctance with which dogmas of religion are discussed, especially when the latter has great propaganda value'.[13] Seventy years later another Italian, Luciano Pellicani, after listing some dogmatic assumptions about a socialist future, wrote that 'they make impossible any critical discussion on the realism or validity of the revolutionary alternative'. He spoke of the 'Reign of liberty of Marx and Engels corresponding to the Paradise of the Christians: it is not describable with the conceptual categories at our disposal – hence the typical refusal of the revolutionary gnostic to speculate about the future society'.[14]

These same problems worry Marxists too. Thus, referring to the vision of the future of the young Marx (at the end of a vigorously Marxist analysis of capitalist crisis), Alain Lipietz wrote of 'the idealist aspect of materialist dialectics', the 'dream' of totally liberated humanity: Marx wrote 'pages as

beautiful and shadowy as the Gospel according to St John: the 1844 manu-
scripts. Indeed behind Feuerbach and Hegel one feels the myth of the Cross
and the Resurrection, called here Alienation and Reappropriation.'[15] Such
'religious' references could be multiplied. Finally, commenting on the Ollman
article concerning Marx's vision of socialism-communism, David Murray, in
Radical Philosophy, agrees with Ollman that 'giving workers . . . a better
notion of what life would be like under communism is essential to the success
of the socialist project', but then attacks him for 'his consistent refusal to
relate Marx's writings to their subsequent use, or even to their practical
relevance'.[16] Murray goes on to criticise the incompleteness and ambiguities
of Marx's own formulations (for example, on the abolition of division of
labour and on the need for a 'directing will' in organising production, matters
which will be discussed at length later), and ends by asking: 'how effective
would this [i.e. Ollman's] account be in persuading people of the desirability
of communism?' His reply: it would be 'a piously dull place . . . the presentation of such a utopia would have the opposite effect to that which Ollman
wishes'.

One might include Debray here: after some fine romantic revolutionary
eloquence, faintly tinged with irony, he asks:

What does all this mean? To do what? At what cost? For what aim?
    Inappropriate questions . . . Impertinent; maybe pertinent from the
outside, but without relevance to the subject. For the acts of the revolutionary are too disinterested for him to lower himself to considering the
usefulness, the results, or the limits of revolution . . . Such questions, apart
from sapping our energy, would deprive the revolution of its entire point by
subjecting it to the contemptible criteria of efficacy, a task undertaken only
by those who do not make revolutions . . .[17]

I have been accused by at least one Marxist-millenarian of being a 'conservative' because I question the validity of the romantic-utopian-religious
elements of the Marxist tradition. I have great respect for faith. The Russian
Christian socialist Levitin-Krasnov wrote: 'If the ideal of a society without
rich or poor, without rulers and subordinates, were not realisable, Christ
would not have given it to us!'[18] This explicitly religious view is at least
internally consistent. But what is one to make of a 'scientific socialism' that
seeks wholly to escape rational discussion as to its own feasibility and working
rules? In any case, it is nonsense to assert that to be a socialist, or a revolutionary for that matter, one must believe in an unrealisable utopia.

Another possible defence of a socialist utopia is to claim that it is valid as a
criterion: this is how a socialist society ought to be. Real life, so it can be said,
will fall short of the ideal, but it should be there in our minds, we should
strive towards it. This would be analogous to the role of perfect competition
and perfect markets in orthodox Western economic theory.

There are two replies to this sort of argument. The first is that to judge *any*
reality by criteria known to be unreal and unrealisable is to condemn *any*
society, to place onself for ever in the posture of a righteous (lefteous?)
oppositionist to any conceivable regime calling itself socialist. Furthermore,

one then loses any basis for critically analysing those regimes which claim to be socialist. Thus what sense is there in accusing Brezhnev and his colleagues of not having 'eliminated the division of labour'? The second is that, echoing Murray, one feels that the 'ideal society' of Marx's romantic imagination is not merely unreal, it would also be dull, of little attraction to either workers or intellectuals.

However, one must not be dogmatic in criticising dogmatism. Let us instead tackle successively certain assumptions which traditional Marxism makes, beginning with the concept of *abundance*, and the related idea of the New Man and Woman.

Abundance, Scarcity and the New Man

Marx appears to have believed that technical progress already made under capitalism had fundamentally *solved* the problem of production, but that the shackles imposed on the forces of production by the capitalist system prevented this from being realised in practice. There are passages in which he speaks of 'the unlimited growth of production', 'the absolute development of social productivity of labour', such as would in fact make possible 'continual relative overproduction'.[19] Marx is well aware that needs expand with rising production. The French economist Tartarin has a sound basis for his interpretation, that Marx saw 'needs as finite and saturable, but rising', that Marx did *not* envisage a stationary golden age, that he spoke repeatedly of the need for an investment fund under communism, that he had in mind 'an economy of the satisfaction of constantly expanding needs'.[20] Evidently there would still be scarcity in relation to need at first, but, it seems, not for long.

Let us define abundance as a sufficiency to meet requirements at zero price, leaving no reasonable person dissatisfied or seeking more of anything (or at least of anything reproducible). This concept plays a crucial role in Marx's vision of socialism/communism. Let us observe the consequences of – and then consider the consequences of not – accepting this assumption.

Abundance removes conflict over resource allocation, since by definition there is enough for everyone, and so there are no mutually exclusive choices, no opportunity is forgone and therefore there is no opportunity-cost. The golden age, a communist steady-state equilibrium, will have been reached. Gradual change, growth, will be simple and painless. The task of planning becomes one of simple routine; the role of economics is virtually eliminated. There is then no reason for various individuals and groups to compete, to take possession for their own use of what is freely available to all. Let me give as an example the supply of water in Scottish towns. Evidently, it is not costless: labour has to be expended on building reservoirs and pipes, purification, repairs and maintenance, and so on. However, there is plenty of water. It is not necessary to regulate its use through 'rationing by price', it is available in sufficient quantity for all purposes. It is not 'marketed' in any meaningful sense, nor is its provision subject to any 'law of value' or profitability criterion. There is no competition for water, there are no conflicts over water (save in some instances arising from private ownership of land, fishing rights, and so on). But this is not so in, say, a town on the edge of the Sahara. There people kill one another over water, because of its scarcity.

If other goods were as easily and freely available as water is in Scotland, then new human attitudes would develop: acquisitiveness would wither away; property rights, and crimes related to property, would also vanish, not because the citizens would have become 'good' by reading Marxist books but because acquisitiveness would have lost all purpose. In other words, Marx did *not* say that, under socialism, there would be no conflicts over the allocation of scarce resources (oil, fish, iron ore, stockings, or whatever), but that these and other resources would not be scarce.

It is my contention that abundance in this sense is an unacceptable assumption. Some Marxists have also seen this. Thus Aidan Foster-Carter has written: 'For Marxists, abundance is out; arguably it was always a meaningless notion, but henceforth scarcity will have to be accepted as more than just a bugbear of bourgeois economics.'[21] Significantly, Foster-Carter is interested in developing countries, and is therefore well aware that over half of the world's population is very poor indeed, that the resources needed to bring them up to the levels already attained by, say, the skilled workers of Western Europe will surely not be available in the lifetime of our children's children. The Brandt Commission report has recently reminded us that 'deforestation at its present rate will halve the world's stock of wood by the year 2000, with increasing carbon dioxide pollution among other effects . . .'. There will be another 2 billion people to feed in twenty years' time, a number equal to the population of the entire world in 1900. Western consumption of energy is 100 times greater, per head, as that in the poorer countries. And so on. Presumably we would all agree that this question must be looked at worldwide, that we are not considering 'abundance' in one or two highly advanced and prosperous countries, defending their riches against the poverty-stricken masses of Asia and Africa!

Let us examine 'scarcity' as a concept more closely. We can distinguish two kinds of scarcity: absolute and relative. The two shade into one another but the difference between them is important. By 'absolute' scarcity I mean that supply cannot be significantly increased even if prices rise. Examples are land in the centre of cities, fish in the North Sea, perhaps oil. Those who take seriously the warnings of the 'Club of Rome' on the exhaustion of non-replenishable natural resources would stress the importance of absolute scarcity, and at least one Marxist, Wolfgang Harich, has drawn far-reaching conclusions which lead him towards an authoritarian (or even Stalinist) 'rationing-of-scarcity' state (*starkes Verteilungstaat*).[22] I will return to this point later. However, there is no need to rest the argument on 'absolute' scarcity in this sense. Let us by all means assume that additional quantities of every important metal, plant and source of energy *could* be procured. But the example of oil shows how this would often be at *increasing cost*, that is, at the cost of forgoing more of other things. Over a fifty-year worldwide perspective, even on optimistic political, geological and technical assumptions, it is surely far-fetched to imagine that there will be enough of all for all at zero price. Saturation of demand for particular products is possible, which might bring them into the same category as water in Scotland. But is it conceivable, can it

be seriously envisaged, that the world's citizenry would be able to take whatever they wanted (even 'reasonably' wanted) from the amply supplied public
stores, and that decisions about production, construction, allocation, would
be taken without having to make mutually exclusive choices?

Given that today most of the people of China and India, which together
number over 1,500 million, live in dire poverty, have the 'limitless-resources'
optimists ever tried to calculate the resource implications of China's millions
eating as much meat as, say, even the East Europeans do today? There is no
point in extending the argument. Those whose faith depends on believing in
abundance will simply ignore these words and cling to Marx's technological
and resource availability optimism. It was quite proper for Marx in 1880 to
attack Malthus and to stress how great are the still-unused resources of the
earth. It is less excusable for Marx's followers, with too rare exceptions, to
take the same line in the 1980s.

Of course, none of us knows what new discoveries will be made, new
sources of energy and synthetic materials or even foods discovered. All that is
being asserted is that the balance of probability is strongly tilted in the
direction of the continued existence of scarcity, the unattainability of
abundance. This by no means excludes improvements in living standards.
Along with them there should be a greater consciousness of yet unsatisfied
needs: cultural amenities, travel, better housing, better-quality food. Indeed,
without rising expectations, new aspirations, one would have a very dreary
world.

Several consequences follow from the survival of at least relative scarcity.

The first relates to the likely behaviour of human beings. It is a common
accusation, made by Marxist 'fundamentalists', that critics of their views
suppose human nature to be unalterable, that man will always be selfish and
acquisitive. Agreed, we must not be unimaginatively conservative. But surely
we must not assume that men turn into omniscient angels either. As already
stressed, it is unreasonable for a Marxist materialist to suppose that men
become good through reading books and listening to speeches. This is the
purest idealism.

It is unnecessary to assume *individual* selfishness, though this too is likely if
there is not enough to satisfy all. People can strive not only for the good of
their (sometimes very extended) family, or tribe, but also for their community
(town, village, commune, *kibbutz*, or whatever), or for the department or
sphere for which they are responsible, whether or not this benefits them
materially. One can see this in the behaviour of such individuals as librarians,
educational administrators, research scientists and a great many others: in
seeking more resources for *their* library, or for nursery schools, or for research
into cancer or astronomy, they may well gain nothing for themselves as
individuals, and they are certainly not selfish hypocrites: they quite understandably identify their sphere of activity with the general good. Most of us
do this. I am plainly of the opinion that writing these lines is a good thing,
that those who read them will benefit, and that this takes priority over other
things which their publishers, readers, or I myself could be doing with the
time and resources being devoted to their publication. But resources (and
time) being finite, *everything has an opportunity-cost*. Something potentially

useful is being forgone. Perhaps it is *more* useful than this book. (Perish the thought! But who can tell?)

It is the belief of the 'fundamentalist' that, in the absence of the distorting effects of private ownership and of the resultant 'commodity fetishism', society (or the associated producers) will know what it is best to do and choose accordingly. I will return at some length to the organisational implications of such a view. Right now my task is simply to assert that, even if it were to be assumed that people wanted the general good, there could be no conceivable way in which it could be operationally defined. By 'operationally' I mean in such a way that it could serve as a guideline for choices regarding production and allocation of goods and services. Conflict over resources under conditions of scarcity arises *both* because people and groups seek their own interest *and* because it is usually not possible to counterpose to this a defined interest of society as a whole. The word 'usually' is important here. I am *not* saying that there are no instances in which the general interest can be seen and can be made to prevail. But even this is consistent with conflict. For instance, even assuming that all agree that a new airport is needed, whoever is within earshot of the projected new airport is bound to protest and propose that it be elsewhere. And the only conceivable situation in which there would be no arguments and restrictions over car-parking is one in which there was ample space for all to park where they wished in our cities (that is, if land in the middle of cities were abundant!), or if there were no cars.

To re-use earlier examples, how can one show that resources used for library A should not go to library B, or for that matter to improve a science laboratory or the diet of children in kindergartens in Kampuchea? Or that the provision of a better telescope for an observatory is more or less important than building a new bridge, growing more carrots, investing in a new cement works, or increasing the size of coffee plantations? As will be stressed later, when we discuss the importance of *scale*, in a big complex society we do not and *cannot* see what precisely is forgone, or who would go without, when we use resources to satisfy the requirements of *our* library, family, factory, or locality. It is, to repeat, *not* just a matter of selfishness or 'human nature', but of information, and of information which *cannot* in fact be provided: how can *anyone* know what is the 'real' opportunity-cost of, say, a research grant? It is like trying to discover what item of British budgetary expenditure is financed by the taxes paid by the citizens of the town of Inveraray. The naive fundamentalist eliminates these problems from his consciousness by assuming abundance, that is, that there will by definition be enough for all these purposes. This enables him or her to regard the entire question of allocational decisions and efficiency as quite unimportant, thereby saving a great deal of otherwise necessary thought, and evading the problems which any really existing socialist economy must face. At this point I should like to echo the words of J. P. Thomas: in a review he spoke of 'solutions which obliterate the terms of the problem, and empty certitudes upheld as necessary for revolutionary struggle'.[23]

This leads me to a further point. Marxists give great emphasis to the class struggle, and are right to do so, so long as it is not assumed that other species of conflict are unimportant. Surely the class struggle is about the division of the social product, which takes a particular form under capitalism, but which can be, must be, the subject of conflict in *any* society in which scarcity exists. Looking at history, it would be foolish and shortsighted not to see that, even in societies divided into classes on the basis of property, the most vicious conflicts sometimes occur not between but *within* the classes, over a wide variety of issues.

The Wars of the Roses saw feudal lords slaughtering each other. Protestant nobles killed fellow-nobles of the Catholic faith in thousands in the Thirty Years' War, and vice versa. In our own century Jewish capitalists went to the gas chambers together with their Jewish employees, and East African native 'bourgeois' expelled their Indian 'class'-mates, which should remind one of the big role of nationalism and racialism in this supposedly civilised century. In 1920 H. G. Wells was asked by Zinoviev to explain the Irish question in class terms, and failed to make Zinoviev understand that there were also other dimensions of importance,[24] which still confuse the situation in Northern Ireland today. White South African or Alabama workers are hardly inclined to show class solidarity with their black fellow-proletarians. There will be more to say about what J. P. Thomas called 'the mythical proletariat, bearer of a new unity of subject and object'. My point is that conflict is not only a matter of class war, involving capitalists, landlords and proletarians, and that it is essential to consider theoretical and institutional means of coping with this fact, under conditions of relative scarcity of means, and not evade the issue.

It will be so even if we assume that the entire population is genuinely anxious to do good. Yet this too is somewhat unrealistic, leading as it does to neglecting the need for both incentives and discipline, instructions and enforcement. It cannot be *assumed* that the right things will be done even if the individuals concerned know what is right. 'Man is by nature a lazy animal', said Trotsky in 1920. He can be lazy also in 1983, and quite probably in 2020 too. People can get drunk, oversleep, avoid disagreeable duties. Or is one to assume that drunkenness is due to alienation, to being deprived of the means of production (though the owners also get drunk!), that sloth, irresponsibility, inertia, indifference, will wither away?

There is also a linked question, likewise to be discussed further, of the relationship between alienation (and also sloth, irresponsibility, and so on) and *scale*. We can identify with a small group of people we know and can meet, with problems and effects we can actually observe; it is another matter if there are hundreds of millions of people, and multiple millions of decisions, great and small, with remote consequences which few can apprehend directly. Diseconomies of scale, economic, organisational, informational, psychological, are among the principal causes of Soviet economic difficulties.

There are 'new leftists' who ascribe the present troubles and confusions of Soviet centralised planning to lack of democracy and workers' power, the implication being that if the present bosses (new bourgeoisie, elite) were removed, and 'the people' ruled, then the sense of common interest would overcome the deficiencies of the economic system, one of which is the distortion of information flows through the interest of the information-providers. Such distortion is real enough. But apart from neglecting the sheer overwhelming complexity of all-embracing planning (of which much more later), the 'new left' critic also overlooks the simple fact that scarcity exists in the USSR and is likely to continue for some time, and that under these conditions information flows are *bound* to be affected, distorted, by the interest of the information-providers, who are in effect competitors for limited resources. This would be so however democratic or undemocratic information-providing institutions actually were. No doubt any of us, 'new leftist' or no, in applying for a research grant or money for travel, would emphasise (and quite sincerely so) the value for society of whatever we are doing, and present the facts with – shall we say – appropriate cosmetics. As already stressed, in a vastly complicated society, we *simply cannot know* who is being deprived for our benefit if our application succeeds. There are, of course, degrees of dishonesty and concealment of facts, in this as in anything else. But to expect unbiased information from those interested in the results to which the information is put is to live in cloud-cuckoo-land. This would not happen if resources were unlimited; but this is where we came in.

The Law of Value under Socialism

Given that economic calculation, opportunity-cost, choice between alternatives, clearly will have to exist, the question is: has Marxian value theory anything to contribute? If so, what? If not, what alternative forms of economic calculation would have to be devised?

We have already examined the proposition that *economics* will wither away under socialism (after a transition period during which, borrowing a phrase which Ollman adapted from Wittgenstein, one climbs up into the golden age and then throws away the ladder). On the whole, the evidence strongly points the other way. We have seen that even Lenin was uneasy with Bukharin's confident prediction that economics and (full) socialism are incompatible. All subsequent experience underlines the evident need to calculate, evaluate, devise criteria for choice between alternatives, at all levels of economic life. Let us take that as proved. What, then, can we make of *Marxist* economics in this context?

Again, a possible answer is: nothing. Marx analysed capitalist relations of production; he was not concerned with calculation, evaluation, criteria, choice, rational decision-making or its organisation, under socialism. Indeed, I would argue that *there is no Marxist political economy of socialism*, just as Hippolyte Simon has asserted that 'there is no Marxist political philosophy',[25] and Althusser that 'there is no Marxist theory of the state nor of revolutionary forms of organisation'.[26] But though no such elaborated theory exists, there are in Marx many indications which are either somewhat utopian or misleading. Generations of Marxists have, in consequence, been misled. For an example, one need go no further than the fascinating (and inconclusive) discussions in Soviet Russia in 1919–20 on 'problems of a moneyless economy'.[27] How, asked several of the participants, are costs to be measured? What, then, would goods be 'worth'?

There are in Marx possible sources of confusion between:

Value
Exchange-value
Use-value
Market-value
'Transformed' values (prices of production).

'Value' is a quantity of socially necessary labour-power. Exchange-value is how value manifests itself in the market, in the form of exchange-ratios between commodities, presumably in equilibrium. Market-value is distinguished from yet another term used by Marx, market-*price*, by the fact that the latter reflects random supply-and-demand fluctuations, while market-value is an equilibrium concept, that is, is equal to the price under normal conditions when supply equals demand (though in Chapter 10 of Volume III of *Das Kapital* Marx allows for an effect of the quantity demanded on the average conditions of production). What, then, is the difference between market-value, exchange-value and prices of production (this last being value transformed to allow for the equalising of profit rates under conditions in which organic composition of capital varies)? They appear to me to be the same. But let us leave this aside, as more important and more relevant issues arise. These are the influence of *use-values*, and the *meaning of the transformation*.

Let us take use-values first. Here, in my view, Marx has himself caused much confusion in viewing *use-values as incommensurate*, and, above all, by an artificial and unjustified *separation* between value and use-values.

At the very beginning of *Das Kapital* we have the following statement:

the utility of a thing makes it a use-value. But this utility is not a thing of air. Being limited by the physical properties of the commodity, it has no existence apart from this commodity . . . The exchange of commodities is evidently an act characterised by a total abstraction from use-value . . . As use-values commodities are, above all, of different qualities, but as exchange-values they are merely different quantities, and consequently do not contain an atom of use-value. If then we leave out of consideration the use-value of commodities, they have only one common property left, that of being products of labour.[28]

Yet Engels, in a well-known passage, wrote that 'it will be the utilities [useful effects, value-in-use] of different products, *compared with one another* and with the quantities of labour necessary for their production, which will determine the plan' (i.e. what it is decided to produce).[29]

Following Engels, Bettelheim has written that in making choices the 'associated producers' will be guided by the 'socially useful effect' (*effet social utile*) of different products.[30] But how can one compare the use-values, whether these be individual or social, when they are not comparable? Marx *might* have said that they are rendered comparable under capitalism only through the market, *ex post* and imperfectly, whereas under socialism society will make comparisons consciously and without the intermediacy of commodity–money relations, and so on. The fact remains that he did *not* say it; what he said was that different use-values are *not comparable*. This glaring inconsistency is a source of confusion still. Thus Shatalin and some other mathematical economists argued, in 1974–5, that use-values, social utility, should guide planners' choices, only to be attacked by Kronrod, who asserted, in line with Marx, that utilities are not comparable, not commensurate, that to assert the contrary is to fall victim to subjective value theory.[31]

Use-value, as seen by Marx, is a necessary pre-condition for any product to have value. Thus labour devoted to some useless purpose is wasted, creates no value. But there is in Marx and in his followers a very great emphasis on the *primacy of production*, and on value as a quantity which relates to the labour used to produce things (abstract, socially necessary, but still *labour*). Of course, Marx was writing of the law of value under capitalism, but, as we shall see, his words have sown confusion in the minds of those who try to devise methods of calculation for a socialist society. Several of the participants of the 1919–20 discussions, for example, put forward proposals for valuation in terms of labour-time, or quantities of labour-and-energy, which in fact measure only effort, and omit the result, the effect, of the effort expended. Yurosky noted a lack of any connection between the expenditure of human or mechanical energy and the end-result, a lack of appreciation that the same amount of effort can produce widely divergent economic effects. Even today Soviet prices have the known defect that they too measure effort, through being based on cost, while, to quote a recent Soviet critic, 'use-values are not counted'.[32] The Soviet economist N. Petrakov criticises this 'cost conception of price' (*zatratnaye kontseptsiya tseny*), and stresses the need to take use-value into account.[33] The French critic Baslé has drawn attention to a major theoretical ambiguity in Marx's argument. If value, if the law of value, underlies exchange relations under capitalism, 'then are these values already determined before exchange, outside of competition, or do exchange and competition cause the values to emerge?' For Marx, values underlie prices, independently of supply, demand and exchange, even though values are 'realised' in the real world *through* exchange. Surely, argues Baslé, Marx should have said that for value to exist one needs production *and* circulation, with competitive markets in which social demand finds expression. Commodities, after all, are (by definition) made for *sale*. The goods can be rejected by the customers in the market, and 'social need, expressed by demand, enters into the definition of socially necessary labour-time'.[34] But it seems to be assumed by Marx (this under capitalism, be it noted), that although value requires *ex post* validation in the market, value is none the less already present when the goods are produced. While a few passages in Marx could be interpreted as recognising that the level of social need (i.e. demand) can affect value, the whole thrust of his argument is to stress over and over again that only the conditions of *production* enter into the formation of value.[35] As Baslé puts it, 'competition and demand are essential to, yet are excluded from, the definition of value'.[36] Marx erected a barrier between the determination of value on the one hand, and demand and use-value on the other. 'There is a contradiction between the *a priori* definition of value and the necessity and social utility which form part of this definition.'[37]

A Marxist economist, Alain Lipietz, faces this problem and, in my view, evades it by a sleight-of-hand. He accepts that 'socially necessary labour' is partly defined by 'social demand'. But then, astonishingly, he blandly asserts that social demand is a function of the class struggle, which determines the structure of consumption and accumulation. He rejects a theory of value based upon 'utility and scarcity' because utility (demand) is not exogenous.[38] Accepting, of course, that income distribution as well as production affects demand, this is still a most unsatisfactory way out of the problem. It still leaves him with a 'quantity-of-labour' theory, with social demand relegated to a quite subordinate role. Bettelheim, as we shall see, is in *this* respect closer to reality, since he does explicitly recognise that Marxist economists have tended to understress use-value.

Quite plainly the same quantity of labour, howsoever reduced to simple labour, howsoever 'transformed', can produce different amounts of use-value. For Marx, the presence of use-value is a pre-condition for value, but there is no recognition in this context that *some things have greater use-value than others*, there is total abstraction from quality *unless* it requires more labour-time to achieve it. Marx certainly knew that exchange-values and use-values will tend to be brought into line with each other in a competitive capitalist market. Thus if A and B fulfil the same need and 'cost' the same, but A is superior to B, i.e. valued more highly by the users, it will command a higher price and/or B will cease to be profitable to produce. Market forces so guide profit-making capitalists that they do not knowingly hire labour-power to make goods which yield below-average profits, or no profits at all.

But what happens if there is no market? Its absence removes the link – imperfect, no doubt, but still a link – between effort and result, between the quantity of labour-power utilised and the use-value it produces. This weakness shows up in the early Soviet discussions: if goods are 'valued' in labour-time (e.g. Strumilin's *tred* of 1920), there is a total absence of any connection between this valuation and use-value, which must then be estimated in other units and in some other way. Quite plainly it would be absurd to aim at maximising labour-values, wrote Shatalin and his friends in 1974–5, because this is a measure of *expenditure*, of effort, not result. Throughout Soviet history, both theory and practice have suffered from this disjunction between value (or cost-based price) and use-value.

Examples are legion. Two machines, for instance, could require the same effort to produce, but if one is more productive, more convenient to work at, than the other, then from every conceivable practical standpoint it is *worth* more. Two tons of coal, requiring the same labour inputs to extract, can differ in calorific value, and therefore in worth. A pretty dress can require the same labour input as an unattractive one. In fact it is quite obvious, is it not, that the knowledge that two baskets of goods have required the same human effort to produce gives us absolutely no ground for believing them to be of the same use-value, *unless* a market is assumed to exist? The very word 'value' (*Wert*, the older Russian *tsennost'*, the French *valeur*) suggests valuation by or for something, or someone. It is absurd, in my view, to accuse the Soviet scholars who have tried to point this out of being victims of subjective value theories. It is plainly the merest common sense. Anywhere, everywhere, *production is for use*. (The capitalist's profit arises only if the customer finds the product 'worth' buying.) It would doubtless distress Marx himself to learn that, a hundred years after his death, men who call themselves his disciples argue about labour-values in the context of deciding valuations and prices in a (so-called) socialist planned economy.

Marxist 'fundamentalists' today have no difficulty in showing that Soviet official formulations on 'the law of value under socialism' are inconsistent with Marx's statements on the subject. Numerous quotations can be found to substantiate this.[39] Thus in *Grundrisse* Marx wrote that 'there can be nothing more erroneous and absurd than to postulate the control by united individuals of total production on the basis of exchange-value, of money . . .'.[40] However, a French Marxist scholar, Chavance, may have gone too far in denying that Marx was interested in the *magnitude* of value. His own quotation from Marx proves only that Marx reproached the classical economists of being interested *only* in relative magnitudes and not in 'the internal connection between value and its manifestation, or exchange-value'. Surely, while this is true, Marx *was* interested *also* in the ratios in which goods exchange, in the magnitude of values and in changes in these magnitudes. Surely this follows from the attention Marx gave to these problems, notably in Volume III of *Das Kapital*. But there may well be a basis for Chavance's criticism of Soviet practice, in that value theory 'has been given a function which is alien to it, that of finding a *practical means* for the *measurement* and *comparison* of different products and different labours'. He then quotes the distinguished theoretician I. Rubin (a victim of the Stalin purges):

> it is not necessary that we seek a practical standard measure of value which would make possible the equalisation of products of labour in the market. This exchange in the market does not need any sort of standard invented by economists. The causal analysis of the process . . . and not the discovery of practically applicable standards for the comparison [of different com-modities, etc.], *that* is the task of the theory of value.[41]

But if, in the real world of capitalist commodity production, the products of labour are related to one another, their 'value' is linked with use-value, and so on, *through the market*, this yet again leaves the would-be analyst of economics of socialism facing a void. When he or she tries to fill it by devising some standard of measure, some attempt to find units of equivalence, there seems no way out but that of using surrogate labour-values, that is, of measuring effort in 'natural' units of some kind, such as hours of labour. Which is where we came in.

Of course, not even the most dogmatic Soviet 'Marxist' actually supposes that one should maximise labour-values, i.e. effort. On the contrary, several formulations, some dating back to 1919–20, some much more recent, speak of the minimising of labour inputs, economy of labour-time, to achieve given objectives. (Given how, by whom? Of this more in a moment.) The difficulty arises when one tries to assign valuations to specific products, to relate them to one another; products requiring more labour and materials thus have a higher valuation, because this is based on costs; demand (utility) does not 'fit' into either the theory or the practice of price-fixing. We will return to the doctrine of economy of labour-time later, in the context of interpreting 'transformation' of values.

One other feature of traditional Marxist 'values' must be mentioned, if only in passing. Since value is based upon a quantity of labour, it is not possible to produce more value unless this quantity is increased. This quite logically leads Alain Lipietz to write the following: during the postwar boom period in France, according to his 'simple caricature' of reality, output, accumulation and consumption (including workers' consumption) trebled, and so did labour productivity, but since total hours of labour worked remained little altered, it follows that the value produced *and* the value of labour-power were unchanged![42] This is strictly correct in Marxian value terms. One wonders – as Joan Robinson also wondered many years ago – whether this is a useful or clarifying definition. (One can see a red thread leading from here to A. Emmanuel and the confusion around the concept of 'unequal exchange', of which more in Part 4 below.)

Returning to Marxian value theory and its influence on economics of socialism, some Marxists would argue that the economists who tried to base a 'socialist' valuation upon the labour theory of value were mistaken. I think they *were* mistaken. The point is that their Marxian training and Marx himself left them with no *alternative*. They were misled by irrelevant theory.

A case can be made for the proposition that the over-emphasis on the primacy of production contributed to the neglect of consumer needs under *real existierender Sozialismus*. One need not go so far as Peter Wiles, who asserted that studies of consumer demand, advocated by some Soviet economists, are actually *contrary* to Marxism. But if one also takes into account Marx's treatment of circulation as unproductive, as not adding to value, this does suggest that doctrine in these matters reinforced the tendency to regard demand (and use-value) as in some sense of secondary importance – though, needless to say, there were other and probably more important reasons for the regime's choice of priorities.

Let us look more closely at the concept of 'economy of labour-time'. Before doing so, one important issue must be tackled. 'Transformation of values' is usually discussed in relation to a quite different problem: that of whether Marx had 'forgotten' to transform inputs. The point is that in Marx prices of commodities would tend to be proportional to values (to the quantity of socially necessary labour-power) only if the organic composition of capital were the same. If it was not, then, since the total capital advanced would tend to command the same rate of profit, 'prices of production' would emerge, which would differ from values: these prices would tend to be higher than values where organic composition of capital is above average, lower if below.

At first sight this may appear to have nothing to do with socialist economics. Yet it is directly connected with the concept of valuations (or cost calculations) in terms of labour-*time*, as suggested by Engels in *Anti-Dühring*, and by many other Marxist or semi-Marxist writers, from Strumilin to Castoriadis. For such an approach is anchored in labour-values, as these are defined in Volume I of *Das Kapital*. The corollary is that 'prices of production', introduced in Volume III. are a capitalist *deformation*, that under socialism 'values' are in this sense reinstated, as they would be if goods were costed (valued) in terms of the labour they contained. (I abstract here from the vexed problem of reducing complex or skilled labour to simple labour.) This does *not* mean that these theorists, any more than did Engels, believed in a theory of value under socialism; but the computations of cost, made by socialist planners or by 'society', would be based on *labour-time*.

A brief digression is now required into the meaning of Marx's 'transformation' of values. What *is* 'transformation'? Three interpretations are possible.

(a) *Historical*   Values predominated at one time, but 'prices of production' are the rule when capitalism develops.

(b) *'Conditional tense'*. Goods *would* exchange at values if organic composition of capital were everywhere equal, but as it is not, they do not.

Rubin spoke of values and prices of production 'not as theories of two types of economics, but the theory of the same economy at two levels of abstraction'.[43] Another way of expressing this idea is first to conceive of capital as a single unit (or the sum of all capitals) extracting a total of surplus-value, and then assuming many capitals and competition; this total would then be divided between the separate capitalists in proportion to the capital $(c+v)$ which each of them advanced.

(c) *A two-stage process*   Goods are produced at their values, which means that capitalists in sectors of low organic composition of capital make higher profits, and vice versa. (This follows from the assumption of a common rate of exploitation.) However, the entire surplus is paid into a sort of enormous joint pot, from which capitalists then draw their share of this surplus, in proportion to the total capital they have advanced.

This last explanation is, for example, that used by Mandel.[44] In my view it is metaphysical: there *is* no pot. Capitalists in sectors of low organic composition of capital do *not* derive the same surplus per employee as those with high organic composition; only the second of the above three interpretations is tenable. However, orthodoxy seems mainly to embrace the third (with some reference also to the first). In this case, the elimination of capitalists and their 'redistribution-of-surplus' pot also eliminates transformation. We are back to surrogate labour-values; calculations in labour-time *replace* calculations in terms of values, i.e. in hours and not in money. Price of production, or its labour equivalent, disappears.

Let us look at the consequences of cost-computations in terms of labour, and its corollary, the 'economy of labour-time'. Strumilin in 1920 faced the logic of this position squarely: 'mankind has only to economise labour-time; materials and energy are inexhaustible'. Commenting on this doctrine, Yurovsky wrote, over fifty years ago: it is not true that materials and energy are inexhaustible, that there are in effect no scarce resources *except* labour; what of land in the middle of towns, or oil-bearing land?[45] Novozhilov remarked, forty years later, that the latest machines must be scarce even under full communism, unless it be assumed that technical progress ceases.[46] One might add: what of time, not labour-time but simply the passage of time, as when it takes six instead of four years to achieve a given objective? (Strumilin tried as follows to allow for time: labour-values fall with rising productivity, so that, by producing today rather than next year, one produces more value. Not really satisfactory, but an ingenious attempt!) Is one to ignore land rent, or capital-intensity, in assessing relative costs of alternative projects? Should land be valued at zero because it is deemed to have no value? Should capital-intensive projects be 'priced' lower, in making calculations, than they would have been if capitalists had been making them? Would this be reasonable, rational, efficient? One cannot but agree with Yurovsky, apropos the use of such devices as rent and interest: only the fact that they 'formed the basis of class income under capitalism can explain the psychological reluctance to use such calculations'.[47]

It is necessary to add that, for Marx, computation of costs in labour-time could be (would be?) only temporary: in a higher phase of communism, when there is superabundance and all work is a pleasure, there would be no point in economising labour.

It will be neither Man's direct labour nor labour-time, but the appropriation by Man of his own universal force of production, it is the understanding and mastering of nature by the totality of society, i.e. the flowering of the social individual . . . When in its immediate form labour will have ceased to be the source of wealth, labour-time will and must cease to be a measure of work, just as exchange-value will cease to be a measure of use-value.[48]

Tartarin comments that this superdeveloped society, when work itself ceases to be important, must be seen as a kind of fuller-than-full communism ('La phase supérieure de la phase supérieure'). The reader will, I trust, excuse me if this totally utopian vision is taken no further here.

To sum up: Marx had little that was relevant to say about computation of costs under socialism (and implied that under full communism costs would not matter anyhow). Marxists who have tried to adapt his theory of value tend wrongly to use 'valuations' in terms of (direct) labour-cost alone, which, so far as efficient resource allocation is concerned, is plainly inadequate, as it ignores scarcity of production factors other than labour, *and* neglects use-value. In Soviet practice, fixing prices by reference to costs, and claiming that this is ideologically the correct thing to do, is certainly a misleading procedure, but Marxist theory provides no guide to finding anything better, and indeed seems to bar consideration of possible alternatives: thus Novozhilov had an uphill struggle to introduce the concept of opportunity-cost, under the rubric of 'feedback costs', because Marx nowhere explicitly recognised opportunity-cost in his value theory (though it is surely evident that alternative uses forgone *do and must influence* decisions on resource allocation). Labour-time can be measured in hours, but it is far from clear, unless one assumes the existence of money, how other elements of cost can be computed and added to a sum of labour-time. Or, indeed, how it is possible to calculate the labour-time devoted to the production of each of millions of products, since, as Bettelheim correctly observes, a product is often the work of all of society and not only of that labourer or group of labourers who have made it . . . Their work involves very large amounts of the work of others, to provide tools, materials and means, which are combined within a highly complex organisation . . . Most are made by workers who also produce simultaneously a great variety of products, so that their contribution to each product cannot be precisely determined . . .[49]

If we consider this last point as a 'merely' technical one, one is then left with another and more fundamental difficulty: how does one compare costs and results? Suppose it is correctly calculated that a tractor and a radio set of given designs require respectively 44½ and 12 hours of simple labour to produce. That tells one literally nothing about their use-value. In a market economy the willingness of the user to pay for the cost of the product, plus a margin for profit, represents its 'social recognition', makes it 'worthwhile' to continue production. Of course in the real world of inflation, uncertainty and instability things are not so simple. But what are socialist planners to do? In the USSR some have long advocated price and rate-of-return calculations which would play this same role, though this has little meaning given the nature of Soviet prices (which neither in theory nor in practice reflect scarcity, demand, opportunity-cost). Such calculations are in any case explicitly condemned by Bettelheim: 'they teach us nothing directly about the needs of development of socialist production . . . At best they could identify productive combinations which, within a given structure of prices, would maximise the surplus value which capital can extract from the exploitation of labour power.'[50]

I would have thought that *any* society (in the real world) should try to increase the difference between cost and result, for that is what the surplus measures (who *gets* the profit is another matter!). But in any event, what is Bettelheim's alternative? Of course *any* price, any valuation system in money terms, is imperfect, and there exist some objectives which it will fail to reflect (external diseconomies such as pollution or congestion, ugliness, disagreeable conditions at work, and so on). We should try to take such matters into account, just as there are decisions – say, the level of provision for old age pensioners, or public parks – to which profit-type calculations should not apply at all. We *should* try to maximise 'socially useful effect', if only we knew what it was and how to measure it. Western economics too has a similar operationally meaningless concept: the social welfare function. It is like Rousseau's *volonté générale*. Harold Laski used to say: 'the trouble is that, if you met the General Will walking down the Strand, how would you recognise it!'

In what units should socialist planners measure socially useful effect, or use-value? *How*, except in money terms, can one compare the use-value of shoes, ships, sealing-wax and cabbages? (Kings will have been abolished . . .) *Who* is to do the comparing? Having done this, how is he or she, how are they, to act so as to implement the findings? If citizens are displeased with the outcome, how are they to argue their case, by reference to what criteria? If the 'law of value' ceases to apply in any of its forms, the task seems to have no theoretical or statistical base. It has no institutional base either. Even Ollman may have introduced a touch of possibly unintentional irony: 'although Marx recognises that demand is elastic, he never doubts that his proletarian planners – whose actual planning mechanisms are never discussed – will make the right equations . . . in deciding how much of a given article to produce'.[51] Needless to say, one does not want a detailed organisational blueprint. What is surely essential is some indication of how hundreds of millions of people will or can decide on what to produce, and necessarily also the production of the means to produce what it has been decided to produce.

Bettelheim, while aware of some of the problems, speaks in terms of what can only be called evasion-slogans – though he specifically admits that many Marxist economists have neglected use-value and resisted marginal calculations where their use was appropriate ('although it follows from the differential calculus'). We have phrases such as 'effective participation of the masses in the elaboration and execution of plans', to ensure that the plan becomes 'a "concentrate" of the will and aspiration of the masses', based upon 'a real economic calculation, a direct measure of socially necessary labour', 'social appropriation'. The fundamental law of developed socialism is 'the law of social direction of the economy', under which one has direct economic and social calculation which does not proceed by the detour of the law of value. This would ensure the 'extension of the field of action of the direct producers, their domination over conditions of production and reproduction'.[52] 'Society', 'the direct producers', should decide. How?

Sixty years ago some of the discussants of Soviet Russia saw the problem but failed to indicate a way out. Thus Kreve's units of labour-time were defined as one hour of unskilled labour fulfilling work-norms 100 per cent, the time being 'socially necessary' and 'purposefully utilised'. Yurovsky, in reporting this, remarked that the model lacked any means of 'determining either social necessity or purposefulness', which in a market model are, of course, determined in the market.[53] Strumilin, in 1920, tried to adapt to the task the notion of diminishing marginal utility: as more is produced, so gradually each additional unit generates less marginal social utility, until eventually the labour effort required to make more of this good ceases to be worth making.[54] This is reminiscent of Jevons, who wrote: 'labour will be carried on until the increment of utility from any of the employment just balances the increment of pain'. Hardly in the Marxist tradition, but an effort to cope with a real problem. Has anyone advanced any further since 1920? Of course, some labour can be regarded as satisfying or even pleasurable, in which case Strumilin's formulation would be unsatisfactory. But the notion of diminishing marginal utility is not thereby rendered irrelevant. Some goods are 'worth' more than others, and their worth is affected by the intensity of yet unsatisfied wants, and therefore also by the supplies available. However, all this still leaves unsettled the important question: in what units should or would the calculations be expressed, and how one is to calculate? Then, equally important, *who* is to do this?

We must tackle the institutional aspect of the question. What possibility is there that 'society' can decide about the product mix, compare alternative sets of ends and means? It must be emphasised that there are very strong tendencies in the Marxist doctrine which (*pace* Yugoslavia) point to a *centralised* all-embracing plan. This is for reasons at once doctrinal and practical. The rejection of 'commodity production' (production for exchange, as distinct from for use), the assertion that 'society' deliberately decides about needs and how to provide for them, makes it hard even to conceive of decentralisation, except in so far as this relates to details of implementation. Who or what institution, *except* at the centre, can consider the needs of the whole society? What *local* authority or committee could do so, when it could only have knowledge and responsibility for its own locality? – and yet, in modern industry, all areas contain numerous units producing for, and drawing their inputs from, other areas. How could the production unit know for whom to produce, what to produce, when to supply it, how it is to obtain its inputs (and from where) unless the planners decide and inform? The resultant complexities will be referred to at length later. All that is necessary to establish is the *centralising logic* of 'production for use', of the elimination of the market.

Perhaps the theory and practice of this centralising logic is contained in the following quotation from I. Rubin:

> In a socialist economy, the relations between members of the society are organised consciously . . . The co-ordination and subordination [*sopodchineniye*] of the individuals is made by reference to calculations made *ex ante* concerning the technical needs of production. This system of production relations represents a closed totality, directed by a single will . . . Evidently, certain changes could become necessary, but these will occur within the system, by order of the directing organs, who will respond to changes in the technique of production . . . But if there is independence or autonomy of separate enterprises, then the transfer of products can only occur in the form of purchase-and-sale.[55]

In other words, one would have commodity production.

Bettelheim too, correctly, notes that commodity production, production for exchange, occurs when separate production units are autonomous, when their activities are not wholly incorporated in the plan. It is this 'separation', and not the factor of ownership, which is decisive.[56] This is a way of expressing Marx's belief that under socialism society will be like a great united workshop. ('All labour in which many individuals co-operate necessarily requires a commencing will to co-ordinate and unify the process'; *Das Kapital*.)

The model has strong centralising implications, but the manner in which 'the associated producers' could decide what to produce, and how they could compare costs with results, was left vague by Marx. Lenin, however, was quite clear in *his* interpretation: 'The whole of society will have become a single office and a single factory . . .', and 'All citizens become employees and workers of a *single* country-wide state syndicate'.[57]

A Digression on Marxian Economics

Since this book is primarily concerned with economics of *socialism*, it is unnecessary to consider certain other ambiguities of doctrine which arise in Marxian political economy. As already pointed out, for Marx 'values' (=socially necessary labour-time) *underlie* prices; the former are essence, the latter are appearance. However, as pointed out by a number of critics, Marx not only 'forgot' to transform inputs in his incomplete picture of the process of transformation, he also from time to time failed to remember that the 'underlying values' are invisible magnitudes, that neither workers nor capitalists can respond to them, for *they* see actual (or expected) *prices*, or wages. This led Marx into his crude initial version of the 'law' of the falling rate of profit: of course *if* the rate of exploitation tends to equality in the sense of being proportional to the wages bill (i.e. to v in the formula $c+v+s$), then naturally an increase in the 'organic composition of capital', i.e. of c, would result in a fall in the profit rate. Note that he did *not* forget the increase in productivity, since this is listed as a factor causing the profit rate to fall. Of course, Marx did list some countervailing tendencies, but he seemed often to forget the fact that there is in capitalism no force which tends to equalise the rate of exploitation ($s \div v$) where organic compositions of capital vary. Capitalists in this model (as also in Chicago) concern themselves with profits, which relate to the total capital advanced, and they and the workers bargain about wages. In equilibrium, competition would indeed tend to equalise profit rates and wage rates, but in doing so would be bound to make rates of exploitation *unequal* as between firms and industries, since no reason exists (given that techniques differ) why organic compositions of capital should be or become equal. Of course in the real world no capitalist would adopt a new labour-saving technique if this did not lead to a rise in $s \div v$, i.e. in his profit divided by his wages bill.

Rosa Luxemburg committed a similar error when seeking to demonstrate, in her highly original book *The Accumulation of Capital*, that capitalism can only survive by expanding into non-capitalist areas and sectors. The imbalances between the two departments on which she based her analysis are in terms of *values*. She ignored the fact that, when shortages and surpluses appear, *prices* change and give rise to corrective trends. She also neglected inter-sectoral financial flows (credits, and so on).

It may well be that profits do show a tendency to fall, and the role of the Third World in maintaining the viability of developed capitalism may indeed be underestimated by conventional analysis. As to the former, we have theories such as those of Glyn and Sutcliffe to the effect that profits fall because of the increasing bargaining power of organised labour, and Joan Robinson has pointed to the importance of Third World markets from the standpoint of economies of scale in production. This is not the place to discuss such theories, but I would only point out that they do not conform to what Marx or Rosa Luxemburg actually said (which of course in no way invalidates them!). Marx's theory of the 'value of labour-power' certainly played no part in his argument about the falling rate of profit, and for Luxemburg it formed the basis of an underconsumptionist view of capitalist crisis: because wages do *not* rise the capitalists cannot find sufficient outlets for the increased output of their industry.

Among other aspects of Marx's theories which could be critically examined,

I will mention one more, directly concerned with his theory of value. The question of demand or use-value as a factor has been referred to already. But what of choice of techniques? When I discussed this question with the Norwegian Jon Elster, he made the point that Marx had to assume that techniques were given and could not be affected by relative prices. I objected that capitalists, in pursuit of profit, *would* be influenced by relative prices of, for example, machines and labour in choosing the method of production. Elster replied that Marx could not even contemplate such a possibility 'because he was a Hegelian'. How so?, I inquired. He replied that if values were 'essence' and prices 'appearance', he could not possibly allow prices to underlie values rather than vice versa. If choice of techniques were affected by price, then prices would be co-determinants of the quantity of labour used to produce a commodity. In an unpublished note, he wrote:

> If the technology depends on prices, and values on the technology, then values no longer have an epistemological independence of prices. Values, prices and technology must be determined simultaneously. If we admit changing preferences, values can even be affected by demand. If a shift in demand induces a change in relative prices, and thus a change in technology, then the change in preferences will have caused the ensuing change in commodity values. (Quoted from 'Lecture notes on Marxism', kindly supplied by their author)

This seems unanswerable to me.

Sancta Simplicitas

It is, unfortunately, part of the Marxist tradition to treat these matters as non-problems, because with the overcoming of commodity fetishism and the contradiction between value and use-value, substituting direct social choice for the 'detour' via the market and the law of value, all will be *clear and simple*.

Let us cite some examples at random. Robinson Crusoe on his island decided directly how to use his labour in relation to the satisfaction of his needs. 'The community of free individuals' will 'consciously apply the combined labour-power of the community. All the characteristics of Crusoe's labour are here repeated, with the difference that they are social instead of individual' (Marx). 'The relations between men in their labour and useful objects they receive will be *simple and transparent*' (Marx). 'Everything will be done quite simply without the so-called value' (Engels). 'Communist humanity will create the highest form of administration of things, where the very problem of collective and individual [decision-making] will disappear as the human beings of the future will do what is called for by the dry figures of statistical calculation. Administration of men will vanish for ever' (Bukharin). 'The function of control and accountancy, becoming ever more simple, will be performed by each in turn' (Lenin). 'To organise the whole economy on the lines of the postal service . . . all under the leadership of the armed workers, that is our immediate [*sic*] aim' (Lenin). 'Capitalism has simplified the work of accounting and control, has reduced it to a comparatively simple system of *bookkeeping*, that any literate person can do' (Lenin; emphasis in the original).[58]

One cannot deny the truth of Katsenellenboigen's remark that these writers were

romantics on this issue . . . The classical scholars of Marxism conceived of future society as a system in which everything would be obvious. People's goals would be obvious, as would the available resources for transforming them into products needed by the population. Marx and Engels evidently pictured future society as an analogous to a nineteenth-century factory, which represented for them a model of organisation, unlike the anarchy of the market mechanism.[59]

It cannot be too strongly emphasised that complexity is not just a quantitative matter: as Marxists should know, quantity passes into quality. Such vital questions as decentralisation and centralisation, plan and market, the interests of the part and the interests of the whole, the identification of the public good, the alienation of individuals, the necessity and dangers of hierarchy and bureaucracy and, incidentally, most of the major problems now plaguing the Soviet economy, all arise directly or indirectly out of the *vast scale and innumerable interdependencies* of the modern industrial economy. It will not and cannot be 'simple'. The economy cannot be planned and run 'like the post office'. It is not just a matter of technique plus accounting-arithmetic, as Lenin (before 1918) seemed naively to imagine.

It may seem unnecessary to analyse the reasons, but briefly one must. In the USSR at this time there are *12 million identifiably different products* (dis-aggregated down to specific types of ball-bearings, designs of cloth, size of brown shoes, and so on). There are close to 50,000 industrial establishments, plus, of course, thousands of construction enterprises, transport undertakings, collective and state farms, wholesaling organs and retail outlets. None of them can produce or distribute anything without the co-ordinated co-operation of the activities of numerous economic units which produce, transport, or distribute. A large factory, for instance, making cars or chemical machinery, is an assembly plant of parts and components which can be made in literally thousands of different factories, each of which has also other tasks and which, in turn, may depend on supplies of materials, fuel and machines, made by hundreds or more of *other* production units. Introduce the further dimension of time (things need to be provided punctually and in sequence), add the importance of provision for repair, maintenance, replacement, investment in future productive capacity, the training and deployment of the labour force, its needs for housing, amenities, hairdressers, dry-cleaners, heating, and the need therefore for building materials, hair-clippers, fuel, furniture . . . 'Simple' indeed! A doubtless sarcastic Soviet author remarked: 'Mathe-maticians have calculated that in order to draft an accurate and fully inte-grated plan for material supply just for the Ukraine for one year requires the labour of the entire world's population for 10 million years.'[60] (Of course, the plan for next year will be ready a few million years before that, but it will not be 'accurate and fully integrated'.)

As we shall see, the Soviet centralised planning mechanism finds itself overwhelmed by these tasks, and numerous unintended distortions and disproportions are the consequence of this. Thus the same source that reported that there were 12 million products also stated that there were 48,000 plan 'positions',[61] that is to say, that the average plan 'position' is an aggregation of hundreds of product variants, which helps to explain why the 'wrong' goods are so frequently produced. It is believed among some Marxist critics of the USSR that the system became bureaucratic through 'betrayal', or through the machinations of Stalin and of self-interested bureaucrats. Trotsky wrote that the early Bolsheviks expected 'the *nachal'nik* [boss] to turn into a simple technical agent' under workers' control, and then in a fine *non sequitur* added that this did not happen because revolution had not broken out in advanced countries![62] He also wrongly identified the power of the bureaucracy with 'control of the sphere of consumption',[63] which is an odd error for a Marxist, taking the effect for the cause. Naturally, the 'bureaucracy' (or whatever one calls the ruling stratum) does not fail to benefit materially from its power: as Trotsky also wrote, 'whoever has goods to allocate never forgets *himself*'. But, given the centralised system, itself the consequence of the elimination of the market, the powerful bureaucracy becomes a *functional necessity*. Lenin, *after* the seizure of power, saw clearly enough that 'enterprises will not be able to function correctly unless there is a united will, connecting all the groups of toilers with the precision of a clockwork mechanism'.[64] Lenin, of course, was against bureaucracy, but *how* is his 'united will' to operate? 'Clockwork' produces the wrong image, since it is mechanical, it ticks without human beings pushing and pulling at the pendulum. But the elimination of the market mechanism requires it to be replaced, by the 'visible hand', by people. One of Marx's more misleading statements referred to the replacement of the 'government of men' by the 'administration of things'. One cannot administer *things*! One cannot address a cabbage or a ton of ball-bearings; one can instruct or persuade *human beings* to grow, make, or transport things.

If thousands, or even millions, of interconnected and interdependent decisions must be taken, to ensure production and delivery of the items which society needs – and this must be preceded by some operationally meaningful set of decisions about what is needed – elaborate administrative machinery is required to ensure the necessary responsibilities and co-ordination. No action can be taken unless three elements are present: *information, motivation* and *means*. A worker or production manager cannot know who needs which products unless he or she is informed. Who is in a position to know? That unit in the complex planning mechanism which is able to calculate requirements (for ball-bearings, lathes, tractors, sulphuric acid, babies' diapers, window-glass, and so on). Then some other departments (numerous *different* departments, because of the scale of the task) have to ensure that the *means* are available, or can be produced, or provided from stock. Even the most 'motivated' worker, manager, or production-planning department cannot ensure that action is taken unless the means are provided, and the means (i.e. the various inputs) are bound to be administered by several other departments. Hence the *paperasserie*, interdepartmental conferences, regulations, delays, inconsistencies, the need to refer questions to higher authority, and other well-known examples of bureaucracy. To denounce it is easy, but it has its vital role in production in a centrally planned marketless economy, and so it grows and 'flourishes'.

Complexity calls not just for many officials to administer it, but requires a *multilevel hierarchy* of offices. This, be it noted, corresponds to a hierarchy of levels of decision. Let me draw up an example. An organisational diagram would correspond to (oversimplified) sketch in Figure 1.1. Thus the decision on production and installation of equipment for pumping stations is a consequence and an integral necessary part of the decision to build a pumping station, which in turn is a consequence of a specific decision about the type and location of pipelines, which is a function of the development plan for oil in West Siberia, which is a result of consideration of the needs for and alternative sources of oil, which in turn is part of fuel policy decision even 'higher' up. Of course, there is a vast number of other such decisions, and – this is of particular importance – at each point there are alternative uses for the products, machinery and labour. The choices made are in their turn dependent on inputs of various kinds (materials, machines, people) which could also be used for other purposes. To achieve the desired result, thousands of people located thousands of miles apart must work together in a network of interrelated activities. The parts must fit together, must *be fitted together*. When the 'fit' is particularly close, then in the real capitalist world the relationships are often hierarchically administered, and do not rely on the looser market mechanism, though the same result is sometimes achieved through subcontracting. (Just as in the car industry some firms make their own carburettors in a workshop they own and run, others have long-term agreements with a specialised component firm which they neither own nor operate.)

The entire project would be brought to a halt if one link in this multilevel chain were to be broken; if, for instance, some enterprise in the food industry were not to send the necessary victuals to the north, or the required metal were not delivered to whoever is charged with making pipe, or the goods wagons were not provided to move the pipe, or the workers to install it, if the heating failed to heat their dwellings, the repair and maintenance workshops lacked tools, and so on. At each level it must be someone's job to ensure that these things are done. They do not happen 'spontaneously', and they are not and cannot be decided by vote, any more than a train crew or station staff can or should decide whether the 12.30 to Manchester should or should not run.

The central organs of a centralised planning system find it very hard to try to keep pace with a huge volume of work. While it is true that in the Soviet case the task was rendered more difficult by the efforts to achieve high growth rates under conditions of shortage ('taut planning'), the nature of the system requires a complex hierarchical structure, with a division of functions between departments and the usual bureaucratic *modus operandi*. The term 'bureaucratic' should be seen as descriptive, not a term of abuse. If an over-worked official responsible for, say, pumps cannot decide on his own initiative

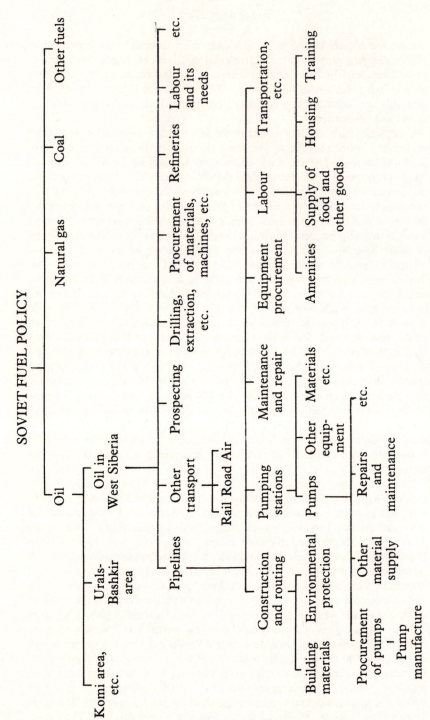

Figure 1.1 *Soviet energy: a decision-making model.*

on a request for supplies to Omsk, this is because he *must* consult those departments who know about other claims for pumps, the possibilities of producing more pumps, the availability of materials for the production of pumps, the spare capacity available at various factories which could be making them, and so on. To see him or her as an elected part-timer, subject to instant recall, is pure fantasy. Evidently he or she has a specialist job to do, a responsibility to carry, in the course of which he must relate with others whose tasks relate to his own, and must fulfil tasks within plans laid down by those above him, whose responsibilities include a wider area.

It is a truism, seldom mentioned in textbooks in East or West, that what appears to be the right thing to do depends in some degree on the area of responsibility of the decision-maker. Earlier in this chapter I referred to the differences of *interest* which must arise whenever there is choice under conditions of relative scarcity. At this point my task is to emphasise the limitations of *information*. I will return to this in the context of Marx's views on the division of labour, but it is important here to stress the effects of the sheer colossal scale of the planning process upon the ability of individuals *within* this process to encompass it. Let us return to the individual whose task it is to ensure the availability of materials for the production of pumps. It does not matter for the present purpose how intelligent, how educated, how conscientious, the person concerned is. It is extremely unlikely that, in his or her specialised capacity, he or she will be able to envisage the problems of transporting pumps, installing and maintaining pipelines, or the advantages of utilising a particular kind of turbo-drill, let alone the fuel requirements of a given industry. He or she may indeed prefer to use leisure hours for some totally different purpose, say, playing the viola. It will be some body, therefore also somebody, 'above' him (or her) who will consider the number of pumps needed and their design and use, and someone 'above' *that* person will relate pumps to the pipelines, the pipelines to the plan for the oil industry, and the plans of those who use oil. As one goes 'higher' one encompasses a wider area, but in doing so one loses precision of detail. The persons concerned with oil in West Siberia have enough on their plate without having the time or the knowledge required to consider the decisions on supply of parts for pump manufacture which was our original individual's responsibility. Self-evident? No, not to those whose reading of Marx inclines them to suppose that it will all be simple, that 'the people', 'society', the 'associated producers' will settle it all in amicable democratic discussion.

At least Bahro sees the point. He writes:

Unless one is prepared to accept that the structure of regulation in interconnected production is objectively hierarchical, the whole problem of socialist democracy can only be raised in an agitational way . . . Technically and informationally, social labour functions are necessarily subordinate to one another.[65]

Unfortunately he does not explain how he proposes to 'overcome' the consequences of the resultant division of labour. But of this more later.

Is there then no possibility for democratic control over the processes of production and circulation? There most certainly is such a possibility, even a necessity, and I will discuss this at length. But first one must make clear that the democratic process will *not* be relevant to a wide category of microeconomic decision-making. Those responsible for making pumps will *not* vote about where they should go. The elected assembly at the centre which will adopt a general plan for society will, *of course*, have neither the time nor the knowledge to concern itself with such a detail as pumps, let alone where any particular consignment should be sent (unless some scandalous situation arises which is brought to their attention). Otherwise, as Antonov wrote, next year's plan will be ready in several million years.

The French radical thinker Cornelius Castoriadis also has a realistic view of complexities, and has come up with an interesting notion of a 'plan factory': specialists in plan-formulations, with the help of computers, would draw up a series of internally consistent alternative plans, between which the democratically elected assembly could choose. He also envisages a consumer goods *market*; much though he shares the traditional Marxist's dislike of 'commodity production', he is unable to see how consumer choice can be ensured, amid a vast range of alternatives, other than by letting consumers spend their income (tokens, in reality 'money') as they think fit. He points out that decisions by majority vote can be positively noxious in this area of decision-making, because minorities too have the right to consumer satisfaction (in other words, it is wrong in principle to decide by, say, a majority of 3:1 not to provide rye bread or classical concerts; if a significant minority desires them, they should have them, and have some means of 'paying' for them). But to this, too, we will have to return. Castoriadis does not extend this principle to producers' goods: these, it seems, will be planned in his computerised plan-factory.[66]

One must, however, remark that the division between consumers' goods and producers' goods, and also between ends and means, presents conceptual and practical problems. Of course, they *are* distinct: a machine-tool and a pair of trousers are, as Marx says, products respectively of department I and department II, producers' goods and consumers' goods respectively. However, apart from the fact that some products are in both departments, depending on what they are used for (fuel, potatoes), consumers' goods cannot be produced without inputs of producers' goods, and a market for the former cannot be effective unless its effects penetrate into the producers' goods sector too (demand for red skirts can only be 'effective' if the clothing industry can effectively demand the required cloth, dyestuffs, zip-fasteners, and so on). Castoriadis's plan-factory would therefore have to be highly responsive to the consumer market, directly and indirectly. Ends and means are also not easy to distinguish. Thus, reverting to the 'fuel' diagram in Figure 1.1, the pumps are a means to an end (pipelines). But pipelines are a means to a 'higher' end (moving crude oil from A to B). Oil is a means to an end, that of providing fuel, but fuel too is a means – *and* an end (i.e. it is used to keep warm, but also in processes of manufacture). This too can be seen as a form of multilevel hierarchy.

These various 'levels' and categories of decision-making should lead one to consider systems analysis and organisational theory. It is worth recalling the name of a pioneer in this field: Bogdanov. He was a Marxist in his own estimation, but most Marxists denounced him as alien to the ideology, not only Lenin but also (for instance) Lipietz. Latter-day Marxists fear the implications of organisation theory – which Bogdanov called *tektologiya* – and they do indeed present problems for socialists. But this is not a good enough reason to evade the issue, which is bound to come knocking at the door whether we like it or not. In any event, the idea of 'simplicity' must be decisively rejected.

The *Ex Ante* Illusion

Marx himself, and many of his followers, stressed the contrast between conscious plan and anarchic market. In a socialist planned economy labour will be 'directly social', that is, it will be allocated in a planned way by society to predetermined tasks, to produce in accordance with needs as determined *ex ante*. This is contrasted with a capitalist market economy, in which expenditure of labour is validated *ex post, a posteriori*, after the event, through the process of exchange. Society will be able to allocate and decide correctly *ex ante*, through planning the use of its resources and allocating labour to the various tasks which are known in advance.[67]

This, in a complex modern economy, is as unreal as is Marx's parallel with Robinson Crusoe. Crusoe (or a patriarchal family unit, another of the parallels used by Marx) can observe directly, and choose between alternatives and their consequences, and there is an immediate link between purpose, action, means and result. Of course Crusoe can make a mistake, such as, for instance, planting a crop in unsuitable soil, but he will see this directly and learn from his experience. All will indeed be simple and 'transparent'.

There are several fallacies involved when one shifts from this simple model to the complex real world of hundreds of millions of people with a complex division of labour.

The first has already been discussed and need be only briefly restated: *how* are society's needs to be articulated, the choices made, and by *whom*? The words 'by society' are literally meaningless as they stand. It is like saying that 'the people' will decide the timetable of the London–Paris air service or the number of onions to be planted. In the real world millions of millions of interrelated microeconomic decisions can only be made in offices (and so by officials). They could fail to reflect needs. It is the purest intellectual abdication to evade this by simply *assuming* that plans *do* incorporate needs, that planners (along with other citizens) have turned miraculously into omniscient angels, that unresponsiveness, inertia, routine-mindedness, rejection of new ideas, *cannot* happen. Perfect information, perfect foresight, are among the most unreal assumptions of certain 'bourgeois' general equilibrium models. As Loasby has pointed out in an admirable book,[68] the assumption of perfect foresight is inherently inconsistent with freedom of choice, since perfectly foreseeable choice is a contradiction in terms: if A and B have any authentic choice, then C and D, whose activities relate to them, cannot know *in advance* what they will choose, and therefore cannot know in advance what *they* in turn will choose to do.

Loasby is attacking general equilibrium theory and bad textbooks based upon it. But his words apply equally to a socialist economy. Surely we cannot assume that plans are correct *ex ante*. Indeed, we cannot even *know* that they were correct *ex ante* unless there is some means of *a posteriori* verification. It is not only a question of action, but also of inaction, that is, both an incorrect response and failure to respond are possible. For all this one needs criteria, and some sort of response or feedback mechanism. This brings one back to use-values, how to measure them, how to enable the *users* – who, after all, are a key factor here – to contribute to the measurement; and, finally, how the evaluation of goods and services by those members of society for which they are intended can affect the pattern of future production. 'Users' are, of course, not only citizens in their individual capacity. A great range of products – steel sheet, boilers, textile machinery, and so on – is made for use in the processes of production.

Later in this book I shall develop further the theoretical, practical and institutional implications of the evident need for *ex post* verification, and ensuring some feedback effect on those who make plans and decide on production and distribution. But right now let us look more closely at how plans are and can be made.

In a sense, decisions even in a capitalist market economy are made as a result of an *ex ante* calculation. The question is only the nature of the information available. It could be the result of a market survey, or an extrapolation of trends. It may be that production is a result of a specific order, that one has a definite *ex ante* contract for a specific customer. Much depends on the nature of the activity and of the product. Thus shipyards generally produce in accordance with an order book, at a price negotiated before production begins, while shoe manufacturers produce in quantity in a more 'speculative' way, hoping that shops and customers will buy the shoes, with a risk that they will not. Restaurants will buy in various materials, and hire labour, in the hope that the customers will come and eat; they *may* prefer to stay at home, or to ask for items which are not on the menu. Any large-scale investment decision is complicated by the time factor: the gap between taking the decision and completion of the investment project may be five or six years, and the capital assets may last another twenty years or more. New techniques, change in tastes, investment decisions taken by others, could upset the forecast (*ex ante!*) upon which the original decision rested. The result could be excess capacity, or insufficient capacity, in relation to needs.

It is certainly arguable that in a centrally planned economy those who take investment decisions have more information, especially about the investment plans of related industries, than is the case in a capitalist market economy. Today's prices are a poor guide to the relative scarcities of six years' time, even if one abstracts from inflation and other distorting elements. (Do any of us know much about what the rate of interest and prices of materials will be in six *months'* time, let alone six years?) But it is self-evident that the passage of time adds to the element of uncertainty in *every* economy, unless we conceive of some sort of static, unchanging equilibrium, and *ex post* verification remains essential, as does *ex post* valuation of the results of productive effort.

In a socialist economy it will surely also be the case that, while ships or power-station equipment can be built or produced by direct agreement with the prospective users, this will not be the case for, say, shoes or onions. They will not be made or grown after each user has indicated his or her desire for them. The socialist producers will therefore, to some extent, be guessing. The plan for shoes and onions *cannot* be known to be correct *ex ante*. The same is true of socialist restaurants. No more than their capitalist *confrères* can they know *ex ante* what the diners will ask for, or whether they will wish to dine at all. They will learn *ex post* whether their preference will be for *canard à l'orange* or haddock and chips – though of course they can base expectations on extrapolation of past experience, as also happens today.

There is in fact only one way of ensuring that *ex ante* and *ex post* coincide: to let the producers determine consumption. That is, the citizens will wear the shoes which it is decided they should wear, all menus will be *table d'hôte* and the customer assigned to specific restaurants. Such a model would be analogous to the army: when I was a corporal I wore the issue boots and uniform clothing, and ate whatever was provided in the mess-hall. This, however, is *not* what socialists mean when they talk of the 'domination of the direct producers'!

This highlights the importance of *choice*. The more choice there is, the less the predictability, for obvious reasons. It is therefore tempting for planners to limit or even eliminate choice, in the interests of good forecasting and the avoidance of the waste which is the inevitable consequence of getting a forecast wrong. In the USSR citizens often have no alternative but to 'take it or leave it'. Soviet managers are attached to their suppliers, have their customers designated, by the plan. Production is in this sense directly for use. There is indeed less uncertainty than in a capitalist market economy, but less choice too. How can the user influence what is produced, in detail, in a centrally planned economy? This is *not* a simple question. By 'detail' I mean not 'footwear', but the shoes one actually wants, not 'food', but a dish one prefers. Plans are aggregated, they have to be, to be reduced to a 'manageable' number. Needs are specific.

An aspect of choice is *competition*. This is not a word that appeals to most socialists, and is no part of Marxist ideas on socialism. Yet if customers are free to seek their sources of supply, then the converse is that producers will seek customers. Unless there are chronic shortages, this would mean that some producers would have difficulty in ensuring full utilisation of their human and material resources when customers prefer something produced by others: there will be empty seats in the restaurant, empty berths in the ship-yards, some shoes no one wishes to wear. Socialists usually deplore competition because it conflicts with the notion of a planned economy; because it is itself a conflict, whereas in a socialist society everyone should co-operate; and because of waste generated by competition. This waste is of two kinds: the empty seats and shipyards represent unused resources which could be used; and competition generates advertising, 'salesmanship' and other such undesirable phenomena.

This, however, is but one example of something of great importance in real life, which Marxist 'fundamentalists' seldom seem to appreciate: that *no* perfect system exists or can exist, that in general all institutional arrangements carry with them advantages *and* disadvantages. One can seldom get something for nothing. Competition has certain positive features: it is a consequence and pre-condition of choice, it also provides a stimulus, to the successful and the laggards alike. Thus the fact of unused capacity, whether in a shipyard or a restaurant, provides a source of pressure to improve quality and service. Advertising is part of an effort to find customers: its opposite can be, in the Soviet Union usually is, indifference to the customers' needs.

Similarly, *central* planning enables the planners to see the total picture, but at the cost of loss of vision of detail. Decentralisation means clarity at micro level, but at the cost that wider effects may remain unperceived. The best solution is bound to be a compromise.

Reverting to competition, one of its positive aspects relates to the need to ensure that there is a remedy for failure. Suppose that a given good or service is not being provided under the central plan, or is in some way unsatisfactory. Means must exist to correct this. Appeals to the central planners, raising the voice, clamour, is one way. Another is to have the possibility of finding another source of supply, or of setting up a new production unit which will be, in effect, in competition with the existing ones.

It is noteworthy that the same thought has occurred to the Hungarian sociologist Ivan Szelenyi. For him it is a matter of great importance that there be alternatives to the central plan.[69] (We will return to his argument in a moment.) A similar point is made by the Soviet socialist dissident Belotserkovsky, who distinguishes between noxious and benign forms of competition, but lays great stress of the *need* for competition (in its benign form), for otherwise there would be no way of ensuring efficiency and responsiveness to consumer needs.[70]

The only possible reply to this on the part of a fundamentalist-millenarian is mulish repetition: Marx was against it, competition is contrary to socialist principles, in a 'real' socialist economy it would not be needed. No doubt also 'the lion shall lie down with the lamb'. We are back in the realm of religious faith.

There is unfortunately also a Marxist tradition which favours *large* productive units. In discussing Maoism, a contributor to *Radical Philosophy* (Sean Sayers) quotes Lenin's dictum: 'small production engenders capitalism and the bourgeoisie daily, hourly, spontaneously and on a mass scale', and concludes that 'the elimination of classes from society absolutely requires the development of the productive forces and the elimination of such small-scale production'.[71] The word 'such' in the above sentence leaves open the possibility that the author envisages other and more acceptable species of small-scale production, though this seems doubtful, as the development of productive forces has earlier been equated with large scale. But one is struck by the word 'elimination'. How? By a 'socialist' police, or by economic competition from large-scale production? (The latter, of course, would mean that small-scale co-operatives, etc., could flourish where there were no economies of scale, or where, for any reason, large-scale state industry failed to provide the desired quantity or quality.) This point seems to me of very great importance, and more will need to be said about it, and about competition too.

Quality and Quantity

Several references have been made to *quality*. This is a concept much neglected also in 'mainstream' economics. But at least the textbook theory of value does have the merit of emphasising the role of demand. The marginal utility school does this to excess, in the sense that it understates the importance of conditions of production. But willingness to pay, valuation by the user, valuation in *money*, are seen as vital. A *better* machine, shoe, steak, will usually command a higher price. But the Marxist tradition is one of *quantitative* planning. Soviet experience shows how the centre cannot cope either with a fully disaggregated product mix, or with quality. The point is that, apart from the sheer impossibility of the centre handling detailed specifications, quality is by no means easy to define. It is sometimes specific: calorific content of coal, tensile strength, and so on; but frequently it is a matter of user convenience, or taste, of attractiveness – in fact value *in use*, valued *by the user*.

We must distinguish here such things as water or electricity, which are homogeneous, flow down pipes or wires and are readily 'plannable', and those products which come in hundreds or thousands of variants: clothes, instruments and implements, vegetables, and so on. It is the beginning of wisdom to realise that the centre *cannot* plan these 'quantitatively', in any meaningful microeconomic sense. Plans in tonnes or square metres are plainly far too crude to encompass the literally millions of varieties and versions of products with use-values that exist.

Trotsky wrote: 'Cast-iron can be measured in tonnes, electricity in kilowatt-hours. But it is impossible to create a universal plan without reducing all branches to a common value denominator.' Here at least he saw the clear limitations of physical planning even of metals and fuels. He was referring to the USSR in the 1930s, but why should it be different in 'real socialism'?

Soviet experience is decisive here. If a plan is expressed in aggregate quantities, the product mix that 'fits' into such a plan (in tonnes, square metres, or for that matter value in money terms) will not, save by accident, be the mix that is actually needed. If, however, contracts between customers and suppliers determine what the micro content of the plan should be, then the economy is no longer centrally planned, since then the totals too (in tonnes, square metres, etc.) are the *consequence* of the negotiated contracts. Productive units (enterprises) are then *autonomous* and, to make a reality of that autonomy, must be free to obtain the inputs which they need by, in their turn, negotiating contracts with their suppliers. But, as we have seen in repeated quotations, the classics of Marxism have not only insisted that all these inter-relationships be 'planned by society', but have pointed out that separation, autonomy, is the very basis of 'commodity production'. Production is then for someone else's use, not one's own. *One then has a species of market economy.* Or rather, since central planners too would have important functions, it will be a *mixture* between plan and market. My own belief is that such a mixture is an essential ingredient of any feasible or tolerable socialist economy, but the very thought might give the 'fundamentalist' apoplexy. For is not socialism, as he sees it, the *negation* of commodity production?

How would he (or she) reply to the above argument? Possibly one answer is to imagine both absolute abundance *and* a species of static equilibrium. All inputs are then as abundantly and freely available as water is in Scotland. Requirements, needs, inputs, techniques, are all known and hardly ever change. Just as the citizen will go to the store to collect whatever goods he or she wants, so the management would fetch the required steel sheet, lathes, sulphuric acid, cloth, pork, cabbages; that would dispose of the problem of the planning of inputs. The workers will then produce the output which 'society' or its customers require. No money would pass, there would be no exchange, no purchase-and-sale. So – no commodity production. Also no complex bureaucratic central planning mechanism. *Et voilà*!

There are comments to be made on this 'solution'. First, it is actually *not* planning; in so far as no role has been defined for 'society' *as a whole*, the centre has no function. It is anarchist rather than Marxist. Secondly, and much more important, it could not possibly work, and not just because there cannot be this kind of abundance. Whose task is it to foresee, to ensure that the inputs are provided to match the outputs, that stocks of everything are adequate? What of investments, and therefore of investment *goods* (building materials, machines)? And since relative scarcity *will* be a fact of life, and since its very meaning is that productive capacity is *not* sufficient to cover all needs (at zero price), what criteria will there be to choose between alternatives? When producers receive requests to produce more than their capacity permits, or than their supply of inputs make possible, then whose needs are the more urgent? Who, in this sort of model, is to know this, and how is he to act on this knowledge, and this without any prices? No valuations of 'socially useful effect', even assuming that we know how to measure it, can possibly be made by the 'direct producers' at the actual place of production. The necessary comparisons between multiple alternatives *can only be made at the centre*. This is so obvious a consequence of the whole concept of 'production for use', 'directly social labour' and 'the elimination of commodity production', that this entire paragraph may seem an unnecessary detour. The point still needs to be made because there remain persons who consider themselves Marxists who refuse to think in terms of practice (though they speak of 'praxis'!). It was a Marxist theorist who wrote recently of the need 'to re-establish contact between Marxist thought and the reality it purported to address'.[72]

To recapitulate: in a complex industrial economy the interrelation between its parts can be based in principle either on freely chosen negotiated contracts (which means autonomy and a species of commodity production) or on a system of binding instructions from planning offices. *There is no third way.* What can exist, of course, is some *combination* of the two basic principles: that is, some kinds of decision could be freely negotiated, others would be subject to binding administrative instructions. In fact these principles *must* be combined, *must* coexist (do coexist under modern capitalism too). Much more will be said on this necessary coexistence later in this book.

Oscar Lange's prewar model is an early attempt to define a division of function between a central planning board (CPB) and management of enterprises. The essential point in the present context is that it is a *market* model, with prices to which management is supposed to respond, though the prices are manipulated by the CPB. The reasons why I consider it inadequate will be gone into later.

Bahro, in his *Alternative*, tries to cope with the problem in a way which shows a degree of both realism and romanticism. It is realistic because he appreciates that the hierarchical nature of a complex modern economy, with all its interrelationships and complementarities, causes bureaucracy and remoteness, hierarchy and alienation; he therefore believes that the complexity, interrelationships, complementarities, should be reduced. His 'communes' should be small and, as far as possible, self-sufficient. One can indeed imagine a village community, or a good *kibbutz*, genuinely deciding directly how to dispose of its labour, how to produce, without having any specialised control hierarchy. But it is romantic because, while such communities could indeed be brought into existence by committed volunteers, modern industry with its scale and specialisation does not permit self-sufficiency. Many things (fuel, metal, machines, cotton cloth, chemicals, vehicles, refrigerators, those foods which cannot be grown locally) will have to be obtained from outside. How? In Bahro's notion of *Zentralisation von unten* the representatives of the communes would meet and hammer out an all-inclusive plan for the necessary exchanges. But these would be *exchanges*, surely, a species once again of commodity production if freely negotiated. If these exchanges are planned centrally, to reflect the needs and priorities of 'society' as a whole, we are yet again with the centralised model, complete with the functionally necessary bureaucracy.

Ivan Szelenyi has argued persuasively for the need to ensure that there be a possibility for citizens to produce and provide goods and services outside the state planning system. He has in mind both the aspect of freedom of work (i.e. the right of people to prefer to work 'outside', with the implication that conditions of work 'inside' must then be such as to attract, and not to repel, the workforce), and that freedom is needed to replace or supplement whatever the central plan provides if for any reason there is failure.[73] One can only escape from the logic of this argument by assuming that planners *cannot* be unsatisfactory, or that one can devise an effective democratic control process within the planning system that can and will put matters right. Needless to say, it is important to try to do this. Experience suggests, however, that this is rendered difficult by the overwhelming complexity of the central plan. When Andras Hegedus speaks of the present Soviet-type system as one of 'organised irresponsibility',[74] one reason why he is right is that where several different units are *co*-responsible for a given outcome it is remarkably hard to identify who should be blamed when something goes wrong. If, in the end, there are insufficient toothbrushes, detergents, babies' diapers, needles and thread, one can (as Brezhnev has done)[75] deplore this, but, given that the failure to provide them is a consequence of the overwhelming complexity of the central plan (and the fact that such 'minor items' are likely to be the responsibility of junior officials without much claim on scarce resources), what better solution is there than to allow groups of citizens (co-operatives, perhaps) to set up workshops to *make* these things?

To this theme too we will have to return.

Division of Labour

This is an area where the romantic-utopian aspect of Marx's thought is particularly prominent, and it should be examined critically. What does 'overcoming' (transcending, *aufheben*) the division of labour mean? What *can* it mean?

Kolakowski summarises Marx's view, correctly, as follows: 'The division of labour leads necessarily to commerce, i.e. the transformation of objects produced by man into vehicles of abstract exchange-value. When things become commodities, the basic premiss of alienation already exists.'[76] Three kinds of 'division of labour' can be identified. One arises out of *specialisation between productive units*: that is, a factory produces stockings, or carburettors, or canned peas, which are intended for the use of others, a situation which leads to exchange, production for sale not production for use; that is, commodity production. Then there is *specialisation as between people*: some are accountants, others are fishermen, plumbers, professors, electricians, clerks, and so on; that is, *horizontal* division of labour. Finally there is *vertical* division of labour, or hierarchy: that between officers and men, commanders and commanded, organisers and organised. Some, like Bahro, lay particular stress in this connection on the division between physical and mental labour, but it should be appreciated that most 'mental' work does not involve command. Workers can thus become alienated for several reasons: because the things they produce are for the use of people remote from them, are not for themselves; because they undertake work that is repetitive and boring (a point to which Adam Smith drew attention in precisely this connection in *The Wealth of Nations*); and because they are subordinates.

Under socialism, the division of labour is to be 'overcome'. How? It is essential to realise that Marx's version is that of a highly productive *industrial* society; he is not envisaging a return to some kind of simple village life of self-sufficiency. If a division of labour in either of the first two senses already leads to commodity production and alienation, and the objective need for a co-ordinating and directing authority (to ensure that the separate activities cohere) also leads to a *vertical* division of labour, then have Marx's definitions any operational sense? *Could* there be a socialism that could overcome alienation due to division of labour in any and all of the above three senses? How can the inescapable separateness of human productive activities be replaced, and by what? What relevance in *this* context has the elimination of private ownership of the means of production? (It is true that it adds another aspect or dimension, in that there is a distinction between owner-employer and non-owner employee, but of course Marx does not assert that division of labour is due to this, rather the reverse.) There is inevitably an air of unreality in a critique of existing society based upon the notion than an alternative exists which does away with division of labour or that specialisation between production units can somehow be 'overcome' by regarding them as in essence one gigantic factory (with local branches, so to speak).

Let us look first at the *horizontal* aspect. There is in this connection a famous quotation from Marx: a person 'will hunt in the morning, fish in the afternoon, rear cattle in the evening and be a literary critic after dinner,

without ever becoming a hunter, a fisherman, a herdsman or critic'.[77] This is
singularly ill-chosen. All these tasks are solitary, some could be hobbies. Most
labour is social labour in the sense that each contributes to joint endeavours
which would be disrupted if someone freely chose to go fishing instead. But
let us rewrite Marx's sentence as follows: 'Men will freely decide to repair
aero-engines in the morning, fill teeth in the early afternoon, drive a heavy
lorry in the early evening and then go to cook dinners in a restaurant, without
being an aero-engine maintenance artificer, dentist, lorry-driver, or cook.'
Then it does look a trifle nonsensical, does it not? Bahro advocates universal
higher education to the age of 22, with everyone taking courses in
mathematics, cybernetics, philosophy and art, but surely he must recognise
that this will not and cannot create omniscience. We could be taught to
understand the problems facing an architect, language-teacher, brick-layer, or
airline pilot, but we would not then be qualified to do their jobs. An operatic
tenor is usually unable to play the oboe, paint scenery, conduct the orchestra,
and it is inherently improbable that he would have any desire, or aptitude, for
tailoring, medicine, allocating ball-bearings, sports journalism, or working in
a slaughterhouse.

What kernel of good sense is there in all this? Surely it is that there should
be *less narrow* specialisation, that people should be so educated as to facilitate
change of jobs if they so wish, that a language-teacher who wants to become a
brick-layer, train-driver, or psychologist, or work on a farm, could have the
facilities to do this – subject only to the criterion of social need (there must be
bricks to be laid, trains to be driven) and aptitude (some people may turn out
unsuitable for certain tasks). The trouble with Marx's formulation is that he
does *not* say that people should be able to change their specialisation, but that
there would be no specialisation at all.

More difficult is the question of *vertical* division of labour. Bahro has been
accused by some Marxists of eliminating the working class, which is unfair:
all he has done is follow through the logic of the notion of interchangeability
of jobs and the elimination of the distinction between labour by hand and
labour by brain, which has the consequence either of turning everyone into
'workers', or homogenising the whole labour force and making them worker-
intellectuals. The comment made above about the need for specialisation
applies also to Bahro's conception, and there is also the question of aptitude,
ability, interest: a good craftsman deserves credit and honour, and may not
want to study philosophy or to be transferred to an 'intellectual' or
administrative occupation.

But these are side issues. The essential question is: how is the obviously
necessary hierarchy of control and co-ordination to be reconciled with the
'overcoming' of the vertical division of labour? How can one avoid the
emergence of the equivalent of an 'officer class', a distinction between rulers
and ruled? Is it a matter of election, delegation, rotation? If management is to
be responsible, then to whom? This last point is by no means a simple one:
for instance, should railway management be accountable to the railwaymen or
to the passengers?

Many quotations can be assembled showing that Marx and his successors
appreciated the need for authority: 'All labours in which many individuals co-

operate necessarily require for their connection and unity one commanding will' (Marx, *Das Kapital*, Vol. III). One needs 'a united will, connecting all groups of toilers with the precision of a clockwork mechanism' (Lenin). 'Co-ordination . . . subordination . . . orders from the directing organs' (I. Rubin, see p. 12 above). Baslé, in citing Marx's image of an orchestra willingly following the conductor's baton, very properly asked how the proletariat can be at the same time the conductor and the orchestra. And it was Lenin, in his otherwise rather 'libertarian' *State and Revolution*, who quoted Engels's 'wanting to abolish authority in large-scale industry is tantamount to wanting to abolish large-scale industry itself'.

How can the centralised nature of the system coexist with the elimination of the planner-administrator, or a reduction of the planner-administrator to the role of technical adviser-executant of the 'associated producers'? What *is* the 'commanding will'? Who issues 'orders'?

An excellent example of enthusiasm causing the enthusiast to leave mother earth behind him is contained in the following passage from the work of Coward and Ellis:

> In China another revolution in ideology is taking place, overthrowing ideas of delegation, management, the handing of power to 'representatives' or 'responsible individuals', ideas which are the keystone of capitalist production relations and bourgeois democracy. They are replaced with ideas of collective decision-making, of active thinking by all the people.[78]

Surely this is the purest romanticism! Not only did this not take place in China, it could not possibly take place anywhere! No delegation? No management? No representatives or responsible individuals? Could even a kindergarten be run in this way? Marx cannot be blamed for Coward and Ellis, *except* in so far as he pointed in their direction in some of his more utopian passages. For Marx, as well as speaking of a 'commanding will', did on many occasions envisage some sort of direct control by the people, with no mediation by or through institutions – without explaining at all clearly how this was to happen. A colleague once called this model one of 'perfect central-isation supplemented by mass solidarity'; this is and can only be hierarchical!

Modern production is complex, integrated. Unless it is integrated, it will disintegrate. The task of ensuring integration and co-ordination – the task of planning – is a difficult and responsible one. It is unlikely that anyone can just take his or her turn in doing it, in between driving heavy lorries and filling teeth. Planners must specialise, be professionally competent people, as indeed must be managers of a production unit (or repair mechanics). Many responsible positions can be filled by non-specialists, but there must be responsibility. With this must go some *authority*, for how can one be held responsible for actions by persons over whom one has no control? This can be a last-resort authority, exercised when persuasion fails, but in the end a ship's captain's orders must be obeyed; 'the editor's decision is final'; building workers erect the building designed by architects, and someone supervises their work; and so on.

One can refer back to the organisational ('multilevel') diagram in Figure 1.1.

Or let us consider an airport, as an example of both vertical and horizontal division of labour. For it to function, the following tasks must be performed:

(*a*) Flying the aircraft
(*b*) Air traffic control
(*c*) Refuelling
(*d*) Procuring and storing the fuel
(*e*) Repairs and maintenance of aircraft
(*f*) Luggage handling
(*g*) Seat reservations
(*h*) Catering on the ground and in-flight (for passengers)
(*i*) Timetables and administration of airlines and their personnel
(*j*) Administering the airport as a whole: repairs, maintenance of runway and buildings, allocation of space
(*k*) Recruitment and amenities for the airport workforce
(*l*) Etcetera.

Each of these functions will and must have someone in charge of it, responsible for it. Responsible to whom? Should the person who organises loading, refuelling, repairs, be responsible to loaders, refuellers, repairmen? Or to the organiser of the airport as a whole? Or to the public who actually use it? Who is to pull all these potentially disparate activities together, to ensure that the right persons are there at the right time, that spare parts, oil, cement for runway repairs and sausage rolls for the cafeteria are ordered in good time? From whom should they be ordered? Which suppliers will supply, and who is to find an alternative if they do not or cannot in fact do so? Who is to ensure that those who make the things which are needed will, in their turn, obtain the means of making them?

The question of authority and responsibility seems more important in this context than that of the distinction between physical and mental labour, since there are many 'mental' tasks which involve little or no authority: pharmacists and radio announcers are not even minor commanders, teachers 'command' only their pupils, while technical changes in industry create definitional overlaps between 'white' and 'blue' collars. A skilled worker and a laboratory technician both have valuable knowledge. *Subordination* is the point, and it is this which always presents dangers: authority can be abused, authority most certainly has been abused.

But the task of devising effective means of democratic control, of guarding against abuses, cannot be tackled from the Marxist-fundamentalist position of assuming that under a 'real' socialism there will be no authority. Nor, of course, can it be tackled by assuming that socialist, working-class government should be subject to no limits (Lenin: 'dictatorship is rule based directly on force and unrestricted by any laws'), presumably because it is inherently incapable of abusing its power. It would be unfair to both Marx and Lenin to assert that the thought of such abuse never occurred to them. Marx envisaged the recall of unworthy representatives, and Lenin's 'party maximum' was specifically designed to prevent party members from feathering their own nests. Yet neither seems to have given much thought to safeguards, perhaps because neither appreciated or foresaw the hierarchical-bureaucratic implications of centralised planning; this despite the fact that their programme envisaged a vast increase in the economic and social role of the state (which was ultimately to wither away, to be sure) and, by eliminating the independent producer and distributor, also vastly increased the dependence of all on the central institutions which were to administer society.

Let it not be thought that my object is to paint a picture of some sort of necessary super-hierarchy, with no possible role for democracy. The object of these last few pages has been to emphasise, first, that *some* hierarchy and subordination are inescapable in organising production – and the smaller the role of producers' autonomy and of markets, the greater must be the role of hierarchy and of bureaucracy. Secondly, I wish to draw attention to the need for a realistic (as distinct from sloganeering) assessment of the role and limits of democratic procedures in economic decision-making. This will be the subject of further discussion later. The essential point is that an elected assembly can only decide on broad priorities, and on the rules within which planners, managers, labourers and specialists work and interrelate. These are important functions, but cannot by their nature concern the microeconomic sphere, except where some major abuse has to be highlighted. Below the centre there are bound to be severe limits placed on the power of *local* or regional authorities, in order to ensure the priority of the general over the particular. Bahro was right to say 'the most difficult thing is control over local and particular special interests'.[79] Local electors as well as local officials quite naturally tend to concern themselves with the needs they know, those of their own locality. Then there are the actual production units: managers' relationships with the workers in a factory raise complex issues, which will require a long discussion, some of it based on Yugoslav experience. Should the manager be elected? How far is rotation feasible, given the specialist knowledge and aptitude which might be required? Should he be responsible to the workforce? Or to 'society' (including the customers)? How can conflicts between management and the workers, or between either or both and the planners, be most effectively resolved? At what level should various species of decision be taken, on the basis of what information? One can go on, but for the present enough is enough. A vertical division of labour there quite evidently will be, and so we will have the problems of authority (and its abuse), discipline, lines of responsibility, and procedures for dealing with failure. Marxist tradition, on the whole, tends to bypass such problems.

Material and Moral incentives

Marx would have certainly agreed that, in the first stages of a socialist society, rewards should be related to *work*, since he clearly said so in his *Critique of the Gotha Programme*. This would still represent a form of inequality, a remnant of 'bourgeois right'. In this first stage, labour-time is the base both of the regulation of production and of distribution to the labourers in proportion to their work. In *Das Kapital* he envisaged this being 'paid' in the form of tokens or vouchers, which would not be money, as 'they would not circulate'.[80]

There are several obscurities here. One is: should rewards be equal for an equal amount of time? Should there be a difference in reward in respect of skill, or physical intensity, and if so, *what* difference? Certainly there seems no suggestion that it be related to the usefulness of what has been done. How does one in fact determine the quantity (let alone quality) of work done by one individual, when it is usually indissolubly linked with the labour of others?

Then *how* is labour to be allocated between different tasks, and who is to do it? Here again it is essential to distinguish the 'patriarchal family', say, and a modern complex industrial economy. It should be recalled that Trotsky and Bukharin (in 1920) both spoke out in favour of *militarisation* of labour – until workers became so conscious of what needed to be done, and so devoted to doing it, that compulsion would no longer have any point.

What are reasonable assumptions to make, under 'feasible socialism', about people's attitude to labour and to what they should be doing? Who will be in a position to know where labour is needed, and how will he or she turn this knowledge into action? Are incentives needed, and if so, of what kind? What could or would the 'elimination of the wage system' mean? What is the meaning of turning money into 'tokens that do not circulate'?

I assume here that real 'abundance', requiring no regulation of consumption (everyone takes from the common stores the amount that he needs, and he determines what he needs), is excluded by the constraint of feasibility, as argued earlier. Therefore the amount that any citizen (as worker, pensioner, child, etc.) *can* claim will have to be limited, by some system of money or tokens, *and* the goods obtained will also need to be 'valued': for example, a woolly toy or fish and chips will require fewer tokens (or less money) than a car or a suite of furniture. Or some other method of limitation would need to be devised: for instance, that a suite of furniture or car might require a permit based on urgency of need. This last method would require a permit office, rules, applications, and so on and surely would, rightly be, very unpopular, except in special cases (e.g. invalids) or in a temporary emergency. I will henceforth disregard it.

Let us begin with an assumption which is, in my view, *not* far-fetched: the vast majority of able-bodied citizens want to work. Only a tiny minority are genuine shirkers. For them – as for a tiny minority of rapists, murderers, the insane – special arrangements may need to be made which need not detain us. The question then is: *what* work, where, when?

Is there any reason to suppose that what workers wish to do will correspond to what needs doing? This is in the context, be it again and again noted, of a complex industrial society with a highly developed sectoral and geographical division of labour, in which it *cannot* be clear why any particular task *must* be this particular individual's or group's responsibility. Furthermore, some work is more unpleasant, involves more 'unsocial hours', than another. For reasons already discussed at length, a necessary horizontal division of labour limits job-interchangeability, so that disagreeable occupations can only be to a limited extent passed round in turn ('You, you and you wash dishes next week'). Should not people be *induced* by material and moral reward of some kind to perform those tasks for which it is otherwise difficult to obtain the necessary labour? Should this then not be systematised into scales of reward?

We will discuss later the principles of such differentiation, but how can incentives – and therefore unequal pay for a given length of work – be avoided, unless there is direction of labour? On all this Marx had nothing at all to say. What he did say, about differentials under capitalism, does not help. Writing of the 'reduction' of labour of different kinds to simple labour, his words were: 'It is clear that the reduction is made, for, as exchange-value, the product of highly skilled labour is equivalent, in definite proportions, to the product of simple average labour.'[81] Here the value of skilled labour-power seems to be derived from the market, from the exchange-value of the goods in which it is contained. But quite apart from circularity of the argument, this is no guide as to what would be appropriate under socialism. The principle of pay 'according to work' in the lower stage of socialism, as he formulated it, is, of course, interpreted in the USSR as justifying wide pay differentials, based on a mixture of criteria: skill, rank, heavy work, location (e.g. in the Arctic), and so on. It is not my task to justify Soviet income differentials. The point is that, if 'according to work' is recognised as having a qualitative aspect, Marx provided no guidance as to what might be appropriate in this respect. Labour-power ceases to be a 'commodity'. This would seem to mean that its value is not determined by any sort of labour market, and this indeed is the position taken by Soviet theoreticians about their economy of so-called 'mature socialism'. However, as Soviet experience also shows, market-type incentives and differentials become necessary to 'allocate' labour in the absence of labour conscription and direction.

It seems inherently far-fetched to imagine the workers identifying selflessly with 'the general interest' (which cannot be clearly defined) and going willingly where they are 'needed by society'. An incentive scheme seems the only conceivable substitute for compulsion. Needless to say, this is no justification for 'traditional' differentials, in which, say, professors earn many times more than slaughterhouse men or bricklayers, while doing much more agreeable work. Many responsible tasks (for instance, being a senior planner, or editor, or the chairman of a soviet) are, or should be, sought after by persons who find pleasure in carrying out these tasks, who would accept the Lenin *partmaksimum* and have no greater material reward than the general run of citizens. (Lenin laid it down that no party member should earn more than a skilled worker, no matter what post he or she held. Stalin abolished this rule.) The decisive factors would be: first, the level of differentials required to elicit voluntary labour effort in the sector where it is needed; and, at least equally important, that these differentials be decided in a democratic way, and not behind closed doors by the beneficiaries, as is the case in the USSR today. By this, of course, I do not mean that 'the people' would determine the income of Bloggs the pilot any more than they could or should decide that ten more tonnes of sulphuric acid be produced. But the principles and limits of income differentiation can and should be decided by elected representatives at some level or other.

Discussion of these matters may be impeded by another 'fundamentalist' blind-spot. Imagine a smallish commune or co-operative, the size of a good Israeli *kibbutz*; say, 200 people. One can envisage a genuine equality of income, with all sharing in times good or bad (no question of 'abundance' need arise). There would be a considerable degree of job-interchangeability, with totally unskilled work taken in turn. Job-allocation would be democratically decided. Elected committees, with rotation and right of recall, could cope with any likely set of problems. And if by chance someone *had* to be designated to do something arduous and unpleasant, a democratic vote would decide on some special compensation (a few extra days' holiday, for instance).

This is all feasible, but with two rather important conditions. The first is that such a society should consist of committed volunteers, that anyone who wishes to live a different sort of life could do so (as is the case with *kibbutzim* in Israel; imagine the effect of making membership compulsory!). The second, and more important perhaps, is yet again scale. People are dividing up tasks they see, among people they know, with consequences that are indeed instantly visible, 'transparent'. It is a naive fantasy to extend this to an industrial society of hundreds of millions of people, unless, of course, one or both of two conditions are met: that the separate small units are largely self-sufficient, and that they interrelate and exchange freely with each other (with 'commodity production' as the consequence).

Another confusion arises from the contrast between workers 'selling their labour-power' under capitalism and their work in a socialist society. A Soviet worker is paid a wage, and certainly feels that some state enterprise or institution employs him, whatever the official ideology may say. Szelenyi, in his already cited article, uses the phrase 'selling their labour-power' in just this context. Indeed, the worker would be justified in feeling that he faces a monopolist-employer, the state, though in practice state-employed managers may bid against each other for his services. The member of an authentic producers' co-operative, or a *kibbutz*, may be expected to regard him or herself as self-employed, but what of one of many thousands working in a state enterprise, which receives plan instructions from the centre about what to produce? The impersonal remoteness of the source of the instructions – made no better if these emerge from a distant computer – contributes to the worker's sense of being, after all, an employee. While in a *kibbutz*-sized co-operative the little community itself can see what needs to be done and can allocate its resources accordingly, this cannot be simple and 'transparent' on a national, let alone international, scale. The question of *who* allocates, by what criteria, subject to what responsibility, to whom, exercised how, these become matters of fundamental importance on which, to repeat, Marx had little of relevance to say.

Then there is the nature of labour reward. The French Marxist Alain Lipietz, in a recent book, has rightly drawn attention to the fact that there is a very substantial contrast between the demands of the real working class – for a higher wage and life-standards within existing society – and the Marxist objective of a new society in which wages as such would not exist.[82] (I have seen the slogan 'Abolish the Wages System' somewhere on a wall in West Germany, but, of course, *not* a factory wall; it was in a university. Most workers would feel that free distribution means that they would have to take what they are *given*.) This brings us back to Marx's 'tokens' which are not money. Why not call them money? Let us look at these tokens and their function. Let us abstract from the basis of how these tokens are earned.

Suppose that 100 such units have been received. What is the recipient to do with them? Presumably he will face a choice of goods in the state stores, whose 'values' will be expressed in tokens. It seems to have been Marx's idea that these would be proportionate to labour-time, presumably with something added to cover what might be called productive and social 'overheads': old age pensions, investment fund, and so on. Thus one can imagine that a chair or a kilogram of sausage might be 'valued' as 12 and 3 labour-hour-tokens, though the actual labour-time devoted to their production might be 9 and 2 hours respectively. The possessor of the 100 tokens decides what he or she prefers to spend them on. At a higher stage, with abundance, one would have 'to each according to his needs', so tokens would wither away.

Several defects of such a system must be apparent, if earlier analysis is taken into account. First, what of supply and demand? In a remarkably 'simple' passage, Marx wrote: 'if it were assumed that the conditions are realised which allow the coincidence between supply and demand, of production and consumption, and in the last instance the (proper) proportions of production . . . then the problem of money becomes quite unimportant . . .'.[83] *Mein Gott! If* the function of money were made unnecessary, then indeed it would not be needed! For what *is*, in the present context, that function? It is to help to bring supply and demand into balance, relating production to consumption, to enable the customer to express the intensity of his or her preferences, *and,* finally, to relate these to the cost of providing the required supply. Thus suppose at the 'price' of 3 tokens there is not enough (or there are too many) sausages. In the short run the alternative to queues or gluts is to alter the token-value. This would also be a signal to the planning organs: produce more of this, less of that. Just as money would be. (In fact these tokens would then become money in all but name.) What does it mean that the tokens 'do not circulate'? Does this mean that I, possessor of 100 non-circulating, non-transferable tokens, cannot pass any of them on to my neighbour as a reward for baby-minding, repairing my radio, or taking me to work in his car? *Why not?* Police would be needed to stop such transactions! And will the 'tokens' which are 'paid' to shops for sausages be used to 'purchase' sausages from the sausage-factory? And then by the sausage-factory to 'purchase' the meat from its suppliers? If not, why not? What alternative is there, which enables the requirements of the consumer to work their way into the system of production?

With a given distribution of income (as egalitarian as the given society chooses it to be), *there is no better way* of enabling citizens to register their preferences than to allow them freely to spend their 'money' (tokens) or their money. If this is denounced by the fundamentalist as a 'market', so be it. As Castoriadis explicitly recognises, no voting system can be a substitute, because, first, the huge variety of preferences makes it an impossibly unwieldy task, and, secondly, as already pointed out, because this is not a matter of majority vote anyhow, since a minority is entitled to be supplied also.

Of course this is very far from *a priori* planning decisions. But, as we have already seen, these are usually impracticable where there is choice. Is this 'market' solution free from defects? No, it is not. But the critic must make a case for a feasible alternative.

The 'Proletariat' and Productive Labour

Bahro has some highly important things to say about the role assigned by
Marxist theory to the proletariat. 'That the proletariat . . . is the actual
collective subject of general emancipation remains a philosophical hypothesis,
in which the utopian components of Marxism are concentrated.'[84] He also
writes that 'Marxist intellectuals have an idealised picture of "the worker"'.
What, he asks, about the ideas and aspirations of the really existing proletariat, their relationship (if any) to its 'real' 'world-historical' aims assigned
to it by the theory? After all, as he also remarked, 'the immediate objectives of
subordinate strata and classes are always conservative'.[85]

Men as different in their ideology as Alfred Meyer, Mihajlo Marković and
Alain Lipietz have in various ways drawn attention to the difficulties to which
this notion of the 'world-historical emancipatory mission' of the proletariat
gives rise.

> How can the industrial working class, being so thoroughly alienated from
> its own human nature, have it within itself to achieve its own
> emancipation?[86]
>
> But Marx did not solve the problem: how will the whole proletariat form its
> common will, make the step from a 'class in itself' towards a 'class for itself',
> win power and run society 'organised as the ruling class'? How will this
> alienated and degraded class build up a consciousness about essentially new
> possibilities, a consciousness that requires enormous general culture and far
> surpasses official academic scholarship? And if a vanguard of the class does
> the job, how to avoid alienation of the vanguard, manipulation of the class
> by it?[87]

Marković is also able to see the vagueness of certain common Marxist slogans:
he quotes phrases like 'all production is concentrated in a vast association of
the whole nation', and 'the public power loses its political character' –
'*whatever this might mean*'.[88]

Lipietz, as we have seen, is troubled by the wide gap between actual
demands by real workers – for higher wages and the like – and the fundamental changes which they ought to want, which include abolishing the
wages system. This, of course, is an echo of Lenin's well-known belief that
socialist ideas need to be brought to the workers from the outside, that left to
themselves workers will confine themselves to 'trade union' demands. Perhaps
he too would have recognised the validity of Bahro's point about the 'conservative' aspirations of most ordinary folk.

André Gorz puts the question rather strongly, as follows:

> Marx's theory of the proletariat is not based upon an empirical study of
> class antagonisms . . . No empirical observation or experience of militancy
> could lead to the discovery of the historic mission of the proletariat, which,
> according to Marx, constitutes its class being . . . The being of the pro-
> letariat transcends the proletarians, it is the transcendental guarantee of the
> adoption by the proletarians of the correct class line.

A question at once arises: who is able to know and to say what the proletariat is, when the proletarians themselves have only a confused or
mystified sense of it? Historically, the answer to this question is: only Marx
was able to know and to say what the true nature and historical mission of
the proletariat really were . . . The proletariat is revolutionary in its essence,
it *must* be, it must become what it *is*.

This philosophic position contains within itself all the deviations:
advance-guardism, substitutionism, elitism, and also their opposites:
spontaneity, 'tailism', trade-unionism. The impossibility of empirically
verifying the theory has always been Marxism's burden, like original sin . . .
The philosophy of the proletariat cannot be legitimised through really-
existing proletarians or through actual events . . . The Hegelian matrix
makes the philosopher the prophet, and his philosophy a Revelation of
Sense and Being . . . No one, and particularly not the proletariat, can decide
the debates which divide Marxists. In the absence of any possible empirical
verification, their divergent political and theoretical theses can be
legitimised only by reference to the Book.

The spirit of orthodoxy, dogmatism, religiosity, are not accidental
phenomena in Marxism: they are necessarily inherent in a philosophy with
a Hegelian structure . . . The theory of the proletariat rests on the texts of
Marx and the words of Lenin. This philosophy of the proletariat is
religious.[89]

All this has implications which merit much fuller discussion, but this is not
the place for it. I will confine myself to drawing a few general conclusions,
which are relevant to Marx's concept of a transition to socialism, and must be
applicable to the 'feasible' socialism to which this book relates.

First, there is the question of the likely behaviour and attitudes of the real
working class. In a hard-hitting article, the Hungarian scholar Mihai Vajda
has pointed out that there is no reason to expect working-class solidarity
except in conflict with the class enemy (and not always then?). With no
capitalists to struggle with, what is it that should link together the interests of
bus drivers, instrument mechanics, brick-layers, street cleaners and cooks?
Or, for that matter, the inhabitants of West Africa with those of the Iberian
peninsula or Malaysia? The contrary view rests on faith alone, and most
obviously so if, as will surely be the case, there are insufficient resources to
satisfy all the needs which these workers, or people in these countries, regard
as legitimate. The workers are not, in Marxist theory, regarded as morally
superior people; they are supposed to liberate mankind by pursuing their own
class interest, which creates a classless society by eliminating the ruling
classes, whether they are conscious of this or not. But, as we have already
noted, the kind of society to which the masses aspire is by no means that
envisaged by Marx. Marx argued that the 'conservative' slogan 'A fair day's
wage for a fair day's work' should be replaced by 'abolition of the wages
system'. But how many *workers* believe this? Nor does experience suggest that
the overthrow of landlords and capitalists results in the final elimination of
the rulers/ruled distinction.

This is because, secondly, there will and must be people who are in charge.

How can the workers rule, *how* can they be 'organised as the ruling class', what can all this mean in practice, in the face of the objective need for hierarchy which Bahro so explicitly recognises? 'One must get beyond the dilemma of choice between 'co-operative-egalitarian or hierarchic-elitist structures', because 'it is illusory to imagine the possibility that informational and decision-making flows *could* be primarily or solely from bottom to top'.[90] Again and again the same problem arises: *what does rule by the workers*, or the dictatorship of the proletariat, *mean*? What *could* it mean? Rakovsky, in a letter written in 1928 in exile, bitterly reflected on the separation from the masses of former workers, affected by the 'professional risks of power'. The personal ambition of workers to rise to the status of rulers is facilitated, appears justified, because of the objective need for individuals to take command. As Vajda pointed out, it is in the interest of each worker so to rise above his fellows, in fact to cease to be a worker.

Thirdly, if workers (to be precise, ex-workers) do rule, will not their 'conservative' aspirations deflect the decisions they take from the aims prescribed for them by Marx and Engels? Real workers are not any less chauvinistic, intolerant, narrow-minded, selfish, than other groups in our very imperfect society. They are certainly less concerned about the rights of women than the middle classes. Oscar Wilde wrote long ago that 'there is only one class in the community that thinks more about money than the rich, and that is the poor'.[91]

A further source of confusion is over who the 'workers' are. This applies also to the definition of the working class under modern capitalism: are they only those engaged in directly productive non-supervisory activities by hand, in which case in many Western industrialised countries they are a minority of the working population? Konrad and Szelenyi, in their analysis of East European societies, rest their case upon a similarly narrow definition of the working class. They then identify the 'intellectual class' with the rulers, and imply that they live on the redistributed surplus, the surplus which has been created by the labour of the 'direct producers'. This, in my view, is a misapplication of Marx's ideas. He distinguished between productive and unproductive labour, but his criterion was that of being employed for profit (except in circulation), so that such 'intellectuals' as the chief engineer of a steelworks would most certainly qualify as productive, whereas a school cleaner or a fireman would be unproductive. So this distinction, whatever its merits or demerits in other respects, does not help Konrad and Szelenyi to make the distinction which matters to them: between those who decide on distribution and redistribution (i.e. the rulers and their acolytes), and the rest. Anyhow, Marx's distinction relates to capitalism, and the mind boggles at regarding all who are not 'direct producers' in this narrow sense as living off the surplus generated by the productive workers, that is, as 'exploiters'.

The distinction between productive and unproductive gives rise to some strange illusions. Thus Becker imagines that, under capitalism, there is a huge waste of labour in what he calls 'the circulatory superstructure'. Indeed, Marx spoke of 'the vast numbers of employments at present indispensable but in themselves superfluous'.[92] But surely this is quite misleading. There are indeed some employments which would disappear: in the stock exchange, for instance. However, *most* activities in circulation are plainly indispensable, though not in the same form, also in a socialist society. Let us take a few examples. A *building contractor* links together various trades and specialist organisations which together erect a building: masons, painters, lift-installers, material suppliers, and so on; and someone must fulfil that task, whether or not the name 'contractor' is used. *Marketing* is a means of finding purchasers (users) of one's product, in a capitalist economy. One must still find outlets for one's output in a socialist economy, or have them designated by the supply-and-allocation plan, and in either case human beings will have to take decisions. *Travel agents* will be needed if people will still wish to book holiday accommodation or seats in planes, even if no actual payment is made. Economy in *retail distribution* has all too often taken the form of providing too few outlets, so that customers have to wait their turn.

Genuine savings of human labour are, of course, possible, through the elimination of waste, but one must not just assume that a system can be brought into being which generates no waste at all. In a modern industrial economy, with high mass consumption and a developed network of services of many kinds, it seems more than a little odd for some Marxists to cling to narrow definitions of the working class, or indeed to assign some special (privileged?) position in their model of socialism to the 'direct producers'.

However, I have great sympathy with the point well made by Ivan Szelenyi: the ordinary worker is all too readily disregarded, in a hierarchical system such as exists in Eastern Europe, and it is a most important object of policy to create the institutional basis for realistic and effective ways of increasing their influence and their rights. In this respect as in so many others, *le mieux est l'ennemi du bien*; by aiming for an unattainable 'workers' power', by indulging (in Szelenyi's words) in 'dreams of general emancipation', one fails to devise means by which workers can in fact exercise their power as consumers and as producers, means which are inevitably limited by practical possibility. These ideas I shall develop later in this book.

The Legacy of Marx: Some Conclusions

I think that it can be demonstrated that Marxist economics is either *irrelevant*, or *misleading*, in respect of the problems that must be faced by any socialist economy which could exist. This is because the very possibility of these problems was assumed out of existence. Attempts to adapt the labour theory of value are doomed to failure, both because Marx did not intend that it be applied to socialism and because of its high level of abstraction. The task is further hindered by an overstress on labour-time and the separation of 'value' from demand, use-value. No hint appears anywhere about how socialist society, or planners acting in its name, could compute use-values and relate them to costs, to effort. The assumption of abundance is far-fetched, when (as the Brandt Commission has reminded us), the number of children to be born in the twenty years 1980–2000 will exceed the *total* population of the world as it was in 1900! The utopian aspects of Marx's ideas, especially the New Man, the absence of conflict between individuals and groups, depend decisively on an unrealisable degree of plenty. Marx also grossly underestimated the complexity of the modern economy (and of society too), and the view that production relations and plans would be 'simple' and 'transparent', that the interests of society would be defined and perceived, was very seriously mistaken. The elimination of commodity production, with production for use and not for exchange, implies a degree of centralisation which has a multilevel, hierarchically organised plan-bureaucracy as its functionally inescapable accompaniment. This in turn conflicts with the aim of meaningful workers' participation in decision-making at their place of work; the concentration of decisions at the centre (with or without computers) must cause alienation. Marx's notions on the overcoming of 'horizontal' and 'vertical' division of labour are wide of any possible application in practice. He left contradictory indications on the need for one directing will *and* on decisions by freely associating producers. He never faced the contradiction between *ex ante* planning and the consequences of choice, which require *ex post* verification of these decisions. He never considered the organisational implications of his ideas. By this I do *not* mean a blueprint or an organisational diagram, but basic principles, such as: the necessary coexistence of centralisation and decentralisation; the need to reconcile inevitable differences of view about what needs to be done; the importance of responsibility and of the implementation of decisions taken, including the provision of the *means* of implementation.

It may be objected that Marx was busily analysing capitalism, that his ideas were never intended as guidelines to the building of socialism, and that therefore the preceding pages are misconceived. To this I must (again) reply: because Marx *did* often indicate features of a future socialist society, if only by contrasting them with specific features of capitalism, his thought developed into an *obstacle* to analyses of economics of any sort of feasible socialism. Doubtless he never intended this, and his famous saying 'Moi, je ne suis pas marxiste' was his warning against his followers' dogmatism. One wishes that more of them heeded this warning.

Let me in conclusion quote two statements.

It is necessary for each state-owned factory, with its technical director, to be subject not only to control from the top . . . but also from below, by the market, which will remain the regulator of the state economy for a long time to come.

The innumerable live participants in the economy . . . must make known their needs and their relative intensity not only through statistical compilations of planning commissions, but directly through the pressure of demand and supply. The plan is checked and to a considerable extent realised through the market. The regulation over the market must base itself on the tendencies showing themselves in it, must prove their economic rationality [*tselesoobraznost*] through commercial calculation. The economy of the transition period is unthinkable without 'control by the rouble'.

This is *Trotsky* speaking. The first quotation dates from 1922 (the 4th Comintern Congress), the second from *Byulleten oppozitsii* in November

1932. The observant dogmatist would instantly retort: 'but Trotsky quite explicitly referred to the transition period. He believed in the ultimate triumph of Marx's marketless socialism.' This is indeed correct, as far as it goes. But must not my observant dogmatist use his mind and go a little further. What circumstances can be imagined in which 'needs and their relative intensity' will be known to the planning organs without the interaction of demand and supply being manifested, in something very like a market, without the need for *ex post* checking of the *ex ante* calculations made in 'planning commissions'? And, let me add, without making romantic leaps into a world of absolute abundance, perfect information and perfect foresight.

There is a long agenda awaiting socialist economists. They cannot even begin to face the real problems unless they openly reject the utopian elements of the Marxist tradition. Marx would surely have revised his own ideas if he had lived a hundred years longer – he would have been a 'revisionist'. There were many things he could not possibly foresee: nuclear weapons, for instance. Great man though he was, he could also just occasionally be wrong.

More probable, surely, than 'abundance' is quite another sort of world, one in which conflicts over scarcity threaten the survival of the human race, in which the pursuit of short-term profit threatens the destruction of the environment. Some species of socialism, on an international scale, may well be the only alternative to disaster – political, economic, ecological, military. But this is conservationist, share-scarcity socialism, which can have little in common with a utopia based upon the assumption of limitless resources.

Sharing Bahro's dislike of what he called *real existierender Sozialismus* in Eastern Europe, I would like to see serious discussion of alternatives. Bahro's own *Alternative* must by now appear questionably feasible even to its author. I feel sure that he, and other honest Marxists, will not be content to remain in a quasi-religious dream world, from which they can sally forth to damn every realistically conceivable form of socialism 'for making compromises with reality', as Debray put it.

Western mainstream economists escape reality by retreating into mathematical abstractions and an artificial world of formulae. Those who claim to believe in 'praxis' should not take refuge in some 'socialist' equivalent of general equilibrium never-never land. 'Marxist scholars have interpreted his doctrines in this way and that. The point however is to change them.'

Addendum: More on Human Psychology and 'Reductionism'

It has been suggested here that the idea of some new 'socialist' man is integrally linked with the concept of abundance, that conflict and self-interest, or group interest, must be assumed to exist unless there is no opportunity-cost, there are no mutually exclusive alternatives. It seems also that to assume away personal selfishness, acquisitiveness, competitiveness, is far-fetched. Let me deal at slightly greater length with the view that this shows lack of imagination, that I am lumbered with bourgeois values.

Few will doubt that not only I, but also the *present* working class, are, in this sense, permeated with bourgeois values. Workers are as acquisitive as anyone else, and the typical agitationist stance of the extreme left does every-thing possible to encourage demands for higher wages, which are the basis of 'consumerism' – the car, colour television set, and so on. The triumph of the extreme left is associated in most workers' minds not with 'the abolition of the wages system' (*l'abolition du salariat*, sounds better in French!), but with additional material income, allegedly denied them by capitalism and capitalists.

Intelligent Marxists would, of course, admit this, as they would readily admit that many real workers have racist, sexist and other prejudices. These they ascribe to the evil effects of a capitalist environment. It will take time, they would agree, to remove the evil effects, the false consciousness, inherited from the past. This, they appreciate, raises awkward questions: who is to do the removing, and does this approach not lead rapidly towards 'substitu-tionism', to a group of inspired Marxist intellectuals leading the real working class in a direction that few workers would spontaneously follow? This is an integral part of Leninism: revolutionary consciousness is to be brought to the working class from the outside. This can lead, has led, to the 'dictatorship of the proletariat' turning into a dictatorship *over* the proletariat. One line taken by those who wish to avoid these uncomfortable conclusions, without making implausible assumptions of universal abundance, is to say that revolutionary struggle and experience will change man. The revolution transforms those who participate in it. It is not the actual workers that exist today, anywhere, with all their prejudices, who would build socialism. The process of over-throwing, then of building, would change them.

This view obviously owes nothing to the study of the actual experience of the Russian revolution. While some devoted workers did indeed throw themselves heart and soul into building a new society, the majority, even of workers, let alone the peasant masses, faced with hunger and cold, became more, not less, acquisitive. According to Kritsman's pamphlet *The Heroic Period of the Russian Revolution*, never did so many people trade and barter as during the period of war-communism, when such activity was supposed to be illegal. Many a Marxist theory concerning the degeneration of the Soviet republic points to the disintegration, the demoralisation, the 'declassing' of the working class at this period. Lenin and the Bolsheviks found themselves exercising dictatorship in the name of the proletariat, over the proletariat, when their supposed class base vanished, or supported their opponents.[93] During the critical period of 1919–21 Trotsky and Bukharin both showed themselves acutely conscious of the need to enforce discipline on the recalcitrant masses, who were apt to pursue sectional interests, or were selfish, lazy, and so on. And this at a time of the most acute crisis, when they might be expected to rally round the party – as, of course, some did.

It may be objected that the years following the Bolshevik revolution were exceptionally harsh, owing to the chaos of civil war. True. But, as Bukharin correctly pointed out in his *Economics of the Transition Period*, any proletarian revolution will be costly in terms of economic efficiency, not only because of the damage done to productive capital by the revolution and its aftermath, but also because of the disruption of established links and organisations, the inexperience of the workers, and so on. It would therefore seem reasonable to expect any violent revolution to lead initially to a decline in living standards.

But in any case the essential point is a different one. Revolutionary dogmatists – Mandel is an excellent example – fail to distinguish between human beings in a situation of acute crisis, and the post-revolutionary society, which presumably will have to develop a routine to cope with everyday life. Mandel once wrote that, for the French workers, a strike was seen as a feast, *une fête*. A struggle, a battle, revolution itself, brings out a spirit of self-sacrifice. But then what? Men may jump into a canal to save a drowning child, but this neither proves that they will cease to be selfish in their normal dealings nor trains them in that direction. My fellow-soldiers in the last war did many brave and unselfish things, but physical hardships merely whetted the appetite for enjoying consumption once the war was over. Nor were Bolshevik commissars immune from this: on the contrary (with honourable exceptions, of course) many succumbed to temptation, and Trotsky and others denounced this at the time. Yet what, as a Marxist, could one expect, even of people who were party members and claimed to be devoted Marxists? *A fortiori*, what of ordinary citizens of all classes?

It seems basically reasonable, therefore, to discuss 'feasible socialism' in which human beings are recognisable, similar to those that now exist. Of course, we must take into account any likely or possible changes in circumstances. But that is a different question, the answer to which does not depend on making assumptions about some imaginary New Man, who, in a choice between his own advantage and that of others, would always choose the latter.

What of changed circumstances? This brings me to the second of the points to be raised here, that of 'reductionism'. This word covers a number of different but related meanings. It is sometimes used to refer to the need, in Marxist value theory, to reduce complex or skilled labour to units of simple labour. But it can also be used to criticise the tendency to reduce complex causal relationships to a single cause, or to identify one aspect of a problem or situation as its 'essence'. In vulgar-Marxism it takes the form of giving some phenomenon, event, work of art, a crude materialist or economic explanation. The more sophisticated Marxists avoid this. But even they are driven to see in material or economic circumstances, and/or in the class struggle, the essential explanation, 'in the last analysis', though certainly allowing for some interaction with ideas, religion, politics and other elements of the superstructure. This can be, often is, accompanied by a tendency to ascribe various evils to property relations, to capitalism. From this it follows that a change in these relations, the elimination of private property in the means of production, will effect a cure.

It has already been argued that this causes difficulty in explaining those historical events in which conflict was primarily between members of the same class. But more relevant to the present theme is the way in which this attitude leads to mistaken views concerning, for instance, racism, sexism, alcoholism, crime, even foul play on the football field, and therefore to an exaggerated and unreal view of the effect of the abolition of private ownership of the means of production on human psychology and on social relations. No one (at least not I) can doubt that property relations and class divisions can contribute to these and other evils in our society. For instance, anti-semitism had its economic roots, the subordination of women is related to property, advertisers persuade people to drink more, people commit crimes to acquire goods or because they are deprived of access to wealth, and the term 'professional foul' has been coined to cover the many cases in which highly paid footballers commit offences while motivated by the large money bonus they would receive for winning. It then turns out that anti-semitism can continue for reasons unconnected with capitalism, that women in the USSR seem to suffer from many of the same disabilities as their sisters in Western Europe, that drink remains a problem regardless of system, that thieving (and bribery) know no ideological boundaries and, finally, that even in those sports where no money whatever is involved there is still some foul play. Of course, one can say that the Soviet experience is irrelevant, that it is not socialism. Thus, to take the first of the examples, anti-semitism can be motivated by the desire to keep Jews out of positions of high rank, and so it could be argued that since there is economic advantage in holding such positions, the motive remains economic. Even accepting this, what can we conclude? If there is competition to acquire positions of influence and honour, and it is difficult to see how this can be or will be avoided, then some will be interested to find reasons to disqualify competitors. Because racial feelings have some rather deep roots, they could enter in the equation, whereas (let us say) the fact that the other applicants come from another part of the country (Yorkshire, say, or Leningrad) provides no basis for prejudice to influence action.

Similarly, some men who are in positions of authority will use their position to secure sexual favours from women, whether or not property relations are involved. If the fundamentalist replies that under socialism no one will be in a position of authority (that 'when everyone is somebody then no one's anybody', to quote W. S. Gilbert), then we are again in the realm of utopia. Naturally, if there is no authority then it cannot be abused. If anyone is satisfied with such a reply, then surely we are dealing with religious faith and certainly not with '*scientific* socialism'.

All this is no reason, needless to say, why we should accept evils and abuses as ineradicable facts of life. We must all hope that they will be eradicated, or at least fully discredited. The point is only that the causes, like the other evils listed above, cannot be 'reduced' in 'essence' to property relations, not even 'in the last analysis'. Under socialism too there will be a need for a referee at football matches.

Another aspect of 'reductionism' has been well described, in a yet-unpublished work, by the *émigré* Czech sociologist Zdenek Strmiska. He notes the 'monistic' way in which Marxism has sought to analyse society; Marx at times had a much more complex view of society, and the two approaches can and do conflict. He notes how the 'monistic, economistic dialectic' affected Marx's view of the relationships between base and super-structure, and that 'this type of dialectic does not allow one to think in terms of the relative autonomy of power relations'. Marx, writes Strmiska, combined the 'monistic-historical' conception with 'accentuation of anti-thetical forms and negations'. This 'recognises only two sets of relations internal to the social system . . . antagonism or perfect functional harmony'. He points to the 'highly ambiguous and reductionist term "negation"'.

The manifestations of an antithetical dialectic are numerous in Marx's analyses. It leads to a simplified representation of two types of societies, class societies and classless ones, with which the whole of Marx's sociology is pervaded, and which, one could say, forms its very foundations. This basic idea generalises, schematises and extrapolates the numerous real or possible differences between various types of society in such a way as to conceptualise classless society as a universal negation of class societies and vice versa; the transition of classless societies into class society and transformation of class societies into classless ones, which takes place on a higher level of historical development, is supposed to lead to a solution of all social and human problems, to communism . . . The real possibilities of change in modern societies are envisaged here in a romantic and many respects utopian manner. The concept of antithesis, imposing itself in the sphere of ideology, is without doubt the source of this orientation.

This antithetical dialectic becomes *negative* or directly *negativist dialectic*, in the interpretation of qualitative social change. The reductionist character of the concept of negation . . . also detracts attention from the actual complexity of social change, socialist transformation primarily, accepting the problems of that transformation as resolved at a moment when their solution enters its decisive phase. The illusion, that a supersession of the old social forms represents the main goal in the realisation of social change, tends not to accelerate the process as it might seem at first glance – on the contrary, it makes it more difficult, robbing the projects of change of much credibility. What is even more serious, it tends to disorient the groups or individuals involved in the process, because the solution to all social problems is seen in terms of mechanistic antitheses of reality, existing in the old system . . . It does not offer a theoretical basis which would permit a definition of the real historical status of the socio-cultural elements to be found in the framework of the old social system of capitalist society: there is no way of determining which element should be eliminated, which retained, and developed, what is to be maintained in transformed shape. Such a perspective allows only with difficulty to distinguish the permanently valid results of the developments of civilisation, especially aspects of the 'superstructural sphere' and historically transitional phenomena, characteristic of capitalist society: which both merge into one another.

. . . A dialectic of this type, enthralled by the conception of antitheses and forgetting the conception of synthesis, anticipates a solution of the contradictions in capitalist society and the building of socialism to be effected most exclusively by the social forces situated at the pole of the social structure, that is, by the proletariat, and bases its strategy on the somewhat controversial assumption of a polarisation of social structures.[94]

This can be seen as one consequence of Marx's philosophical adaptation of Hegel. As Charles Taylor pointed out, Hegel's analysis of the contradictions of human existence leads to a species of higher reconciliation (*Aufhebung*), through the intervention of a supernatural *Geist*. Marx the materialist rejected *Geist*, but in doing so he had to substitute man. 'The revolution would abolish bourgeois society and hence the laws of its operation, and a united class of proletarians would take over and dispose freely of the economy it had inherited . . .' But 'Marx seems to have been oblivious of the inescapable opacity and indirectness of communication and decision in large bodies of men, even in small and simple societies, let alone those organised around a large and complex productive system'. This 'prevented Marx from seeing communism as a social predicament with its own characteristic limits . . .'. This leads to 'a wildly unrealistic notion of the transition as a leap into untrammelled freedom' . . . 'Marx held a terribly unreal notion of freedom, in which the opacity, division, indirectness and cross-purposes of social life were quite overcome'. Taylor agrees that one should not ask for a blueprint of communist society, but one can and must 'ask in general terms how we envisage men's situation to have changed, what constraints, divisions, tensions, dilemmas, struggles and estrangements will replace those we know today. Not only does classical Marxism have no answer to this; it implies that the answer is "none": that our only situation will be that of generic man, harmoniously united in contest with nature. But this predicament is not only unbelievable, but arguably unlivable.'[95]

Notes: Part 1

1 B. Ollman, 'Marx's vision of communism: a reconstruction', in *Critique*, no. 8, 1978.
2 L. Trotsky, 'Chto takoye SSSR i kuda on idyot', mimeo., 1936, p. 36.
3 See A. Nove, 'Is the Soviet Union a class society?', *Soviet Studies*, October 1975, for my own views (also reprinted in my *Political Economy and Soviet Socialism*, London: Allen & Unwin, 1978).
4 C. Bettelheim, *The Transition to a Socialist Society* (Hassocks: Harvester, 1975), p. 23. Engels wrote: 'with the seizing of the means of production by society, production of commodities is done away with' (*Socialism, Utopian and Scientific*).
5 N. Bukharin, *Ekonomika perekhodnogo perioda* (Moscow, 1920). Translation taken from Adam Kaufman's essay 'The origin of the political economy of socialism', *Soviet Studies*, January 1953.
6 E. Preobrazhensky, *Novaya ekonomika* (Moscow, 1925). Translation from B. Pearce, *The New Economics* (Oxford: Clarendon Press, 1965).
7 L. Baslé, 'L'élaboration de l'économie politique du socialisme en URSS, 1917–54', thesis, Paris-Nanterre University, 1979.
8 *Leninsky sbornik*, no. 10, 1929.
9 R. Kosolapov, *Sotsializm* (Moscow, 1979), p. 219.
10 X. Richet, *Cahiers du CEREL* (Paris), no. 18, 1980.
11 A. Brody, *Proportions, Prices and Planning* (Budapest: Akadémiai Kiadó, 1970).
12 A. Mattick, *Marx et Keynes* (Paris: Gallimard, 1972). In English, *Marx and Keynes* (London: Merlin Press, 1969).
13 E. Barone, 'The ministry of production in a collectivist state', in *The Economics of Socialism*, ed. A. Nove and D. M. Nuti (Harmondsworth: Penguin, 1972).
14 L. Pellican, in *Controcorrenti*, January–March 1976, pp. 32, 40.
15 A. Lipietz, *Crise et inflation: pourquoi?* (Paris: Maspéro, 1979), pp. 304, 366.
16 D. Murray, in *Radical Philosophy*, Summer 1979, p. 22.
17 R. Debray, *L'Indésirable* (Paris: Editions du Seuil, 1975), pp. 111–12.
18 A. Levitin-Krasnov, in his *SSSR: demoktraticheskiye alternativy* (Achberg: Achberger Verlag, 1976), p. 225.
19 K. Marx, quoted from Pleïades edn, Paris, Vol. 2, pp. 802, 1032.
20 R. Tartarin, 'Gratuité, fin du salariat et calcul économique dans le communisme', paper presented at the University of Paris I, 5 October 1979.

21 In *Sociology and Development*, ed. E. de Kadt and G. Williams (London: Tavistock, 1974), p. 93.
22 See O. Flechtheim, 'Kommunismus ohne Wachstum', *Wirtschaft und Gesellschaft*, no. 4, 1978, pp. 415–21.
23 *Radical Philosophy*, Summer 1979, p. 35.
24 H. G. Wells, *Russia in the Shadows* (London: Hodder & Stoughton, 1921), p. 78.
25 *Esprit*, November 1977.
26 Quoted from D. Buxton, *Radical Philosophy*, Summer 1979, p. 30.
27 A fascinating description of the debate may be found in L. Yurovsky, *Denezhnaya politika sovetskoi vlasti* (Moscow, 1928); see also Baslé, op. cit. (n. 4), vol. 1.
28 K. Marx, *Capital*, Vol. 1 (New York: International Publishing Co., 1967), ch. 1.
29 F. Engels, *Anti-Dühring*, emphasis mine.
30 C. Bettelheim, *Calcul économique et formes de propriété* (Paris: Centre d'Etudes de Planification Socialiste, 1970).
31 *Ekonomika i matematicheskiye metody*, no. 6, 1974, and nos 1 and 2, 1975; and (Kronrod's attack) *Planovoye khozyaistvo*, no. 8, 1975.
32 D. Valovoi in *Pravda*, three relevant articles: 11, 12 and 13 November 1978.
33 N. Petrakov, *Khozyaistvennaya reforma* (Moscow, 1971), and other works.
34 Baslé, op. cit. (n. 4), pp. 761–2.
35 This is the position adopted by R. Rosdolsky, in his *The Making of Marx's Capital* (London: Pluto Press, 1977), and it seems correct.
36 Baslé, op. cit. (n. 4), p. 763.
37 ibid., p. 56.
38 Lipietz, op. cit. (n. 15), pp. 276–7.
39 Apart from Bettelheim's works, there is also a valuable doctoral dissertation by B. Chavance, 'Les bases de l'économie politique du socialisme', Paris-Nanterre University, 1979.
40 K. Marx, *Grundrisse* (Harmondsworth: Penguin, 1973), pp. 158–9.
41 Chavance, op. cit. (n. 39), p. 279; his emphasis. Rubin's work will be quoted directly, see note 43 below.
42 Lipietz, op. cit. (n. 15), pp. 326–7.
43 I. Rubin, *Ocherki po teorii stoimosti Marksa* (Moscow, 1923).
44 E. Mandel, *Marxist Economic Theory* (London: Ink Links, 1968), pp. 159–60.
45 Yurovsky, op. cit. (n. 27), p. 118.
46 V. Novozhilov, in *Primeneniye matematiki v ekonomicheskikh isslevodvaniyakh*, ed. V. S. Nemchinov (Moscow, 1959), p. 165. The book has appeared in English as *The Use of Mathematics in Economics* (Edinburgh: Oliver & Boyd, 1964).
47 Yurovsky, op. cit. (n. 27), p. 118.
48 Quoted from Tartarin, op. cit. (n. 20), p. 24.
49 Bettelheim, op. cit. (n. 30), p. 30.
50 ibid., p. 25. See also my critique in Nove, op. cit. (n. 3).
51 Ollman, op. cit. (n. 1), p. 18.
52 Bettelheim, op. cit. (n. 30), p. 134.
53 Yurovsky, op. cit. (n. 27), p. 105.
54 ibid., p. 109.
55 Rubin, op. cit. (n. 43), pp. 10–11.
56 Bettelheim, op. cit. (n. 30), pp. 53, 70–1, *passim*.
57 V. Lenin, *State and Revolution* (London: Lawrence & Wishart, 1933).
58 See K. Marx, *Capital*, Vol. I (in some translations the words are 'simple and intelligible'); F. Engels, *Anti-Dühring*; N. Bukharin, *Economics of the Transition Period*; V. Lenin, *State and Revolution* and many of his other works.
59 A. Katsenellenboigen, *Studies in Soviet Economic Planning* (White Plains, NY: Sharpe, 1978), p. 123.
60 O. Antonov, *Dlya vsekh i dlya sebya* (Moscow, 1965), p. 23.
61 *Voprosy ekonomiki*, no. 12, 1977, p. 5.
62 Trotsky, op. cit. (n. 2), p. 57.
63 ibid., p. 78.
64 V. Lenin, *Sochineniya*, 5th edn (Moscow, 1962), Vol. 36, p. 157.
65 R. Bahro, *Die Alternative* (Cologne: Europäische Verlagsanstalt, 1977), in English as *The*

Alternative in Eastern Europe (London: New Left Books, 1973). These quotations are on pp. 201 and 521 of the German edition.

66 C. Castoriadis, *Le Contenu du socialisme* (Paris: Editions du Seuil, 1979).

67 Marx and Engels repeatedly argued thus, e.g. in *Capital*, Vol. II, ch. 10, and in *Anti-Dühring*.

68 B. Loasby, *Choice, Complexity and Ignorance* (Cambridge: Cambridge University Press, 1975).

69 I. Szelenyi, 'Whose alternative?', Flinders University, 1980.

70 V. Belotserkovsky, *Svoboda, vlast' i sobstvennost'* (Achberg: Achberger Verlag, 1980).

71 *Radical Philosophy*, Spring 1980, p. 24.

72 R. Samuel, *New Statesman*, 15 February 1980.

73 Szelenyi, op. cit. (n. 69).

74 A. Hegedus, *Socialism and Bureaucracy* (London: Allison & Busby, 1976).

75 *Pravda*, 28 November 1979.

76 L. Kolakowski, *Main Currents of Marxism*, Vol. I (Oxford: Clarendon Press, 1980), p. 172.

77 K. Marx, 'The German ideology' in *Collected Works*, Vol. V (London: Lawrence & Wishart, 1976), p. 47.

78 Quoted from a critical review in *Radical Philosophy*, Winter 1979, p. 8.

79 Bahro, op. cit. (n. 65), German edn, p. 537.

80 K. Marx, *Capital*, Vol. II (New York: International Publishing Co., 1967), p. 358.

81 K. Marx, *Critique of Political Economy* (Harmondsworth: Penguin, 1976), p. 31.

82 Lipietz, op. cit. (n. 15), p. 353.

83 K. Marx, quoted from Pléïades edn, Paris, Vol. 2, p. 204.

84 Bahro, op. cit. (n. 65), German edn, p. 233.

85 ibid., p. 174.

86 A. G. Meyer, *Marxism* (Cambridge, Mass.: Harvard University Press, 1970), p. 84.

87 M. Marković, 'Stalinism and Marxism', in *Stalinism*, ed R. Tucker (New York: Norton, 1977), p. 312.

88 ibid., p. 303; emphasis mine.

89 A. Gorz, *Adieux au prolétariat* (Paris: Editions du Seuil, 1980), pp. 22–4.

90 Bahro, op. cit. (n. 65), German edn, p. 521.

91 O. Wilde, 'The soul of man under socialism', in his *De Profundis and Other Writings* (Harmondsworth: Penguin, 1973), p. 28.

92 J. F. Becker, *Marxian Political Economy* (Cambridge: Cambridge University Press, 1977).

93 For instance, see Neil Harding, *Lenin's Political Thought*, Vol. 2 (London: Macmillan, 1980).

94 From Z. Strmiska's unpublished paper 'The social system and structural contradictions in societies of the Soviet type', submitted to a conference in Paris ('Le Printempts de Prague') in October 1981, by kind permission of its author.

95 C. Taylor, *Hegel and Modern Society* (Cambridge: Cambridge University Press, 1979), pp. 149, 153, 154.

Part 2

Socialism and the Soviet Experience

Introduction

What can and should socialists learn from the experience of the USSR? Its official theorists designate the existing situation as one of 'mature socialism', while claiming, with Stalin, that the Soviet Union entered into the socialist stage in the 1930s. The next stage will be communism.

This raises a whole series of questions. There is the Soviet experience viewed historically: the 'war-communism' period, NEP, the various theories and controversies of the 1920s, the Soviet model viewed as a model of rapid industrialisation of a backward country, and so on. It can be considered against the background of Marxian prophecy: that is to say, we can compare Soviet socialism at any of its stages with what Marx envisaged. We could apply Marxist theory to the USSR, but in doing so, we should undertake a double process: not only using Marxist ideas on socialism as a criterion for judging the USSR, but also seeing how far Soviet experience might throw some light on the validity of the Marxian criteria. We could also look at Soviet planning as a technique, its achievements, weaknesses, limitations, efficacy, its potential for reform. Then socialist theorists must inevitably look at the political economy of the USSR from the standpoint of the rights of the working masses, the extent of their control over their leaders, over the means of production, over the disposal of the product – at political and economic democracy. Once again, this should be done without adopting utopian criteria: thus no one would seriously wish to criticise Soviet criminal law or constitution on the grounds that, in a truly socialist society, law, crime and the state will have withered away. Similarly – for reasons abundantly explored in Part 1 – it would be naive and pointless simply to denounce the USSR because there are elements of hierarchy, because some are managers and others are managed – in other words, there is a vertical division of labour. But a critical *and* realistic appraisal of Soviet experience could be of considerable assistance to clear thought about the relationship which *could* exist in a socialist society, without making any absurd or far-fetched assumptions. Then there is one other important question, that of *economics*, or economic laws, under socialism. Here too there are Soviet discussions, there is Soviet experience. Nor should the views of minority groups be neglected, whether these belong to oppositions within the party or to (especially economic) specialists outside it.

However, there is also the relative scarcity of paper and of the readers' (and author's) patience. Most of these questions could be the subject of a book.

There are in fact two French doctoral dissertations beside me as I write this, one by Baslé, the other by Chavance (both referred to earlier), devoted wholly to the discussion of economic laws and the law of value, which together run to just about a thousand typed pages. I have myself written perhaps as many pages, in books and articles, about various aspects of the Soviet economy and of economic history. Far more than this has been written by other authors. The literature on Soviet-type economies is vast and is growing. So Part 2 of the present book will seek to draw lessons and conclusions from aspects of Soviet experience which will have been documented (by this author and by many others) in other works, with only occasional direct reference to illustrative material.

Externalities and 'Internalities'

As an example of how I shall proceed, let me take the argument that under socialism it will be possible to internalise externalities, that is, to decide by reference to the general interest. Under capitalism, the profit of each separately owned unit can contradict the profitability (interest) of the whole. One can transcend this fragmentation if the means of production are commonly owned. Or can one?

Soviet experience suggests that this is far more difficult than might be supposed. Externalities arise not because of separation of ownership, but because of separation of decision-making units. Even in a university, room-allocation or timetable changes by one faculty office can have deleterious effects on students in other faculties, effects which are external to the faculty office in question. What is taken into account depends on the area of responsibility of the decision-maker. This is partly due to interest (the decision-maker will be judged by how well he or she carries out his/her prescribed responsibilities), and partly due to information flows (effects external to the office concerned may simply not be known to the decision-maker).

Given the magnitude and complexity of the task of planning and managing a modern industrial economy, it is inevitable that the task be divided between different offices, departments, ministries, regions, and so on. This is the institutional foundation of what a massive Soviet literature describes pejoratively as *vedomstvennost'*, 'departmentalism'. The other frequently mentioned disease is *mestnichestvo*, 'localism'. Brezhnev and others have repeatedly criticised both these manifestations of the priority of partial over general interest. There is abundant evidence of pollution of air and rivers, and local soviets have at least as much difficulty in enforcing zoning and other town planning regulations as the authorities of any Western conurbation.

One reads almost daily of some ministry or department neglecting the interests of some related or complementary activity, because it is beyond its 'departmental barrier'. There is a strong tendency to self-supply. Thus each of twenty-five ministries engaged in construction in the Pavlodar *oblast'* seeks to set up its own quarry and building materials factory (*Pravda*, 26 December 1980, to cite an example that happens to be to hand).

The difficulty faced by the centre in 'internalising' all the externalities, in identifying and enforcing the general interest, is evidently closely connected with the sheer scale of centralised planning, which is also the cause of the necessary division of function between departments and local bodies. To consider everything in the context of everything else is plainly an impossible task. At departmental or local level the 'general interest' is not and cannot be unambiguously visible, or even visible at all. Imagine that one is an official responsible for allocating sheet metal, or for building a petrochemical complex, or manufacturing precision instruments, or controlling the movement of trains in the Ukraine. One's task is determined by plan-instructions, and/or norms, and the efficiency of one's operation will be judged by how well one has carried out the instructions and responsibilities. It is inconceivable that the official could evaluate, at his or her level, the 'external' consequences of this or that action, e.g. of supplying A rather than B.

So Soviet experience points to the importance of boundary-lines of responsibility, their effect on perception and on decision-making, the *impossibility* of avoiding the issue of external economies and diseconomies, the difficulty of reconciling partial and general interest. How much of this, it may be asked, is due to the specific features of the *Soviet* system? One hears voices from the 'new left' to the effect that Soviet experience is irrelevant, it is not 'real' socialism. One of their arguments is precisely that, in the USSR, differences of interest exist between different strata, workers and managers, managers and planners, leaders and led; different industrial and local officials are at odds with one another. While this is indeed so, can one envisage a situation in which the general interest *would* be universally perceived and identified with? For reasons already examined at length in Part 1, this seems to me a utopian and unreal conception. Nor could grass-roots democracy make the problem any easier to handle.

But this does not mean, of course, that any form of feasible socialism *must* reproduce the deficiencies and distortions of the Soviet system, in this or a number of other respects (for instance, in the relations between management and workers). It is also the case that organisational rearrangement can mitigate some of the problems, by altering areas of responsibility. For instance, the Soviet leadership is now (1981) considering ways and means of putting agricultural machinery design and production, and also storage and transport of farm products, under one organisational umbrella together with agriculture. Of course this would not eliminate the 'boundary' problem, it would change the boundary. Perhaps more significant is another and different point. Many of the problems of the Soviet-type economy are in some way or other connected with shortage, with a sellers' market situation. This exacerbates all the other problems: thus fear of not receiving needed supplies of so-called deficit products is one reason for self-supply, and it is shortage which makes it all too easy for the producers to neglect the requirements of the users. Shortages, it may be argued, are a consequence of the priority of growth, of the strategy of 'catching up and overtaking' – a consequence, then, of specifically Soviet policies.

Shortages and the Sellers' Market

So let us now pass to an examination of the causes of shortage. This must be distinguished from scarcity, the latter being a situation in which demand *unlimited* (by either price or rationing) exceeds supply, while shortage means that individuals (factory managers or consumers) with a legitimate claim on resources cannot obtain what they want or need, even though they have the money. Shortages can be due to natural causes (e.g. a drought), to unforeseen circumstances (events abroad), to imperfect foresight (e.g. demand was under-estimated, supply overestimated), to deliberate policy (as when retail prices are not increased, though demand is known to exceed supply), or to an overambitious plan which exceeds the resources available (but is meant to have a 'mobilising' function).

There are several works published in Eastern Europe on the subject of shortage, chronic or recurrent. The most important are by Kornai[1] and Bauer.[2] They identify social-political pressures which result in overtaut plans. (In so far as these concern investments, they will be further discussed later in Part 2.) It would be theoretically possible to envisage a socialist society in which such pressures would be less strong, but, unless we were to imagine a state of abundance, they must surely be present. In the real world there will be unsatisfied aspirations, and the existence of democratic institutions will not reduce such pressures; on the contrary! This is quite apart from government's own commitment to growth, a commitment which is also associated with full employment of material and human resources. Full employment is, of course, of great significance, especially when one contemplates the alternative, which is unemployment. It is not an advertisement for the efficiency of capitalism if a sizeable proportion of productive capacity and personnel is inactive. However, it can (I believe) be shown that full employment *must* entail shortage. This is a consequence of (inevitably) imperfect foresight. Unless one assumes a static economy, there is bound to be change: in tastes, techniques, preferences. At microeconomic levels these *cannot* be precisely foreseen. Any major investment takes many years to complete, and then has many more years of life before it. Workers and engineers acquire specialised skills, which may or may not be needed ten years hence. So we may be sure that, even if macro equilibrium exists between requirements and resources, there would be *some* shortages, which, because of full employment, cannot be speedily made good.

Let me give two examples. Suppose that there are a thousand different spare parts for vehicles of all kinds, and suppose that the planned supply in aggregate exactly equals planned demand in aggregate. Or suppose that the number of seats in restaurants, and the total number of dishes to be served in them, exactly equals total demand but that no *extra* unused capacity exists. It is *certain*, is it not, that some shortages would occur? Say, there would not be enough of a given type of carburettor or radiator-cap, not enough seats in certain restaurants, not enough duck or apple tart, even while some other items were in excess supply. Kornai argued long ago that the negative features of a sellers' market situation must exist unless it is difficult to sell, unless the seller (supplier) finds it necessary to take trouble to satisfy the needs of the customer.

This, too, is an important aspect of Soviet (and not only of Soviet) experience. Where the supplier is in a strong position *vis-à-vis* the customer –

whether because of shortage or because the supply plan ties the customer to this particular supplier – the latter tends to neglect the requirements of the user, *and* finds that it is actually beneficial to do so. In the Soviet system the supplier is usually designated by the supply plan, and is therefore in a position of an absolute monopolist. Even if others produce this same item, the manager is not (legally) entitled to transfer his custom to them. The rules do empower the customer to refuse to accept goods which are not to specification, but ample evidence exists that such powers are used sparingly, under conditions in which the slogan 'take it or leave it' applies. It should be possible to envisage a socialist economy in which one is free to negotiate freely with suppliers, and we shall be considering this later. (Just such a reform has been proposed in the USSR, and there was mention of it in the decree published in 1965, but it has not in fact been adopted.) But the condition of shortage is one of the principal reasons why the material-allocation system exists. We know from wartime experience in the West that there too it led to the negative phenomena associated with a sellers' market.

Shortage, then, is due partly to the full employment of resources, partly to the commitment of the centre to rapid growth, and partly to the efforts of sectors, departments, ministries and localities to acquire resources for their various purposes. *Because* it is known that resources are scarce, that goods may not be available, for production and consumption alike, everyone tends to hoard, to buy whatever non-perishable goods may be obtainable, and this exacerbates the shortages. The power of the supplier, under sellers' market conditions, still further weakens the already weak position of the customer *vis-à-vis* the producer.

Shortage is the consequence of the Soviet version of inflation. In theory this should be excluded. Demand for producers' goods is *planned* demand, limited not by the money supply but by the system of material-allocation (one can have the money in the bank, but the bulk of materials and machines are, in fact, 'rationed'). Consequently, a balanced plan excludes the very possibility of inflation. In the case of consumers' goods and services, the total incomes of the population appear to be largely determined, and paid out, by the state and its institutions and enterprises. Supply is planned, prices are determined by state organs, so there *should* be balance. In practice this does not happen. Partly the imbalance is a micro imbalance, that is, some materials, machines, foodstuffs and manufactures are in short supply and others are in excess supply, owing to errors, unpredictability and inflexible prices. However, massive evidence points to the existence of macro imbalance too. In the producers' goods and investment sectors too many projects are started, for reasons to be examined when we discuss investment, and many producers complain that they are ordered to deliver more than they can produce. In the case of consumers' goods, incomes tend to be equal to or sometimes exceed plan, output is well below plan, and there is reluctance to increase the general level of prices. So, as a result, as a *Pravda* editorial frankly admitted,[3] incomes increase much faster than supply, and the rapid increase in saving bank deposits and a rise in prices of foodstuffs in the free peasant markets are consequences of the frustration of would-be purchasers.

A further point worth making is that so-called commercial criteria can be highly misleading and even perverse when the producer can exercise monopoly power. If, for example, the producer is urged to cut costs, it is sometimes all too easy to pass them on to the customer. Thus Soviet machinery producers are notoriously unwilling to take responsibility for installation, maintenance and repairs; for them these are 'avoidable expenditures', that is, they can be passed on to others. Goodwill is gained through a reputation for quality and prompt service, and goodwill is valuable – under competition. Since to acquire goodwill involves cost, in the absence of competition it has no 'commercial' value. Quality can be expected to deteriorate. Or take the example of a monopolist retail trade organisation. How is its efficiency to be measured? By profits? By labour productivity? By turnover per shop? By all these measures, it 'pays' to have customers stand in line all day and every day. A city's buses show 'better' economic results if they are jammed with passengers. I have made these points in discussing certain naive formulations of 'commercial' criteria for British nationalised industries, but they also apply to the 'East', and it is perhaps no accident that an article of mine on the subject was reprinted by a Hungarian periodical. I shall return to these questions when considering nationalised industries.

Planning Indicators and the Evaluation of Performance

The question of evaluating efficiency leads to the problem, familiar to most students of the Soviet economy, of *success indicators*. Plan-instructions have to be expressed in units of measurement: tonnes, square metres, millions of roubles, thousands of pairs, and so on. In any instance where there is a product mix, or different types or dimensions, plan indicators must of necessity be *aggregated*. As has already been noted, there are about 12,000,000 different products if these are fully disaggregated. There are in all some 48,000 plan 'positions'. In other words, the *average* 'product' which is the subject of a plan-instruction is an aggregate of 250 sub-products. These cannot be the subject of systematic plan-instructions because of the 'curse of scale'; there would be far too much information to handle. When a road transport enterprise receives a plan, in its fully disaggregated form it should include instructions as to what load every one of the several hundred lorries should carry every day, and where to.

But an order aggregated (e.g. in tonne-kilometres) incites the recipient to act in a particular way. If the measure is tonnes, this rewards weight and penalises economy of materials. If the measure is gross value in roubles there is benefit to be derived from making expensive goods, using expensive materials. Tonne-kilometres incite transport undertakings to carry heavy goods over long distances. Examples of wasteful or otherwise irrational practices designed to fulfil plans (in Russia the phrase is *delat' plan*, literally 'do the plan') could fill several bound volumes, all the examples being taken from Soviet publications. That so well-known and well-studied a problem still resists solution is proof enough that it is genuinely difficult to solve. The basic contradiction arises from the simple fact that the centre *cannot* know in full detail what is in fact needed by the customer, and yet the entire logic of the

Soviet system rests upon the proposition that it is the duty of all subordinate management to obey the plan-instructions of the centre because these supposedly embody the needs of society. In practice, the detailed specifications can generally only be determined in negotiation between producer and user, with or without the intermediacy of trading organs. But instead of the plan being the sum total of the detailed requirements, the detailed requirements have to be made to add up to the predetermined aggregated total. As Brezhnev (among others) has noted, the user has insufficient influence on production – and the 'user' is not only the consumer-citizen but also industrial, agricultural and other state enterprises.

Soviet experience proves also how difficult it is to plan and define quality, as against quantity. One can issue an order – produce 200,000 pairs of shoes – and this is identifiable and enforceable. To say 'produce *good* shoes, that fit the customer's feet' is a much vaguer, non-enforceable order. (Similarly I can be meaningfully instructed to give fifty lectures, but it is not so easy to enforce an order that I give *good* lectures!) It also shows the severe limitation of planning in physical quantities. The same number of tonnes, metres, pairs, can be of very different use-values and fulfil widely different needs. In any event, quality is a concept frequently inseparable from use; thus a dress or a machine can be fully in accord with technological standards, but still not be suitable for a particular wearer or factory process. How can this problem be overcome if plans are orders of superior authority (the central planners or ministries) and not those placed by the users?

The 'success indicator' problem is a major unsolved question, and is worthy of much closer attention than it can receive here. As noted already, it is exacerbated by the sellers' market and suppliers' monopoly, which frequently force the customer to accept goods of a quality or specification quite different from his desires and preferences. This applies both to producers' and to consumers' goods. Thus many machinery-manufacturing enterprises have obligatory plan targets in tonnes and in roubles; construction enterprises have plans expressed in roubles expended; labour productivity is usually measured by dividing the number of workers into the gross value of the output. As a multitude of Soviet sources attest, this inclines the producers to select the more expensive variants. Similarly, plans expressed in tonnes actually penalise those enterprises which succeed in using less metal, and this at a time when metal is particularly scarce! Output targets for intermediate goods and services have the inevitable effect of stimulating waste; one should produce a given final output with the minimum use of intermediate goods (i.e. of inputs), yet this would bring penalties to the enterprises and ministries producing such goods. The system also lends itself to some outrageous abuses: thus the 'service' organisation *Sel'khoztekhnika*, which (*inter alia*) supplies machinery to agriculture, levies charges for transport, delivery, assembly and testing, even when the farms have to send their own transport for machinery parts and assemble and test them themselves.[4]

All this is an integral part of a major problem, itself in two parts: how to incorporate micro demand into instructions passed down from hierarchical superiors; and, in more general terms, how to plan in aggregate quantities. For a serious socialist economist it cannot be enough to smile at the very numerous anecdotes of unintended forms of waste and of misfits between supply and demand. For what is the alternative, short of allowing 'horizontal' relationships between supplier and customer (with or without the intermediacy of trade organs) to determine the product mix? But this is a market solution.

There are two kinds of exceptions to the rule that microeconomic demand fails to have the required influence on supply, that plan indicators do not and cannot indicate just what is needed. One of these relates to homogeneous commodities, which may be termed 'plannable', of which electricity is the best example. A figure such as '100 kWh' is unambiguous and clear, unlike 100 pairs of shoes or 100 spare parts for tractors. The other concerns those cases in which the centre is itself the customer, and can directly demand that its demands are met: this is the case with armaments. Of course armaments are also a very high priority, but not all high-priority sectors fare well under the centralised system: thus there is no doubt at all about the importance which the top leadership attaches to technical progress, but to translate this desire into operational 'micro orders' has proved remarkably difficult.

The 'Curse of Scale', Innovation and Bureaucratic Fragmentation

Soviet experience underlines both the necessity and the dangers of a multiplicity of plan targets in a non-market economy. Output plans must be backed by the allocation of inputs and, since most factories' output consists of products which are inputs for other factories and sectors, 'the plan' becomes an interlocking multiplicity of instructions on production and allocation. It is important to distinguish between the current operational plan, which the Russians call *adresnyi* (i.e. an order with a name and address), and the longer-term plan, which is and can only be of a much more general and aggregated kind. Thus a five-year plan contains a target for, say, steel sheet and footwear, but this is not yet operational: there is no order yet for any specific production unit to produce any specified thing.

It is inevitable that production plans are issued from offices other than those responsible for material allocation. It is also obvious that if to produce a good requires ten different inputs, these are likely to be allocated by ten different offices, each of which is also responsible for allocating the item in question to other economic sectors that use it. Consequently there is an immense task of co-ordination, to ensure that, at microeconomic operational level, production and inputs plans are coherent and consistent. Be it noted that input-output techniques can only be of limited use in this task, and this for two reasons. One is, again, aggregation: the variety of inputs is too great to be incorporated in full detail in an input-output table. The other is that allocation (and information flows) relate to administrative units, and these do not and cannot coincide with product designations.[5] The sheer complexity of the task ensures that it is never completed, and numerous instances arise when supply and production plans are inconsistent. Plans then require changes in the course of their implementation, which is why the desired objective of *stable* plans has never been achieved.

But output and inputs are only part of the process of planning. Labour, the wages bill, profits, investments, payments in the state budget, technological change, economy of materials and fuel, labour productivity, cost reduction, value (gross or net) of turnover, the fulfilment of delivery obligations, and other items (such as a reduction in size of office staffs) figure or have figured on the list of compulsory plan objectives. These too can contradict one another, and conflict with output plans, or with the production of goods actually required by the users. To cite but one of a mass of examples, a change in the output plan halfway through the year is often unaccompanied by any consequential change in the financial or labour plan, and there is even a phrase, *vozdushnyi val*, 'gross-output made of air', to designate a production task for which inputs are not provided.

Faced with an evaluation procedure which is above all concerned with plan fulfilment, and with uncertainty about supply and possible changes in plan, the management understandably tends to seek plans which are easy to fulfil (or avoids the risk of receiving plan orders which may prove unfulfillable) and overapplies for inputs, hoards materials and labour. Faced with the knowledge that this is the likely behaviour-pattern of management, the planners tend to proceed on the basis of past reported performance. This in turn causes cautious managers to avoid 'excessive' improvements in performance, which could cause them to be given excessive tasks in the next plan period.

Technical progress, indeed change of any sort, causes difficulties, and this for several reasons. First, the planners themselves base their instructions on past performance, and input-output tables (material balances too) are inherently conservative, reflecting *past* technical coefficients. Secondly, technical progress, either in the form of a new type of product or a new method of manufacture, will usually require some change in inputs, or in the output plan, beyond the power of management and requiring permission from one or several planning agencies. Finally, all innovation involves risk, and risk is not rewarded. Indeed, risk-aversion is (unintentionally) rewarded.

An intelligent critic, N. Voslensky, has pointed to an interesting contrast in this respect between the USSR and the West. In the USSR innovation has to be 'introduced'. The Russian word, *vnedreniye*, implies that it requires effort, a push from above. In the West, on the contrary, one had industrial espionage, and efforts have to be expended to prevent one's rivals learning about one's innovations.[6] The reason for the contrast must be competition, which exists in the West even in sectors (such as the chemical industry, for instance) in which giant monopolists may seem to be dominant; whereas in the USSR it is no accident that many plays and novels feature the obstructionist director who resists innovation: he has very little incentive to do otherwise. I am reminded too of a Czech economist who was once asked in conversation: 'Why is a capitalist monopoly so much more enterprising than a socialist monopoly?' His answer: 'There is nothing so monopolistic as a socialist monopoly.'

A further obstacle is the fragmentation of machinery production. Many machines and instruments are made by enterprises under a large number of different ministries, all of which are also engaged in a variety of other production activities. This applies both to industrial equipment and to consumer durables such as refrigerators, and also to farm machinery of many kinds. To give just one example, in 1975 materials-handling equipment was made by 380 enterprises under 35 all-union and republican ministries![7] There are many complaints about non-interchangeability of parts, lack of desirable standardisation and lack of any clear line of responsibility for quality or technological improvements. A devastating analysis by S. Kheinman tells us much about inefficiency and waste in the design and production of Soviet machinery; about the almost incredible degree of fragmentation of production and also of repairs, causing inefficiencies in the use of machines and skilled labour; and about the high cost of many components, as well as poor quality of equipment.[8] This, along with many similarly critical articles, helps to explain the need for the USSR to import modern technology on a large scale.

Management is in fact placed in an anomalous position. On the one hand, its task is to fulfil plan-instructions, supposedly embodying the needs of society. On the other, these plans are frequently inconsistent and ambiguous, and in any event the management's own proposals influence the instructions which it receives. 'Many orders are written by their recipients', a Hungarian economist once remarked. So management is in fact in a position to make a whole number of choices, but its performance is evaluated in terms of plan fulfilment, and so it is constrained to use its powers to demonstrate that it has succeeded in terms of the success indicators of the plan. This frequently is to the detriment of quality and of satisfying user needs.

A Soviet author has calculated that in a year there is a total of 2,700–3,600 million plan 'indicators' determined at all levels – 2.7–3.6 million at the centre, and 70 per cent of these concerning material allocation and supply.[9]

What has all this to do with factors specifically Soviet? Surely the difficulties and distortions are the consequences of *scale*, are various kinds of manifestations of *diseconomies of scale*. As already argued in the section on Marx, it was (to some extent still is) unfortunately the case that Marxists have vastly underestimated the complexities of centralised planning. Barone and Mises can be said to have seen the genuine difficulties clearly, and it was an East European economist who once said that, in a future socialist common-wealth, a statue to Mises might well be erected! Those who choose to attribute the distortions of the planning system to bureaucracy and lack of democracy have put the cart before the horse. Given the aim of substituting planning for the market, administrative resource allocation for trade, the visible for the invisible hand, *central* control becomes an objective necessity. Given the immense complexities, one requires a complex bureaucratic structure to take a multitude of interconnected decisions which, of their nature, are not a matter for democratic voting. In no society can an elected assembly decide by 115 votes to 73 where to allocate ten tonnes of leather, or whether to produce another 100 tonnes of sulphuric acid.

This is not to deny that there are economic policy decisions that *ought* to be democratically arrived at, and I will devote many pages later on to discussing this question. A case can be made for the proposition that the functional logic of centralised planning is closely associated with a one-party type of hierarchically organised despotism. This is because of the immense power wielded by the state's production-and-allocation mechanism (and the absence of countervailing power, when everyone is so dependent on the state), and also because the bulk of the state's functions become economic-managerial, and there seem to its controllers to be some very good reasons why these highly complex functions should not be disturbed by the unpredictabilities of volatile voting by the masses. And those who ascribe the problems to alienation must face the fact that this too is a diseconomy of scale: decisions are taken at levels remote from ordinary people. It has already been argued at length that this remoteness is due to the very nature of centralised planning, of a marketless economy. So is hierarchy, which arises because decision-making *is* hierarchical, but which then has profound social effects, including the emergence of institutionalised privilege. This is one reason why a model of socialism free of such defects will have to be based on direct links between economic units, that is, on commodity production, on exchange, with some form of market. Soviet experience is, in my view, conclusive on this point – though one should never forget that external economies and diseconomies may remain unperceived at levels below the centre.

Indeed, the numerous lacunae, inconsistencies and uncertainties in the plan, especially the unreliability of material supplies, lead not only to 'self-supply' (i.e. wasteful duplication) but also to unofficial horizontal links between enterprises, a network of personal relationships, supply agents known as *tolkachi* ('pushers', or 'expediters'), and also corrupt practices. Lack of data does not allow any of this to be quantified, but ample 'anecdotal' evidence exists which suggests that these phenomena are very widespread, and that they are the consequence of the malfunctioning of the planning mechanism, a malfunctioning which seems to me an inescapable consequence of the sheer scale of the task, and of the size and multiplicity of the hierarchical organisation which has to cope with it.

The Hungarian *émigré* Gyorgy Markus has called this 'the third economy, that of the personal-informal relations of assistance in case of shortages . . . existing between the various members of the bureaucratic apparatus'. This he distinguishes from 'the second economy', which is the tolerated (or unsuppressed) private enterprise which provides or redistributes goods and services for the consumer, filling gaps left by the clumsy and overcentralised official plan structure.

The tendency of management (and others in charge of sectors) to overstate material requirements, to hoard, to manoeuvre so as to 'fulfil' plans, may appear to be due to their failure to identify with the general interest. As Markus points out, they are indeed 'exhorted all the time to give priority to the "interests of the state". This is undoubtedly their *duty* . . . but it is not the *task* for which they are directly responsible. As a matter of fact, even if they *wanted* to act in a "disinterested" spirit, they would not know how to do it: they have no systematic information about the real situation in all those fields not under their direct control.' And in the bargaining process which accompanies plan disaggregation and implementation, their claims for resources represent an 'attempt at the most optimal conditions for the fulfilment of those tasks which the plan specified'. Inevitably, in the bargaining process at all levels 'the balance will always be further tilted towards the largest, most centralised and politically most powerful organisations, independently of actual economic demand, not to speak of the needs of the population'.[10]

Hierarchy has its purely economic aspect too. Let us take as an example a product which appeared on Brezhnev's list of so-called *melochi* (minor items) in short supply: toothbrushes. In capitalism the firms which make tooth-brushes do so because it is profitable. In the Soviet model they are made because a planning office so decides. Who, then, is responsible for tooth-brushes? One must suppose that the official is a fairly junior one. So, under conditions of shortage, in the competition for scarce resources he or she carried less weight than a more senior official in charge of, say, wool cloth or electronics. With too many items to handle, the planning mechanism inevitably tends to identify some as priority. Indeed, the production and delivery obligations imposed on management specify what is called *vazhneishaya produktsiya*, the most important products. An influential Soviet economist, D. Valovoi, has pointed out that some items not on the 'most important' list are in fact complementary to those that are. And some figure on the list of those that Brezhnev described as *melochi*.

Another problem which has proved difficult to solve deserves a brief mention. This is the contradiction between basing central planning on industrial sectors and on regions. Obviously one cannot do both at once: if steelworks or electronics factories are subordinated to the appropriate ministry in Moscow, then the regional authorities can have only very limited power over economic activities in their area, which causes problems with regard to regional co-ordination: each ministry looks after its own subordinate units and potential local economies of scale are not realised. However, as experience under the Khrushchev regionalisation reform of 1957 (*sovnark-hozy*) abundantly proved, placing the enterprises under the authority of regional or local bodies does even more harm: supplies to other regions and the planning of specific industries on a national scale inevitably suffer. In 1965 the industrial sector, 'ministerial' structure was restored. However, much criticism has been directed at the resultant lack of regional co-ordination, particularly evident in places such as Siberia, where large-scale developments in previously empty areas require the co-ordinated activities of enterprises under many different ministries; a number of so-called 'territorial production administrations' have been set up, some of which overlap the existing provincial boundary-lines (neither provinces – *oblasti* – nor the fifteen republics are convenient units for planning purposes). As a result there is still considerable confusion about lines of responsibility and authority.

Another difficulty with the ministerial form of centralised planning arises from the fact that the same goods are made in enterprises under a number of different ministries; the example of materials-handling equipment has been cited already, but the same is true of many other items, from refrigerators to ploughs. The vast range of products made by modern industry makes it difficult to distribute the task of organising their production between a finite number of authorities.

Is It Planning?

Several authors of the most diverse political views have stated that there is in fact no planning in the Soviet Union: Eugene Zaleski, J. Wilhelm, Hillel Ticktin.[11] They all in their very different ways note the fact that plans are often (usually) unfulfilled, that information flows are distorted, that plan-instructions are the subject of bargaining, that there are many distortions and inconsistencies, indeed that (as many sources attest) plans are frequently altered within the period to which they are supposed to apply, partly to take the unexpected into account, but also to justify the claim to 100 per cent fulfilment of a plan reduced (at enterprise level) to the level of actual achievement. The outcome often differs both from the intentions of the authors of the plan *and* from the needs and desires of the users. So – how can all this be 'planning'?

Zaleski has produced a large and scholarly volume, in which he is able conclusively to demonstrate that, over many decades, not only were long-term *and* short-term plans underfulfilled, but target figures were not seldom missed by very substantial margins. Plans of every sort were repeatedly altered. His statistical appendices document all these facts with unparalleled thoroughness. He then concludes that the economy was not planned in any meaningful sense, that planning agencies, ministries and managers adapt as best they can to circumstances, and that therefore the economy was not planned but *managed*. Wilhelm takes a similar view, but he also gives emphasis to the fact that the plans themselves are affected by consumer demand, that they are based on the actually achieved level, and so on, which would not be the case if this really was 'planning'.

Ticktin believes that planning should conform to the original ideas of Marx and Lenin on the subject, and that wasteful bureaucratic 'planning' does not deserve this name. The economy is 'administered'. He also strongly opposes anything resembling 'market socialism'.

My difficulty with the Zaleski formulation is perhaps mainly verbal. All that he says is correct. It demonstrates the existence of great inefficiencies, gaps between outcome and intention. If this intention is called a 'plan', then this is bad planning. By the same token it is bad management. The existence or non-existence of a plan cannot be demonstrated by showing that a large gap exists between the original objective and the result. If most of what actually happens does so because the officials and managers are trying to fulfil plan orders, the fact that many will fail in this does not transform a planned economy into an unplanned economy.

Wilhelm's approach is logically consistent. If planning is defined as he defines it, as a set of consistent and enforceable objectives laid down by the central authorities, then it is easy to show that many objectives are not enforceable or not enforced, or mutually inconsistent; many of the objectives are influenced or even determined by pressures and circumstances which affect the orders given by the centre; and so on. In a later and as yet unpublished version of his argument, Wilhelm comes close to asserting that consumer choice and planning are *definitionally* incompatible. His conclusion follows from his premises, but one can and should question the premises. My argument is that the deficiencies and imbalances, and distortions due to group interest too, are the inescapable accompaniments of the endeavour to plan centrally, and that central planning is the inescapable consequence of trying to organise a socialist economy along non-market lines. It follows that in Wilhelm's terms centralised planning has not existed because it *could* not exist.

Ticktin never explains how his non-market, non-bureaucratic planning would or could work. So it is difficult to discuss his implied model. (On one attempt to do so, I was met with the reply: 'The very notion of a model is un-Marxist!') That Soviet-type planning differs radically from that envisaged by Marx is, of course, true. For reasons developed at length in Part 1 of the present work, it could not possibly conform to what Marx *did* envisage!

Class Structure, Labour, Wages and Trade Unions

A Soviet theorist, Kosolapov, has sought to argue that a worker in the USSR is a co-owner, that since he does not sell his labour-power he employs himself, and the consumers' good he buys is 'in essence an issue of his share in the social product', even though Kosolapov himself states that some workers do not see things that way.[12] In fact surely it is the case that the 'we/they' division is very real, and is perhaps equally felt by the rulers and the ruled, the managers and the managed. There is a quite sizeable literature on the nature of Soviet society, on whether those who rule are a 'class', or a stratum, or an elite, whether the system is 'state capitalism', whether the workers are 'exploited', and if so, by whom. I have joined in this interesting discussion elsewhere,[13] and this is not the place to pursue terminological-definitional matters. Let us content ourselves with noting that the hierarchical Soviet model is one in which persons of high rank acquire power over resources, and over other persons. Or it might be more accurate to say that the inherently hierarchical nature of the decision-making process ensures that the holder of a particular rank in the hierarchy does have such power, just as, in an army, a battalion or division must have a command structure, independently of the ambitions of a particular holder of this or that senior rank. The central authorities' power includes that of defining the privileges that go with rank, and also the power to prevent any public reference to and discussion of such privileges. For example, everyone knows that party and state officials of a defined seniority have access to special shops where goods unobtainable by ordinary citizens can be bought at low prices, but censorship prevents any mention of this in any publications.

Who are the rulers, the class(?) that governs? This is a question which admits of no unambiguous answer in any society, and the Soviet model in this respect is both more and less clear than that of the West. More so because, thanks to the *nomenklatura* system of appointments and the carefully graded ranks of an all-embracing hierarchy, most posts of significance and the persons holding them are identifiable. It is as if there were a universal civil and military service: senior officers can be seen to be such. By contrast, in a typical capitalist society there are many independent hierarchies, alongside property-owners large and small. However, in the Soviet system one is still left with no satisfactory basis for *defining* rulers. Again taking the military rank parallel, are they senior officers (colonel and above), or *all* officers, or anyone with any command role whatever, which would include corporals? Is a foreman on a building site to be included, or the manager of a rural retail store? Equally important, what, for a socialist, should be the criterion for judgement? Is the very existence of a distinction between rulers and ruled already evidence of the non-socialist nature of the Soviet Union? Is it therefore implied that a complex modern society, with or without a market mechanism, can operate without rulers, or with individuals holding posts of authority by rotation? Even if one believes that elections to the Supreme Soviet should be genuine (which they are not at present), should industrial managers, planning officials, chief engineers, ships' captains, newspaper editors, also be elected, and if so, by whom? Presumably in the real world of tomorrow factories will need to be managed, or newspapers edited, and so on. I have referred to these questions before and will return to them later; for the present it is enough to pose them.

Linked with them is another question: in assessing the role and nature of the ruling class-stratum-elite, is one to consider their *power*, or *what they do* with the power that they exercise? Or to put it another way: are the rulers 'exploiters' because they determine (within limits, of course) the way resources are allocated, and therefore 'appropriate the surplus'? Or does the surplus they appropriate consist of their own excessive material and non-material privileges? (And what *are* 'excessive' privileges?) Suppose that the Soviet authorities decide to invest in housing, or in a factory to make sausages, or in fertiliser to improve the potato harvest, or in rural health clinics. Let us further assume that these measures benefit the masses. Does the fact that the decisions are taken by the 'elite' make them exploitive, a form of appropriation of the surplus extracted from the workers? Would a genuinely paternalistic despotism be exploitive because despotic, or exploitive because not genuinely parternalistic? There is no need to dwell further on these matters. I do not raise them to justify any aspect of the Soviet system, but because if the existence of the distinction between rulers and ruled is to be a feature of 'feasible socialism', then it is not the existence of rulers, but their relation to and responsibility towards the rank-and-file, and the nature of the decisions they take, that should be the basis of an adequate critique. As has been argued earlier, one cannot devise safeguards against abuse of authority under socialism if one believes that under socialism there will be no authority.

The Soviet managerial model is authoritarian, in that management is appointed, and has no responsibility to its own workforce. The so-called 'production councils' (*proizvodstvennye soveshchaniya*) appear to have little significance. Supervision is from above, not from below. The Yugoslav 'self-management' approach is rejected (and not without reason, as we shall see). It is important to note the close connection between the rejection of the market and the system of upward managerial responsibility. Within a model of centralised non-market planning, the task of management is to fulfil plan orders received from above, and this predetermines the command relationship between the manager and *his* subordinates. With relatively few decisions taken at the level of the factory or shop, even genuinely elected representatives of workers would have so little to decide that they would probably not bother to attend meetings. As Brus has several times pointed out, meaningful workers' participation requires decentralisation of decisions to the level at which they can meaningfully participate. Of course, meetings are held, suggestions and criticisms (from below) are supposed to be welcomed, but management is in theory and in practice in command. Its powers are constrained not only by party (and to some extent trade union) organs, but also by the unorganised response of the workforce. Soviet experience shows that management finds it difficult to cope with go-slows, absenteeism, drunkenness, petty pilfering; it would be quite wrong to imagine that a terrorised labour force does what it is told. Under conditions of shortage, as we have repeatedly noted, there is a sellers' market. There is a labour shortage, and a worker is usually free to resign and go elsewhere. The Soviet state may be a monopoly-employer, but the state is for practical purposes a large number of separate units which compete with each other for labour. Influence from below, though unorganised, is therefore greater than it might appear.

The determination and enforcement of wage and salary scales raise a number of problems in Soviet experience. The first is the principle or criterion to be adopted. The words 'to each according to his work' are no more than words. In theory the scales should reflect skills, responsibility and the burdensome or unpleasant nature of the work (subject to a minimum which has been increased significantly in recent decades). It is in fact very difficult to put actual numbers to those very general considerations. Thus should medical practitioners and teachers receive half the pay of bus-drivers? Should semi-skilled workers in the chemical industry earn twice as much as those in retail trade, or a manager three times as much as an engineer? Who is to tell, and on what basis? In practice pay rates must be modified by the conditions of the labour 'market', i.e. supply of and demand for different kinds of labour in different areas. Thus, under conditions of labour shortage, let us imagine that the pay of brick-layers or metal-workers in central Siberia is not attractive; since they are free to move, the workers in these categories *have* to be offered more, or plans will be unfulfilled. This will mean either that the central regulations will change, or that they will, whenever possible, be evaded by management in collusion with the workforce. One moral to be drawn from Soviet experience is that central income determination is frequently ineffective, that actual income relativities differ significantly from tariff rates (through piece rate and bonus payments, etc.) and also that evasion is easier in some sectors and occupations than in others. Thus key priority projects and areas are more likely to be allowed extra, and a worker on piece rates is far more likely to be able to exceed his tariff or basic rate than, say, a bookkeeper or librarian. The effective control over wages is the so-called wages fund, that is, the limit placed on the total wages bill of every enterprise and institution.

Soviet experience suggests that material incentives are needed, but also that the desirable income relativities are hard to define and harder to enforce. It would seem that – as has already been argued – pay differentials are an integral part of any system in which labour is not directed, and is free to move. The alternative to inducement is compulsion, and inducement implies incentives and therefore inequality. This is not meant to imply that the actual degrees of income inequality (and other privileges or handicaps) conform to principles appropriate to a socialist society, but clearly giving such principles operationally meaningful definitions is a highly complex task to which far too little attention has been given by socialist theorists, in and out of the Soviet Union. Criteria apart, it is also an important question to determine *who* should decide. The government? An elected assembly? The market, suitably modified? What role should be played by the trade unions? It is only proper to add that income distribution is in a mess at points far west of the Soviet border.

Before returning to the issue of trade unions, a few words about women. Soviet ideology has always laid great stress on female equality, and there is equal pay for equal work. However, the average rate of pay of women appears, from incomplete evidence, to be as much below that of men as in capitalist countries of Western Europe, and men fill the overwhelming majority of senior positions. Nor is there any trend towards changing this situation. This certainly should lead us to question the views of naive feminists who attribute female inequality to 'capitalism'. It seems as if male and female attitudes, and the obstacles and handicaps which women face in their careers, are somewhat similar on both sides of the ideological barrier. Given the typical attitude of most male workers to women, there was in fact no reason to expect that the rise of workers (or rather ex-workers) to leading positions would be of any special benefit to 'women's liberation'. The situation has been exacerbated in the Soviet Union by the low priority enjoyed by those sectors which particularly cater for women's needs (e.g. retail distribution) and indeed by those which tend to employ a large proportion of women. Much more could be said on this topic, but this is not the place to say it.[14] The moral seems to be that socialist feminists should derive from the Soviet experience the need to think hard and long about the causes and remedies of women's inequality in income and status, and of course some feminists have been doing just this.

Soviet trade unions have long been party-controlled adjuncts of the state planning system, responsible also for administering social insurance. Independent trade unions had been snuffed out by 1921. This is not the place to discuss early controversies about the *ètatisation* (or even militarisation) of the trade unions. The point is that they had from the first a dual role, that of acting as a 'connecting rod' between the leadership and the masses, mobilising the workers for the fulfilment of state plans and policies, *and* that of protecting the workers and furthering their interests. Should the workers need protection from a workers' state? Lenin answered that the state did have bureaucratic deformations, and neither in theory nor practice is it denied that workers' rights *can* be disregarded by management; it is the duty of trade unions to ensure that rules are observed. Furthermore, there is evidence, for instance in Mary McAuley's well-documented study,[15] that the union branches can and do act in a protective capacity. However, they have tended for many years greatly to stress the mobilising function, so much so that trade union officials are often seen as part of the official establishment. Events in Poland in 1980 highlighted this: workers felt that 'their' trade unions were official stooges, which was not surprising, as their officials (above works level) were in effect party nominees, on the *nomenklatura*, responsible therefore to those above them, not to the members. In the USSR one does not ever hear of any union making a demand (or even the politest request) for higher wages.

This said, Soviet *and* Polish experience raises in one's mind a number of unanswered, perhaps unanswerable, questions. *Should* trade unions in a socialist society militantly demand more for their members? Is there not a likelihood of conflict, of clashes between sectional and general interest, especially since, as we have already observed, there is no generally accepted and objectively 'correct' standard for income distribution? Even in the West, various unions which ostensibly fight the employers are in reality leap-frogging over each other, redistributing incomes also away from other workers. In the USSR or Poland it remains true (and *not* only official propaganda) that any important gain in material welfare requires higher output and higher productivity, that without it higher wages can lead only to inflation and that work stoppages diminish output and tend to depress the level of real incomes.

So, while being rightly critical of the unrepresentativeness of Soviet-type 'trade unions', socialists should think carefully about trade union reforms. Romantic Marxist-fundamentalists may imagine that workers in a 'real' socialist society will show solidarity and pursue the interests of society as a whole. For reasons discussed at length earlier, this is surely an illusion under conditions of scarcity (the achievement of meaningful abundance under effective workers' control would surely eliminate the functions of trade unions, as well as those of the state, but then we are back in never-never-land). The dilemma posed by the power of sectional interest in any kind of socialist society is a real one.

Agriculture and the Peasants

A whole volume could be written on this theme. A most important aspect relates to the treatment of the peasantry by the almost wholly urban party, both in the so-called 'great debate' of the 1920s and in the collectivisation drive that followed it. Both of these questions are fundamentally linked with that of the 'building of socialism' in a backward country with a peasant majority. This is by no means an issue only of historical interpretation, since there are 'socialist' or 'Marxist' governments in many developing countries where the peasants are numerically predominant. Is it appropriate, is it acceptable, to treat the peasants and their interests as mere objects of policy? One consequence is (was) to subordinate all nominally democratic institutions to the one party, which considers itself engaged in the role of transforming society against the will of the majority. In retrospect, one of the causes of the rise of Stalinist despotism must be seen as the emasculation of any democratic counterweight to the party machine, an emasculation justified in the eyes of the Bolsheviks by their position as an embattled minority in a peasant petty-bourgeois swamp. Indeed it was Trotsky who noted that too much democracy in the party itself was dangerous, since petty-bourgeois ideas could penetrate it from outside.[16]

Collectivisation, Soviet style, is surely a disastrous course, disastrous economically (production and efficiency suffer) and disastrous politically (mass coercion, 'justification' of terror, cruelty, and so on). The deportation of the 'kulaks', i.e. of the bulk of the successful and hard-working peasants, did serious damage, and it is surely no accident that such a procedure was not followed even in those countries which in other respects followed the Moscow line. It is essential to distinguish *agricultural co-operation* from the Soviet-type of *collectivisation*. The vital differences are: voluntary as against compulsory membership; and self-government as against control from above. Historically, Soviet collectivisation was associated with the mobilisation of resources for rapid industrialisation (whether it in fact contributed to capital accumulation in the 1930s is a controversial subject, but that this was the intention is disputed by no one). The process was essentially coercive, and unaccompanied by material inducements, since the latter were simply not available at a time when all efforts were directed to the building of heavy industry. The nominally co-operative and democratic structure of collective farms (the management was, formally speaking, elected and responsible to the members) was negated by the fact that the local party nominated the management. The farm was subjected to compulsory delivery quotas and to binding instructions on a wide variety of topics, ranging from the date of sowing and the area to be sown to wheat to the number of cows and the planned yield and deliveries of milk. This too was partly explicable by the lack of material incentives. Unlike state enterprise workers, who were guaranteed their wage, collectivised peasants were 'residuary legatees', in that their pay, in money and kind, depended on how much was left over after the state took its share, at low prices; and the average income was very much below that of urban workers. Indeed, most peasants survived because they were allowed a small private plot and some private livestock. Under these circumstances, collective work and 'sales' to the state did not 'pay', indeed could have the effect of diminishing the real incomes of peasants.

But more recent experience shows that the lack of incentives was not the whole explanation. In the last two decades there has been a very substantial increase in agricultural procurement prices and in peasant incomes. Over half of all arable land is now cultivated by *state* farms, and the collectives now pay a guaranteed minimum 'wage' to their members. Yet the practice continues of imposing compulsory delivery quotas and issuing operational orders to the farms. State farm management was and is appointed from above, and collective farms' management (the chairman and the committee) are still 'elected' on the nomination of the party authorities. Indeed, the tendency is to try to incorporate agriculture more closely into the centralised planning system, with much talk of 'agro-industrial complexes'.

So while poor Soviet agricultural performance until, say, 1960 could be attributed to neglect, underpayment, underinvestment and exploitation for the benefit of industry, this is no longer the case, and any remaining deficiencies exist in spite of massive investments, high priority, much better incomes for the producers and large subsidies. There has, undeniably, been an improvement in production and productivity, but no one seriously questions the proposition that Soviet agricultural performance has been disappointing.

The extent of the shortfall in production has been exaggerated by price policy: shortages of many foodstuffs become visible when they are under-priced relative to demand, for reasons and with consequences to be discussed later. But productivity is still low by international standards, and here again we must examine the reasons, distinguishing the consequences of specifically Soviet methods and policies from those which relate, or could relate, to socialism in general.

One must return at once to the issue of diseconomies of scale, already discussed at a more general level. Socialists were already arguing at the end of the last century as to whether economies of scale applied to agriculture. One of the heresies of Bernstein, the original revisionist, was that he claimed that smallholder peasant agriculture had strength, that large-scale capitalist production had disadvantages in agriculture. Since his day, of course, the size of farms in Germany and elsewhere has increased and the number of peasant cultivators has declined. However, mechanisation has greatly added to the effectiveness of the large family farm, and facilitated highly capitalised agriculture undertaken by a small labour force. It is noteworthy that while Soviet factories resemble their Western counterparts, and their internal structure is largely predetermined by technical necessity, Soviet collective and state farms have no parallel outside the area where Soviet political influence is or was dominant.

What does Soviet experience tell us about diseconomies of scale in agriculture? One important point concerns internal management, and the related problem of incentives. Farms are big. This is not just a matter of area, though this is considerable (17,200 hectares of farmland, 5,300 of sown area for state farms; 6,600 hectares of farmland, 3,700 of sown area for collective farms, i.e. very large, in 1980). These large farms usually cultivate many crops, keep many kinds of livestock and have a labour force of 500 and more scattered in numbers of villages and hamlets. Given the nature of agricultural work, there is a major difficulty of ensuring supervision. It is unnecessary to follow a peasant proprietor or working farmer around to ensure that he does his job properly, as he is directly interested in its outcome. But the many and varied tasks on a mixed farm can be done well or badly, and this may remain unnoticed, the consequences unseen. Thus if ploughing is carelessly done, the effects on the next harvest (which is also affected by weather, weeding cultivation, and so on) are unattributable. The large size of the farms, and the sad history of the treatment of the peasantry by the Soviet authorities, contribute to a strong sense of alienation, of lack of commitment. A Soviet author once wrote: 'to kill the peasant's love of private property we had to kill his love for the land'. It has proved difficult to replace this by meaningful material incentives. Incentives exist, of course, but repeatedly produce perverse results. Thus if tractor-drivers engaged in ploughing are rewarded for the area they plough (and for saving fuel, and avoiding breakages), it 'pays' them to plough shallow. Repeatedly one reads in the Soviet press about the ill-effects of incentives linked with plan fulfilment. Rewards can also depend on chance circumstances, on whether the plan target is easy to reach and on favourable weather. (If there is a drought no amount of hard work can avoid financial penalties for failing to reach the target, and prices paid to farms will not rise in years of shortage – indeed, with bonus prices paid for extra sales, the opposite may be true.) Compared with the family farm, the Soviet variety requires a much larger administrative structure. Of course, this is true of all large-scale business in all spheres, but economies of scale in agriculture are peculiarly hard to realise.

The lack of commitment of the peasantry to their work, and inadequacies of mechanisation, have led to the rapid increase in the scale of the annual 'mobilisation' of labour to help with the harvest. According to a Soviet source, the numbers involved in 1979 exceeded 15 million (!), which was 2·4 times more than in 1970.[17] The individuals in question are industrial workers, clerks, students, soldiers. . . . The disruption this causes to the rest of the economy must be considerable.

In a perceptive paper, Michael Ellman reminds us that Marx himself, and also both Kautsky and Lenin, grossly overestimated the economies of scale (and ignored the diseconomies of scale) in agriculture. 'The efficient large-scale organisation of labour requires efficient planning, administration and book-keeping work which is unnecessary under peasant or smallholder farming.' He also rightly notes that 'the great difference between agriculture and industry as far as economies of scale are concerned can be seen clearly by looking at the experience of capitalist countries'. Under Stalin the underpaid peasantry were virtually attached to the land ('semi-serfdom'), but the much higher pay and the issuing of internal passports to peasants have not resolved and cannot resolve the problems of material incentives: 'This results from the sequential nature of much agricultural work, the fact that it is spatially scattered, the heterogeneous nature of the resources (e.g. fields of different quality), and the erratic and seasonal nature of the inputs (e.g. precipitation and temperature). Moreover there is no fixed or easily predictable relationship between output and inputs.' This calls for flexibility, adaptability, initiative, at the grass-roots. Instead, he rightly points out, there is 'apathy'. Marxist theory had 'exaggerated expectations concerning the gains from abolishing private ownership'.[18]

Problems are exacerbated by interference with farm management from the party and state authorities. Agricultural planning is complicated by the infinite variety of land, and the need for flexible decision-making in a sometimes very fickle climate. Crop rotations must be carefully adhered to if land fertility is to be preserved and (in some areas) land erosion avoided. Soviet agricultural history abounds in examples of centrally directed campaigns imposed on the farms through the party-state apparatus. Some are hardy annuals: sowing, harvesting, delivery to the state, at dates determined by officials anxious to report completion to Moscow and not by conditions down on the farm. Then there have been 'Stalin's plan for the transformation of nature' (forest shelter belts), Khrushchev's maize campaign, the mass use of peat-compost pots, 'overtake America in the production of meat and milk', amalgamation of farms into larger units, and now (1981) the formation of agro-industrial complexes. There is repeated interference in the choice of and area under particular crops. In some years management is forbidden to slaughter even one head of cattle without written permission. And, finally, the practice continues of imposing compulsory delivery quotas, and of arbitrarily varying them, though it must be emphasised that prices are now much higher. These practices have been publicly criticised, but persist.

With the progress of mechanisation the problem of the link between agriculture and its industrial suppliers becomes more acute. This is a special case of a general weakness: the customer's lack of influence on production. Farm management puts its purchase requests to an intermediary body, *Sel'khoztekhnika*, which then seeks to obtain the needed machines, spare parts, and so on, from the agricultural machinery industry. A massive volume of published complaints testifies to the fact that machines are too often of poor quality, unsuited to local conditions, with insufficient spare parts, while many requests are not met at all. *Sel'khoztekhnika*, and yet another 'service' agency, *Sel'khozkhimiya* (the latter responsible for fertiliser, liming, weed-killers, etc.), are bitterly criticised for fulfilling plans in terms of roubles, instead of seeking to act in the manner best calculated to increase harvest yields. Since farms generally lack well-equipped workshops and skilled labour, many tractors, combines and other equipment are out of action, or need to be 'cannibalised' to 'produce' the missing spare parts. The specialised press repeatedly complains of *nekomplekstnost'*, i.e. of lack of complementary equipment, of unbalanced mechanisation which creates bottlenecks at other stages of a complex production process. Thus powerful tractors are produced, but not the attachments which should accompany them. Planners find it difficult to relate production and allocation to the highly varied needs of farming in a vast country. Inevitably the task becomes fragmented: thus the production of fertiliser is decided in a different office from that which is concerned with bags, transport, storage and the machines that spread the fertiliser, with the notorious consequence that fertiliser piles up in the open at railheads. There are many other 'lacks': hard-surfaced roads, packaging materials, ordinary roofing.

Mention must be made of the private plot. For a generation and more this was the main source of most peasants' food (bread-grains apart) and cash income. Work for the collective in those years was analogous to *barshchina*, work for the lord under serfdom, i.e. virtually unpaid labour. To all intents and purposes the peasants were tied to the land, in that they were not issued with internal passports, without which they could not legally change their residence. Things are different now. Not only is payment for collective and state work much higher, but at long last peasants are being issued with passports. However, the private plot continues to play an important role: in 1978 it provided over 26 per cent of all agricultural production.[19]

It is sometimes asserted that, since only 3 per cent of the land is privately cultivated, this shows that the private sector is eight times more productive than collective and state farms. This is not a legitimate calculation, for two reasons. First, private livestock accounts for two-thirds of the output, and its fodder mainly comes from collective and state sources. Secondly, on a restricted amount of land the peasants understandably cultivate high-value crops, and obviously a field planted with onions or grapes will yield a higher value than a field of the same size under oats or rye. The yield of comparable crops on private land *is* higher, but not in the proportion of 8:1. It is higher because of a concentration of effort, sweat and manure on a small area. It does not follow that the same yields would be achieved if the area were substantially increased.

It is important to note that the private sector produces so much despite great handicaps. Fodder is often difficult to obtain. Simple tools are scarce, and there are literally no machines adapted to the needs of smallholdings, so that techniques are primitive. The present (1981) policy is to favour private plot production, so the situation may change.   Many complaints are published about the difficulties of marketing, and these difficulties also apply to the farms. They are due to poor transport facilities, and lack of roads, storage capacity, or interest on the part of state and co-operative trading agencies (and the non-existence of professional traders).

Some of the deficiencies of the Soviet model relate directly to centralised 'non-market' planning, and its many consequences. If the management has no basis for determining what should be produced – and land can produce many different things – then the planners must. Yet the very variety of types of land, and ways in which it could be used, virtually ensure that the plan orders will frequently be unsuitable for the specific conditions of the given locality. Similarly, farms cannot just purchase their inputs, they must apply for them and take what is allocated, which once again leads to predictable errors and omissions. The large size and complexity of farms is due partly to ideological preference, but also to the desire of the overworked planners to reduce the number of the units to which they have to issue instructions. Remedies, to be effective, must surely enlarge the decision-making functions of those on the spot, both farm management and the sub-units within the farm, to reduce the size of the giant farms, to stimulate peasant interest in the outcome of the work they do, and to allow the farms to purchase the inputs they need, as well as the provision of the required infrastructure. It is interesting in this connection to study the much more successful Hungarian experience. The key contrasts are, first, the absence of compulsory deliveries, and therefore the much greater freedom of farms to choose what to produce and what to sell; secondly, almost total freedom to purchase inputs; thirdly, much greater flexibility in internal organisation and in organising the work of peasant members; fourthly, the successful incorporation of the private sector in the production of food, with adequate supplies of fodder, equipment, well-organised marketing facilities, and so on. In my view none of this is inconsistent with a properly understood socialism, but this is not how Soviet (and many 'new left') ideologists see things.

Investment Decisions and Criteria in Theory and Practice

These have several aspects. There is the volume of investments, the share of accumulation in the national income in relation to current consumption. Then there is the complex question of investment criteria: how to judge which investments are appropriate, rational, efficient. Also of great importance are: who decides what, by reference to whom, and what can and should be the role of the democratic process and/or of interest and pressure groups of various kinds. Finally, there are problems of planning and implementation: how to ensure that the necessary means are available to carry out the intended programme, and then ensure that this (and no other) programme is in fact carried out.

How much should be invested? What balance should be struck between present and future needs? It is only in the more formalistic Western textbooks that this question is 'resolved' by phrases about 'the time preference of the community', since in practice personal savings play a subordinate role as compared with the savings of institutions and the reinvested profits of firms. In any event, in a socialist society a major part of investments must clearly be the responsibility of the planning organs, based on a political decision, taken in the last resort by the political authorities. There is no 'scientific' basis for determining the scale of capital accumulation. Should net investment be 10 per cent, 15 per cent, 25 per cent, or the national income? It must depend on the level of development already achieved, on the perceived urgency of expanding productive capacity, social overhead capital, and so on. The role of the democratic process, in determining how much to invest and in determining broad priorities, seems both important and desirable. Indeed this is fully recognised in the USSR on a formal level: the five-year plan and the annual plan, which incorporates investments, are voted on by the elected Supreme Soviet. The snag, of course, is that the vote is always a unanimous formality, as indeed are the 'elections'.

No historian of economic thought should overlook the remarkable pioneering ideas of the economists of the 1920s on development strategy and investment criteria. Some were political figures, such as Preobrazhensky, others were non-Bolshevik specialists, of which Bazarov was a distinguished example. Indeed an early contributor to the development strategy debate was an anti-Bolshevik, writing in an area occupied by the Whites during the civil war, Grinevetsky, and Lenin knew of and used his ideas when discussing plans for 'the electrification of Russia' as early as in 1920. War and civil war had interrupted Russia'a industrialisation. The triumph of the Bolsheviks had led to the elimination of capitalists and landlords, and therefore meant that savings and investments were to be primarily the direct responsibility of the state. Thus, at a time when Western economics was uninterested in growth and development, Russian thinkers of many political hues or none had to blaze their own trail. The debates coincided with a period in which small-scale private enterprise coexisted with the state sector, and one aspect of the discussions centred on how (and whether) this coexistence could continue – how the resources needed for investment could be 'pumped over' from the private sector, that is, primarily from the peasantry. I can do no more here than underline the importance of the arguments of the period and refer interested readers to the literature.[20]

The dissolution of the so-called New Economic Policy, and the elimination of the private sector (and of nearly all the most talented economists), followed (and was partly caused by) the increase in state investments which was taking place in 1925–7, even before the adoption of the first five-year plan. Even this comparatively modest increase – modest in comparison with what was to follow – caused the gravest strains and shortages and proved incompatible with market equilibrium in a mixed economy, that is, with the principles of NEP. There then occurred, under Stalin's first five-year plan, an investment boom of unprecedented dimensions, which caused massive disproportions and a steep decline in living standards. This tendency to over-invest has been repeated in other communist-ruled countries, and has led to political and economic crises, and also the 'socialist' equivalent of trade cycles, as well as contributing to the chronic sellers' market and shortages which were discussed earlier.

Under Stalin the balance between current needs and investment in the future was tilted very strongly in favour of the latter. In view of the hardships it can cause to the present generation, this strategy is closely connected with the elimination of democratic institutions and the emasculation of the trade unions. It may be argued that Stalin in 1930 had very urgent reasons to press ahead with a huge investment programme with priority for heavy industry, owing to the sense of isolation and external threat. But the same excesses were committed afterwards, in Poland, Romania, Hungary, Czechoslovakia, not once but repeatedly. Poland's investment boom of 1971–5 led to economic catastrophe and political upheaval. The causes of the Hungarian crisis of 1956 were also connected with the effect of the investment programme on living standards. Much greater sufferings, including real famine, occurred in 1932–3 in the USSR, due partly to the crazy investment tempos and partly to the effects of collectivisation of agriculture; but there the police and the terror were sufficient to maintain order.

What drives the political leadership to over-invest? Various theories have been put forward, some of a psychological nature. A Soviet critic once asserted that Stalin wished the great works of Stalin to be visible from the planet Mars – a kind of pyramids complex. While this is of doubtful validity, it is by no means incorrect to note the predisposition of the leadership to build for the future; indeed, the official aim of 'building communism', requiring, according to orthodox doctrine, a great enlargement of productive capacity, does point to a preference for tomorrow over today. But if this helps to explain the desire for new factories and mines, it cannot be the explanation for the large-scale public buildings, a preference which reminds one of ruling classes of pre-capitalist times.

The large and spectacular has taken precedence over the small, and there was (and is) persistent undervaluation of routine maintenance. Here too one notes the strong desire for 'showmanship', what the Russians frequently refer to as *pokazukha*. This can be seen as an aspect of the success indicator problem, success in this instance meaning an activity which is big, and visible from above. This, and not only a belief in economies of scale, can account for the many instances of 'gigantomania'. The average size of Soviet enterprises is in fact very much larger than is the case in the West, where alongside the giants there are many thousands of small firms. Another reason for the reluctance to set up small units is that it complicates the process of planning: orders have to be issued to larger numbers of managers, so that it seems simpler to have large factories and/or to merge small ones. Yet, as has been pointed out, for instance, by the Soviet economist Kvasha, there is a clear advantage in certain specialised tasks being carried out by small productive units. This is apart from the argument put forward by André Gorz, to the effect that large-scale industry is inherently alienating, that 'small is beautiful', a theme to which it will be necessary to return.

Gigantomania was (and to some extent still is) accompanied by neglect of minor but essential investments, for instance, the persistent lack of what the Russians call *malaya mekhanizatsiya*: auxiliary tasks, such as loading, unloading, repairs, materials handling, storage, are seldom adequately mechanised, and this causes much waste of labour. Prosaic but useful techniques may be neglected for what appear to be irrationally trivial reasons: a Soviet newspaper once reported that an inventor who claimed to have devised an efficient button-holing machine for the clothing industry was met with the reply: 'In an age of Sputniks, you come along with a button-holing machine!'

This brings the discussion closer to the issue of investment criteria. A Western profit-making firm will decide to develop or use whatever it believes to be profitable, whether it is a button-holing machine, a gramophone turntable or a machine for putting tops on bottles. In the USSR the preference for the grandiose and neglect of 'minor' matters spring from lack of clear criteria for decision-making. Space forbids even a brief analysis of the huge Soviet and non-Soviet literature on investment criteria in the USSR, and the many discussions on the subject. After decades in which the purest 'voluntarism', a 'refusal to calculate', to use the words of Jean-Michel Collette, seemed to prevail, practical planners found that choices had none the less to be made, and that in a choice between techniques the one with the shortest pay-off period should be chosen, other things being equal. It was argued that there should be a cut-off point, beyond which the proposed investment should be adjudged inefficacious. However, several points of great importance remained in dispute, and for good reasons. One was the question of whether the chosen criteria should be identical throughout the economy, or vary by sectors. This was essentially a matter of how to cope with priorities. This in turn had two sub-aspects. One was that *past* priorities had caused great unevenness between the profitabilities (rates of return, pay-off periods) of investments in different industries; to redistribute investment in accordance with a single criterion would cause major imbalances. The second was how to take *present* priorities into account. Example: does the urgent need for energy imply that a lower rate of return should be adopted for energy, or should the criterion be formally identical and a case made for exceptional treatment for energy? The practical outcome in the two formulations might be the same, but there is a point of principle involved: should objective criteria be recognised, or should one alter the criteria in line with the chosen policy?

Reference to energy should remind us that Western theories on investment criteria are neither satisfactory nor complete. If the world is really to face a shortage of energy towards the end of the 1980s, this in itself constitutes a powerful argument for more investment in this sector, whatever may be the current rate of interest and the actual rate of return on investments in energy at present prices. Of course, we all *ought* to be using the 'shadow' prices which reflect the probable scarcities of seven and more years hence, but these in turn are a consequence of (fallible) calculation as to future supply-and-demand conditions. Calculations about future shortages (input-output, material balances) need not be confined to energy. In so far as, in their major investment decisions, Soviet planners reflect not only general policy priorities but also anticipated shortages (of anything from sheet metal to sports shoes), they should not be regarded as 'irrational' if, in a conflict between rate-of-return and material-balance calculations, they give precedence to the latter.

The above might seem to downgrade, or even ignore, the role of prices. This is not my intention. One must agree with Kornai that, while price information is indeed essential, decisions are not taken on the basis of price information alone (especially bearing in mind the vital role in any major investment decision of uncertainty about the future). To cite Kornai again, while it makes sense to say that if the price of a certain type of cotton cloth has risen, more should be invested in its production, no one is likely to say, in East or West, 'The price of electricity has fallen, let us therefore invest less in power stations'.

Accepting this, it is still necessary to stress the waste occasioned by the nature of Soviet prices. Since – as will be shown – they do not reflect relative scarcities of means, or use-value, or demand, it is clear that all calculations aimed at minimising cost, or maximising effect, are doomed from the start, since the monetary units used in the calculation fail to measure what they ought to be measuring. All this is quite apart from the presence or absence of a rate of interest, and of the rate chosen.

Many a socialist critical of Soviet practice, from Trotsky to Bettelheim, has rightly criticised arbitrariness, has urged the need for rational calculation. But how is one to judge whether a decision is arbitrary or irrational save by reference to some objective criteria? In a choice as to whether to invest in A, B, or C, or whether to produce more of A by methods X, Y, or Z, how can the calculation be made other than in some kind of meaningful prices? How can one avoid having to take time into account too? Evidently, if a project takes two years longer, but economises in the use of some scarce material, there must be some means of comparing the advantages and disadvantages. But the relevance of Soviet experience in the area of prices raises many more issues, and must be put aside for the moment.

Let us pass on to the question of *who* decides what to invest in. One element of Soviet experience must be mentioned first, since it is often overlooked. It may be best illustrated by quoting a conversation with a Soviet specialist, who said: 'There is a large literature on investment choice, but often there is in fact no choice, as the project-makers have only drafted one project.' Other economists, for example, Krasovsky, have strongly criticised the large and bureaucratic *proyektnye organizatsii*.[21] Design bureaux, quantity surveyors, engineers capable of selecting appropriate machines and other such specialists are an important part of the investment process. Whoever chooses can only choose between alternatives that are elaborated by specialists. These also require criteria. If the project-makers have to fulfil plans expressed in millions of roublesworth of projects, this incites them to opt for expensive variants.[22]

The place at which decisions are taken must naturally depend on the relative magnitude and importance of the proposed investment. It may be the top leadership (say, in a decision to develop oil and gas in north-west Siberia, or to launch the virgin lands campaign), or a minister, or more junior officials at the centre or in a locality. The interests and motives of ministerial and other officials below the topmost levels affect the nature of proposals made, the total number of projects started, the speed with which they are completed and much else besides. Here, as in many other instances, Soviet experience underlines the extent to which, in a nominally highly centralised and hier-archically organised system, proposals made and information supplied from below, and the implementation of orders given, are all substantially affected by subordinates; but also that, given the criteria by which they are judged, the actions of subordinates can have deleterious effects.

One of these is an aspect of the problem of externalities, already discussed. Anyone below the centre can see only a part of the whole picture. A ministry faced with the task of increasing output of, say, farm machinery will tend to save expense and trouble by placing its manufacture in an already-developed area, where the social overhead capital already exists, which may well conflict with the objectives of regional policy and may cause bottlenecks for transport or excess demand for local labour.

A different problem arises out of the commitment of subordinates to large investment programmes of their own. The motives vary. One is the familiar one of 'empire-building'; a party secretary, a minister, a manager, gains in status (and in some cases also salary) if his bailiwick expands. But one need not assume selfishness. As argued in Part 1, people identify sincerely with their area of responsibility: whether it is fertiliser, housing in Tomsk, medical services, artillery, washing-machines, or the development of minerals in Yakutia, genuine reasons exist for more investment. Those in charge of the activities concerned will press for an allocation, authorisation, credits. It is important to note that there is no real cost involved: the 'price' of the invest-ment for the recipient is all but zero.

This is obvious in those instances in which the investment is financed by the centre, by outright grant. It is also the case if the retained profits out of which the investment is financed would otherwise have to be transferred to the state budget. But even if there is a capital charge, or the investment requires an interest-bearing credit from the state bank, this does little to discourage over-application for investment resources. Among several reasons for this, two stand out. The first is what Kornai has called the soft budget constraint: in the end deficits will be covered and no one will be allowed to go bankrupt. The other is that in the end it is not clear who is to be held responsible if the given investment proves to be an error; by the time this becomes known there would probably be a new director. The tendency to over-invest therefore arises *both* because of the centre's own ambitious growth targets *and* because of the efforts of subordinate units to expand, of local bodies to undertake public works. It is, of course, the task of the supreme planning organs to prevent this, to ensure that there is balance between the investment programme and the resources necessary to complete it. But this seldom happens.

In virtually every year since 1930 a Soviet leader has deplored what is called *raspylenie sredstv*, the 'scattering' of investment resources among too many projects. Measures are taken to prevent this, to concentrate on completing what is already started, but the ineffectiveness of these measures is attested by the fact that they have to be repeated, while the percentage of uncompleted investments rises. The result is very long delay in commissioning new factories, houses, and so on. Pressure from above sometimes has paradoxical or even comic results: *Pravda* reported in 1980 on projects certified to be operational but which were not in fact completed, and the excuse given by local officials was that they had strict orders to reduce the percentage of uncompleted construction! It is plainly in the interest of sectoral and local officials to start as much as possible, and to try to divert resources to projects of particular interest to them, and it is equally plain that the central co-ordinating power is unable to combat this tendency effectively. As is so often the case, the centre is able to ensure that a few key activities are given priority, but cannot cope with the task of controlling everything.[23]

Mention has already been made of fluctuations, 'trade cycles', these being closely connected with over-investment and its consequences. In the smaller countries, heavily dependent on foreign trade, the balance-of-payments constraint (excessive deficits, debt, etc.) compels a downturn in investment, but in due course the upward movement is resumed, with (apparently) no lesson learned from the previous crisis. The case of Poland is a particularly striking instance, and will be discussed in greater detail in Part 3.

In the USSR such a 'classic' cycle-'stop' occurred in 1932–3, but in more recent years it has been more a case of chronic shortage (and construction delays) than a pronounced cyclical trend, at least at macro level. It is quite another matter if one looks at sectors. There one sees grossly excessive investment upswings, for instance, in the chemical industry in the 1958–65 period. These arise for a reason which it is important to analyse, however briefly: the fact that, in a centralised planning system, any important change of structure requires a decision at the very top, but the need for such a decision will only be perceived (by the very busy men at the summit) if the need is very urgent indeed. Until that moment, working with material-balances or input-output tables, the planning officials naturally tend to preserve the existing pattern, partly because input-output tables are of their nature conservative, reflecting the past, and partly because these officials do not have the authority to make structural changes, which inevitably affect vested interests: one needs a decision at the summit. Let us take the Soviet chemical industry as an example. By the mid-1950s it was woefully backward: production of fertilisers, plastics and detergents was very far below need, and below Western levels. So Khrushchev decided to launch a great campaign to catch up. Over-investment occurred on a massive scale: plans surpassed the possibilities of training personnel, designing (or importing) and installing the machinery, and so on.

It should therefore be a matter of concern to socialist economists that necessary structural changes should not be delayed by the degree of centralisation. One must also assess realistically the time available at the summit to digest information and to take decisions, and then to ensure that they are in fact implemented.

It must also be recognised that in any realistically envisageable situation there will be many conflicting interests involved, each trying to put the best possible case for a larger share of the investment 'cake'. The Soviet economist Maiminas has suggested that one way of limiting the distortions that this can cause is to devise a procedure by which those who draft variants of a project must be distinct from those who select, and a separate body then authorises the necessary financing, all to ensure that information flows and decision-making are kept as clear as possible of prejudice due to interest.[24]

It is also important to appreciate that, in the competition for resources, victory is likely to go to the sector which has the biggest political 'pull', the best hierarchical connections, the most senior and influential boss. As already argued, whoever is in charge of toothbrushes (or an economically backward province, say, Tambov) is bound to have less 'pull' than the official in charge of metallurgy, or of Sverdlovsk province. So instead of bias towards anticipated profitability one has a bias in favour of the already big and powerful, and this helps to explain the chronic under-investment in consumers' goods and services, as well as in 'small' equipment of many kinds (*malaya mekhanizatsiya*), and this despite repeated attempts by the top leadership to redresss the balance.

Finally, the tendency to adopt over-ambitious investment plans is an important cause of Soviet-type 'inflation'. Planned demand for producers' goods (building materials, machines and also labour) exceeds actual supply. This would cause prices to rise if they were free to do so. Since they are not, there is shortage, and this gives rise not only to the delays already mentioned but to semi-legal forms of barter, bribery and other unplanned or downright criminal phenomena.

On the positive side, we must note the fact that centralised planning does give to those who plan major structurally significant investments an overview of the whole economy, and an insight into its probable future needs, which are a source of potential strength, especially if seen against the background of the plain inadequacies of Western theory and practice.

Prices in Theory and Practice

Soviet experience underlines the importance of prices, and also the difficulty of devising a relevant theory and an appropriate price structure. Let us look at theory first. In 1920 it was still believed by many comrades that prices as such were a dying remnant of a moribund capitalism, that they could and should be speedily done away with. Various theories emerged as to alternative means of calculation: combined human-effort-and-energy units, or units of labour (*tredy*), and so on. Reference has already been made to these efforts, and to the difficulties which any such approach faces: in particular how to relate effort to result. In due course money was 'rehabilitated', though there was a period of ultra-leftism during the years of the first five-year plan (1928–32) when it was again downgraded. This was when the Central Statistical Office was renamed the Central Office of National-Economic Accounting (TsUNKhU), because the word 'statistics' suggested unplanned, random and uncontrolled phenomena. Linked with the discussions on prices were deeper-lying issues connected with the role of the 'law of value' under socialism, the applicability and relevance of the labour theory of value. This debate still continues. Thus in 1979 it was still being argued that in Soviet conditions a product is not a 'commodity', but only looks like a commodity, just as a worker receives only what looks like a wage, but is in principle his share as co-owner in the social product.[25] Others, naturally, take a very different view.

Of course, there is a close link between theory and practice. The real question is: what *role* should be played by what the theorists call 'commodity-money relations' in a Soviet-type system? We must examine this, and then also discuss the effects on economic efficiency of the price system which has actually operated.

In 1943 an authoritative article published in *Pod znamenem marksizma* declared that the 'law of value' operated in the Soviet economy, albeit in 'transformed form'. The point was to stress the existence of 'objective economic laws', which had to be taken into account by planners, though the content of these 'laws' was left vague. In 1952 Stalin himself, in his last published work, revised this doctrine. The 'law of value' was now confined to those transactions in which there was purchase and sale, such as in retail trade, or when the state bought grain or cotton from a collective farm. Transactions *within* the state sector, for example, the 'sale' of iron ore to a steel-works, or leather to a footwear factory, was not a real sale, since the state remained the owner. This resembled what we would call a transfer price. But Stalin accepted that such prices, and the cost calculations which they made possible, were useful and necessary. He supported *khozraschyot*, economic accounting, essentially because it made possible evaluation of performance and the avoidance (or identification) of waste in the process of carrying out planned tasks.

Within three years of Stalin's death a number of economists began to question these propositions, for good reasons. While it was impossible to deny that prices within the state sector were a form of transfer prices, it was deemed essential to stress that they too were subject to economic laws, had to be in some sense 'rational', and so within the ambit of value theory. There followed several years of argument about the relationship between Marxist value theory and actual Soviet prices, which in retrospect must be seen as a blind-alley. This was because the protagonists were trying to apply Marx's value theory to circumstances which were most certainly never in Marx's mind. It would never have occurred to him that socialists would try to *fix* prices in accordance with 'values'. He was well aware that he had been analysing a market economy, in which prices fluctuate, in which they play an active role in determining the use of capital, land and labour, under the influence of supply and demand. As we have already noted, his 'values' were analytical abstractions, which (he claimed) underlay the visible phenomena of price, but which were not and could not be identical with actual prices. Similarly, prices-of-production (as presented in Volume III of *Das Kapital*) were a part of formal analysis of an equilibrium situation in a market economy. Both were exclusively cost-based.

Evidently, if prices were to influence decisions, choices between alternatives, it was essential that they reflect relative scarcity (of means of production as well as of objects of consumption), utility and demand. This would be so at whatsoever level the decisions were taken, whether central planners or enterprise managers made the choices, in so far as price relations affected these choices. The more far-sighted economists recognised that one cannot take decisions based *only* on price information (I have already cited Kornai to this effect), and I recall also a saying of Kalecki's: 'The stupidest thing to do is not to calculate; the second most stupid thing to do is to follow blindly the result of one's calculation.' The information contained in prices is, however, indispensable in the choice of both ends and means. Quantitative planning is evidently inadequate, since it in no way permits a comparison of costs of alternatives. How should one generate electricity? Should the power stations be large or small? Is it prohibitively costly to invest in coal mines in north-east Siberia? What type of insulating material is cheaper? Is it worth investing in a new process for producing sulphuric acid? One cannot answer such questions without using prices of some kind, whether real or shadow, and the prices so used must reflect costs, which in turn reflect relative scarcities of means. Of at least equal importance is the use of prices in decentralised decision-making, as a means of conveying to the producers the relative urgency of user demand. It is therefore not surprising that all those Soviet reformers who stress the need to allow management to be free to choose its product mix and to purchase the needed inputs also advocate supply-and-demand-balancing prices. A market-type reform requires market-type prices.

A French theorist, Pierre de Fouquet, has put his finger on an important point when he writes of

the loss of the significance of exchange. In capitalism, exchange is a deter-minant phase of the social process of production to the extent that it is precisely through exchange that production acquires its social character: production is then socially validated by the valuation [*valorisation*] of the various labours incorporated in it. It is as a commodity that the product acquires its (exchange) value. In state socialism, exchange, in so far as it depends on the plan and not the market, is reduced to a technical phase of the production process. The social validation of the product is deemed to be present from the first, so to speak on principle . . . As for its value, it is essentially determined by planning . . .[26]

Herein lies an essential element of the problem. What de Fouquet calls the 'administrative, state, accounting value' replaces the valuation of a commodity by its potential purchasers. This would make sense if the planners who confer this value (fix the price) were, or could be, aware of the social value of each product. This brings us back to the earlier discussion of a basic weakness in Marx's view of a possible socialism: how can planning organs, on behalf of 'society', determine *ex ante* the value (value-in-use, naturally) of what has been produced, unless and until the potential user is directly involved in the process, and in fact can say 'no'? Once again, the hierarchical and undemo-cratic nature of the Soviet political system, though a factor of undoubted importance, is not the cause of this particular problem. For how can millions of users value millions of products by voting (except, of course, 'voting with the rouble')?

The essential theoretical point was made most fully by V. V. Novozhilov, and it is expressed or implied in the title of his book *Izmereniye zatrat i resultstatov*, 'The Measurement of Costs and Results'. Able (and younger) economists such as Petrakov and Karagedov developed his ideas. They and others criticised what was called *zatratnaya kontseptsiya tseny*, prices based on costs, which disregarded results, utility, effectiveness.[27] Novozhilov and his successors stressed the vital significance of feedback, *obratnaya svyaz'*, the influence of consumers, and of the relative scarcity of means, on prices and valuations. Indeed, even Brezhnev spoke of the urgent need for the customer to have a greater influence on what is produced, though he and his senior advisers derived no price theory (or practice) from this insight.

These ideas as well as the (linked) theories of the mathematical pro-grammers – of which more in a moment – were attacked by a coalition of dogmatists and traditional planners. The dogmatists (for instance, Kronrod, Boyarsky) pointed to the alleged contradiction between such price theories and the labour theory of value, some of them insisting that value in Marx depends only on effort (human labour, albeit socially necessary) and not on utility. An attack was mounted on anything which suggested marginalism, or a subjective theory of value. The practical planners insisted that disequilibria between supply and demand be corrected by *their* decisions, and not by the price mechanism (or only if they so decided). The price reform now (1981) in progress is on traditional lines: cost-plus, with discussion centring on 'cost-plus-what?' The reformers' ideas are still being effectively resisted.

Let us now look at the consequences of the pricing system actually adopted, concentrating on points of principle rather than on specific anomalies (of which there are quite a number in all countries and systems). If prices do not reflect relative scarcity of means, then whosoever chooses between means, to achieve a given end, can be misled. Actions which appear to be 'cheaper', to save labour and resources, may in fact be wasteful. The exclusion from costs of a charge for use of scarce land must also cause distortion in cost calcula-tions. At least equally important is the fact that if prices do not balance supply with demand, this means either rationing (administrative allocation) or standing in line. In Soviet practice, rationing ('material-technical supply') applies to producers' goods, with familiar consequences: a great burden on the planning organs, frequent mismatching between production and supply plans, difficulty in securing deliveries of the needed specifications. Organs responsible for allocation lack criteria in choice between alternatives. In deciding whom to cut when supplies are short, they usually proceed by applying crude priorities ('the most important') or arithmetical allocation based on past performance. Frustration and irrationality are the common result. Prices which do not reflect either demand or relative scarcities are also useless as a guide to what to produce. There is then no connection between profitability (or other success indicators) and the product mix desired by the customer, no link through prices between demand and supply. In the case of consumers' goods and services, Soviet experience clearly shows the dis-advantages of underpricing. It shows also, as does Polish experience, that price rises are intensely unpopular, and so it *appears* to be politically safe and socially fairer to keep prices low, especially those of necessities. If, for example, there is not enough meat at the price of 2 roubles per kilo, then the low-paid can afford it if they can find it, while if it is sold at 4 roubles then the better-off will benefit.

But is this in fact so? The Hungarian sociologist Ivan Szelenyi has argued that raising prices to a level at which supply and demand balance benefits the working class. The reason is that, if supply is short at the official price, the upper strata of society will usually find ways to obtain what they need, in special shops or by other backstairs means. Certainly in the USSR it is shortage at official prices which is the source of much of the privilege of the privileged: *they* can obtain what ordinary people cannot, and at low prices too. This explains why there is no pressure from the ruling stratum to raise prices to supply-and-demand-balancing levels. As for the ordinary citizen, his or her ability to get scarce goods at low prices depends on luck, or on having the time to wait in line. Then, of course, there are the other familiar aspects of a sellers' market: 'conditional' sales ('you can have these herrings only if you also buy five bottles of mineral water'), petty bribery, black markets, and so forth. It is thus by no means obvious that a policy of pricing goods low in fact benefits the low-paid (unless there is strict rationing).

The whole problem was well put by the already-cited Hungarian *émigré*, Gyorgy Markus:

> As long as the whole country is not transformed into one enormous camp of labour with a strict system of rationing, so long as individuals have some choice between the administratively offered jobs (at set wages) and available consumption goods (at set prices), the economies in question necessarily represent a dual picture of *administratively centralised production and atomised consumption* . . . following different principles of economic activity, being submitted to discrepant 'logics'. The economy can function as a whole, of course, only because these two spheres are interconnected; primarily but not exclusively by the administratively regulated markets (or pseudo-markets) for labour-power and consumption goods . . . [But] both these markets have an essentially non-pricing character . . . Changes in demand for articles of consumption do not lead through a feedback mechanism of prices to a readjustment of the structure of production.

In the absence of such equilibrating forces, the central apparatus must try to achieve some degree of balance by administrative intervention.[28] So the existing system of prices renders necessary the existence of the central apparatus – which is possibly why it has (so far) resisted a change in the principles of pricing.

The same point is made by Selucky: 'the direct feedback between production and consumption (the market) has been abolished'. The link is through the planning apparatus, which forwards 'plan targets' to the producers. 'Since every working man is simultaneously both a producer and a consumer, his economic essence is split into two parts: as a producer he reacts to the targets of the plan, while as a consumer he tries to satisfy his material needs and interests through his effective demand' – and he calls the resultant contradictions and frustrations 'the alienation of man from his wages'.[29]

There is one other important aspect of Soviet experience with regard to pricing. This is the sheer volume of work involved. Estimates of the number of prices, fully disaggregated, range from 10 to 12 million. It is essential to appreciate that actual prices must be fully disaggregated. There is no such thing as 'the price' of footwear or of agricultural machinery, only prices of specific kinds of shoes or ploughs from which an overall price index can be derived *ex post*. If millions of prices are to be fixed, whoever determines or approves them must collect information (on costs and on demand), information which needs cross-checking, in view of the possible interest of the information-providers in higher prices. This is a hugely labour-intensive, time-consuming task. A general review of prices is therefore undertaken at long intervals (e.g. 1955, 1967, 1981), which means that, even if they do bear some relation to cost in the first year of their operation, they soon cease to have such a relation as costs alter. Furthermore, even if it were decided that prices should be flexibly adjusted to changes in supply–demand relationships, it would be quite impracticable to do this administratively, that is, through price control by the government and/or the planners. There would simply be far too many prices to control. This, let it be stressed, is not an argument against all forms of price control; what is being asserted is that it is impossible to control *all* prices without creating a very large number of unintended irrationalities and anomalies. Some of these arise because central price control deprives the customer and the supplier of the possibility of negotiating a price (and related specifications) which suits the circumstances of the case.

In other words, the proposition that one can flexibly control millions of prices is plainly incorrect. This, as we shall see, is one of the points overlooked by advocates of the so-called Lange model of socialist planning. Of course it is possible, probably even desirable, to control the prices of, say, energy, steel and bread, and it is also necessary to prevent monopoly powers being used to increase prices. But a comprehensive, all-inclusive system of price control cannot be either flexible or rational in any terms, because of scale. It also seems that no socialist (*feasible* socialist) society can be realistically envisaged without prices. Their existence is the necessary accompaniment of relative scarcity, opportunity-cost, choice, the need to calculate costs and to relate effort to result, to have an economic link between demand and supply, criteria for decentralised decision-making. The objective need for a price mechanism is not the consequence of the specific features of Soviet-type 'socialism'.

Turning now to a less basic but nevertheless important aspect of Soviet experience, one must mention not only the vast complexity of the task of comprehensive price control, but the virtual certainty of evasion. By this I do not mean black or grey markets or the so-called 'second economy', though of course these too exist. The point is rather that the official price index, official prices, become distorted. This arises from the coincidence of several factors. One is price control itself, the prohibition of unauthorised price increases. Another is the possibility of changing the product mix, by producing some new good or service. Still another is the existence of plan targets expressed in monetary aggregates. Finally, there is the sellers' market: to sell is easy, to buy is more difficult. Under these conditions it is possible, indeed it is almost certain, that price control can be evaded by introducing a new product or model, which, so it will be claimed, is of better quality, while withdrawing cheaper varieties from production. Soviet price and volume indices are undoubtedly affected by this, causing an understatement of price rises and a corresponding overstatement of volume increases, but to an extent which none can precisely measure (some new and dearer products *are* genuinely of better quality!). The only 'cure' for this disease is to eliminate excess demand and the sellers' market.

Mathematical Methods and Programming

Over twenty years ago I heard Danzig present the principles of linear programming at a seminar at the London School of Economics. An eminent neoclassical economist remarked (with dismay) that this technique would be particularly applicable to socialist countries, should make them more efficient. The reason, as he saw it, was that they, unlike us, had an objective function, or an authority that could define the objective, and programming techniques would enable the authority to calculate the most effective means to achieve the given (determined) ends.

He need not have worried. Soviet economists too were attracted by the potentialities of programming, the advantages of computerisation. Did not Mises and Robbins argue that socialist planning was impossible because of the number of simultaneous equations to be solved? And did not computers solve such equations by the million in the twinkling of an eye? Input-output techniques had been developed in America by Leontief, and those in Russia who wished to adapt these techniques to Soviet planning did not fail to point out that Leontief was a graduate of Leningrad University, who had already as a young man showed an interest in the first primitive Soviet efforts to draw up a 'balance of the national economy'. As for linear programming, Kantorovich's remarkable pioneering work dates back to 1939, and he very properly received the highest international recognition. Soviet mathematics is of excellent quality, and so if these methods could resolve the problems that face centralised planning, we must suppose that ways to apply them effectively would have been found. Why have they not been?

An important factor is the definition of the objective function. What is it that is to be maximised, or minimised, and how does one measure the result? A large and extremely interesting Soviet literature exists on the issue of the objective function. It turns out that this raises insuperable problems. It is one thing to solve a specific allocational problem, such as the best use of means of transport for given purposes under given constraints. It is quite another to do the same exercise on the scale of the whole economy, the whole of society. The party's general economic policy objectives are too general, too diffuse, to serve as an operational criterion. If asked by the leadership to produce a programme which contains optimal targets for 1990, the economic profession cannot escape the problem by taking the targets adopted by the leadership as its optimisation criterion. After all, the leadership asks the advice of economic profession about what these targets should be! How is one to distinguish means from ends? Various proposals are mooted: maximise the national income; maximise labour productivity; minimise costs for a given set of outputs; and so on. To maximise human welfare is altogether too vague, and the more intelligent Soviet specialists never forget that some aspects of welfare (leisure, quality of life, environment, etc.) do not figure in national income statistics. But in the Soviet case even the purely material part of welfare is poorly reflected in aggregate statistics. This is a consequence, *inter alia*, of cost-plus pricing. With prices fixed by authority, on the basis of costs, to maximise an aggregate in such prices will maximise effort, not result. It is evident that society will not fail to differentiate between two baskets of goods which have in common only the fact that they 'cost' an equal amount of effort to produce. It may be easier to expand the output of products which yield less satisfaction than do alternatives, but this would fail to find expression in the prices used. Also choice may be objectively incompatible with maximising growth.

The whole notion of somebody defining an objective function rests on the incorrect assumption that there is only one actor. But, as Malinvaud has pointed out: 'to regard the decision process as the solution of a mathematical programme assumes a single decision-maker. But this is never the case. Actual processes involve many participants whose interests inevitably conflict.' In the same volume the Yugoslav economist Radmila Stojanovic writes: 'The problem of finding an answer arises when there are conflicting objectives, such as is the case in all social systems.'[30]

Kantorovich and other leading Soviet mathematical economists envisage a means of overcoming the price problem by means of what he has called 'objectively determined valuations'. Plan determination interacts with price determination, the valuations reflecting the scarcities in relation to the plan programme and vice versa. Appropriate valuations would emerge for land, minerals and other means of production, as well as final products of every kind. Of course, this would not ensure that the plan programme itself was optimal, but the valuations would be those appropriate to the plan and would affect the choices made by the planners. Thus if variant A of the draft plan implied a high degree of scarcity, and so a high shadow-price, for steel or copper, this would lead to the conclusion that a redrafted plan with less steel and copper (and more of the more abundant substitutes) would reduce real cost, and free resources for other purposes. It seems to me that Kantorovich's 'objectively determined valuations' are the prices appropriate to evaluation in terms of so-called planners' preferences, that is, they are those prices (or shadow-prices) which correspond most closely to the scarcity relationships and pattern of demand implied by the adopted plan targets. This would also fit the definition adopted by Novozhilov: by iteration one should seek to minimise costs in the production of a given set of outputs, and then, by further iteration, use any additional resources that can be identified to increase total output, or rather total value-added. As a number of Soviet economists have pointed out, at macro level the aggregate measure to be used as a criterion is valued-added (measured in the appropriate prices), since it is the best, or least imperfect, measure of the product available for distribution. At micro level, that is, at that of the enterprise, profitability could serve as a criterion, since the level of wages and salaries can be taken as given, and so profits can be regarded as the excess (surplus) of the value of the result over the value of the total inputs. Whereas at macro level the division of the total value-added between personal consumption and other uses is itself a variable.

The concept of planners' preferences has meaning at macro level (e.g. their choice between investment and consumption), or in certain instances also at 'lower' levels (e.g. priority of energy as against textiles, or for the works of Brezhnev rather than those of Dostoevsky, or a desire to limit the sale of vodka). However, it is important not to treat actual output as necessarily conforming to planners' preferences, save in the tautological sense that what is produced is to some considerable degree determined by 'the plan'. For reasons already discussed at length under the heading of diseconomies of scale, the centre seldom knows exactly what needs to be done in disaggregated detail, and what is actually provided may not accord with anyone's conscious preferences (as when sheet steel is made too heavy in order to fulfil a plan in tonnes). I would draw a further conclusion from these facts. If the centre did know precisely what was needed, there would be every justification for giving it the power to order that it be done. If it is known in advance that precisely n units of product X need to be produced, it seems somewhat pointlessly roundabout to adopt a model in which the centre achieves this result indirectly via the price and market mechanism. The whole experience of the centrally planned economies indicates something quite different: that without a price and market mechanism the centre is deprived of vital information about what is most urgently needed, *and* that the micro detail would in most cases have to be decided at lower levels, closer to the suppliers and their customers.

Disaggregation is in fact one of the main difficulties which arise in the use of programming techniques in planning. The number of plan indicators has to be kept to manageable levels. Let us again take as an example agricultural machinery. It would probably appear in a programme – linear or non-linear – as one item. Yet there are hundreds of types of agricultural machinery; the price of none of them could be derived from an aggregated programme, nor indeed would such a programme tell us how many of each type were required, what new models should be adopted, or precisely what inputs of what specification should be supplied, and to whom. In other words it is inconceivable to 'mathematicise' the complexities of current operational production-and-supply planning and thereby secure a more efficient operation of the centralised system. True, very interesting efforts have been made to decompose aggregated plan programmes, to devise schemes for multilevel programming, in which decisions at one level can be used as parameters and/or constraints at lower levels. However, even their authors would admit that the applicability of these schemes in practice is not great. One also recalls the opinion of a Hungarian economist who noted that the most hidebound and conservative bureaucrat is infinitely more flexible than the most flexible computerised programme.

All of this in no way precludes the widespread use of computers in most calculations, or to arrive at optimal solutions of partial, limited questions, such as a transport problem, or that of loading a given set of machine-tools, which were the context of Kantorovich's original discoveries. To repeat, Soviet mathematical economists are on a very high professional level, and it is only right to learn from their experience about the limitations of computers and programming. We cannot exclude the possibility of further large advances in computer technology, but as of now one sees the formidable obstacles that face models of 'mathematical socialism'.

Growth and Full Employment

Soviet experience can be interpreted as a model of rapid industrialisation, without private capitalists and landlords, with many of the crudities and errors attributable to backwardness, and/or to the impact of specifically Russian traditions and political culture. It can also be regarded as pointing a way which developing countries could follow, even while it could be argued that the Soviet planning system has ceased to be appropriate to an increasingly sophisticated and complex industrial economy. In this respect the evidence points in a direction contrary to the assertions of some dogmatists, who hold that the need for market-type decentralised decision-making arises out of backwardness, with the implication that a more advanced economy *could* be the subject of efficient comprehensive quantitative planning. The reverse is surely the case. Centrally determined priorities, though over-brutally imposed, can be seen as having played an important role in making possible a speedy industrialisation, under conditions of isolation and military danger. To say this is not to apologise for Stalin's excesses, some of which were directly counter-productive (the arrest of many engineers, when such skills were highly scarce, to mention just one example).

Even when 'deflated' to remove various sorts of statistical exaggeration, Soviet industrial progress *was* certainly rapid at least to the end of the 1960s. So was the pace of recovery after war-damage. Most impressive also was the performance of war-industry in 1942–5, after the terrible shock and disruption occasioned by the German occupation of many of the principal industrial areas. It is also a positive factor that the urban unemployment which characterised the 1920s in the USSR itself, before comprehensive planning was introduced, and which has caused so much under-utilisation of material and human resources in the capitalist West, was brought to an end. Rapid and forced accumulation was achieved without having as its by-product the enrichment of owners of land or capital, and without the diversion of resources for all species of secondary and (from the standpoint of the priority of industrialisation) wasteful purposes: advertising campaigns, imports of luxuries, and so on. So the model has a rationality, linked with backwardness, and with lifting oneself up by one's own bootstraps. It may be objected that material privilege was acquired by a 'new class' of rulers, who simply took the place of capitalists and landlords. But from the strictly economic point of view this had (and has) a much lower direct cost, in that the standard of life even of fairly senior officials was nowhere near that of, say, a Mexican or Kenyan entrepreneur. Having a four-roomed flat instead of a room in a communal apartment, the use of an official country cottage, access to a 'closed' shop, give the Soviet official important privileges relatively to ordinary mortals, but these are but a fraction of the riches at the disposal of a fairly successful business man.

From the left one can imagine indignant protests: this may or may not be a development strategy, but it has nothing to do with socialism as Marx envisaged it. Some denounce the very notion of 'socialism in one country', in the sense that socialism to be real *has* to be international, a point to which it will be necessary to return. From left, right, or centre it could be objected that the close association of Soviet experience with rapid industrialisation of a backward isolated country (*and* with terror and despotism) limits the relevance for socialism of this experience. Presumably socialists should be concerned with envisaging normality, not a siege economy. This is indeed a serious point, and readers should be reminded of the spirit in which these pages are written: it is always important to bear in mind that the problems or difficulties discussed may be peculiar to the specific circumstances of the Soviet Union.

The *measurement* of growth is complicated not so much by statistical sleights-of-hand as by the fact, already referred to, that aggregate totals in Soviet prices do not measure use-value, the price indices that are used tend to understate price rises, and various forms of waste (e.g. unnecessary goods transportation to fulfil a plan in tonne-kilometres) are included in 'output'. But this is not the place to discuss statistics.

Foreign Trade

It is not surprising that there is little about foreign trade in Marx's scattered remarks about socialism (though it is known that a volume of *Das Kapital* was planned which would deal with the subject of trade under capitalism; Marx's death came first). Presumably there would be some species of world socialist commonwealth, in which all would draw freely from the common pool of abundantly available products, though one can read into Marx the possibility that he envisaged separate socialist communities interrelating in some undefined comradely way. It is difficult enough to envisage a medium-sized country being planned as 'one gigantic co-operative workshop'. The world is bigger yet! It is possible, therefore, that the separate but allied socialist commonwealths of the imagination might enter into some sort of exchange. Bukharin and Preobrazhensky's *ABC of Communism* can be read in this spirit.

Anyhow, the USSR, Czechoslovakia, China, Cuba and the rest exist as separate 'socialist' states and trade with each other. There is also trade with capitalist countries. It seems reasonable for us to envisage 'feasible socialism' as a state of affairs in which many countries coexist in some sort of (let us assume it is friendly) relationship, and exchange with one another. Therefore Soviet trading experience is not irrelevant, in particular trade within the Soviet bloc, within the countries of Comecon, which now include Mongolia, Cuba, Vietnam, as well as the European countries of the Soviet sphere.

Several negative features have been widely commented on. First, although various resolutions on integration have been adopted, the plans of the separate Comecon countries have been drafted separately; while the bilaterally nego-tiated delivery obligations, and a limited agreement on specialisation, have been incorporated in the national plans, no one has claimed that this consti-tutes effective joint planning. In a centralised and complex industrial economy of a non-market type the sectoral lines of subordination lead to the centre of each country, so that joint planning requires co-ordination at the topmost level. Under conditions of shortage, the fear that priority might be given to domestic users predisposes planners against dependence on supplies and (especially) components from other Comecon members. So, although trade does take place on a substantial scale, many sources in the USSR and other Eastern countries complain that the advantages of the international socialist division of labour are not adequately realised.

One reason why they are not is the prevailing bilateralism and non-convertibility. The cause of bilateralism lies once again in the centralised nature of planning and allocation. Trade agreements have to be incorporated into the plan. Thus a contract to deliver goods wagons from Czechoslovakia to the USSR involves the central planners of both countries: those in Czechoslovakia must ensure the delivery of the needed inputs to the enterprises charged with making the wagons, while the wagons are entered in the Soviet rail transport plan. The means of paying for this (e.g. a quantity of iron ore) must then be found and incorporated in the Soviet plan for the given year. Mere possession of currency does not mean that the possessors can claim the goods they require: these have to be the subject of administrative decision. Below the centre, in a centrally planned economy, even a country's own currency is non-convertible. Thus a manager in Omsk cannot obtain an allocated commodity from one in Tomsk, even if he has the necessary roubles, unless in possession of a planners' allocation certificate. *A fortiori*, he cannot turn these roubles into crowns and buy from, say, Prague, unless there is a bilateral agreement to cover the transaction. This is the issue known as the 'non-convertibility of goods'. This procedure turns into bilateral barter. Multilateral barter is theoretically possible, but has proved difficult to organise.

Barter at what prices? This has been a major bone of contention, and has contributed to and complicated the practice of bilateralism. At what prices, at what exchange-ratios, should socialist countries supply each other? Marxian values? This is quite unsatisfactory, for several reasons. One relates to the use in any transaction, external or internal, of a price into which relative scarcity and demand do not enter. But there is a further complication. What is the meaning of Marxian values in an international context? A lively controversy has arisen over so-called 'unequal exchange', involving (*inter alia*) A. Emmanuel and C. Bettelheim.[31] This relates directly to trade between developed and developing (rich and poor) countries, and raises such questions as: does West Germany, say, 'exploit' India through trade, since the prices are such that the product of an hour of German labour exchanges for two or more hours of Indian labour? The complexities of the argument need not detain us; these concern such issues as organic composition of capital and labour productivity. The point is that these differ widely between socialist countries too. By these criteria, are the more developed socialist countries 'overcharging' the poorer and less developed ones? Are *these* the relevant criteria? If not, what are?

A prolonged study has failed to come up with any sort of 'socialist market prices', and the solution has been to base transactions upon *capitalist* market prices, as the one objective criterion. To iron out fluctuations it has become the practice to use capitalist 'world market prices' averaged over the previous few years. A remark made to me by a Czech economist may be quoted in this context: 'When the world revolution comes we shall have to preserve at least one capitalist country. Otherwise we shall not know at what prices to trade.'

But the use of such prices in a 'socialist' market leads to plainly undesirable consequences. The price relativities may more or less reflect the demand–supply relationships of the capitalist world market. They in no way reflect the demand–supply relationships among socialist countries, or the relative scarcity of particular goods. Furthermore, there is virtually no connection between these prices and the domestic prices and costs of any of the countries concerned. Nor, finally, has there been any serious attempt to align their domestic price structures to each other's, or to the exchange rates in use.

This enormously complicates all and any calculations of comparative advantage, of the profitability of specific trade deals. It also means that some goods are much more valuable to both the recipient and the seller than is indicated by their prices. These are then termed 'hard' goods, and bilateral barter involves not merely overall bilateral balancing, but balancing by category of 'hardness'. With such prices convertibility is out of the question. In Hungary, where management has wider powers of decision and where an attempt has been made to abandon administrative allocation, steps have been taken to align domestic and world market prices at a realistic exchange rate. However, Hungary's 'new economic mechanism' is something of an anomaly within the Eastern bloc.

This whole controversy on trade and prices can be regarded as a special case of the wider issue of the role of markets and the price mechanism. It will certainly be necessary to return to these matters later in this book.

The Cost of What Is Missing

So far we have been examining the effects of methods, policies and administrative arrangements that exist. It would be improper, however, not to count the cost of what does not exist. Few can doubt that this too is serious. I have in mind the virtual elimination of small-scale autonomous enterprise, whether private or co-operative, and the absence of professional traders.

The inflexibility and lack of enterprise of Soviet internal trade is notorious. This can only partly be due to its low priority and poor pay, which must affect the quality of the personnel it recruits. There has been persistent difficulty in devising relevant criteria of efficiency and productivity under conditions of shortage and monopoly, and with fixed retail margins which do not establish any link between profitability and consumer demand. If, for example, farms offer to supply perishable fruit and vegetables, which are in fact in demand, and the fixed margins make it financially unattractive to handle them, the retailers will try to avoid doing so. And no private trader can fill the gap. Suppose, for instance, there are apples and tomatoes in Krasnodar, but a shortage of these in Rostov. It is not legal for some enterprising citizen to buy them in Krasnodar and re-sell them in Rostov at a profit: this might well earn him four years' imprisonment as a speculator.

Similarly, suppose that there is a shortage of toothbrushes, safety-pins, piston-rings, babies' diapers. It is not possible for citizens on their own initiative, jointly or severally, to set up workshops to produce these commodities for sale. Private craftsmen can function, but in a strictly circumscribed way, and they cannot employ others or form a co-operative workshop. Nor can a citizen who thinks he can cook well decide to open a restaurant.

In a remarkable novel, unpublished in the USSR, Vasili Grossman puts the following words into the mouth of a simple Russian prisoner (prisoner of the Germans, as it happens):

> I wanted since childhood to open a shop, so that any folk could come in and buy. Along with it would be a snack-bar, so that the customers could have a bit of roast meat, if they like, or a drink. I would serve them cheap, too. I'd let them have real village food. Baked potato! Bacon-fat with garlic! Sauerkraut! I'd give them bone-marrow as a starter . . . A measure of vodka, a marrow-bone, and black bread of course, and salt. Leather chairs, so that lice don't breed. The customer could sit and rest and be served. If I were to say all this out loud, I'd have been sent straight to Siberia. And yet, say I, what harm would I do to people?[32]

What indeed? (emphasis definitely mine!).

In Hungary many restaurants and shops, even when state-*owned*, are leased to private individuals, who operate them freely as small family businesses and are even allowed to employ a limited number of persons. There are also large stores and supermarkets operated by the state. It seems to do no 'harm to people' to have state, co-operative and private side by side. One returns again and again to the thought, expressed by Marx, that modes of production pass from the scene only when they have exhausted their potentialities. Nowhere in the communist-ruled world have small-scale production and distribution, for and through the market, exhausted their potentialities. On the contrary, they have to be kept under by prohibitions and by repeatedly invoking the criminal law. Yet nowhere does Marx say that the petty bourgeoisie should be eliminated by a 'socialist' police! Later in this book I shall discuss the many problems that must arise out of the coexistence of plan and market, state, co-operative and private activities. Soviet experience demonstrates the inadequacy of what might be called the police solution, the frustration of potential petty entrepreneurs and of their potential customers. It suggests that there is plenty of room for spontaneity, for freedom to fill gaps in planned production and to respond to user requirements without involving the complex bureaucratic structure. If the state-planned provision is adequate, there is usually no incentive for the 'privateer'. Thus, to take a Soviet example, in the (limited but important) free market for foodstuffs one will seldom find any peasants selling butter if butter is available at the official price in state shops. If, however, there is an insufficient supply of 'state' butter, it makes it worth the peasants' while to sell it, at a higher price of course. Soviet law and practice recognise this as legitimate, so long as the peasant is selling his own produce. This principle could with great advantage be generalised across a wide range of goods and services. Why not a private or co-operative workshop making toothbrushes? Why not an unofficial travel agency? Or a café? Yet the very word 'spontaneity' (*samotyok*) is a dirty word to Soviet official ears, as is the word *chastnik* ('privateer'). It is thought to be highly objectionable if private enterprise turns out to be very profitable, although the size of the profit is usually a measure of the extent of the failure of the official distribution network, and profits can (and should) be subject to a progressive rate of tax.

The unresponsiveness of the existing system to user demand is built into its very nature; it arises from its own complexity and from the dominance of production ministries, who issue commands to enterprises and evaluate their performance, and also from the consequences of a sellers' market. It is only to a limited extent a question of human attitudes: as has repeatedly been noted, even well-motivated directors, planning officials, or retailers are frequently unable to act, because other offices and departments are needed as suppliers, allocators, authorisers. This in turn arises not out of some abstract love of bureaucracy, but out of the functional necessities of a system based on directive planning and administrative allocation of resources.

One might even enunciate the following paradox. The power of the state and party is both too big and too small. It is so big as to prevent the emergence of autonomous and spontaneous activity, or free associations and organisations; it fragments and isolates. But it is itself fragmented, and has the greatest difficulty in ensuring co-ordination of its own activities. While it is nominally in command of almost the entire micro sphere, it is evidently unable at this level to secure the necessary link between supply and demand, or indeed to impose discipline on labour, management, or its own officials. The system model assumes omniscience and omnipotence, and many of its problems arise because neither exists.

Conclusion: Centralised Planning and Democratic Socialism

It is impossible for anyone seriously concerned with the future of socialism to ignore the political and social aspects of Soviet reality, and their link with the economic system. Despite the apparently massive participation of citizens in low-level 'representative' organs, authority resides in a hierarchy of party and state officials who recruit to their ranks by co-option. For reasons just advanced, they are not all-powerful, especially in the micro sphere, but their power is sufficiently great and pervasive to offend deeply the principles of socialist democracy, including the principle which allegedly underlies the Soviet Union's own institutions – democratic centralism, which implies an *elected* leadership. It does seem that the despotic nature of central power is much enhanced by the nature of the economic system. Thus a strict state monopoly of printing presses and editorial offices facilitates (along with the censorship) a dreary homogenisation of news and comment. It is easy to blacklist 'undesirables', to deprive them of employment, if the state is the only employer, and the damage is the greater when unofficial ways of earning a living are illegal. The great poet Mandel'shtam and his wife, out of favour and penniless, dreamt of owning a cow, for that would give a degree of personal independence even when poems displease the powers that be: at least one could drink and sell milk. The fact that the party-state machine is mainly engaged in planning and managing the economy also provides a *raison d'être* for a one-party state, to ensure stability for long-term planning, undertaken (naturally) for the good of all of society. The hierarchical structure of the planned non-market economy is paralleled by a similar hierarchical structure of society as a whole, and no Marxist should be surprised that this is so. The power of the party-state leadership over resource allocation facilitates the diversion of a part of these resources for the benefit of the ruling stratum itself, and these and other kinds of privilege and inequality are then hidden from view and never publicly discussed.

Markus, in his already-cited article, notes the apparent perversity of some decisions. Thus, while genuinely anxious to increase agricultural production at least cost, the Soviet-type regimes have consistently disregarded the fact that the most cost-effective sector is private, then collective-co-operative, and the least effective are state farms. Resources are in fact poured into state farms, to a lesser extent into collectives, and least of all is done for the private sector, which is usually obstructed. This, writes Markus, reflects the systematic preferences of the apparatus for 'the maximisation of material means under the global disposition of the apparatus of power'. This is so, but the question arises, what if the minimal degree of efficiency which the apparatus itself requires comes into conflict with 'its being able to retain control over the means invested'?

Markus, and many other writers, notably Bienkowski,[33] have also stressed the unfortunate economic effects of the political domination of a self-perpetuating oligarchy which claims dominance over all spheres of human activity and thought. This has a whole series of adverse effects: on scientific research; on the possibility of grass-roots innovation in any field; on the quality of leading personnel, often chosen for their 'political' qualities (i.e. for conformism and loyalty to the leadership, or a particular leader), a process which could be likened to the survival of the unfittest (unfit, that is, for efficiently carrying out the assigned task). This is apart from diseconomies of scale, which have been examined at length earlier. Perhaps insufficient attention has been paid in the preceding pages to the impact of specifically *Russian* factors: the despotic political past; the weakness of spontaneous social forces (which partly explain the rise of despotism and are partly explained by it); economic and social backwardness; and the way in which these elements were reinforced by Leninist politics and the exigencies of civil war and 'socialist construction'. It is hardly an accident that a Russian poet, Voloshin, wrote: 'Peter the Great was the first Bolshevik'. I have also given emphasis to these matters in other works.[34] We can argue about the relative weight of the past in our explanation and understanding of the present, but that it has some considerable explanatory importance can hardly be doubted, even if it cannot be measured – any more than Japan's remarkable economic achievements can be analysed without reference to the specific features of Japan and of the Japanese.

Political-ideological considerations apart, the student of Soviet economic performance cannot but be struck by the fact that various negative phenomena have become more widespread. There is an increasing feeling among the Soviet economists themselves that drastic changes are essential. It is not just that growth has slowed down, that plans are not fulfilled. Shortages have become more serious, disequilibria and imbalances, which always existed, have reached intolerable levels, and by 'intolerable' I mean that the leadership itself is alarmed and is not prepared to tolerate them (though it has yet to devise a cure). One is told repeatedly by the highest in the land that efficiency is essential, that this is a period of 'intensive' growth, that higher labour productivity, rational investment choice, technical progress, are vital, that waste of resources must be sharply reduced, that production for plan statistics must be replaced by production for user needs, that the shortages of food and transport bottlenecks which now (1981–2) beset the economy are matters of the gravest concern.

No one who reads the Soviet press can doubt the high priority which the leadership gives to correcting these and other defects. However, since they still reject the 'market' model, the reforms they are announcing cannot possibly cure the disease: tighter central control, the imposition of centrally determined 'norms' (normed value-added, normed material utilisation, etc.), stricter allocation of a longer list of materials and machines, exhortation to achieve higher quality of planning and of production, more severe penalties for non-fulfilment of (planned) delivery contracts, and so on. While no one would deny that some aspects of the system could be made to function more efficiently, the basic problems are either untouched or actually exacerbated by 'reforms' such as these. The chronic crisis of the centralised system may be reaching its acute stage, with consequences as yet unforeseeable.

From all this it follows that our further examination of 'feasible socialism' will be concerned with how to avoid the overconcentration of power and the overcentralisation of management, and the diseconomies of scale, which have been among the major defects of Soviet-type socialism. Inflexibility, inefficiency, human alienation and the unrepresentative nature of authority are part of the same unattractive package. Of course the USSR was a pioneer and faced grave difficulties, and it would be foolish simply to denounce it without seeking to understand causes and circumstances. It is also absurd to ignore its experience, as if the negative features that existed were due merely to human wickedness (or to 'socialism in one country'). From Soviet experience there is much to be learned. But it should be possible for socialism to present a much more human and acceptable face.

A Short Digression on 'Ideology'

Discussion of Soviet policy on almost any topic, from foreign policy to economic reform inclusive, often reaches a point at which someone asserts: they do this, or do not or cannot do that, because they are guided or influenced by their 'ideology'. No doubt they are. However, what *is* their ideology? This is by no means a simple question to answer, and some of the attempts to answer it represent circular argument of an almost classic kind.

So: what *is* Soviet ideology? The sayings of the founding fathers? This is hardly a satisfactory definition, in view of the many departures from these. As we have already had numerous occasions to observe, some of these departures were, so to speak, inescapably necessary, since a number of the assumptions made by Marx and Lenin were contradictory or unrealistic: thus the division of labour has shown no sign of withering away; planning is the task of a complex and hierarchically organised bureaucracy, and not 'the associated producers'. Less necessary, though of course not accidental, are a number of other elements of Soviet reality which may be said to conflict with Marx's ideas: Russian nationalism, the refusal to allow free trade unions, the preservation of capital punishment, strict press censorship, pseudo-'elections', and so on. Even the one-party state was never mentioned as a possibility by Marx, or (until 1917) by Lenin either, though it is certainly a most important (the most important?) Soviet political principle. Under Stalin a law was passed forbidding marriages between Soviet citizens and *any* foreigners; while this law has been repealed, such marriages remain notoriously difficult still, though this is surely in conflict with 'internationalism' of any variety. The list can easily be lengthened.

My object is not to score cheap propaganda points, but to clarify the issue. If these and many other patterns of organisation and behaviour exist, do they show that 'ideology' is disregarded in practice? Not so, argue some of the Soviet Union's bitterest critics. The above examples, they would say, are misleading. We must identify and define the *real* ideology. Some sayings of the founding fathers have no operational significance. The real ideology can be deduced from what the regime actually stands for, what it does. Thus in these terms the one-party state, censorship, hierarchy, privilege, the suppression of workers' rights to organise, nationalism and militarism, are essential elements in *the* 'real' ideology of the Soviet regime.

Without entering into the merits of these propositions, let me stress the circularity of the argument. For what this type of analyst does is to *deduce the ideology from actions and policies*, and then to assert that the actions and policies are determined by (or are at least consistent with) the ideology! *Quod'erat demonstrandum?*

Surely this will not do at all. I do not wish to deny that something called 'ideology' affects the perceptions and behaviour of the Soviet leadership, but to define its role and practical influence is a very difficult matter indeed. Just as in foreign policy the great-power interests of the USSR (or of the latter-day Russian empire, if one prefers) are inextricably mingled with, and may even override, considerations of a more ideological kind, so the evident reluctance of the party hierarchy to accept economic reform could be due primarily to their self-interest as controllers of the economy, rather than to what Marx said about 'commodity production' under socialism. In both these instances the legitimation or justification of policies and actions make reference to principles enshrined in the sayings of the fathers, but this is far from showing that it is these sayings that determined or even had a major influence on what was decided. Of course, as also in Christian doctrine, biblical texts are many, sometimes contradictory, capable of differing interpretations, some are conveniently forgotten or rediscovered. No doubt the upbringing and party training of the responsible party officials does have an effect on what they do.

But it would be wholly within the 'materialism' tradition to accord primacy to the interests of classes or strata, and I believe that this approach is more likely to be fruitful. Thus, applied to such an issue as economic reform, if the powers-that-be become convinced of its practical necessity in their own interest as they conceive it, the right ideological texts will be found to justify whatever it is decided to do. Indeed, such texts and interpretations exist already, in the work of such Soviet economic reformers as Novozhilov, Petrakov and others.

It may help to clarify a necessarily complex issue to take a historical example: the forcible collectivisation of the peasantry in the USSR in 1930–3. Was it due to (a collectivist) ideology? Then what of the clear statements by both Engels and Lenin about the vital need to avoid coercing the peasantry? So well known were these statements that Stalin, and official Soviet historians, had to pretend that the process was basically voluntary, apart from some errors by overzealous comrades. The need to lie can be seen as a gesture towards the power of ideology, but by the same token the action cannot be ascribed to it. It can of course be argued that, since collectivisation of peasants played and plays a major part in policy, in the USSR and in most of its allies, it is an integral part of Soviet ideology, but this conclusion involves the fallacy, mentioned above, of deducing theory from practice and then ascribing the practice to the theory. (And one cannot legitimately escape from this by intoning a formula about 'the unity of theory and practice'!) The following elements of an explanation seem to me to fit both the facts and the prevailing set of ideas.

(*a*) The industrialisation strategy required increased and secured marketings of farm produce.

(*b*) The level of forced savings needed to make rapid industrialisation possible precluded reliance on normal market incentives to obtain this produce.

(*c*) There *was* an ideological as well as a political hostility to what could be called the 'kulak solution', i.e. getting the extra produce by encouraging the growth of a prosperous property-owning peasant stratum. (Note that this closed off the most promising practical alternative to collectivisation, and thus had the 'negative' effect of making the latter seem the only solution to the problem.)

(*d*) The belief in planning, a negative gut-reaction to the market, the view that the petty-bourgeoisie is the class enemy, the equation of planning with tight state control over production and distribution, *and* faith in the existence of big economies of scale in agriculture, all played their part. So did the deep distrust of the peasantry on the part of the almost totally urban party. Opinions can differ as to how much weight should be assigned to these many elements in the chain of causation, and also as to the contribution that agriculture actually made to capital accumulation, bearing in mind the adverse effects on production of forcible collectivisation, the losses in live-stock, and in peasant lives too. The point is just that it would be much too simple to assert that forcible collectivisation followed inexorably from Marxist or communist ideology (though it was undeniably one element which cannot be ignored). Any orthodox Marxist who decided *against* such a policy would have no difficulty in finding numerous texts to support him.

Perhaps an even better example is China. If Mao's 'leap forward' and cultural revolution were products of ideology, what, then, were the inspirations of those who tried to undo the first and are undoing the second of these? All concerned claimed to be orthodox, or else creatively developing the allegedly unchanged body of doctrine.

It is also important in this context to cite the Polish social philosopher Bienkowski. Among the many stimulating thoughts which his book contains is one concerning the internal dynamic and logic of institutions in general, despotic institutions in particular. Another is the role of the given country's political culture and traditions. Just as certain aspects of Stalinism may reflect Ivan the Terrible and Peter the Great (and even Nicholas I) more than Marx, so Mao's cultural revolution has – he suggests – some deeply Chinese roots.

In any event, 'pure' ideology, even if it could be defined, never is and never can be the sole factor in any decision in the real world, which always has to do with practical exigencies of some kind. Perhaps, then, we could best see ideology as colouring the spectacles through which reality is seen; or, changing the image, one might see it as a set of blinkers, which cause the wearer to reject, not to see as practical, certain solutions which might otherwise be objectively possible. All this is *not* to deny that ideas affect human actions, in the USSR or anywhere else. However, ideas evolve, ideas can be reinterpreted, elements of doctrine can be dropped, in response to circumstances, even while men seek to shape circumstances in the light of their ideas.

Notes: Part 2

1 J. Kornai, *Economics of Shortage* (Amsterdam: North-Holland, 1980).
2 T. Bauer's book as yet exists only in Hungarian. A good summary of the arguments, using the ideas of Kornai, Bauer and others, is by G. Markus, 'Planning the crisis: some remarks on the economic system of Soviet-type societies', *Praxis International*, no. 3, 1981. For a summary in English, see T. Bauer, 'Investment cycles in planned economies', *Acta Oeconomica*, vol. 21, December 1978.
3 *Pravda*, 3 September 1979.
4 *Pravda*, 1 October 1981 and 24 December 1981, and *Novyi mir*, no. 7, 1981, have printed such criticisms.
5 See A. Birman and L. Tretyakova, in *Soviet Studies*, no. 2, 1976.
6 See his book *La Nomenklatura* (Paris: Belford, 1980).
7 V. Lebedev, *Planovoye khozyaistvo*, no. 11, 1975, p. 12.
8 S. Kheinman, in *EKO (Ekonomika i organizatsiya promyshlennogo proizvodstva)*, nos 5 and 6, 1980.
9 E. Maiminas, *Protsessy planirovaniya v ekonomike*, 2nd edn (Moscow, 1971).
10 Markus, op. cit. (n. 2), pp. 248–9, 255.
11 E. Zaleski, *Stalinist Planning for Economic Growth* (London: Macmillan, 1980). J. Wilhelm, in *Soviet Studies*, April 1979.
   H. H. Ticktin, in several articles published in his journal *Critique* (e.g. no. 9).
12 R. Kosolapov, *Sotsialism* (Moscow, 1979), pp. 219, 234, 271.
13 See my *Political Economy and Soviet Socialism* (London: Allen & Unwin, 1978).
14 For a valuable detailed study, see A. McAuley, *Women's Work and Wages in the Soviet Union* (London: Allen & Unwin, 1981).
15 Mary McAuley, *Labour Disputes in Soviet Russia* (London: OUP, 1969).
16 L. Trotsky, in his speech to the 12th Party Congress.

17 E. Manevich, in *Voprosy ekonomiki*, no. 9, 1981, p. 60.
18 M. Ellman, in *World Development*, nos 9/10, 1981, pp. 982–8. There is a valuable survey of the whole subject by K.-E. Wädekin, *Agrarian Policies in Communist Europe: A Critical Introduction* (Totowa, NJ: Allanheld Osmun, 1982).
19 G. Shmelev, in *Voprosy ekonomiki*, no. 5, 1981, pp. 66–71, gives these and other data. For the best study in depth of the subject, see K.-E. Wädekin, *The Private Sector in Soviet Agriculture* (Berkeley, Calif.: University of California Press, 1973).
20 J.-M. Collette, *Critères d'investissements et calcul économique* (Paris: Cujas, 1964); A. Erlich, *The Soviet Industrialisation Debate* (Cambridge, Mass.: Harvard University Press, 1960); N. Spulber, *Soviet Strategy for Economic Growth* (Bloomington, Ind.: Indiana University Press, 1964); A. Nove, *An Economic History of the USSR* (London: Allen Lane, 1969); E. Preobrazhensky, in *The Crisis of Soviet Industrialisation*, ed. D. Filtzer (White Plains, NY: Sharpe, 1979); and E. H. Carr and R. W. Davies, *Foundations of the Planned Economy* (London: Macmillan, 1969).
21 V. Krasovsky, in *EKO*, no. 1, 1975, pp. 18–19.
22 They were again criticised more recently, on similar lines; see V. Krasovsky in *Voprosy ekonomiki*, no. 1, 1980, p. 110.
23 For a good account of this trend, see Markus, op. cit. (n. 2).
24 Maiminas, op. cit. (n. 9).
25 Kosolapov, op. cit. (n. 12).
26 'Marxisme et socialisme étatique', *Revue d'études comparés est-ouest*, March 1981, pp. 97–8.
27 See for example R. Karagedov, *Khozraschyot effektivnost i pribyl* (Novosibirsk, 1979); N. Petrakov, *Khozyaistvennaya reforma* (Moscow, 1971).
28 Markus, op. cit. (n. 2), p. 252; emphasis his.
29 R. Selucky, *Marxism, Socialism and Freedom* (London: Macmillan, 1979), pp. 38–9.
30 E. Malinvaud, in *Methods of Long-Term Planning and Forecasting*, ed. T. Khachaturov (London, 1976), p. 34, and R. Stojanovic, in ibid., p. 152.
31 Further discussed in Part 4.
32 Quoted from the magnificent novel by V. Grossman, *Zhizn' i sud'ba* (Lausanne: L'Age d'Homme, 1980), p. 205.
33 W. Bienkowski, *Theory and Reality* (London: Allison & Busby, 1981).
34 See, for example, 'History, hierarchy and nationalities', in my *Political Economy and Soviet Socialism*, op. cit. (n. 13); and also the first part of my book *Stalinism and After* (London: Allen & Unwin, 1975).

Part 3

Reform Models: Hungary, Yugoslavia, Poland, China

Some 'Revisionist' Critiques

There have, of course, been efforts by Marxists of many schools to discuss possible solutions to problems to which Marx paid little attention. I can well imagine a number of individuals, who would regard themselves as non-dogmatic Marxists, being dissatisfied with the treatment accorded to the Master's doctrine in the earlier part of this book. They could well say that the essentials of Marxism consist of a *method* of analysis (as Lukács argued sixty years ago), though of course a method which is integrally linked with the aim of human emancipation through the achievement of (feasible!) socialism. It does not mean that his various statements with regard to socialism (or anything else) *must* be accepted by his followers. It can reasonably be held that Marx, were he alive, would most certainly have modified his doctrines in the light of experience. Just as his views on war would hardly have remained uninfluenced by the emergence of nuclear weapons of mass destruction, so we can imagine him studying with care the experience of those countries which have tried to plan their economies.

Similarly, it is possible for Marxists deliberately to put aside the utopian aspects of Marxist thought, seeing in them the influence of nineteenth-century romanticism, while retaining the essentials of his methods and aims, using his methods to show the irrelevance of this romanticism to the achievement of practical socialist objectives. Another way is to point to inconsistencies in Marx, which his followers are not obliged to reproduce. For example, Harding[1] has pointed out that the Marx of 1848–50 repeatedly advocated the strengthening of state power over virtually all aspects of economic life, including the creation of labour armies in industry and agriculture, while the Marx of *Civil War in France* (1872) was writing eloquently of the smashing of the state machine and its replacement by highly decentralised self-governing associations. Harding argued that this underlay a similar contradiction between Lenin's authoritarianism and the libertarian utopianism of his *State and Revolution*. Or one can undertake exercises in redefinition. Thus the withering away of the state can be held to relate *only* to the state's functions of class domination and class coercion, which do indeed vanish by definition if class domination is ended, but the state's many other functions can be held as necessarily persisting in any conceivable society.

A point similar to Harding's was made by Selucky: Marx's economic model of socialism was highly centralised, the political model highly decentralised; yet on Marx's own showing, how could such a political superstructure rest upon this economic base?[2]

The 'non-dogmatists' would have no difficulty in accepting the validity of most of the criticisms which have been made here concerning Marx's actual propositions about socialism, but would not regard these criticisms as destroying the validity of Marxism, any more than they 'prove' that socialism is either wrong or impossible.

It may be useful, therefore, to consider first one of the best-known economic models of a possible socialism, that of Oscar Lange.[3]

This model must be situated in its historical context. Lange was answering the arguments of those who, like Mises and Robbins, asserted that socialism was impossible because it placed too vast a burden on the shoulders of the central planners. Lange did not deny that the burden *would* be impossible if they had to take all microeconomic decisions, but there was, in his view, no need for this. In his model the consumer is free to choose, and it is the duty of the planners to respond to consumer choice. There is relative scarcity of means in relation to ends. He therefore assumed that there must be prices, and that the level of prices affects the behaviour of the consumers, and that of the producers too. That is to say, the production units (enterprises) are influenced by prices and profitabilities, acting in a way similar to that of a textbook entrepreneur, tending to equate marginal revenue with marginal cost. The Central Planning Board (CPB) is responsible for investments, and presumably also for investment goods and industrial materials too, since in the Lange model there is a market only for consumers' goods. The CPB keeps its eye on stocks. If a shortage threatens, prices are raised, if stocks are abundant they are lowered, by a process of continuous *tâtonnement*. Prices of consumers' goods in the market are free to fluctuate. It therefore becomes unnecessary for the CPB to issue specific instructions as to the product mix, as there would be a large measure of automatism in the functioning of the system. The CPB imposes a parametric function for prices. It is possible, wrote Lange, to imagine the CPB arbitrarily deciding what to produce, and then disposing of these goods by fixing the appropriate market-clearing prices, but Lange (writing in the 1930s) discounted this possibility. In a democratic socialist society these preferences would embody (reflect) the interests of the citizenry.

Lange himself recognised, when he returned to postwar Poland, that his model could have no practical application (in his last years he was attracted by the possibility of computers and cybernetics). A critical look at the model may help us to see its limitations.

In some respects, it is a step in the right direction, in that it explicitly recognises the need for a market in consumers' goods, as the inescapable consequence of consumer choice (save on far-fetched assumptions about abundance of all things), and also recognises that the CPB cannot (and need not) handle micro detail. However, the boundary between market (consumers' goods) and planners' control (investment goods) is a dubious one. Apart from the fact that the Lange model of 1935 does not incorporate growth, there is the problem, which must be faced, that a market for ends is unworkable unless there is a market also for means. Lange may have silently assumed firms which are vertically integrated, but this is rare in the real world, and indeed undesirable: a major weakness of the Soviet system is constituted by the tendency of firms and industries to produce their own components, procure their own materials. Let us imagine a socialist footwear factory. It requires leather, nails, glue, machines, fuel. It cannot respond to user demand unless those who provide leather, glue, nails, machines and fuel can in their turn respond to user demand. In other words, the logic of the model requires market response of those who make and sell producers' goods. One would require supply response from them all, which in turn means that at least some investments be made on producing units' initiative. Thus suppose demand for item X rises, so does price, but there is insufficient unused productive capacity, so that it is only possible to increase supply by installing new machines in a new workshop. This, plainly, is investment. Unless such an investment is made, the higher price would simply serve to increase the profits of the producers to no useful purpose. Of course, one can imagine the CPB responding by providing the necessary resources, but then one is back to the now-familiar difficulty of a CPB overloaded by current production-and-allocation decisions, the very matter which the Lange model was supposed to resolve.

Another snag relates to external economies and diseconomies, other than those *within* the given sector, which the model ignores, except in so far as they are silently regarded as being within the purview of the CPB. Nor can it cope with increasing returns. It is also not clear why the managers of Lange's enterprises should act in the way prescribed, unless so impelled by competition. He hardly discusses motivation, the destination of profits, or the role (if any) of the workers. But perhaps the most important issue relates to the place, the role and the effectiveness of the price mechanism. It seems impossibly complex for the centre to determine literally millions of prices. While Lange does envisage that prices of consumers' goods could be varied in bargains between firms and customers, producers' goods also number many millions. A large number of these too must surely be determined by negotiation, which would be concerned also with detailed specifications, modifications, delivery dates, and the like. This is particularly important in the case of machinery, involving new products and technical progress. A product has many aspects and dimensions in the real world, for goods and services alike. There is a certain 'textbook naivety' about imagining the CPB responding to signals about surpluses and shortages of particular goods by modifying their prices, both because there are too many prices to handle *and* because (as Kornai has pointed out) few decisions can be based upon price information alone. In a moment we shall be considering the Hungarian experience, also based on the market principle, which must be regarded as more relevant for our purpose than the very interesting and pioneering model imagined by Oskar Lange nearly fifty years ago.

More recently we have had the work of Ota Šik and also of Wlodimierz Brus. In their very different ways, both, while starting from a Marxist standpoint, recognise and stress the many disadvantages of centralised planning, and recognise also that the only practicable alternative involves the market mechanism in some form. Neither for a moment denies that there are bound to be difficulties, both technical and social-political, in devising an appropriate mix of plan and market. Both would certainly reply that, in the real world, there inevitably are difficulties and contradictions, as indeed is so. We shall be discussing these at length in the 'constructive' part of the present book.

As was mentioned also in the Preface, the writings (and criticisms) of Brus have been very helpful in clarifying my own ideas. He has also written intelligently on Chinese economic reform discussions, comparing them with those of Eastern Europe. Brus has provided some extremely cogent criticisms of received doctrine (e.g. on 'commodity fetishism'), and has had much of great importance to say about remedies to the existing state of affairs, which certainly imply an alternative model.[4] Šik has gone further, and produced a long book containing a rather fully elaborated model of an alternative economy, neither 'soviet-socialist' nor capitalist.[5] Since his book is over 800 pages long, the remarks that follow cannot even begin to do justice to his ideas on 'the third way'. Though certainly influenced by his own Marxist training, he is influenced also by his negative experiences in his native Czechoslovakia, so much so that the word 'socialism' frequently appears in inverted commas, accompanied by reference to the Soviet version towards which he has (understandably) great antipathy. However, his third way *is* in fact a democratic-socialist way, and should be seen as such. He is concerned with 'overcoming the contradiction between wages and profits', the 'democratisation and humanisation of the economy'. Capital assets of large firms are to form an indivisible fund (he calls this *Kapitalneutralisierung*), with a management or supervision committee (*Aufsichtsrat*), elected by the workforce. Medium-sized firms could be mixed, with some of the capital private. Small firms would still be private. Current operations of all three would be based on the market mechanism. Competition would be encouraged, monopolist tendencies combated. Profits would be devoted partly to the expansion of the firm's capital, partly to profit-related bonuses for the workforce, in proportions which the political authority would determine in the light of its growth and incomes policies. Reasonably enough, Šik emphasises the role of democracy in electing the government, choosing plan objectives. He proposes not 'profit maximisation' but 'profit optimisation' as his efficiency criterion, with much emphasis on quality of life and the desirable balance between investment and consumption. Presumably 'optimisation' in this context is the level required to provide the desired surplus.

This is no place for a lengthy critique of these ideas, though a critique of a kind will be implied by my own rather different ideas in the final part of this book. With many of his propositions one can agree, though perhaps their author has underestimated the practical difficulties (I mean economic-organisational, not political) of implementing his proposals. There may be some contradiction between his notions of participation (or self-management) and scale. It is surely easier to achieve a sense of 'belonging' if the firm is small than if it is large. Yet it is precisely in the large firms that he expects the greatest extent of self-management (they become *Mitarbeitergesellschaften*). He appears to have in mind the desirability of encouraging small entrepreneurs, and his definition of medium and small firms is one which envisages the owner or co-owner being the working manager as well as risk-taker. In my own 'model' I also provide for small-scale 'working entrepreneurs' who might

hire a few workers, but envisage that many small and medium-scale enterprises would be co-operative. Otherwise it may well turn out that the
economy will in fact remain largely private, while some large-scale sectors
would inevitably acquire a monopoly position and so could not be left to
uncontrolled self-management. However, Šik would doubtless be the first to
agree that his ideas are controversial, that his proposals (like all others)
contain disadvantages as well as advantages. His attempt to sketch out a
future alternative to capitalism and to Soviet-socialism should be welcomed.
Critics are under the obligation to do better; no simple task, this, as soon as
one tries to move from ideological slogans into the contradictions and complexities of a possible real world.

Less satisfactory is the way in which Hegedus and Bahro handle these
questions. Both are hostile to centralised bureaucracy, but neither develops
any alternative model. Bahro mars a highly realistic and critical analysis of
East European reality by hoping for an 'overcoming' (*Aufhebung*) of the
division of labour, which would somehow relegate the problem of plan *v.*
market to the status of unimportant detail. Labour then becomes 'homo-
genised'. He recognises quite specifically the hierarchical implications of
modern industry and of planning, but if everyone has an all-round education
and is therefore interchangeable and jobs rotate, there need (in his view) be no
social hierarchy based on professionalism and specialisation. For reasons
already discussed at length earlier, all this seems beyond the bounds of
feasibility.

There are a number of others who, starting from Marxist premises, have
developed ideas which are highly relevant in the present context. Even
Trotsky, whose modern followers tend to regard the market as the devil's
invention, could write (and repeatedly) that one needs a combination of 'plan,
market and democracy' to combat bureaucratic arbitrariness. True, he was
discussing what he called 'the transitional epoch', but the word 'epoch'
suggests that he did not see this as a short-term expedient, even while
retaining his faith in the ultimate Marxian vision of full communism. More
recently a number of Soviet reforming economists have discussed in a most
interesting way such problems as optimal decision-making structures, from
which emerges an irreplaceable role in the microeconomic realm, alongside
planning, for market relations: for instance, Petrakov and Karagedov.[6] An
émigré who has remained a socialist, Belotserkovsky, has been mentioned
already as seeing the necessity of producer and consumer choice and 'positive'
competition between autonomous units.[7] The Hungarians Ivan Szelenyi and
Janos Kis, though they differ in many respects, have questioned the relevance
of what some regard as Marxian dogma. They show awareness of the negative
effects of substituting the visible for the hidden hand, stress the implications
of producer and consumer choice, note that Marxian value theory (which was
related by its author to a model of capitalism) would require significant
modification if one were to use it in a transitional or any sort of socialist
economy. The dangers posed by a market are not denied, but there are no
solutions without dangers or disadvantages. No model can be discerned in
which the market can be eliminated without even greater danger and
disadvantages.

The Hungarian Reform

Hungary's experience shows all this clearly. In examining Hungarian experience, it is necessary to abstract from specific circumstances of the time: for instance, the adverse terms of trade after 1973, or the complications due to the failure of Hungary's Comecon partners to adopt similar reforms. What can Hungary's experiment with the 'new economic mechanism' tell us about the consequences of strengthening the market mechanism and eliminating (at least in part) the centralisation of microeconomic production and allocation decisions?

In 1968 the Hungarian leadership adopted a measure which greatly strengthened the role of the market mechanism, dismantled the administered material allocation system and abolished the compulsory plan targets in relation to output and assortment. It was intended to link domestic prices with those on the world market, so that, subject to import duties and certain other restrictions, enterprise managers could buy and sell across borders. Prices were partially de-controlled. Managerial bonuses were linked to commercial results, to profits. Investments were henceforth to be financed mainly by interest-bearing credits, with the enterprise responsible for around half of all investments. In agriculture the imposition of compulsory delivery quotas was discontinued, and a wide range of non-agricultural activities was undertaken by the collective (co-operative) farms. Private enterprise on a small scale was allowed, in towns and in villages. Central planning was to be confined to 'macro' magnitudes, together with key sectors such as energy and transport. There would still be, for instance, quinquennial plan targets for specific products, but these would be indicative and not obligatory.[8]

The so-called New Economic Model was not consistently applied, and there was some retreat from its full rigour. There were many cases of direct central intervention, including *ad hoc* subsidies, directions to deliver to specific customers (e.g. to Comecon partners under bilateral agreements), limits placed on imports and on co-operative enterprise. This is not the place to go into the many modifications and policy zigzags which followed the original reform of 1968, though it should be borne in mind in assessing its significance that it was not fully or consistently applied. The question we shall now put is the following. Given that the reform was designed to overcome the principal defects of Soviet-style centralised planning, how far can it be said to have succeeded? Which of these defects can therefore be curable by 'Hungarian' methods?

A most valuable survey was presented by Kornai in his lecture to the Irish Economic and Social Research Institute.[9] He, like most others, claims that the reform of 1968 was reasonably successful. But certain stresses and strains have come to light. Perhaps the most important for us are those that he enumerates which concern a contradiction between principles of efficiency and those of what he calls 'socialist ethics'. Thus any system of incentives, if it is to be effective, must be associated with inequalities, and if it is linked with profit is bound to conflict with the principle of equal pay for equal work. As we shall see in discussing the Yugoslav model, the problem is exacerbated by the fact that profits and losses may be due to reasons totally unconnected with efforts of workers or management of that particular firm. In Hungary one has seen strong 'equalising' pressures, to pay subsidies to (or otherwise rescue) the laggards, the unsuccessful. The management itself seeks help: 'lobbying begins . . . Personal connections are used', to get tax allowances, subsidies. Bankruptcy is avoided. Conversely, large gains are frequently not allowed to accrue, through taxes or changes in the rules. While entrepreneurship and risk-taking should be rewarded, the risk of innovation is worth it 'only if success can bring a large gain'. But 'in post-reform Hungary the economic leader cannot lose a lot, but he cannot gain a lot either. There is no scope for any great advance. The firm with uncommon or provocatively high profit will be "tapped". The levelling of incomes involves also more or less the levelling of performance.'[10]

He goes on to point to the contradiction between the socialist principles of solidarity and security, of full employment, and efficiency. Once again, no bankruptcies, no closures, therefore no effective 'punishment' for inefficiency. Competition was and is limited, its effectiveness 'softened', yet we know that profit-oriented firms require competition, to prevent them from increasing their profits at the customers' expense. Security of employment is naturally much prized, and is a positive phenomenon, but an 'easy-going, lazy attitude', problems of discipline, become hard to deal with. He does not fail to mention also the issue of externalities. Since these are particularly significant in investment decisions, this is one good reason why the central planners must play a role in any major decision of this sort, and are also involved in investments undertaken on the initiative of firms as providers (or non-providers) of credits and other financial assistance. However, this causes bureaucratic delays and a degree of irresponsibility: if mistakes are made, whose fault is it, and what can one do about it anyway? Decisions in the real world are influenced by many considerations, including string-pulling and lobbying. Central planning officials, like others, 'are not the philosophers of Plato's ideal state endowed with wisdom soaring above society. They are real people, living in the midst of society, linked by a thousand threads to their colleagues active in economic life.'[11]

Kornai very properly concludes that there is no 'solution', no convenient nostrum that will 'cure' all diseases. We will continue to live in an imperfect world, and any reform is bound to contain defects as well as positive features. He shows that one serious obstacle to the smooth functioning of the Hungarian reform was an excessive number of changes in rules and regulations, changes no doubt designed to stop or forestall various undesirable acts, but which had the effect of causing confusion in the minds of management, since they could not adjust to constantly changing rules of the game. He ends with a warning which seems entirely justified: some reformers, or analysts of reform models, imagine that there is a sort of 'reform supermarket', and from its shelves one can pick the best features of various models, while leaving the rest. This is not in fact possible. The choice is between packages, the contents of which are functionally or logically interrelated, and some of which are bound to cause difficulties.

As already argued more than once, life is necessarily full of contradictions. Some, it is true, are so contradictory as to be non-functional, or self-destructive. Thus some reform packages have come to grief, in the USSR and elsewhere, because of major internal inconsistencies: for instance, one cannot rely on the profit motive if prices are uninfluenced by use-value and demand, and relaxation of price control and of administrative allocation of inputs will fail to achieve the desired results if there is a sellers' market (excess demand, physical shortage).

One very important lesson to be learnt from Hungary is that not only is the elimination of excess demand necessary, but it is possible, and possible even in situations in which it involves unpopular price rises. It was necessary for the Hungarian economic policy-makers to overcome political fears and the pressures of those who, disliking market-type reforms, were willing to use the unpopularity of price increases to discredit them. It is an important political-social fact that reforms of the Hungarian type encounter strong resistance, and it is remarkable that Hungarian reformers have met with some success in their efforts, in contrast with the almost total failure of similar efforts in other communist-ruled countries. 'Reform-mongering' (to use a term coined by Albert O. Hirschman) is no simple matter. This raises the question of the various strata and interest groups affected positively or negatively by a greater reliance on the market mechanism, a question we cannot pursue here.

Of quite vital importance is the whole question of how *prices* are or can be determined. Soviet experience shows conclusively that central control over all prices is quite inconsistent with flexibility or indeed with any rational use of the price mechanism: there are too many prices to control. In Hungary it has been found possible to de-control a large number of prices, most notably in the producers' goods sectors. Prices of most machines, semi-manufactures, many materials, are free; others are subject to maxima; only a minority are tightly controlled from the centre, and such control is justified partly on social grounds (for consumer necessities) and partly because of the need to prevent abuses of monopoly power in what is after all quite a small country. Linked with this is the question of the relationship between foreign trade prices and domestic prices. The original intention of the reform was to merge the two: subject to some exceptions and to import duties, enterprises would be free to buy their inputs and sell their output inside or outside the country. This has been only very partially realised in practice, for a number of reasons that need not detain us. One of these was the worldwide inflation which accelerated after 1973, and which led to the emergence of a very large gap between internal and external prices, and of a complex system of subsidies designed to maintain price stability. This policy was abandoned in 1980, when internal prices were sharply raised, and a new attempt was made to establish a closer relationship with world market prices (though the method used is of questionable logic and effectiveness). It is, of course, neither possible nor logical to have domestic prices subject to free negotiation *and* to align them with 'world' prices unless there is much greater freedom of trade (especially for imports) than is possible for Hungary in its present balance-of-payments difficulties and given also the importance of its links with the centrally planned economies in Comecon. However, the object of the present section is to discuss the operational principles of the Hungarian model, rather than describe those difficulties which were due to external causes. It is worth

noting in this context that many Hungarian economists stress the considerable importance of *informal* controls over prices and other decisions: thus
management is given to understand that large rises in prices charged to
Hungarian customers for goods free of price control would give rise to
disapproval. Very large profits are viewed with disfavour. Given that management can be dismissed (or promoted) by party or higher administrative
instances, and frequently needs to apply for various permits and authorisa-
tions, such informal controls can have considerable effect. None the less, they
must be distinguished from Soviet-type centralisation. It is one thing to be
formally free to act, subject to spasmodic interference from superior
authority, and quite another to be unable to act without changes in obligatory
output and allocation plans. There is no doubt whatever that Hungarian
directors have far more decision-making powers than their Soviet equivalents,
even though these are not as great as the formally adopted model implies.

It should perhaps be added that central interference is not necessarily
wrong. Some Western work on the Hungarian economy takes it for granted
that, in the event of conflict, the management's view is the economically
rational one. No doubt this is often so, but it *need* not be so, given the possible
existence of informational economies of scale and externalities. In Hungary,
as elsewhere, the centre sees the wider consequences of local action, but sees
detail less clearly. In Hungary, as elsewhere, *some* types of decision can with
advantage be subject to central decisions or veto. There is also the question of
a possible conflict between centre and enterprise because of differences in
time horizon. According to O. Gado, managerial interest in short-term profits
(with subsidies if possible) is too great. 'Methods for creating long-term
interests have not yet been evolved.'[12]

An important role in practice is played by the banking system. Approxi-
mately half of the total investments are decentralised, in the sense that the
decisions 'belong' to enterprises, and this is a logical consequence of the
nature of the model: the centre is responsible for decisions to create new
enterprises, and for major projects, as well as for social service investments,
while firms invest to expand production or to adjust it to changing demand
prospects at home and abroad. In practice the state planners can exert
influence on decentralised investments through the banks: few enterprises
have sufficient reserves of their own; they have to borrow, and the bank has
the task not only of ensuring the economic soundness of the project, but also
of seeing whether it 'fits' into the economic strategy of the government, as well
as avoiding unnecessary duplication. The government can encourage decentralised investments by making it known that credits will be readily available
for particular activities. Here again, central guidance can have positive
results, and foreign observers have commented favourably on the high quality
of the work of Hungary's investment banks.

There are a few further remarks to be made about the Hungarian
experience. It has already been noted that the logic of the reform requires
competition, as the original resolution introducing the reform quite specifically recognised. But, quite apart from being out of line with traditional
socialist ideology, competition is also inconsistent with the interests of those
who do not win. Management and workers join in begging the government to

intervene. Yet competition, to be effective, requires that there be penalties for failure. Even in a society with a highly free-enterprise ideology, similar pressures develop. Then, of course, there are sectors where economies of scale (technological or organisational-informational) favour very large units which, especially in small countries, acquire a strong monopoly position. We will discuss later the difficult question of how then to define efficient operation when monopoly power is present, but in both East and West it is recognised that a case exists for state regulation, to avoid abuse of this power.

Does reliance on the market mechanism make for excesses of inequality? As the quotations from Kornai demonstrate, the implementation of the reform showed a tendency to avoid the over-rewarding of success (especially managerial) and the penalisation of failure. However, there are some very substantial inequalities in Hungary, and it is interesting and relevant to consider how far they were due (if at all) to the 'market' elements of the reform. It is necessary to recall that the Soviet system also generates inequalities. Large bonuses are paid to management in both cases, the key distinction being: what criteria are used to determine the bonus? In the 'traditional' Soviet centralised model, the bonus relates to plan fulfilment, i.e. to obedience to orders received from above. In the 'Hungarian' model it relates notionally to the satisfaction of customer requirements, reflected in the customer's willingness to buy and in the resultant profits. In either case the bonus may be more or less deserved, and in principle there is no reason linked with the chosen model why bonuses should be higher in the one case than in the other. As for 'hidden' benefits (perks of various kinds), these exist in some degree in all systems, Eastern and Western, but one must bear in mind that the absence of physical shortage, due to the presence of supply-and-demand-balancing prices, eliminates one form of privilege of great importance in the USSR: access to goods and services unavailable to most citizens, at the low official prices.

Hungarian experience of incomes policy and wage control is of great interest, and provides useful evidence of problems likely to be encountered if there is decentralisation. Wage scales are centrally determined, as are skill differentials and the rules for bonus payments. However, as Soviet experience shows, actual wages are always to some degree a matter of local decision, whatever is the formal position. Piece rates, promotion, re-grading, can be used to pay extra to attract or keep labour. The Soviet method of control, as we have seen, relies heavily on a planned wages fund 'limit', and also on linking total wages to the value of output (since 1981 it should be the value of *net* output). The Hungarians wished, understandably, to relax these inflexible controls: enterprises responding to market opportunities should be allowed to recruit the necessary extra labour without having to seek permission to exceed the planned wages fund. There should also be some link between wage levels and profits, but since *within* the firm the model is an 'authoritarian' one (i.e. management is in command), it seemed appropriate to make profit-related bonuses apply particularly to managerial staffs. They would take the risks, they would make the decisions. Reflecting this, the original 1968 version of the reform laid down limits to profit-related bonuses to be paid out of the so-called 'sharing fund': 80 per cent of monthly salary for managers, 50 per cent for other senior personnel, 15 per cent for workers. In case of loss, managers could have 20 per cent of their salary deducted, while workers were guaranteed their basic wage rates. This gave rise to widespread dissatisfaction, illustrating one of the problems highlighted by Kornai: fairness, the egalitarian tradition, seemed to be ignored. A jest of the period is reproduced below. Kádár, the party leader, visits a factory and asks the manager: 'Have you had a bonus under the economic reform, and what have you done with it? Reply: 'I bought a country cottage, and the rest of the money I put in the savings bank.' He asks the chief engineer the same question. Reply: 'I bought a car, and the rest of the money I put in the savings bank.' Finally Kádár asks a worker. He replies: 'I bought a pair of shoes.' Kádár: 'And the rest of the money?' Worker: 'The rest of the money I had to borrow from my mother-in-law.' (These rules were later modified.)

The government was conscious of the need to avoid a wage explosion under conditions of comparatively full employment. Increases were limited to given percentages, and while enterprises were not actually forbidden to exceed this limit, they faced severe financial sanctions (additional taxes) if they did. By Western (and Polish) standards the rise in money wages was effectively contained, despite the fact that worsening terms of trade compelled the government to increase retail prices faster than wages towards the end of the 1970s. The detailed methods by which this was achieved are worthy of careful study. But one wonders if they could be effective in the face of militant independent trade unions.

Commitment to full employment went with the inevitable difficulties in persuading workers to move where they were needed, or in imposing redundancies where labour-saving machines were installed, which led to a combination of labour shortage in some sectors and overmanning in others. In the absence of compulsory labour direction, which would be intensely unpopular, *and* with little or no unemployment, such problems are bound to arise. Granick, in the course of a very valuable analysis of the Hungarian situation, stresses that this was not only a 'full employment constraint', but also 'protection of jobs from changing product demands, and from alterations in technology which affect the skill composition . . . of the labour force'.[13] (We all want flexibility, so long as it affects others.)

There *are* large inequalities of income in Hungary, but they seem to be due not to salary-and-wage disparities in the state sector (which are no greater, or may even be less, than in 'unreformed' centralised economies in Eastern Europe), but to various forms of private enterprise. These activities range from private medical practice to shops and small-scale private and co-operative manufacture, craftsmen, cafés, car repairs, construction gangs and a variety of other provisions of goods and services, some of them undertaken by state-employed persons to earn extra (in 'the second economy').[14] Hungarian laws are more liberal than the Soviet, and most of the so-called second economy is legal. Thus, while in the USSR it is a crime to employ anyone to make something for profit, and all private trade is outlawed (except to sell one's own produce), in Hungary one may employ, say, half a dozen workers to bottle mineral water or to put roofs on private houses, and much else besides. There are co-operative enterprises, in industry as well as in agriculture, and agricultural co-operatives undertake industrial and service activities on the side. Obviously, all this gives very considerable opportunities for making money. 'Moonlighting', secondary occupations for workers, is a widespread phenomenon, introducing further elements of inequality. All this provides a dilemma for socialists. What should be their attitude? I return to a point made earlier: if the economic situation is such that individuals and groups can profitably undertake small-scale provision of goods and services, should they be prevented from doing so, by a 'socialist' police? Suppose that private or co-operative enterprise of this sort nets a high profit for those undertaking it. Is this an indication that they should be stopped (arrested? deported?)? Or is it sufficient to impose a graduated income tax, and encourage competition as a means of reducing prices and profits (whether from state enterprises or from other private and co-operative ventures)? On the whole, the Soviet tendency was to call in the police. The Hungarians too sometimes resorted to legal restrictions, as when (in 1972) they set some limits to the business activities of agricultural co-operatives. However, the official policy has been on the whole a tolerant one, and in 1980 it was decided to lease most small state shops to private operators, as this was seen as a cheaper and more efficient way to deal with retail distribution. Many restaurants also operate on this principle. Evidently all this heterogeneous activity can yield windfall gains, along with a risk of loss. Clearly this is inconsistent with egalitarianism. It is equally clear that economic loss would follow from the application of restrictive measures. Not only economic loss, but also human frustration would result. I would like to introduce the notion of producers' preferences, i.e. how people prefer to work, which will be taken up again in Part 5. Excessive incomes can be taxed, and competition from other 'privateers' and co-operatives is a better method of combating overcharging than by bringing in repressive laws.

The Hungarian economic mechanism has no place for workers' self-management. The trade unions are of the usual East European type, totally unlike both Western trade unions and the Polish 'Solidarity' union. Hungary has avoided any serious unemployment, and there has been no labour unrest. Under all these heads there are problems for socialist theory and practice. What influence ought the workers to have over decision-making? Should managers be accountable to the workforce, or to their hierarchical superiors? What effect on efficiency, and on the standard of living of the masses, would a militantly 'free' trade union have? Let us leave these matters aside, but bear them in mind.

Can the Hungarian experience be seen as a success, from which socialist theory and practice should learn positive lessons? It is certainly of great interest to socialists, as I found when called upon to lecture on the subject in Peking. It has also attracted attention from reform-minded Soviet economists. The question is: how can one measure success? If one confines one's attention to macroeconomic aggregates, or to productivity comparisons (e.g. tonnes of steel per steel-worker), the answer seems quite indeterminate.

The reform has made little difference to aggregate growth rates, which eventually declined at the end of the 1970s for reasons external to Hungary (a very sharp worsening of terms of trade) and not directly connected with the reform. Statistics are incapable of measuring improvements which take the form of a closer link between what is produced and what the user actually desires. They measure how much is bought, not consumer satisfaction.

Let me illustrate this with an (imaginary) example: suppose that, before the reform, a factory made 1,000 shirts at 100 forints each. They were of unattractive design and the colour faded on washing. Suppose that, as the result of the reform, 1,000 shirts were made, at a similar cost and at a similar price, but the customers liked the colours, which did not fade. There is a 'growth' of zero. Yet there is a clear gain. Or take another, and quite realistic example. In Hungary there is a wide choice for the consumer, with very little time spent waiting in line. In the USSR the choice is much more restricted, some goods disappear from the shops for months on end, and it is often necessary to wait in line. Yet how does one incorporate this in a comparative measure of living standards?

Let us now examine the Hungarian experience more closely, beginning with the position of the consumer.

Here the advantages seem overwhelming. Supply and demand have tended to balance at the existing prices. There is not a sellers' market, and there is some incentive to acquire goodwill by pleasing the customer. Time spent on shopping is no greater than in capitalist countries, and this sort of 'cost of consumption' is not to be ignored.

This result is a consequence of a price policy which has important implications. Hungary is a relatively poor country and, especially in the face of worsening terms of trade, it has been necessary to increase retail prices to a level which has upset many citizens, though without leading to riots, as was the case in Poland. Voices were raised in favour of tighter price control, and the opponents of the New Economic Mechanism claimed that the policy of higher prices was contrary to the interests of the working class. However, if one contrasts the price policies of Hungary and the USSR, it may be observed that the Hungarian consumer of any class gains immeasurably from being able to choose what to buy without having to waste time and effort on finding scarce products. The (dissident) Hungarian sociologist Ivan Szelenyi has argued that, in fact, the high prices at which demand and supply balance are in the interests of the working class, because, if there is shortage, the 'administrators' of this shortage become back-door beneficiaries. One cannot repeat often enough a quip of Trotsky's: if men have anything to distribute, they never forget themselves. One must clearly distinguish between an emergency rationing scheme, to ensure minimal fairness in times of war and disaster, and a model for normal weekdays, so to speak. The emergency provides not merely a generally acceptable reason for the existence of shortage, but also a moral climate within which cheating is reduced to relatively small proportions. But if goods are in short supply, at established prices, for decades, and if, in addition, there is no formal rationing, then all kinds of distortions occur, and the beneficiaries (and victims) are scattered in a random way. Apart from the officials who get their supplies by the back door, some poorly paid shop assistants are able to 'earn' sizeable extras by diverting supplies, and various forms of corruption and unofficial barter flourish. The worker family without connections and with little time to stand in line is more likely to be a victim than a beneficiary. The mere fact that in Hungary it is generally possible to buy what is needed through the proper channels, the ordinary shops, is an automatic insurance against much petty corruption: there is no point in using bribery to get what is in any case available – available at its own proper price.

All this underlines the inadequacy of our statistical tools. The key problem lies in the economic meaning of non-market state-fixed prices, in which economic aggregates are measured, prices which do not reflect use-value or user satisfaction, either in theory or practice (as has been pointed out several times). The aggregate thus measures cost (effort), not result. We also know that the Soviet planning system generates waste by penalising economy in materials, intermediate goods and services (e.g. by insisting on fulfilment of plans in tonnes, tonne-kilometres, and so on). Thus the Soviet steel industry may be 'efficient' in its operation, but much steel is wastefully utilised. The output of textiles, shirts, or washing machines may be of inferior quality, or not accord with consumer tastes. Suppose that the effect of reform is to reduce waste and to cause output to be of better quality, better related to user requirements, so that there is less frustration, fewer hours are spent standing in line, and so on. This will find little or no expression in the official statistical aggregates.

In the nature of things one cannot measure such improvements. Thus suppose a purchaser prefers to buy X and buys Y because X is unobtainable. Statistics merely record the purchase of Y, which looks like a revealed preference but is not. The extra satisfaction which is derived from actually finding X is not even conceptually definable: who can tell in what degree the consumer prefers X to Y? (To complicate matters further, there is a special satisfaction obtainable by one who succeeds in finding a 'deficit good', which cannot be felt if the good in question could be bought at any shop without trouble.) There is therefore an evident risk of being accused of coming to favourable conclusions on 'anecdotal' evidence. There seems no alternative to taking the risk. Supplies both to industry and to the consumer do flow more freely, queues are few, and quality and choice compare favourably with Hungary's neighbours.

The importance of the so-called second economy can be held to demonstrate weaknesses and gaps. But these same facts can be seen as a form of desirable realism. In the knowledge that the state planning system cannot cope effectively with certain activities, the regime tolerates (sometimes even encourages) 'secondary' ('parallel') work which fills these gaps.

There are, of course, weaknesses too. Some Hungarian reformers attribute these to the incompleteness of the reforms, to arbitrary interference by ministries, to errors of price policy, and of course also to the strains caused by imported inflation, worsening terms of trade, and the like. These had effects both direct and indirect: they directly worsened the economic situation, and indirectly strengthened the hands of those who sought remedies by tightening control over production and prices, in ways inconsistent with the reform. But there is one lesson which, in my view, can be learnt from Hungary's imperfect reform. There is all the difference in the world between not being allowed to decide and having that right, even though from time to time one's superiors interfere with its exercise. Thus a Soviet firm cannot obtain inputs without an allocation certificate, and it always has an output and delivery plan imposed from above. The Hungarian firm, in principle, can choose what to purchase and from whom, and has no imposed output and delivery plan as a rule. True, ministries and party officials may issue orders: buy this, produce more of that. But the central authorities have neither the time nor the personnel to do so continuously and systematically, and so the management can act autonomously, by reference to economic criteria, most of the time. This is decisive and, despite modification and backslidings, this is still an essential difference from the Soviet centralised model. It should also be noted that there has been no significant unemployment; indeed, labour is often short.

One sector of unmistakable success is *agriculture*. The reader is referred back to the analysis of Soviet, and also forward to Yugoslav and Polish, agriculture, with which the Hungarian experience contrasts very much to its advantage. The key elements which account for this seem to be the following.

(*a*) *Price and procurement policy* Prices are negotiated with farms and are such as to elicit the required quantities without having to resort to compulsory delivery quotas. The farms thus find the expansion of production and sales to be profitable. At the same time, retail prices of food are sufficiently high to eliminate queues and a sellers' market. To illustrate the importance of this last point, one has only to observe that, according to the Comecon statistical annual (1980), meat consumption per capita in Poland was about 10 per cent higher than in Hungary, yet in Poland there was a serious 'shortage', while in Hungary meat was 'plentiful' – but of course at higher prices. This cannot be disregarded, especially if Hungary's success is seen in terms of apparently plentiful supply in the shops and in the markets (with prices in the latter no higher, as a rule, than those in state shops).

(*b*) *Operational autonomy of farms* In the absence of compulsory delivery quotas, or of imposed targets for sown area, output, number of head of livestock, and so on, farms can decide at their own level what to produce, and of course are freed from the petty tutelage from state and party officials about how and when to sow, harvest, or whatever. Therefore there can be proper adjustment of a farm's activities to the infinite varieties of soil and climate, and to other local circumstances (such as availability of labour and equipment).

(*c*) *Freedom to purchase inputs* The absence of a system of material alloca-tion, plus a reasonably flexible market environment, means that farms can choose freely whether and what to purchase (machines, fertiliser, fodder concentrates, building materials). Of course, this requires the industrial producers, and also importing agencies, to respond to demand, and this they are to a considerable extent free to do. Limitations on this freedom usually relate to foreign trade: thus pressure is exerted to buy more farm machinery from the USSR and less from the USA. But, despite this, the wide range of choice of inputs, the fact that they are usually available, represents a contrast with the situation both in the USSR (where inflexible administrative allocation prevails) and in Poland (where availability has been very restricted).

(*d*) *Non-farm occupations* Although no longer quite free to undertake all kinds of non-agricultural 'sidelines', the co-operative farms and their members can choose among a wide variety of occupations, ranging from car repairs and construction to the manufacture of components and other small-scale industrial production. (The principal limitation is on the *employment* by the farms of outside labour for these purposes.) These activities contribute to incomes (and to total output) and ensure round-the-year employment.

(*e*) *Peasant incentives, and private activities* Last but far from least, the farms have been able to use a variety of schemes to encourage peasants in their collective labours, taking into account local conditions and peasant preferences. It generally 'pays' the peasants to work well, and the level of pay is reasonably high. Furthermore, peasants have no difficulty in spending their money, whether on consumers' goods or on building materials or tools. The private sector can develop without obstacles, with the peasants encouraged to own and fatten livestock, and free to sell it on contract to the state food industry, or through their farms, or market it themselves (or eat meat and drink milk themselves, of course). They can freely purchase fodder and small tools. So complex are the arrangements within the farms, so vague the dividing-line between collective and private activity, that it is sometimes impossible to say which is which.

Of course there are problems also in Hungarian agriculture. Thus some critics argue that the farms have grown too big, with the chairman out of touch with the rank-and-file peasants. Costs are high. Peasant incomes have risen faster than productivity. But all these seem minor in comparison with the achievements. These contrast not only with the situation in the USSR, but also with what occurred in Hungary itself when Soviet-style collectivisation was crudely enforced upon the peasants in the first half of the 1950s. Surely there are morals to be drawn: peasants can be persuaded to work, management can genuinely manage, within co-operative agriculture. The better-off peasants, instead of being labelled kulaks and persecuted, were drawn in, and given responsibilities, in the second (more flexible) wave of collectivisation which began in 1958 (the peasants had largely dismantled the earlier Soviet-style collectives in 1956). Let there be no mistake: the second wave of collectivisation could not be described as voluntary. Perhaps it could be described as a sugared pill. Be this as it may, it was swallowed, and the subsequent arrangements worked to the reasonable satisfaction of the peasantry *and* of the urban consumer of farm products (though some of the latter complained about both the 'excessive' incomes of the peasants and the price of food; you cannot please everyone!).

To sum up: Hungary's experience shows clearly both the advantages and the difficulties which follow from an attempt to introduce what can be called 'market socialism'. On balance the positive features seem to predominate, and this despite some major inconsistencies in the application of the New Economic Mechanism. It is very important for anyone thinking seriously about 'feasible socialism' to study carefully the economic and social history of the Hungarian reforms, and also their effects on the political structure.

Yugoslavia and Workers' Self-Management

As in the case of the USSR, one must try to distinguish those aspects of the

Yugoslav model which are specific to the political realities of Yugoslavia. It is a country with wide disparities in income, productivity and culture between north and south, and one with serious divisions between different nationalities. We must try to separate out those features of Yugoslav experience which seem to be of general application.

There is a sizeable literature on the subject. Ward, Vanek, Horvat, Tyson, Meade, Bergson, Milenkovich and Sirc[15] have discussed it at various levels of abstraction. Some of this has been very abstract, perhaps too abstract for our purposes. Thus some of the models have assumed perfect competition, and/or that techniques are given. I recall a paper in which it was 'rigorously' established that a rise in price could cause a labour-managed enterprise to reduce output. When I objected that this could hardly happen in practice because the firm concerned would lose out to its competitors, I was coldly informed that on the assumption of perfect competition the firm would be (by definition) unconcerned with the actions of its competitors! (Or, of course, its customers' goodwill?) Of course, abstractions are necessary, and it is certainly worthwhile establishing the formal differences in maximising behaviour as between the labour-managed firm, in which workers' incomes depend on the financial results of its activities, and one in which the maximand is profits, or whatever is the maximand for a Soviet manager. What *does* a Soviet manager maximise? To say that he seeks to maximise his bonuses under constraints is to say very little, since the 'constraints' can be so vitally important. (For example, he must fulfil certain orders and plans which do not earn bonuses, he must obey orders emanating from influential party and state officials even if these conflict with bonus-maximising, and so forth. No simple formula will do.) But we should still try to identify the difference between Soviet managerial responses and those of a Yugoslav manager responsible to a workers' council, in so far as this responsibility is real. We must not lose sight of the experience of the real world, nor assume away some key and relevant variables. Thus, to take one example, if one is interested in the effect of 'self-management' on unemployment, it is surely inappropriate to assume that techniques are given, since the essential point might be precisely a tendency to choose labour-saving, capital-intensive techniques.

In real-life Yugoslavia the workers' councils' powers are limited, by state regulations (including regulation of prices) and by political intervention through the so-called League of Communists (i.e. the party). None the less, certain tendencies can be discerned which justify a series of generalisations.

There is, first, the question of income distribution. This in turn has a number of aspects. The first is one which arises in all our societies, but can be seen in its most acute form where workers' incomes are supposed to be directly linked with the commercial results of 'their' enterprise. This inevitably creates tensions between two divergent principles, or perhaps even three: payment by commercial results, payment in relation to productivity and equal pay for equal work. If the notion of workers' self-management is to have meaning, then success or failure must affect income. Income will then vary significantly according to whether the enterprise is or is not commercially successful. But this depends on a variety of causes, many of them quite outside the control of the workers: market fluctuations, imposition of a tariff by a foreign country, and so on. It may indeed have very little to do with effort, or with productivity. The latter is essentially a quantitative measure: a worker or group of workers produced 100 units last year, 120 units this year, therefore productivity has risen by 20 per cent, and according to the concept of relating pay to productivity they would seem to be entitled to an increase. But it is possible that net revenues have not increased, because of a fall in price, increase in costs, or some other cause. Finally, there is among workers the not unreasonable feeling that work of the same quality and intensity deserves the same reward, whatever may be the commercial result of the given enterprise's operations. Suppose (let us say) you are a lorry-driver, and you drive a 10-tonne lorry from Zagreb to Skopje. Why should your pay be different from that of another lorry-driver, driving the same type of lorry the same distance, merely because of differences in the commercial performance of this or that firm?

These species of contradiction are inescapable whenever payment is related to a firm's success. Yet if it is *not* so related, then where is the workers' material interest in the success of 'their' firm? Would they then not be indifferent to the profitability of their firm's operations? The dilemma is an objective fact, and any form of self-management with material incentives will have to live with it. It must be noted that this is not the same problem as that of income differentiation *within* a firm; it would arise even if all its personnel were paid the same. It seems likely that the problem is less acute below a certain size of labour force. Imagine, for example, a co-operative of ten workers, providing any good or service, from drawing-pins to interior decorating. Any differences in income between them and others are much more likely to seem acceptable, since a small group such as this can more readily relate their direct personal effort to result. This is more remote when there are a hundred variegated workers, let alone a thousand or more.

The effect of the contradictions described above, combined with a tendency for workers' councils to be under pressure to distribute higher incomes, has been to stimulate wage inflation. Some earn more, others wish to catch up in the interests of fairness and parity. Of course, wherever incomes are lower than the recipient would like (i.e. in all countries) there is pressure for more. In the USSR this is more or less effectively resisted by a combination of imposed wage tariffs and planned limits on the wages fund of enterprises. In the Yugoslav model the share-out of the net income of the enterprise (net of material costs, taxes, and so on) is for its own elected council to determine. The temptation is to distribute the bulk of it, and then to finance investment by borrowing. This would be the normal course of events, unless prevented either by state-imposed regulations (which are, so to speak, external to the model) or by party-political control exercised within the enterprise.

In the most recent years there has been pressure to reduce inter-firm income differentiation, through a so-called 'social contract', and this has had some negative effects, in that it is inconsistent with the principles of the model. Successful firms now have sizeable surpluses, which can seldom be effectively invested, while the less successful must be subsidised, or borrow from the bank to cover their deficits.

It had already been observed that 'participation of rank-and-file employees in the more important policy-making areas was almost nil'.[16] But this by no means excludes continuous pressure for higher incomes, which the 'key position of management' cannot allow it to ignore.

The workers as a collectivity lack any economic interest in the long term, to balance the evident advantage of a short-term share-out of whatever net revenue is available. As Sirc correctly points out, this arises from the fact that the workers are in no sense co-owners or shareholders. They did not contribute to the initial capital of the enterprise, or indeed to the decision to bring it into existence in the first place. Conceptually they are involved (through their elected representatives) in its management, and they share in its net income, but only for as long as they work for it. When they resign to go elsewhere, or when they retire, they have nothing to sell, and so no material interest in the value at that time or in the future of its capital assets. In Yugoslavia, as elsewhere, there is considerable labour turnover. Only a minority of the workers can realistically identify their interests with that of 'their' enterprise for the whole of their working lives.

This has several consequences. One relates to responsibility for investment decisions. No one can say that the Yugoslav model is one of under-investment, since the statistics show that both the volume of investment and the rate of growth are high by international standards, higher than in most of the countries which follow the Soviet model. But so is the rate of inflation, since these investments are superimposed upon the high share-out of net incomes, and borrowing to finance investments (whether by enterprises or by local authorities) can and often does outrun the resources available and the limits of sound decisions. Extra resources can be provided by the printing-press (increase in money supply, with the obvious consequences) and by imports (and so a large balance-of-payments deficit and foreign debt). Suppose the investment proves a loss-maker, who can be held responsible, and in what sense? In practice one cannot close down the enterprise, or make it bankrupt. One cannot hit the workers' pocket, not only for political reasons but because most of those actually working at this time probably had little connection with the decision to invest. The manager can be replaced, but he (rarely she) too may not be responsible for the incorrect decision, either because he was not then the manager, or because it was the vote of the workers' council that was decisive. So one could all too easily have not only too much investment but also misdirected investment; market signals and institutional arrangements do not create a coherent whole, even if there is no arbitrary interference with prices.

The investment is all the more likely to be both misdirected and excessive when there is arbitrary interference with prices, an increasingly artificial exchange rate *and* a low rate of interest. Recently the rate of interest has been a quarter of the rate of inflation! Furthermore in Yugoslavia, unlike even the USSR, there is no capital charge (i.e. no annual payment to the state related to the value of fixed assets). Obviously under such conditions the extent of resource-misallocation can be enormous, unless there is systematic control by some central planning body. But no such control exists, and indeed the centre lacks authority, while the republics dispute over resources and sometimes duplicate each other's investments. Controls, when imposed, tend to be sudden and disorganising: a total price freeze, or a ban on all 'unproductive investments', to cite some recent examples. These result in a strange mixture of distorted market and spasmodic state intervention (which can hardly be called 'planning').

Yugoslavia's experience suggests that the desire to participate is by no means universal. Many workers and other staffs are not keen to sit on committees, to acquire the detailed knowledge that would enable them to be in any significant sense co-managers. It is for this reason above all that the management has very considerable power. It is tempting, but misleading, to attribute this lack of interest to faults in the system. A man or woman who works conscientiously may have other interests: the family, football, philosophy, do-it-yourself electronics, or playing the cello, for instance. Indeed, most visions of socialism rightly emphasise the need for diversification of interest. Then it must be appreciated that to participate seriously in decision-making one must do one's homework. The manager and his immediate associates are aware *ex officio* of the relevant economic and technological circumstances. The instrument mechanic, brick-layer, lorry-driver, may be assumed to be skilled and intelligent workers, worthy of the highest respect, and with intimate knowledge of instruments, bricks, driving. They will not, in their professional capacity, be acquainted with the demand pattern for the product of their firm, or alternative sources of supply of materials, or relative costs of variants, or the economic advantages of this or that innovation. Only a small minority is likely to make the effort. So it is not surprising that the Yugoslav experience points to the limitations of participation, to the fact that workers and their representatives are concerned most of all either with income distribution or with detail, such as the provision of clean towels in the washroom or a better arrangement of a specific production task or process. The same experience has been reported from a study of Hungarian producers' co-operatives: few persons other than the manager are concerned with the enterprise as a whole.

It is in the nature of the self-management model that it must rely greatly on the market mechanism, on self-interest of the production units. It therefore follows that the issue of external economies and diseconomies is bound to be relatively neglected. The interest of the part *can* conflict with the interest of the whole. The profitability of one unit may be a misleading criterion. Yugoslav experience strongly suggests that these factors can be ignored at one's peril, that one can overcompensate for the admittedly serious deficiencies of overcentralisation. What of complementarities and indivisibilities? There have been instances of myopia, of the fragmentation of systemic links. Thus one part of the railway system cannot be evaluated without regard to the effect of its operations on the traffic and revenue of other parts of the system. A research institute may or may not be profitable *as such*. Does the research department of Imperial Chemical Industries make a profit for itself? Presumably its existence is advantageous for its parent firm, and this cannot be known without a calculation made at the level of the larger all-embracing unit. Yugoslav experience provides numerous instances of the disadvantages of over-decentralisation. Economics of socialism must never overlook this particular problem, since one of the most effective arguments for socialism is precisely the frequency with which private (or partial) benefit can conflict with the general welfare. It therefore follows – it therefore *will* follow – that an efficient socialist economy must be an amalgam of plan and market, centralisation and decentralisation, control and local initiative. Yugoslav practice has varied at different periods, and this provides the interested scholar with many detailed examples worthy of study, which can only be touched upon in very general terms here.

It is a fair generalisation that central planning has been weak in Yugoslavia, due perhaps to the conflict between republican and federal powers. Far too little seems to have been done to bridge the gap between richer and poorer areas, though the difficulty in doing this should not be underestimated. Thus there is a great difference in natural fertility between the soil of the Vojvodina in the north and south Serbia or Herzegovina, so that for the same effort the peasantry will obtain a far higher income in Vojvodina, a difference which will not be corrected by an explicit differential rent, as there is no rent. For social, geographical and purely economic reasons it is more profitable to create new factories in the already developed areas of the north. The greater the stress on market and profitability, the greater the danger of perpetuating regional imbalances inherited from the past. At the same time an effort by the centre to locate new industries in the underdeveloped south meets with indignant resistance from those in the north who (understandably from their point of view) regard this as an unsound and wasteful use of *their* money. The centre seems to interfere in the investment process both too little and too much, and critics are unanimous only in seeing major irrationalities in the use of investment resources.

Then there is the vexed question of unemployment. It is repeatedly and correctly pointed out that this is one of Yugoslavia's most pressing and chronic problems. Even with a large number of workers 'exported' to West Germany, many are out of work. Is there a connection between the self-management model and unemployment?

It seems certain that there is, and it has been demonstrated formally. Compare a capitalist, or a Soviet manager, with a workers' council, assuming that the council is interested in maximising net revenue per worker. Income of workers according to the model is based upon the sum arrived at by dividing net revenue by the numbers employed. There is no material interest in taking on extra labour if the effect is to diminish this figure. It is easy to visualise that in an otherwise identical situation a capitalist concerned with profit, or a Soviet manager anxious to fulfil plans, would employ additional labour. Similarly the desire to maintain or increase net revenue per worker would influence investment choice in the direction of labour-saving variants. It must be added at once that practice shows also the reluctance of self-managed enterprises to *shed* labour: workers do not vote for redundancies. However, expansion is most 'profitable' when there is the least number of additional sharers in net revenue.

In one of his analyses Sirc points to another relevant factor, given a specific feature of the Yugoslav institutional structure, one to which we have not hitherto referred. This is the existence of a limited private sector. The point of the word 'limited' is that there is a maximum number of employees, usually ten. Under these conditions, the private entrepreneur who wishes to expand can only do so by capital-intensive, labour-saving methods.[17] One appreciates the motives of those who insist on setting limits to the size of private enterprise; we shall in due course have to consider both the reasons why small-scale private activities should be allowed, and the extent to which it is possible to allow them within a socialist society. It may be that size is not to be defined by number of workers, but rather by the value of capital assets, for then there would be no disincentive to employ some of the unemployed.

Evidently the Yugoslav system has not been able to surmount the contradiction between the need to provide work and the material interest of enterprises (self-managed or private) in economising labour. It is noteworthy that this high level of unemployment has coexisted with a high rate of industrial growth, a large volume of investments, inflationary pressure, that is, with conditions that might be expected, in the absence of disincentives to employ, to create a shortage of labour.

There is another lesson to be learned from Yugoslav experience, and in certain respects from the *sovnarkhoz* (regional council) experiment in the USSR also. This is the possible negative effect of the granting of powers over resources to regional bodies, whether these be national republics, cities, or districts (communes). It might seem that this would represent an improvement on central control: closer to the people, potentially more democratic. But there are serious disadvantages. Let us take as an example a factory, making, say, cement, or metal rods, or trousers. In the centralised model its output and its customers are determined by the planners, and in a complex modern economy the customers (as also the factory's own suppliers) are scattered over many regions. In the market model the management negotiates contracts with suppliers and customers in many parts of the country and perhaps outside it, devises investment projects, and so on. Where, then, is the role of the local authority? What interests is it likely to express? Its role is clear enough if local resources are used to satisfy local needs. But otherwise, given that its interests and the information at its disposal relate only to its own area, the local authority is almost inevitably prone to intervene to press the claims of the locality. In fact the more democratic the local institution is, the *more* likely this is to happen. In the USSR and in Yugoslavia, despite criticism, and despite the role of party officials as (supposedly) representative of the general as against the particular interest, diversion of resources occurs in ways which can conflict with economic rationality howsoever defined. There were even some cases in Yugoslavia of a local authority levying a sort of export tax upon goods sent outside its area, a sales tax on outsiders, and this practice had specifically to be outlawed. A cautious approach to local/regional powers over resources seems to be justified by experience. At the same time we know that centralisation of the Soviet type tends to weaken regional planning and fragment complementary development plans relating to an area. There is no simple solution. (There never is!) We learn from experience where the shoe pinches, where problems are likely to arise.

In the field of foreign trade, Yugoslavia tried to 'liberalise', aiming at a convertible dinar, with the labour-managed firms free to deal across borders. Yugoslav citizens were allowed to keep foreign currency accounts in the

Yugoslav banks. However, despite large remittances from abroad, and substantial revenue from tourism, the Yugoslav balance of payments moved heavily into deficit, and there is now (1982) a frighteningly large foreign debt. In part this is a consequence of large and sometimes unsound investments, in part it is a consequence of an overvalued dinar. The effect has been to compel the authorities to impose restrictions on imports, which vary from republic to republic, since (incredibly) they seem to control the bulk of the foreign exchange. Again, what was supposed to be a sort of free market has been turned into a mixture of improvised 'stop-go' controls, which cannot be called a plan. Some imports can be paid for by obtaining dinar from the bank at the official rate, but some enterprises are entitled to retain part of their export proceeds, and then sell some of this currency to other firms (*de facto*, as in theory what they do is to import on behalf of the other firm), at a rate that is negotiated and can be two or three times the official rate. The dinar is thus only partially convertible, there is no single exchange rate (except for tourists), and there seems now to be an uncrossable barrier between foreign exchange held by persons (a very large sum, estimated as close to $8 billion) and the foreign exchange available or allocated to firms.

Yugoslav economic performance was undoubtedly affected adversely not only by erratic price control but also by intervention at republican and local level, which went so far as to set up 'regional barriers to the free flow of goods and factors of production', creating what Tito himself called 'small protected markets'.[18] A further consequence of the deliberate weakening of the centre was that only a small part of total investments were effectively planned or financed by the centre, a serious defect in a country characterised by very uneven development. This could only be partially corrected by the provision for compulsory exchange of information on investment projects. The endeavours to arrive at 'social contracts' (or 'social compacts') also ran into difficulties owing to the power of republican and local interest groups. 'Interregional optimality was hindered by barriers to capital mobility which encouraged banks, enterprises, and republican and communal governments to keep capital resources within local boundaries', with 'the emergence of "political" factories', duplication, and so on.[19]

In a recent discussion in Belgrade the view was expressed that 'self-management was becoming a screen behind which the real decision-makers in the political sphere are hiding'. Professor Maksimovic roundly declared that the basic laws currently in operation are such that 'they establish an economic system that cannot function'. Branko Horvat stated that these basic laws 'are not only bad but unworkable', and pointed to many contradictions, adding that 'the whole conception of the basic organisations of associated labour is wrong because it leads to fragmentation and disorganisation of the economy'. The necessary degree of planning is absent. Yet there is much 'intervention', which, Horvat said, has severely limited the autonomy of the enterprises.[20]

There is widespread belief in Yugoslavia that the system as it is today cannot continue. Its functioning depends on the market, yet a variety of improvised controls, price freezes, import restrictions, exchange rate variations and negative interest rate, plus political interference with the income distribution of self-managed enterprises, adds up to a bundle of contraditions. The looming crisis in the balance of payments requires a firm policy at the centre, but, especially since Tito's death, the centre has insufficient power to act. It would seem that a crisis may come to the boil before this book is published. If so, it should be noted in how many respects reality has fallen short of the 'Yugoslav model'.

This may be a suitable place to stress that this apparently long list of difficulties and deficiencies is *not* intended to 'prove' that the Yugoslav system is wrong or mistaken. It has achievements to its credit. The standard of life compares favourably with its 'centralised' neighbours. Belgrade and Zagreb must seem highly prosperous to most inhabitants of Romania, Bulgaria, the Soviet Union. Growth has been impressive, even if sometimes distorted and costly. With all its shortcomings, the experiment with 'workers' self-management' has been of great importance; there is much that anyone interested in socialist economics can and must learn from it. Here and elsewhere, we must never forget that perfect systems exist only in books, that the real world in East and West abounds in irrationalities, misallocation, mis-employment of resources, various forms of waste. In the real world, whether socialist or not, some intractable problems and contradictions will exist. Indeed, it is well that this is so, for a world without contradictions would be an intolerably dull place, and social scientists would be threatened with unemployment. I can only repeat that we must learn from the things that go wrong, in the hope that by doing so we will diminish the ill-effects of predictable troubles.

Private Agriculture in Yugoslavia and Poland: Peasants and Farmers

Yugoslavia and Poland are the two countries in which, while the urban economy is predominantly 'socialist', the peasantry is predominantly private. It is worth devoting attention to the effects of this, and also subsequently to contrasting the performance of smallholder agriculture not only with the collective and state farming of the USSR but also with the different experience of Hungary.

Neither Yugoslavia nor Poland can be a good example of effective private agriculture, whether the measure is cost or productivity. In particular, Polish peasants have not only failed to respond to rising demand for meat, but a growing deficiency of grain has led to rapidly rising imports, at a time when the balance of payments was (and is) under heavy strain.

It cannot be our purpose here to examine the current economic problems of Poland or Yugoslavia for their own sake. The question we must put is: what can be learned from the experience of these two countries concerning the viability of smallholder peasant agriculture? This should be contrasted with the many deficiencies of large-scale collectivised and state agriculture. Could they all be inefficient? Then what is the answer to the agricultural problem?

One possible answer to this puzzle is suggested by one simple (and fairly accurate) statistic: in many parts of Poland the average size of holding is 5 hectares, whereas on similar land in the Soviet Union we have state and collective farms of 5,000 hectares. Perhaps 5 is too small, 5,000 too large. In Yugoslavia the *average* size of a peasant holding was only 3·9 hectares in 1969.[21] This may be a significant clue to one of the principal defects of Polish and Yugoslav agriculture: formal rules and informal pressures (and fears) prevent the formation of economically viable and efficient units. That is, in some cases the household is simply forbidden by law to possess more than 10 hectates of land; or there is fear that to grow too big would be to attract undesirable attention from party officials fearful of the emergence of a new bourgeoisie. The latter point reminds one of the principal contradiction in the peasant policy of the party in Soviet Russia in the 1920s: basing agriculture on the 'middle peasants', treating the successful and prosperous as 'kulaks' and so as class enemies, meant that enterprise brought danger to the enterprising; agricultural production was to be based on the moderately unsuccessful ('middle') peasant. This conflicted with the urgent need for higher marketings of farm produce.

If one also considers the impact of state-controlled purchase prices, which have acted as a disincentive, and also the relatively low retail prices which (especially in Poland) were heavily subsidised, and the inadequate supply of machinery and equipment (again especially in Poland), it is not surprising that agricultural performance lagged behind the requirements of the economy. A disproportionate share of resources has gone into the relatively few *state* farms.

Several issues of general importance arise as one further considers the issue of private agriculture. One is the very wide range of forms of land tenure, and of population density, in different countries, which must be taken into account before drawing any practical conclusions from various countries' experience. Thus in, say, the Canadian prairies small numbers are engaged on large, highly mechanised farms, while in Eastern Europe (or, even more, in China and India) there are large villages and a much larger number of cultivators. Quite different techniques, habits of mind, patterns of labour utilisation, emerge. It is plainly futile to imagine that, say, Canadian agricultural organisation could be introduced in India, or Poland, or vice versa. The impact and possibilities of co-operation also differ very widely. It is one thing to consider the advantages of production in common by villagers, though in Russia we have seen how disastrous was the attempt to impose it from outside, by coercion, even though there had been a tradition of communal tenure. It is quite another to try to devise it where there are scattered farmsteads, even of the Scandinavian, let alone the Canadian, type. When the soviets imposed the *kolkhoz* system in the Baltic states, they sought also to eliminate the farmsteads (*khutora*), to drive the peasants into village settlements. Still other possibilities exist in the immediate aftermath of a land reform in a country of giant landlord estates, *latifundia*.

In Poland and Yugoslavia individual peasant ownership predominated, most landlords having been expropriated long before the communists took power. In both an attempt was made to collectivise, and in both it was abandoned. The existing compromise seems unsatisfactory, and the most obvious solution seems to be to allow the private peasant sector to expand, i.e. to increase the average size of farms, with a higher level of mechanisation.

The market is, and presumably would remain, the basic link between agriculture and the urban sector, as it was in the USSR in the period of NEP. This does not necessarily mean a reliance on the spontaneous and uncontrolled market, which is not allowed to operate in the West either. Economic theory knows of the 'cobweb', the persistent disequilibria which can be engendered by the price mechanism in agriculture. Furthermore, sharp variations in prices have a direct effect on the incomes of the producers, and in all countries where peasants and farmers have influence this causes strong pressure for some species of price support scheme. In the Stalin period the interests of peasants were disregarded, and prices were fixed not as a means of supporting the producers, but rather as a means of extracting resources from them, as a form of taxation. This is no longer the case, however, even in the USSR.

In West and East alike attempts to control agricultural prices have led to anomalies of various kinds, and no doubt any socialist regime will have to try to reconcile a number of mutually inconsistent objectives in its price policy, as virtually all regimes have had to do.

More perplexing still will be other dilemmas. In a country with large collective and state farms of the Soviet type, there seems little or no advantage to be gained from adopting Polish-style smallholder agriculture. Polish peasants complain that they were undersupplied with inputs, that prices paid to them were too low, and they lacked confidence in a regime that seemed very unsympathetic to their needs and aspirations. No doubt even small farms could produce more under less unfavourable circumstances (look at Japan!), and to this extent the Polish experience should not be seen in too negative a light. None the less, the record of Poland and Yugoslavia is not reassuring. What, then, should reforming socialists be advocating? Should it be a system of free (or freer) co-operatives of the Hungarian type? Should there be various species of farms coexisting, depending partly on producers' preference and partly on the nature of the productive activity? Peter Wiles used to speak of 'left-wing crops' and 'right-wing crops', and this is not a bad way of highlighting the fact that mechanised cultivation of wheat on the prairies might call for very different scale and organisation, compared, say, with the cultivation of vines or onions.

Then what of a country, be it Poland, or for that matter Denmark, France, Canada, where farms of varying size are owned and operated by a family, with a little hired labour? Once again, we would have to take producers' preferences into account. A voluntary co-operative is no doubt excellent. A good Israeli *kibbutz* is run by committed enthusiasts, with anyone who does not like the communal principle free to leave. Forcible collectivisation is surely to be avoided. Neither Marx nor any sensible socialist did, or should, envisage coercion of small producers as the appropriate solution; it should not be the job of a 'socialist' police. But let us return to the lessons which Poland and Yugoslavia teach us. The chosen mode of production must realise economies of scale where they exist, must no obstruct efficiency. Strict limits on size can have deleterious effects, whether size is measured in hectares, in livestock numbers, or in the value of capital assets. Yet to have no limit on size could well lead to an undesirable concentration of agricultural production and land in the hands of a few private entrepreneurs.

What of the potential of coexistence of state, collective *and* private agriculture? (State farms exist in both Poland and Yugloslavia, and while in Poland they appear to have operated inefficiently, in Yugoslavia their yields are much higher than those of peasants, though allowance must be made for the fact that the state farms are mainly on much more fertile land.) Should socialists oppose private farms which employ no or little hired labour? If producers' co-operatives are efficient, if they accord with the desires of the peasants or farmers, then of course there would be a legitimate preference for such units in socialist ideology, but would this need to be reinforced by prohibitions or strict limits on individual agricultural enterprises?

I must admit to a deep prejudice against the use of police to prevent people from producing goods and services which others want and are prepared to pay for (unless, of course, they are noxious as such, like drugs). If large-scale production is indeed more efficient, it would not need extra-economic coercion to prevent the private farmer from competing. But if, say, wheat, maize, milk and butter are amply supplied by large farms, but private enterprise finds it advantageous to supply mushrooms, raspberries, green peppers and goat's milk cheese, or indeed if individuals can be more efficient in the production also of milk and butter, it would surely be wrong to stop such production in the name of socialism.

Then there is another issue, applying equally to individual *and* co-operative (collective) farming, which relates to differential rent. Some areas of land are naturally more productive, more conveniently located, than others. It follows that productivity will tend to vary. The same effort, the same skill, produce more in one place than in another. Such contrasts are particularly great in Yugoslavia, though they exist in some degree in all countries. Left to themselves some individuals and co-operatives will therefore be (undeservedly) much more prosperous than others. How can this be corrected? In a model in which agriculture is undertaken by wage-earners, in which the wage of tractor-drivers, milkmaids, and the like, is centrally determined, differences in net revenues can be absorbed through financial redistribution, within a ministry or via the state budget. This method is inapplicable to individuals and co-operatives. It should be possible to deal with this question by a differential land tax, and this is done in some East European countries (in the USSR a more clumsy method is used: lower prices are paid to farms in areas of greater natural fertility). However, experience in many countries, including also China, shows that what ought to be seen as differential rent does in fact find expression in peasant income differentials.

Finally, let us devote a little attention to a concept introduced a few pages back, that of 'producers' preferences'. The words 'consumer preferences' are more familiar. In one sense, this is as it should be. The object of production is to satisfy need, and in a conflict between producer and consumer about *what* should be produced the consumer is generally right. But this does not and should not apply to the question of *how* it should be produced, under what conditions of work. The citizen who wants milk, cabbage, pears, is entitled to have his needs satisfied. But if the producer prefers to work in a family unit, derives satisfaction from being in charge of his or her own work, does not want to join a large collective operation, *and* if this preference does not adversely affect the quantity and cost of milk, cabbage, pears, should we not take this into account? We shall return to this theme later. Maybe socialist economists should recognise that small can be beautiful, and be acutely conscious of the many forms taken by diseconomies of scale.

Of course, there is a great deal more to be said about self-management, but it is being postponed until Part 5.

The Polish Experience: the Road to Catastrophe

The inadequacies of Polish smallholder agriculture, referred to above, must be seen in the context of an economic crisis which culminated in catastrophe in 1980–2. This book is not intended to be a description of events or an economic history. None the less, it would be appropriate to look at what has happened in Poland, if only to see if any more generally applicable lessons can be drawn. Was the catastrophe due to peculiarly Polish circumstances, or is it the first stage of the disintegration of Soviet-type economies?

Poland had the good fortune to possess three distinguished socialist economists: Lange, Kalecki and Lipinski. Various proposals to reform the centralised planning system were discussed in and after 1956. For reasons which must be largely political, no effective reform was adopted, and the measures taken were half-hearted and contradictory. There is a good description of these measures and an analysis of why they did not work by W. Brus, to which interested readers can refer.[22] Apart from the inadequacies of the reform measures, there were two other 'negative' factors, both political. One was the isolation and unpopularity of the communist leadership in a country deeply Catholic and traditionally anti-Russian. The other was the adoption of exceptionally unsound policies for investment, prices and incomes, policies which would have demolished even the best-laid scheme for reform of the economic mechanism.

Already in 1956 there had been a popular outburst against the hardships caused by over-investment in the preceding period (as well as against the pro-Moscow communist leadership of the time). Gomulka came to power amid scenes of popular enthusiasm. Workers' councils were created, a new spirit seemed to be arising. Fourteen years later, hopes had been disappointed. Workers' councils had been emasculated. Investments were again increased. Cultural and economic controls were tightened. An attempt by Gomulka to increase food prices in December 1970 led to riots and strikes (although food prices were indeed too low). After some shooting Gomulka resigned and was replaced by Gierek, who reversed the price increases and then launched the disastrous policy of simultaneously increasing both investment and consumption by very large percentages. Investments rose in the five years 1971–5 by 130 per cent, and money wages by over 60 per cent, this being sustained by massive borrowing from the West. By 1976 it was essential to change course. An increase in food prices was more necessary than ever, since Poland could not sustain so high a level of subsidised consumption, especially of meat, and the subsidies represented a big burden on the state budget. Gierek's attempt to increase prices in the summer of 1976 led to yet more riots, and he hastily backed down. The next four years were years of drift to disaster, with ever-rising debts, food shortages, and imbalances and disequilibria in many sectors. Remedial action was urgent, but politically impossible. Poland became a big grain importer, at a time when the balance-of-payments situation went from bad to worse. The high expectations raised by the artificial boom of 1971–5 were sadly disappointed. In 1980 yet another attempt to increase food prices contributed to the disintegration of authority, the rise of the 'Solidarity' trade union, the resignation of Gierek and his replacement first by Kania then by Jaruzelski, amid far-reaching discussion of political and social renewal and of drastic economic reforms.

Meanwhile there was a continued drift towards economic catastrophe. Output fell sharply, partly because of strikes, partly because of the exhaustion of foreign exchange, food shortages and supply bottlenecks. 'Solidarity' became a powerful economic and political force, elbowing aside the official 'trade unions' and achieving an effective veto on government action.

There was talk of a government of national salvation, with the participation of the party, 'Solidarity' and the very influential Catholic Church. However, formidable obstacles stood in the way.

One was political. On one side was the party's claim to undisputed political leadership, with as a corollary its control over basic economic policy and over appointments (i.e. the Polish version of *nomenklatura*). Some of the leaders were very unwilling to compromise on this, and they were reinforced in their obstinacy by pressure from Moscow, which was increasingly alarmed by the turn of events. On the other hand, 'Solidarity' inevitably became the focus of all political opposition, in the absence of any other legal opposition organisation. In its ranks were trade unionists anxious for higher wages and shorter hours, nationalists, many sincere socialists, many equally sincere anti-communists. Its democratic and free assemblies gave expression to a wide range of mutually inconsistent views. It was too much to expect the emergence of a coherent policy from so heterogeneous a group, even if circumstances had been normal.

But circumstances were far from normal, for economic catastrophe was here. Rationing had to be introduced, rations reduced, prices (at long last) increased. As output and exports fell, imports had to be slashed. Living standards had to be cut, key priority sectors protected. So, even if the party leaders and 'Solidarity' had a clear idea of what sort of economic reform should be adopted, it was hard to see how it could have been adopted in the chaotic situation which existed, and which provided strong reasons for continuing rationing and the reinforcement of central control, rather than extending the use of the market mechanism. Consequently no coherent economic policy, other than coping with immediate emergencies, came from either the government or 'Solidarity'. The latter was in any case split on the issue of whether it should take responsibility for harsh measures which, it was argued, were a result of the errors and incompetence of the party leadership.

By December 1981 the political claims of 'Solidarity' (free elections, a free press, legitimate opposition), the continued drift towards economic disaster and the evident powerlessness of the government to enforce any policy, together with demands from Moscow to re-establish order, led Jaruzelski to launch his repressive 'coup'. Martial law enforced by military officers, with the party apparatus pushed aside, represents a quite new situation, and the outcome is far from clear at the time of writing. Perhaps the military will impose much-needed reforms in the end. (They are asserting now, January 1982, that this is their intention.) It seems pointless to guess what will happen next.

Let me instead answer the question raised earlier: is Poland a sign of things to come? What lessons can be drawn from Polish experience?

The following points could be made in reply.

(*a*) Poland's leadership adopted an economic policy of possibly unique unsoundness, and the resultant destabilisation was all the more risky because the political foundations of the regime were so weak. Romania, by a different route, also arrived at a critical economic situation in 1981, but authority and the police were strong enough to prevent the emergence of any opposition.

(*b*) Opposition in Poland (unlike, for example, Hungary and Czechoslovakia) was based very largely on the working class, and therefore took a trade union form. This had the 'advantage' of causing much ideological confusion in the ranks of the party, supposedly the vanguard of the working class. It had the disadvantage that such an organisation developed primarily negative power: it could stop the government from acting and embarrass it by making political demands, but neither its structure nor the convictions of its mass membership facilitated its taking responsibility for policy.

(*c*) The experience of the 'Solidarity' union raises in very sharp form the question of the role of trade unions in societies claiming to be socialist, and in societies genuinely socialist too. In its first manifestations, alongside fully justified complaints regarding conditions of work, 'Solidarity' demanded higher wages, shorter hours and no rise in food prices which, taken together, were impossible in the economic conditions of Poland. Its actions contributed to a further decline in productivity. Understandably, as a focus of all opposition, it began to make political claims also, but without a coherent or united economic policy or the will to take responsibility (as indeed is not the task of a trade union). An important question arises as to the aims of the mass of the membership of 'Solidarity'. They certainly had no desire to restore capitalism. There was a lack of confidence in management at all levels, political and economic, a widespread demand for workers' councils, a generalised feeling that fundamental reforms were needed, with no consensus about the *sort* of reforms that were wanted (e.g. on the role of the market mechanism). This raises more general questions about obstacles to economic reform, and of the attitude of the masses to them, which will be discussed later.

(*d*) The lack of legitimacy, in the eyes of the masses, of the government and party, the leadership's ineptness and/or lack of commitment to necessary change *and* its unwillingness (until December 1981) to use force or terror meant a continued drift towards catastrophe.

(*e*) Other countries share Poland's 'systemic' weaknesses, and the contradictory attitudes of both the ruling stratum and the masses to economic reform. However, Poland's combination of official incompetence, 'illegitimacy', popular anti-Sovietism and Gierek's economic adventurism is not to be found elsewhere, which is not to deny that grave economic problems exist in other countries, not least the USSR, which *could* have political consequences.

G. Markus, the Hungarian philosopher who now teaches in Australia, recalls that socialism was supposed to 'overcome and liquidate the cyclical, crisis-ridden character of capitalist economic development'. The existence of cycles in Eastern Europe has been noted by a number of economists, including T. Bauer and J. Goldmann, but nowhere has it been taken to such extremes. Markus writes:

> Indeed one has only to look at the present state of the Polish economy, which can be compared to a country devastated by global war, to see the extent of destructive economic fluctuations possible under a regime where there exist no economic *or* social mechanisms of direct control over even the most mind-boggling mistakes of planning undertaken by a hierarchically organised apparatus ruling over the whole society.

It was in Poland that 'The whole social malaise of East European societies exploded with unexpected force and clarity'.[23] Will the other countries heed the lesson and avoid the Polish disease? Is the unreformed economic-political system capable of immunising itself against it? I do not possess a crystal ball.

China: Leap Forward, Cultural Revolution and Reform

It may be appropriate to return to the ideas of Coward and Ellis, already quoted in Part 1: 'In China another revolution in ideology is taking place, overthrowing the idea of delegation, management, the handing of power over to "representatives", or "responsible individuals", ideas which are the keystone of capitalist production relations and bourgeois democracy.' This represents in somewhat extreme form a misunderstanding both of the 'cultural revolution' and of the practical possibilities of any real-world situation. Many 'Marxists' shared this misunderstanding. Charles Bettelheim bases his theoretical critique of the Soviet system upon contrasting the supposedly successful class struggle and building-of-socialism in backward China with the doctrine that socialism required the development of productive forces. This latter doctrine he called 'economism'. Of course it was the Menshevisks (and the latter-day Kautsky), not the Bolsheviks, who believed that the Russian revolution had been premature because of the underdevelopment of the productive forces; but the Bolsheviks gave top priority to industrial growth after the seizure of power, and certainly saw in growth a pre-condition first for socialism and then for the advance towards communism. Bettelheim is, of course, quite right to stress the idea that 'Soviet power plus electrification' (i.e. Lenin's shorthand for industrialisation) was not a *sufficient* condition for the building of socialism, but was it not a *necessary* condition? No, Bettelheim replies, that too was 'economism', as was demonstrated by the cultural revolution in China, where a real socialism was being created in a very backward country, where the class struggle had priority over economic development: being Red was more important than being expert.

Bettelheim himself has been rethinking his position. He would now surely agree both that the 'cultural revolution' did not take the form that Marxist theory envisaged, *and* that much damage was done by it, which must now be painfully repaired by Mao's successors.

What lessons can be learned from China's experience?

In the period 1949–57 the Chinese planning system evolved in the direction of copying the Soviet model, and progress was assisted by a sizeable volume of Soviet aid. While all large-scale and much small-scale industry was nationalised, the authorities were conscious of the need to use scarce entrepreneurial capacity, and there were many instances of former capitalist owners continuing to run their factories as managers. Urban co-operatives were encouraged. The peasants were collectivised by stages (after a rather bloody anti-landlord campaign), and there was little damage done to agriculture in the process, in contrast with Soviet experience, probably because the Chinese communists had operated from rural bases, and so had been much closer to the peasants than their comrades in Russia had been. None the less, collectivisation was also a coercive process in China. The preferences of the peasants were not taken into account.

Production in town and village rose rapidly, and one important reason for this was simply *order*, replacing the chaos, civil war, foreign invasion and domestic war-lords which had been plaguing China for a hundred years. It was no accident that the main centres of industry before 1949 had grown up in areas under Japanese control, such as Manchuria, or in foreign concessions (especially Shanghai), where order *was* maintained.

Then came 1958, and with it the 'great leap forward' and the split with the Soviet Union. The 'great leap' may have been Mao's attempt to find a Chinese road forward, utilising the vast size of its rural population. However, there is a parallel with the strategy adopted in the USSR in 1929–32, which also involved the adoption of extremely ambitious growth targets and the mobilisation of the masses. In both cases the warning voices of sanity were denounced as 'right-wing deviations', and there was immense waste of effort. There were differences too. Thus there was no Soviet equivalent of the backyard foundries and other excesses of rural small-scale industrial plants. These proved impracticable and, along with excessive mobilisation of peasants for public works, diverted attention from agriculture and led to a serious food shortage. There was also the creation of the 'people's communes', with attempts to introduce extreme forms of communal living and to restrict or even abolish the peasants' rights to private plots and livestock. By 1959 there was such chaos and confusion that economic statistics ceased to be published (limited publication was not resumed until 1979), and the 'leap' was abandoned. Apparently Mao's personal position was adversely affected, with power passing to Liu Shao-chi and Chou En-lai, whose more moderate policies made it possible to repair the damage and to resume progress. However, the system remained highly centralised. Thus state enterprises retained virtually none of their profits and most materials were centrally allocated. Urban co-operatives were brought under such tight control that they came to be in a position similar to that of state enterprises. Though there was talk of decentralisation to provinces, in practice Peking controlled the bulk of industrial production. In the villages, the communes' productive functions were reduced, with agricultural production organised by 'brigades' (corresponding in size and importance to Soviet collective farms), or even in 'teams', subdivisions of brigades, though controversy continued over their respective roles, and to this day this is a subject of some confusion: incomes are supposed to be based upon each team's net revenues, but these revenues are partly the result of what the team has been ordered to cultivate by the brigade or the commune, so that wide disparities in income are due to circumstances extraneous to the work or efficacy of the team. Private plots were again tolerated. But private enterprise in towns was rendered virtually impossible.

Progress was interrupted by the launching of the 'cultural revolution'. Its history has been written so far mainly by its victims or opponents, and this must be allowed for. It had a number of elements, which, though linked, should be carefully distinguished. One was the effort by Mao to recover his dominant position, to defeat Liu, who controlled the party machine, by mobilising a mass movement against them, accusing them of being 'capitalist roaders'. This line of attack involved an appeal to the most radical elements, to the revolutionary spirit. It developed into a vicious attack on culture, and perhaps the most lasting damage was to education, numerous sources testifying to a ten-year gap which had adverse effects both on culture and on technological training. Thousands of intellectuals were sent to the countryside for 're-education' and hundreds of colleges and research institutes were closed or disrupted. Mao encouraged the zealots, though in the view of some observers (Jack Gray, for instance) they went further than he had wished.[24] There were attacks (sometimes physical) on management, and many instances of officially fostered indiscipline. Though wage inequalities persisted, there were spasmodic campaigns against so-called 'bourgeois right', a stress on the supposedly superior notion of moral as against material incentives. In the villages too there was a revival of anti-private-plot measures.

The role of the army, of Lin Piao (and his mysterious death), of the so-called Gang of Four and their relationship with Mao himself at different stages of the cultural revolution, raise questions far beyond the scope of the present work. It is clear that the cultural revolution was very unpopular in many quarters, and especially in its last years was a cause of serious economic damage, the full extent of which cannot be measured until more statistics are available.

After Mao's death, policy changed. When I visited China in 1979 reform was in the air, the priority of economic development over ideological radicalism was reasserted and efforts had begun to repair the damage to education and culture. At first it was thought possible to adopt a large-scale industrial modernisation programme, relying on substantial imports of Western technology. These plans were quickly shelved in the face of daunting obstacles: there were major economic disequilibria, agriculture was in urgent need of material inputs and incentives if the population of close on 1,000 million was to be fed, and incentives for peasants meant the rapid expansion of light industry. Major modernisation programmes would have to wait. 'We one-sidedly sought high speed and high accumulation rates, and hankered after large-scale capital construction. In relations of production we gave undue stress to the transition to a higher level of ownership of the means of production.'[25] Noting that the productive forces are still 'very backward', the present official policy goes on to re-emphasise the priority of agriculture and of light (consumers' goods) industry, the shift of heavy industry towards providing the means of production for the consumers' goods industries, and the increased attention to be paid to services.

Reforms are being introduced which have the aim of strengthening the market mechanism, though it is far from clear yet how far they will go. Public ownership is to remain predominant, but there is repeated criticism of the 'premature transition to a higher stage of ownership, disregarding the actual level of productive forces and wilfully raising the degree of socialisation', that is to say, the elimination of co-operatives and private enterprise, when objective circumstances favoured their continuation. Consequently it has been decided to loosen controls in agriculture, to give 'the 800 million peasants for the first time [sic] the right to select different systems of responsibility for agricultural production, which determines the forms of labour organisation and the ways of distribution according to work. The plots for private use may be enlarged or even doubled, increasing from 7 to 15 per cent of the total cultivated area.' In cities the so-called 'individual economy, which was once regarded as the "tail of capitalism" and the small-scale co-operative economy which had been looked down upon are all being encouraged by the new policy'.[26]

China is an exceedingly poor country. Its population is close to 1,000 million, yet its arable land area is only half of that of the Soviet Union. Its poverty is a function of the fact that its 800 million peasants can only just feed themselves and the existing cities. China's experience, positive and negative, is of the very greatest interest and relevance especially to densely populated less developed countries (LDCs). It is of particular value to compare its progress with that of India. While growth rates have not greatly differed, China may claim an advantage in the eyes of socialists, in that no one actually starves and there are no very rich people. India's democratic voting is a disadvantage in tackling such deeply ingrained causes of inequality as the caste system. China, in turn, is seeking to study and learn from the experiences of other planned economies, which is why I was invited to lecture in China on the Soviet and Hungarian economies. As for the viability, or indeed the final shape, of the new model which China is now seeking, it is far too soon to make any comment on what is still a very fluid and rapidly changing situation.

China is, of course, an ancient state with the longest continuous history of any. As in the case of the Soviet Union, revolutionaries did not and could not start with *tabula rasa*, and the habits of centuries had their effects on both leaders and led. Bienkowski, whom we have already quoted, has much to say about 'the Chinese experience', and forecasts the emergence or maintenance of an 'egalitarian despotism' which was also an aim of Chinese emperors. One need not agree fully with Bienkowski's analysis, but it would be foolish indeed to refuse to recognise that there could be peculiarly Chinese solutions to economic, political and military problems, and that socialist principles and slogans would take very different forms when translated into Chinese. At the same time, as has been stressed earlier, the problems themselves have much in common with those encountered in other countries. They cannot be resolved or overcome by writing them in Chinese characters.

Notes: Part 3

1 N. Harding, *Lenin's Political Thought*, Vol. II (London: Macmillan, 1981).
2 R. Selucky, *Marxism, Socialism and Freedom* (London: Macmillan, 1979), pp. 74–8.
3 Lange's seminal article has been reprinted many times, including in *The Economics of Socialism*, ed. A. Nove and D. M. Nuti (Harmondsworth: Penguin, 1972).
4 Among Brus's many works are *The Market in a Socialist Economy* (London: Routledge & Kegan Paul, 1972); *Socialist Ownership and Political Systems* (London: Routledge & Kegan Paul, 1975); and 'Political systems and economic efficiency', *Journal of Comparative Economics*, no. 4, 1980.
5 O. Šik, *Humane Wirtschaftsdemokratie: ein dritter Weg* (Hamburg: Albert Knaus, 1979). See also his earlier *Die dritte Weg*, which appeared in English as *The Third Way* (London: Wildwood House, 1976).
6 N. Petrakov, *Khozyaistuennaya reforma* (Moscow, 1971).
7 V. Belotserkovsky, *Svoboda, vlast' i sobstvennost'* (Achberg: Achberger Verlag, 1980).
8 The best account in English of the reform in its original shape is in *Reform of the Economic Mechanism in Hungary*, ed. I. Friss (Budapest: Akadémiai Kiadó, 1969).
9 J. Kornai, 'The dilemmas of a socialist economy: the Hungarian experience', Geary lecture (Dublin: Irish Statistical Society, 1979).
10 ibid., p. 9.
11 ibid., p. 18.
12 *Reform of the Economic Mechanism in Hungary 1968–71*, ed. O. Gado (Budapest: Akadémiai Kiadó, 1969), p. 21. Among Western analyses, of particular value is D. Granick, *Enterprise Guidance in Eastern Europe* (Princeton, NJ: Princeton University Press, 1976); *Hungary: A Decade of Economic Reform*, ed. P. Hare, H. Radice and N. Swain (London: Allen & Unwin, 1981); B. Csikos-Nagy, 'The Hungarian reform after ten years', *Soviet Studies*, October 1978; I. T. Berend, 'Current Hungarian economic policy in historical perspective', *Acta Oeconomika*, vol. 18, no. 2, 1977.
13 Granick, op. cit. (n. 12), p. 247.
14 See the study by Agota Dezsenyi-Gueullette, 'L'économie parallèle à l'est: le cas hongrois', *Revue d'études comparatives est–ouest*, June 1981, pp. 25–40, and the comments on the role of the second economy in G. Markus, 'Planning the crisis: some remarks on the economic system of Soviet-type societies', *Praxis International*, no. 3, 1981.
15 The following appear to me as of particular interest: A. Bergson, 'Market socialism revisited', *Journal of Political Economy*, October 1967; B. Horvat, M. Marković, R. Supek and H. Kramer (eds), *Self-Governing Socialism: A Reader* (New York: IASP, 1975), 2 vols.; B. Horvat, *The Yugoslav Economic System* (White Plains, NY: International Arts and Sciences Publishers, 1976); J. Meade, 'The theory of labour-managed firms and profit-sharing', *Economic Journal*, March 1972; D. Milenkovich, *Plan and Market in Yugoslav Economic Thought* (New Haven, Conn.: University Press, 1971); L. Sirc, *The Yugoslav Economy under Self-Management* (London: Macmillan, 1979); L. Tyson, *The Yugoslav Economic System and its Performance in the 1970s* (Berkeley, Calif.: Institute of International Studies, University of California, 1980); J. Vanek, *The General Theory of Labour-Managed Market Economies* (Ithaca, NY: Cornell University Press, 1970); J. Vanek (ed.), *Self-Management: Economic Liberation of Man* (Harmondsworth: Penguin, 1975); B. Ward, 'The firm in "Ilyria"', *American Economic Review*, no. 48, 1958. (Also relevant is E. Domar's essay 'The Soviet collective farm as a producers' cooperative', *American Economic Review*, no. 56, 1966.
16 J. Županov, in Horvat *et al.* (eds), op. cit. (n. 15), p. 82.
17 L. Sirc, 'Notes on the practical working of cooperation and partnership', in *The Political Economy of Cooperation and Participation*, ed. A. Clayre (Oxford: Oxford University Press, 1980).
18 Tyson, op. cit. (n. 15), pp. 4, 11.

19   ibid., p. 13.
20   *Ekonomiske politike*, 3 November 1980, and *Duga*, 13 September 1980 (grateful thanks to Dr Sirc for these references).
21   V. Stipetić and V. Tričković, in *Food Policy*, August 1980, p. 175.
22   See his contribution to *The East European Economies in the 1970s*, ed. A. Nove, H. H. Höhmann and T. Seidenstecher (London: Butterworth, 1982).
23   Markus, op. cit. (n. 14), pp. 240–1.
24   For a valuable analysis of Mao's policies from a critical socialist viewpoint, see M. Selden and V. Lippit (eds), *The Transition to Socialism in China* (White Plains, NY: Sharpe, 1982).
25   Xiao Zhen, in *Beijing Review*, 10 August 1981, p. 14.
26   ibid., p. 17. See also C. Lin, 'The reinstatement of economics in China today', *China Quarterly*, March 1981.

Part 4

Transition

Some Introductory Remarks

'If you do not know where you are going, all roads will lead you there.' So goes a modern saying. *The* 'revisionist', Eduard Bernstein, wrote that 'the goal is nothing, the movement is everything'. It is therefore a little dangerous to discuss the problems of transition before answering the question: transition to what? I disregard the danger, however, for two reasons. One is that, while the goal is not and cannot be 'nothing', bitter experience teaches us that means affect ends. If to get some version of socialism clear to an incorruptible fanatic leads through blood and terror, requires a prolonged one-party despotism, strict censorship, and so on, then we may be reasonably confident that the road will *not* get you there. We might arrive at something which will be *called* socialism, in which anyone who suggests that this is not so would be courting instant arrest. We may have some idea of the direction in which we wish to go, but the final destination is bound to be affected by the nature of the journey. Indeed, whatever the goal, there cannot in social life be a literally *final* destination (except ultimate extinction, I suppose). Marx in his more romantic moments may have envisaged full communism as a stable golden age, but most Marxists (and surely also Marx himself in unromantic moods) would probably agree that while there is life there is contradiction, that the ideas of what constitutes socialism will alter with experience, that conflicts will not cease to exist. It would be silly to *assume* that such conflicts and contradictions would be 'non-antagonistic'. Marx was right in refusing to discuss detailed blueprints of a future socialism, though, as argued at length earlier, he was wrong in many of his indications about the economics (and politics) of an envisageable socialist society.

Part 4 divides itself into three main sections. In the first we shall consider some ideas and experiences of a transition from a developed or semi-developed capitalist society. In the second, the question of how to move from Soviet-type 'socialism' towards something more acceptable ('socialism with a human face', if one would like a familiar label). In the third section I shall take up the issue of 'developmental socialism', but not at the length which the subject doubtless deserves, and this for the following reason. 'Developmental socialism' is bound to be underdeveloped 'socialism', geared to the task of modernisation of the productive structure. This could be held to apply to Stalin's Russia, of course. As we saw, the French socialist thinker Charles Bettelheim thought that the Bolsheviks were guilty of the deviation which he called 'economism', which consisted of believing that the basic task was to develop the forces of production and that this would lead to socialism, whereas in his view, Mao's China was proving that a correct class line would enable even a very backward country to build socialism. Priority, he thought, should be given to class struggle and cultural revolution. Subsequent developments in China must have shaken Bettelheim's beliefs, except of course that he was right in one respect: economic growth in no way guarantees the triumph of socialism, even if the government is in the hands of a party which claims to be building it. Marx long ago, and correctly, pointed out that a share-poverty 'socialism' is bound to be an abortion, that if one shared out poverty then soon things would return to 'the same old rubbish'. Engels, in a famous passage, wrote that 'the worst thing that can befall a leader of an extreme party is to be compelled to take over the government in an epoch when the movement is not yet ripe for the domination of the class he represents'.[1] From this it follows that he believed, rightly, that material abundance, or at least an end to penury, was a *sine qua non*, a necessary (but not sufficient) condition for any sort of socialism that he could envisage. As I suggested at the very beginning of this book, economic development in the name of socialism has strong attractions for many in the Third World, for reasons we can or should understand. However, in the 'constructive' final part of this book I shall be concerned with 'feasible socialism' in an industrialised, modern country.

The use of the singular will at once cause dogmatic hackles to rise. Socialism in one country? Impossible!

Given the time-scale which underlies this entire study ('conceivable in the lifetime of a child already conceived'), universal, worldwide socialism is surely a far-fetched fantasy. Of course, just as we have a West European common market today, so it is possible to envisage a socialist customs union or federation which embodies a number of countries. This is not utopian, and is evidently desirable. It is anyhow rather pointless to consider 'socialism' in one small state, such as Austria or Belgium. The debate on 'socialism in one country' in the Soviet Union in the 1920s is often interpreted in a confusing way. The USSR was very large indeed, but isolated and underdeveloped. The protagonists, and many subsequent commentators, did not distinguish clearly between the following possible reasons for a negative answer:

(*a*) *Power, external* Given the overwhelming military and economic preponderance of the capitalist world at that time, Soviet Russia would be defeated unless there were world revolution.

(*b*) *Power, internal* Given that the peasants were numerous and the proletariat was small, given also the problems of capital accumulation, the effort to build socialism in Russia in isolation would fail.

(*c*) *Definitional* Socialism is defined as international and worldwide.

It is, of course, possible to combine all of these. Thus a critic could argue that, by turning in on itself, by devoting a disproportionate effort to the military sector, by using mass coercion against the peasant majority, the USSR in its Stalinist guise can be said to have built a 'socialism' which good socialists should reject. However, there is a vital difference between asserting that the USSR could not build socialism because of external and internal obstacles, and *defining* socialism so that it could not be achieved in *any* one country, whatever the circumstances and obstacles. Anyhow, no one doubts that in the transition period a country or countries will be trying to move towards socialism with external economic relations very much on the agenda, with a degree of dependence on the outside world. To repeat, if one were to assume that socialism is only possible on a world scale, this amounts to denying its possibility within a century, or at all, and ensures that the dogmatist who makes such an assumption will be able to reject any and every real embodiment of a socialist idea – a posture recommendable to those who wish to be in eternal opposition, but not otherwise very useful.

Transition I: From Capitalism to Socialism

No developed capitalist country has ever become socialist in any acceptable sense of that word. Of course, a number of countries under social-democratic rule have adopted a series of social reforms and expanded the nationalised sector. But it would be stretching the meaning of words too far if we were to speak of a Swedish socialist republic – and not only because it is a kindgom! (To say this is not to criticise or denounce what has been achieved in Sweden.) We have seen a number of attempts to lay the foundations of a basic change in property relations and in the social structure, and discussions as to how to proceed are very much on the agenda; for instance, in France before and after the election of Mitterand, and in Britain within the Labour Party. There had earlier been the experience of the French Popular Front government of 1936–7, and also that of the Popular Unity in (semi-developed) Chile, both ending in failure. It so happens that these, and also Portugal, were the subject of an interesting and original analysis by S. C. Kolm, published in a symposium.[2] As a student I attended the giant 14 July demonstration in Paris in 1936 and, in much more mature years, taught in Chile in the last year of Allende's ill-fated presidency. My analysis of Chilean policies and their consequences forms part of a published symposium.[3] The pages that follow owe something to Kolm and to my own experiences and ideas. Of course I appreciate that these are controversial questions. Opinions should differ, and certainly will.

There are some typical and dangerous misapprehensions commonly held by those on the left of the left, and which can lead to disasters, both political and economic. Since disasters should be avoided, these matters should cause concern also to individuals located far further to the left than the present writer.

The first relates to income redistribution and its relationship to productivity. It is widely believed that the welfare of the poorer sections of the community can be significantly increased by taking from the rich. Unfortunately, several difficulties arise. Thus part of the wealth of the rich cannot be redistributed. For example, a painting by Van Dyck can be confiscated or hung in a museum; it could be sold abroad and its proceeds distributed, but only once. A privately owned firm can be nationalised, with or without compensation, but it cannot be distributed either, though its future output could be. A privately owned château could be turned into a public museum, but not distributed to the poor. Though a few families could be lodged in it, its contribution to the housing problem would scarcely be appreciable. Land, of course, *can* be redistributed, and land reform is both possible and desirable. However, in many leading Western countries (e.g. France, West Germany, Scandinavia) either the bulk of cultivated land is already in the possession of peasants, or, as in the USA, there are no peasants.

The redistribution of *income* is complicated by the relatively small number of the really very rich. Let us suppose that, say, in Britain, 20,000 high-income recipients each have an income of £20,000 a year to spend on luxuries. (Note that any income that is saved and invested would probably also have to be saved and invested by a socialist government, and so would not be available.)

$$20,000 \times £20,000 = £400 \text{ million}$$

This large-looking sum would give the average wage-earner in Great Britain 50 pence a week or so, the equivalent of ten cigarettes. This is no reason for tolerating the existence of super-rich people. But the fact remains that their excess incomes, if redistributed, will make no decisive difference to the material welfare of the masses. Yet left-wing propagandists almost invariably cause their supporters to believe otherwise: *faire payer les riches*, let the rich pay. This sets up a unrealisable expectation, ensuring future disappointment.

In practice, when governments do try to achieve redistribution, they have to affect adversely the interests of a far wider group of people than the very rich. This is rendered necessary if sufficient revenue is to be raised. This, however, has political consequences, of which more in a moment.

Some also seem remarkably unaware of the consequences of 'nationalisation without compensation' of the big companies. Again they must be mesmerised by their own propaganda about the small group of super-rich ('les deux cent familles') who are supposed to dominate and own the large corporations under 'monopoly-capitalism'. The important role of big business men is undeniable, but what is overlooked is the importance of institutional investors, among them the big insurance companies and pension funds. Their investments are doubtless managed by financiers, but the savings are those of many millions of people, many of them trade unionists, who would not take kindly to losing them. Indeed, a sizeable portion of those who are members of the working class on any reasonable definition (i.e. who sell their labour-power, and hold no senior managerial post) own some property: a house, a car, other expensive consumer durables, pension rights, insurance. A policy posture that ignores this can lose the support of a large segment of the working class, even in countries where (unlike America) there is a traditional working-class attachment to socialist sentiments. Political and social realism also requires the recognition of the fact that there is a large class or stratum which considers itself middle class (even if in terms of property relations most of them could be seen as workers). Some have low- and middle-level supervisory tasks, some are specialist technicians and engineers, computer programmers and other kinds of skilled office staff, small shopkeepers, working owners of small businesses in a wide range of activities. The last of these may be seen as small capitalists in the strict Marxist sense, but they also work, and they are not a negligible quantity, numerically, politically, or economically. Chile was brought to a halt by a strike of lorry-owners: it turned out that, on average, each owned 1·5 lorries! While certain small businesses, notably shops, have been declining in number, it must surely be recognised by non-dogmatic Marxists that the old simplified notion of proletarianisation, of a polarisation of society between a small class of monopoly super-capitalists and the mass of workers (whose misery brings about their revolutionary class-consciousness), has *not* been borne out by history.

A 'wealth tax', and more severe taxation of inheritance, are attractive ideas, which also sometimes have quite unintended effects. It is one thing to hit large fortunes, or vast landed estates, but quite another to break up medium-scale or small businesses. Yet just this can happen. The super-rich go to live abroad, while the successful farmer or small factory-owner finds that he has to sell off part or all of his property to pay the 'capital transfer tax' or whatever is the contemporary equivalent of an inheritance tax. Limited companies are not so penalised, since they are impersonal (*sociétés anonymes*, as they are called in France), and therefore in the physical sense immortal. So the paradoxical and quite undesired result is to break up small and medium-scale family businesses or farms, while leaving the big corporations unscathed, thereby actually assisting in the process of concentration of capital. A levy on personal accumulation of wealth is indeed desirable, on grounds of social equity, but if this levy is confined to very large fortunes, the yield will be disappointingly small, while if lowered to a level at which the yield would be substantial it will help to alienate the middle classes. It has, however, definite symbolic significance. Such a tax has been introduced by the Mitterand government in France, and its effects are worthy of careful study.

In Marxist journals the notion of 'de-skilling' has been discussed; this is the view, also to be found in Marx, that machinery replaces skilled workers and, so to speak, homogenises the rest into a pool of universal unskilled labour. Surely, while machines eliminate some skills, they create the need for others, replacing a great deal of manual work in factories, on building sites and in offices. It is sometimes said that the new species of 'skilled work' is repetitive and boring, but then so was much of the unskilled heavy work which the machines have replaced. The driver of a bulldozer is not more bored or less skilful than the dozen or more navvies or coolies with picks and shovels. There are, it is true, examples to the contrary, and it is sad to register the fact that some skills have indeed been vanishing. Let us just say that the effects on skills of technical progress are indeterminate.

Some, for example, the late Nicos Poulantzas, have sought to save the purity of class analysis by defining 'workers' very narrowly: non-supervisory, manual, 'productive' (i.e. essentially working in factories and mines and construction). But in developed countries this is a minority of the working population![4] A socialism introduced by and on behalf of a minority class hardly accords with the Marxist or any other socialist tradition (except in so far as the Leninist model is applied, but this relates to countries with *peasant* majorities, and not, of course, to Western Europe, or even to semi-developed countries such as Chile).

Of course, mass unemployment is quite another matter. It now threatens all working strata: small business men, skilled engineers, factory workers. This is indeed a major issue, and we shall be discussing it in a moment.

But let us return, after this necessary detour, to income or wealth redistribution. It is no accident, it follows from all that has been said above, that serious measures of redistribution cannot be confined to taking from 'the rich', as the amount so obtained would make no significant difference to the poorer segments of the community. Therefore, to obtain the needed resources, it is necessary to hit and to hurt the middle strata too. Let me cite a parallel derived from Soviet policy towards the peasants in 1928. Faced with a grain shortage, the authorities decided to use coercion against the 'kulaks', the so-called rich peasants, in the name of the class struggle. They were said to be holding the Soviet regime to ransom, hoarding grain, and so on. It turned out that the rich did not have enough grain, and the campaign inevitably hit the so-called 'middle peasants', indeed the majority of the peasantry, for only thus could the necessary quantity of produce be procured.

In Russia the resultant discontent could be, and was, suppressed, by methods which we are surely not prepared to defend, or to tolerate. No socialist in the West should advocate a policy which envisages a police state coercing the majority. One sometimes wonders if some of our extreme-left intellectuals ever undertake a realistic class analysis of their own countries.

There does exist a solution that makes possible an improvement in the material conditions of the poorer section of the community, without entailing an attack on the interests of the middle strata: higher productivity, a larger cake. Where there is under-utilisation of productive resources, as in Chile in 1970 or in many countries today, a 'larger cake' can be the short-term consequence of reflationary (or inflationary) policies, though the longer-term effect must not be exaggerated. But even in this form, this whole approach has never stood high on the list of priorities of the West's left-wing groups. Indeed, the very phrase 'a larger cake' is apt to elicit cries of derision. Why?

First and foremost, it is because of the priority given to the class struggle, and the view of industrial relations as a zero-sum game. This was touched upon at the very beginning of this book. Higher output under capitalism seems to strengthen the class enemy, increases profits, may also increase unemployment, as when five workers with a new machine can do the work formerly done by ten. It is common for militants to demand wage increases 'without strings', often by percentages vastly in excess of any rise in productivity in the given industry or in the economy as a whole. Their motives and degree of understanding vary: some sincerely believe that they are redistributing income away from the capitalist class, and indeed neo-Ricardian theorists provide a kind of rationale by their treatment of the division of GNP between wages and profits: what one gains the other loses. There are also pseudo-Keynesians, who believe that higher wages for producing the same output stimulate demand, and are surprised to find the gains eliminated by cost-based price rises. The more intelligent revolutionaries well understand that the wage demands they are making cannot be met, or that if they can it is only through increases in prices. In so far as it is not just a question of sectional interest (i.e. leap-frogging, getting ahead of other workers in the wages 'league'), they see militancy, strikes, inflation, the closing of factories, as contributing to the breakdown of the system. They act as enemies of it. British and American planes, or IRA terrorists, who blew up factories in the Ruhr, or in Belfast, did not wish to increase productivity. The aim was to destroy, to cause demoralisation and collapse. As one dogmatist put it: 'We must demand higher wages, then still higher wages, until finally we destroy the wages system.' Not many of their fellow-citizens wish for this outcome; most would surely oppose it if they understood it. Still, the aim is logically pursued: these extreme-leftists wish to overthrow the system, they wish it *not* to function, they have every interest in causing productivity to fall, as this would 'sharpen the struggle'. For them, 'the worse, the better', until they seize power in a true socialist proletarian revolution. *Then*, of course, productivity becomes important; they believe it *will* increase, when the masses are no longer exploited, are freed from the shackles of capitalism, and so on (though they usually have not the remotest idea of how a complex industrial economy operates, or could operate, and treat such studies with open contempt).

It is worth noting that in the early years of the Soviet regime the 'left' also opposed the Soviet government on this issue. I am not referring here only to the conflict over the militarisation of labour and the trade unions, but also to the more 'normal' conditions of the mid-1920s. When the leadership put productivity high on the list of priorities, Zinoviev retorted: how could one exhort the workers to raise productivity when wages were still below pre-revolutionary levels! They were, of course, but the causal link seems to have escaped his attention, a typical blind-spot. So it is not just a matter of division of spoils with the capitalists, it is a whole mental attitude. One hardly needs reminding, in Britain, that nationalised industries suffer quite as much as the private sector from unreasonable wage demands and restrictive practices. This includes such non-commercial sectors as the hospital service, for instance. So nationalisation as such does not resolve the issue. Indeed, given the belief that the state can print any amount of money (while private business does in the last resort go bankrupt), it can make matters worse, so far as productivity is concerned. But I shall have more to say about nationalised industries in a moment.

A preoccupation with income redistribution and a lack of preoccupation with productivity is associated with opposition to wage control and a pre-disposition to believe in the desirability and efficacy of price control. Even if the need for a wages policy is recognised, it is then made conditional upon strict price control. This is in a context in which the policies pursued – for instance, higher welfare and other social expenditures, as well as higher wages – lead to increased inflationary pressures. Prices of necessities, so it is argued, must be held down as part of the process of income redistribution; to increase them is to benefit the better-off at the expense of the poor.

The consequences of price policies can be far-reaching, even decisive. I have argued elsewhere (e.g. in *An Economic History of the USSR*) that the price policy pursued in the period 1926–8 would have wrecked the New Economic Policy even if no other decisions had been taken. Price control made its contribution to the economic disasters in Chile. It played an important part in the Polish catastrophe. In the form in which it is advocated by some of the Labour left in Britain it would certainly lead to trouble here. May I stress that this is *not* meant as a condemnation of all and any price control, especially in times of crisis or emergency, when it (and rationing too) may be essential. In more 'normal' situations too price control is justified where monopoly power is strong. But it is no recipe either for efficiency or for the combating of inflation. Worse, it has profound social and economic consequences, usually unforeseen, and political consequences too, especially in a mixed economy (in a Soviet-type system prices also cause trouble, as we have seen).

A good example of an obstinately blind mentality is provided by typical Labour councillors (not all of them of the extreme-left by any means) faced with the self-evident fact that rent control plus security of tenure for tenants diminishes the supply of rented accommodation, thereby imposing hardships on anyone not already in rented accommodation. All they can ever see is that it is an anti-landlord measure, therefore good. All kinds of specious arguments are then trotted out, for instance, that rented accommodation would have declined in any case.

One should distinguish a price subsidised for social reasons at which supplies are sufficient to meet demand (let us say vitamins for pregnant women, or the Paris métro) and a price at which supply and demand do *not* balance. The goods concerned could be anything: steel, timber, meat, footwear. The consequences inevitably are either shortage or administered allocation (rationing). The introduction of consumer rationing in peacetime is intensely unpopular. Shortages are sometimes tolerated in the name of equality, because a higher price appears to favour the rich. But low prices favour the black market, and the rulers and administrators are tempted to allocate what *they* need to themselves, avoiding the long lines that wait outside shops. The private manufacturing and services sector finds great difficulties in obtaining supplies, and is in turn suspected of evading price controls and supplying the black market. Dealers, traders, also corrupt officials, make fortunes. This is held to call for still tighter controls and punitive measures, which must still further alienate the middle strata. In Chile they grew angry both as consumers (I heard housewives banging saucepan lids nightly in protest at food shortages) and as producers or traders. Conditions are created in which success in obtaining a licence or an allocation becomes a means of enrichment, either by sale at inflated prices on the side or by barter. It becomes worth a house-owner's while to bribe or otherwise induce a tenant to leave, since the value of the house increases hugely with vacant possession. The extremists use these facts as arguments for tighter controls, municipalisation of rented property, measures against private traders, and other acts which are bound still further to antagonise the 'middle'. In Chile food in short supply was distributed in some working-class areas by the so-called JAPs (Juntas de Abastacimiento Popular). This not only infuriated the middle classes, but left out a large number of the poorest who were not in regular employment or happened neither to be organised nor resident near a functioning JAP.

Universal price control is highly difficult to administer even if there is no significant private sector, as Soviet experience abundantly shows. Partial price control, for essentials only, tends to divert effort and resources from essentials to the more profitable non-essentials. Extremists than blame capitalists and traders and demand stricter measures, prosecution, wider nationalisation. The mixed economy operates in a market environment, and disruption of the market cannot but cause confusion and loss, and shortages. (As I am writing this the British Labour Party is committing itself to 'price control', to no control over wages, *and* saying it intends to help small businesses! *Gott im Himmel!*)

Shortages can be mitigated for a time by imports. This brings me to foreign trade and payments, a sector where the negative consequences of the policies outlined above would become speedily apparent, and must react back upon the internal economic and political situation. Chile in 1971–2 is a classic example, but France in 1936–7 followed the same pattern – and so would Britain under Tony Benn. Higher wages increase industrial costs and reduce exports. At first the higher demand may stimulate a domestic mini-boom and reduce unemployment, but the stimulus to imports will be greater. Even if the flight of domestically owned capital can be checked, foreign capital will be withdrawn, worsening the balance-of-payments situation further. Import controls will have to be introduced, with results that are bound to disappoint those who desire them and, if severe, cause further disruption and increased discontent.

As a sizeable part of the Labour left believes in import controls as a solution to British problems, it is worth spelling out the reasons for anticipating negative, indeed highly dangerous, consequences. One would be a breach of whatever trading pact or customs union the country is involved in (EEC, Andean pact, or whatever), and also of a number of commercial treaties and agreements. These would have to be renegotiated, presumably on a bilateral basis, if *selective* import controls are intended, selective both by product and between countries. The hoped-for results of import controls are the stimulation of those domestic industries particularly affected by foreign competition, and the saving of foreign currency. But the degree of interdependence and international specialisation is grossly underestimated, if indeed studied at all. A large number of specialised machines and components used in British manufacture are imported. A large number of (different) British machines and components are exported to be used in foreign manufacturing (for example, in Swedish cars). Some multinationals make certain models or products in Britain, some of which are exported, while other models are sent to Britain from abroad. As for consumers' goods, some are hardly made in Britain at all, and many that are (e.g. textiles, clothing, footwear) are imported largely from developing countries and Eastern Europe. It hardly seems to be behaviour appropriate to an internationalist ideology to play 'beggar my neighbour' and cause loss to other and poorer countries' workers – though this attitude is typical of trade unions in many lands.

It must be added that some economists of quite moderate political complexion, such as Wynn Godley at Cambridge, persist in advocating import controls, claiming for them advantages which could hardly materialise in practice. The 'macro' assumptions underlying their analysis have been devastatingly criticised by Paul Hare,[5] and it may be no accident that Hare is known as a leading expert on the Hungarian economic reform, and so is well acquainted with the trading practices of Eastern Europe. He points out that Godley's model incorporates implausibly optimistic assumptions about the behaviour of wages and prices, the supply response of industry and the reactions of foreign countries. There is no sign that he and his friends have done any of the necessary 'micro' homework, that is, exploring the consequences of import duties and/or quantitative restrictions on particular industries or the supply of particular commodities. It is even argued that a sizeable import duty on most if not all manufactures (say, at the rate of 30 per cent) would not lead to higher prices, higher wage demands and higher inflation, or to the devaluation to which such an import duty is seen as a preferable alternative. Godley himself favours non-discriminatory import duties, but many on the left envisage discrimination, and are usually quite unaware of the bureaucratic nightmare that is implied by the negotiation of bilateral quotas for thousands of different products with hundreds of different countries, which would be highly damaging to a country heavily dependent on foreign trade.

I have nowhere seen an attempt to work out the detailed consequences of serious, all-embracing import controls. Presumably most food and raw materials, and most semi-manufactures intended for further processing, would be exempt. In the British case, leaving the Common Market would enable some foods to be imported much more cheaply, which would be an important gain (the consequences to British farming would be devastating unless large subsidies were paid). But let us just take the group of products 'textiles, clothing and footwear'. A full list of such products runs into hundreds of thousands of designations. In many instances the cheapest items in the shops are imported, from a variety of countries such as Taiwan, Korea, Hong Kong, Brazil, India, Romania, Poland. What is proposed? A tariff of, say, 50 per cent? Global quotas? Specific quotas negotiated with each of these countries? Quite apart from the problems of negotiations and of reprisals, what would be the effect on domestic supplies, prices, wage claims and inflation? Or suppose that certain imported steels are 30 per cent cheaper than the domestically produced variety. Ban the import? Impose a 30 per cent duty? Would this not add to the cost of steel used in British industry? With what consequences in costs and competitiveness? Should we ban imported liquors – and expect no one to take reprisals against Scotch whisky? As for machinery, have any of the advocates of import controls actually examined in detail what is imported, what can be made here, what consequences would follow from restrictions? All this needs micro quantification. By this I do not mean that someone has to work out the exact future value of imports of doll's eyes from China or Peru, but one really must consider the scale of the intended cuts in imports in relation to the practical possibilities. Otherwise one would be adopting the typical posture of a conservative councillor who *knows* that massive savings can be made through the elimination of 'waste in government'. Of course there is waste in government! Of course some savings can be made in imports, some British industries could revive if adequately protected. Let me give an example. The cotton cloth industry in Lancashire has been declining for many years. Can imports be cut? Of course. Suppose that a sizeable proportion comes from India and China. As already pointed out, this could damage the interests of poor countries. But in addition these countries may well discriminate against British exports. If we put a ban on West German salami, Mercedes cars and radios, what would be the effect on British exports to West Germany of confectionery, Metros and tractors? What happens to non-discriminatory undertakings enshrined in GATT and a long list of 'most-favoured nation' clauses? How many Labour left-wing advocates of import controls have seriously considered such questions? It is an unfortunate effect of the Godley ('Cambridge') model that it purports to answer them, though in fact it either makes optimistic and highly question-able assumptions (e.g. on prices and wage claims) or simply ignores them, by remaining at the 'macro' level.

Some of the above arguments relate specifically to the British situation, and it may well be that some of the protagonists would not extend them to other and more industrially successful countries. Thus Cripps stresses Britain's 'industrial senility', urges a strategy of 're-industrialisation', expresses alarm – not without reason – about what the situation will be when North Sea oil supplies are exhausted, and sees 'limits on import penetration' as necessary in the context of state-financed industrial expansion.[6] One can envisage situations in which measures of this sort would be justified, together with control over export of capital. It would also be desirable to use for industrial and other productive investment the huge sums which so-called institutional investors dispose of, notably the pension funds and insurance. Protection for 'senile' industries would protect traditional inefficiencies, but would or could be justified in the context of a major modernisation programme. In a country such as West Germany the above arguments lose much of their force, and one can scarcely imagine that the 'Cambridge' school would advocate them there.

These are *not* arguments against all forms of protection, nor are they intended to exclude *ad hoc* restrictions when an import flood threatens a particular industry: Japanese cars are a familiar example. But as a generalised and apparently long-term 'solution', in the form in which it appeals to the left-extremists, it is a recipe for chronic crisis or disaster for a country which *must* import raw materials and food and whose manufactures *must* be competitive. Godley's plan is intended as a short-term solution of our immediate problems, and is in this respect different. It is one thing to administer a 'siege economy' in time of crisis, another to envisage some British version of the state monopoly of foreign trade.

The intended or unintended effect of the policies of the Labour left would be the suspension of the convertibility of the currency, strict controls on foreign exchanges and devaluation. Judging from precedents elsewhere, some would then advocate multiple exchange rates (varying by degree of 'necessity' of the import, 'necessity' being determined by government officials), and a sizeable gap must then develop between the official and the black market rate. Amounts doled out for travel abroad would have to be cut. There would be loud denunciation of currency speculators. Prices of imports would rise sharply, or would need to be allocated between users by government agencies, again administering a priority scheme. This was in fact familiar in Britain in wartime, when it was indeed essential. The attempt to divide important from less important is familiar also in Soviet planning experience, as is administrative allocation. The cost and defects are notorious.

All this would hit not only big business, but also the middle, the small business community, professionals of all kinds.

The combined effect of all these policies is bound to be to drive the political centre to the right. (In Britain fear of the consequences of such policies is driving part of Labour's own supporters to the new SDP–Liberal alliance). In Chile the alienation of the petty-bourgeoisie in 1971–3 was a major factor in the overthrow of Allende by a military coup. Most Chilean left-wing exiles recognise this, and stress that this alienation had not been intended, and indeed it was not. Allende had perhaps a clearer view than the Labour left has in Britain of the vital political importance of these strata, and Chilean communists had too. It was the combination of excessive wage increases, price controls and the balance-of-payments crisis which forced the government to take measures which hit the economic-political 'middle'. Kolm, in discussing both Chile and France, correctly points out that a left-wing victory in elections is only possible if the centre moves left. The effect of the sort of policies outlined above is to push the centre to the right. In France in 1937 this led to the erosion of the Popular Front majority, a rightward shift in the parliamentary balance; in Portugal to the disintegration of the left; in Chile – to a coup.

A left-wing government with socialist aims can act in one of two ways. One is to attempt a gradual shift in economic power away from big business (national and multinational) in alliance with small business (or at least keeping it neutral). Nationalisation raises questions to be discussed in a moment, but is clearly an important way forward. The government's supporters will seek immediate gains in the form of higher wages and improved social services. Some way *must* be found to keep these within the limits set by actual gains in productivity. This may prove the biggest obstacle of all. Trade unions pursuing the narrow sectional interests of their members may well clash with government. Political (socialist) influence in the unions would be necessary, unlike the paradoxical British situation in which unions' power over Labour's politicians has actually been strengthened. Since there would be a mixed economy, with a large and important private sector, market forces must be allowed to function, and not be disrupted by a combination of price controls, import restrictions and material-allocation. Limits on wage increases will clearly be vital, and by no means easy to achieve, in the face of strong pressure from the extreme-left. Then and only then can there be a likelihood of not losing power at the next election to a mighty right-wing backlash.

There is an alternative strategy, which may well be in the minds of thoughtful left-extremists. There *would* be no next election. In Chile in 1972 I had a long argument with Andre Gunder Frank. I pointed out the consequences, which were plainly already visible, of the policies being pursued. An increase in 'real wages' by 30 per cent in one year was a recipe for disaster. Reserves were exhausted, shortages were growing worse, and so on. Frank replied that the policy of immediate benefits would have made sense if it had been used as a springboard for the effective revolutionary seizure of power, but that of course President Allende was not a revolutionary, and so the consequences would indeed be disastrous.

The idea, then, would be to take advantage of a temporary leftward swing of opinion, reinforce it with some immediate distribution of benefits which would empty the treasury and exhaust reserves, and then take political action to prevent the right backlash from lashing, by appropriate changes in the constitution towards a 'people's democracy', plus the strengthening of the 'socialist' police, the creation of a workers' militia to replace or fight the army, and so on.

A variant of this strategy can be studied in Czechoslovakia in 1945–9. This too was a country with a large middle class, an independent peasantry, and a tradition of parliamentary democracy. The communists went into the election of 1946 promising full support for the small manufacturers, traders and peasants; they repeatedly stated that only the big monopolists and wartime collaborationists would have anything to fear. They scored the highest vote of any communist party in a free election. Within a very few years small businesses had been forcibly liquidated, the peasants compulsorily collectivised and any protesters taken to concentration camps. The strains and stresses which developed as a result (*inter alia*) of price control and (party-controlled) trade union demands were used as pretexts to eliminate private enterprise, which was presented as consisting of speculators and black marketeers. Of course, this was only rendered possible because the Communist Party held the levers of power.[7]

Let me hasten to add that I do not suppose that Benn and the majority of Labour's left wing have the slightest intention of taking this sort of action, which makes it all the more important and relevant to take into account the probable consequences of their policies. The above-cited article by Kolm should be required reading for them. But, as Hegel is alleged to have remarked, the only lesson to be learned from history is that no one learns lessons from history. It is one thing deliberately to engineer a crisis in order to benefit from its consequences, to achieve 'irreversible' changes, that is, to acquire power to prevent opposition from opposing. It is quite another to generate a crisis unintentionally, and then find to one's astonishment that the enemies of socialism are the chief beneficiaries of one's policies.

If any left-wing socialist has read so far, he or she may be saying: this is propaganda for the new British Social Democratic Party, if not simply anti-socialist. To this my reply would be: wherever my sympathies in fact lie, the fact remains that policies have certain consequences, and it is wilful blindness to refuse to consider them soberly and anticipate them. A sad *émigré* in Mexico after the coup told me that Chilean left-wing intellectuals had spent much time in denouncing international finance and the multinationals, but unfortunately had never studied what their actual role was, and what would happen if links with them were broken.

A critic might reproach me for having devoted no space to the actions of anti-socialists, who would surely seek to obstruct, if not sabotage. Indeed, the opposition will oppose. This can be taken for granted. My object was to point to certain policy errors which would have the unintended effect of assisting the opposition in its task.

While this book was being written, Mitterand took power in France, with a comfortable parliamentary majority (Allende in Chile was handicapped throughout by being in a minority in Congress). By the time this book is published we shall know much more about what Mitterand will do. It is my hope and expectation that he will do his utmost to avoid the errors that have been described above. (Alas, he seems to be on the verge of committing some of them!)

Some Thoughts on Nationalisation

Nationalisation of the British species arouses no enthusiasm, in the minds of most socialists *and* anti-socialists. It would probably be agreed that hopes which reposed on nationalisation have been disappointed. Conservatives hold that this is due to defects inherent in nationalisation, that private enterprise based on private ownership is inherently superior. (Mrs Thatcher's government tried to ensure that this was so by preventing essential investments and ordering the nationalised industries to sell off their more successful undertakings.) Obviously, socialists cannot agree. Yet the kinds of nationalisation frequently encountered in Western countries cannot give them satisfaction. Let us examine the problems involved.

The original notion was that nationalisation would achieve three objectives. One was to dispossess the big capitalists. The second was to divert the profits from private appropriation to the public purse. Thirdly, the nationalised sector would serve the public good, rather than try to make private profits. Be it noted that the last two objectives could easily contradict one another: there would be no profits to be diverted to the public purse. To these objectives some (but not all) would add some sort of workers' control, the accountability of management to the employees.

Capitalists are indeed dispossessed, in the sense that they no longer control, but it has usually been found necessary to compensate them, if only for reasons already referred to. (Many institutional investors operate with moneys advanced them as insurance premiums and pension contributions by quite ordinary citizenry.) So interest payments appear as major financial burdens, and the distribution of wealth is not significantly affected. If policies are followed which seek to avoid price rises under conditions of inflationary pressure, losses are probable, as certainly happened in Chile, so that, far from benefiting the exchequer, there is danger of these industries becoming a financial burden. As already indicated, there is also a danger that the workers will demand higher wages regardless of the financial situation, since in their eyes the government has a bottomless purse, and a printing-press. This not only happened in Chile, it happened under Labour and Conservative governments in Great Britain. Many steel-workers and the miners and their unions not only show themselves unmoved by financial deficits of 'their' public corporations, they are also quite indifferent to the fact that if costs go up and they then demand a ban on imports, other British industries will see *their* costs rise and become less competitive, with higher prices for the consumer. Or, if they do realise it, they simply demand subsidies, from the (bottomless) public purse.

But there are other and equally serious matters to consider. What should be the efficiency criteria under which nationalised industries operate? Who should determine them? What should be the relationship between management and the political organs of the state? I have written quite a few words on this subject,[8] but some of them 'belong' here, in the context of the tasks of a 'transitional' government.

When in 1945–6 the Labour government nationalised a number of industries its members had hardly any ideas as to what criteria should govern their operation. Thus Shinwell, the minister responsible for coal, admitted that he started with an empty desk. The industries should serve the public, should put social considerations high on their list of objectives, presumably should cover their costs and operate 'efficiently'. But these worthy aims were vague. Clearly, inefficiency means that resources needed elsewhere are unnecessarily wasted. What, however, *is* efficiency?

Part of the answer depends on the presence or absence of competition, *and* on the nature of the good or service provided. Let me illustrate with examples. The Renault car company belongs to the French state. It operates in a competitive environment, in France and in export markets. There is no reason why its operations should not proceed on normal commercial criteria, subject to what could be regarded as normal limits (e.g. conditions of work acceptable to the labour force, environmental protection rules observed, and so on). The essential point is that competition, the right of the user to choose alternative sources of supply, should normally ensure that efforts will be made to satisfy the customer. (True, in the event of failure, there would be claims for a subsidy and for protection, but this is a natural reaction even if the firm in question is privately owned: capitalists and workers hold the begging bowl together. Nor is this always wrong.)

A very different example is water. By long tradition, and rightly so, water authorities consider it their duty to supply water regularly to households, and this overrides profit-and-loss accountancy. No one would say: 'To supply the new suburb with tap water does not pay, so let no water be supplied.' Water is, of course, a homogeneous commodity, H_2O. Everyone uses it. Consumer choice is limited to such issues as fluoridisation. Consumer needs are clear: clean water should flow from the tap. It is customary to cover costs by levying a local tax or rate. Costs should be minimised, on condition that the above objectives are safely met. So, although water supply is a monopoly, criteria for water authorities seldom give rise to any economic or political controversy.

This cannot be said of a wide range of nationalised industries, whether these produce goods or services. Let us see why.

In most of the economy, goods and services can be provided in a number of different types, with quality an important variable. User demand varies too. So does the degree of monopoly power of the nationalised industry concerned. Of course, total monopoly is rare. There are usually substitutes, some close, some less so, some from private sources, some from other nationalised undertakings. None the less, some monopoly power is frequently encountered, and the larger the portion of the economy that is nationalised, the greater it is likely to be.

In this context we must see the ambiguities of such terms as efficiency, commercial operation, the public good. Labour and Conservative governments in the 1960s tended to see these three objectives as one: efficiency equals commercial criteria equals the public good, since the 'efficient' use of resources is in the general interest. Economic advisers were chosen who advised accordingly: subject to very general guidance as to objectives, management was to behave in the same way as private enterprise was supposed by the textbooks to behave, except that target rates of profits were substituted for profit maximisation. Investments had to meet a 'cut-off' rate of return, derived from the profitability of private investment, with due allowance for inflation. In the British experience none of this was done quite consistently. Thus some prices and charges were uncontrolled, in other cases the government's approval was necessary. This in turn was given by reference to different criteria at different times: on some occasions price rises were deliberately minimised, while under Mrs Thatcher orders were given (for instance to the Gas Board) to charge higher prices than the management considered necessary.

There was also very considerable inconsistency and confusion with regard to the division of responsibility between government departments and the management of the particular industry. The latter understandably argued that, if it was to be judged by financial-commercial criteria, then it had to be allowed to take decisions. It would be unreasonable for it to be directed to provide some good or service at a loss, and then be judged adversely because profits fell. It would also be unreasonable to judge it by the quality of the service it provided (e.g. fast punctual trains) if investments which it considered necessary for the purpose were disallowed by a government department because, in its judgment, it would not meet the target rate of return on capital. Similar issues were discussed at length in a NEDO (National Economic Development Organisation) document,[9] and the questions of mutual responsibility and authority proved extremely complex. The recommendations finally made evoked protest from management of the industries concerned, and were not implemented. I shall not dwell on the details; I refer to this only to draw attention to the difficulties encountered.

More important, in my view, is the inherent ambiguity of the criteria already referred to. It is a weakness of conventional monopoly theory that it concentrates attention on two variables only: quantity and price. This omits a large number of other dimensions, such as quality, punctuality, after-sales service and reliability, to name but a few. Many of these can be subsumed under the term 'goodwill'. In a competitive environment, if you have to wait in line for an hour in a shop, if the television-hire firm fails to respond to a call to repair your set, if razor-blades are blunt, if the steak is tough, then you, the customer, can go elsewhere, and the knowledge that this is so, that loss of goodwill is commercially damaging, provides the manufacturer or trader with a material inducement to satisfy the customer. Very few textbooks on economics mention goodwill (Samuelson briefly refers to the fact that it is a saleable asset, but does not discuss it in any other way; most others do not refer to it at all), and indeed hardly any textbooks have an index entry for 'quality'. The reason is not hard to find: conventional microeconomics prefers to treat each product as homogeneous, and each transaction in isolation; or, more precisely, they are related to the market and not to each other. The fact that one act or omission by a firm reacts upon the profitability of other acts of the same firm is untidy, unquantifiable, inelegant, therefore best ignored.

Yet in our context it is vitally important. Suppose the customer cannot go elsewhere, or the only available substitutes are inconvenient and expensive. Then there is no particular advantage in goodwill. We are back to some of the most familiar deficiencies of the Soviet-type system: it is possible to fulfil plans (whether these are expressed in terms of a profit rate, in quantity, or in value of turnover) at the customer's expense. Goodwill costs money and effort to acquire and keep. Under monopoly conditions this ceases to be advantageous for the enterprise concerned, whether nationalised or private. Let us recall some examples: a line of customers in a shop improves its 'productivity' per shop-worker, lowers costs per unit of sale, increases profits. So does overcrowding on public transport. It 'pays' to keep the customer waiting until it is convenient and least costly for the firm to send the repair men to put right that TV set. If razor-blades are blunt then, unless he grows a beard, the user will have to buy them more frequently. And so on.

To counter this it is necessary to begin by seeing clearly two things. First, that the conventional textbook picture of commercial behaviour by real firms is dangerously oversimplified and, secondly, that nationalised monopolies cannot function 'efficiently' unless their performance is related to *duty, purpose, function*. How this is best defined and enforced is a question which is complicated in practice, and varies greatly in different sectors. It is indeed difficult to balance these matters against the financial considerations which are also an integral part of efficiency criteria.

Let me give an example of the incorrect doctrine at its most extreme. Evidence was given to the Select Committee on Nationalised Industries of the (British) House of Commons in 1968. The late Denys Munby, an influential Oxford economist, observed that the head of London Transport considered that he had a kind of social contract with Londoners, and Munby's reaction was to assert that with such a conception it is not possible to provide transport for London efficiently, that 'it made no social or economic sense'.[10] Surely it would be more correct to say that, without such a concept, efficient operation of London Transport would be devoid of meaning! Imagine a firm operating a fleet of lorries to transport their own goods, and then detaching the concept of efficiency from the task of punctual and reliable transportation of the goods in question!

Governments in the 1960s and 1970s unfortunately also tended to accept criteria which downgraded the importance of complementarities, what could be called systemic elements, as well as externalities. Of course, their existence was not denied, and cost-benefit analysis was sometimes used to justify otherwise unprofitable investment, such as London's Victoria line. But these were seen as exceptional. Yet it is precisely here that nationalisation should show advantages over fragmented private enterprise. Instead, the tendency has been to fragment, to insist that each separate activity and investment should 'pay', to denounce 'cross-subsidisation' as evidence of misallocation of resources. One could describe this as the 'externalising of internalities', instead of vice versa. (Mrs Thatcher's government is trying to compel nationalised industries to sell off profitable complementary activities, but this is probably due less to incorrect economics than to ideological prejudice.) An elementary example will illustrate the situation in which denial of 'cross-subsidisation' is evidently fallacious, and at the same time emphasise the element of system. Imagine a railway or bus network that just covers its costs, at a standard charge. Since costs per passenger-mile vary widely, half of the network will appear not to pay, while half more than covers its costs. Are we then to close the half that does not pay (unless it is 'subsidised on social grounds'), or are charges to be varied in accordance with varying costs per passenger-mile? Either solution would be incorrect, because it disregards the indivisibility-complementarity aspect of the *system*. Investment or current operational decisions can be related to the system. Marginal decisions within a network of interrelated activities are multidimensional. Needless to say, it *may* be rational to close down some part of the system, but the decision should be taken in the context of the effects on the system as a whole.

Another British example of muddled thinking on nationalised industries relates to the Post Office. Ever since its foundation it has been run as a government department, directly under a minister. This is still so in most of the world, even in the USA. Why? Because governments appreciate that its functioning has a direct effect on both human welfare and commerce (printed catalogues, parcels, telex, etc.) which relates only very indirectly to the profitability of specific postal operations. In other words, so important are externalities (*and* cross-subsidisation) that it is considered essential to regard profit-and-loss as subordinate to its public service aspects. Who turned the British Post Office from being a government department into a 'commercial' corporation? A *Labour* government!

If even the posts are to be regarded as primarily a commercial activity (subject, to be sure, to the obligation to deliver letters even to outlying islands), if the criteria of the operations of nationalised industries can be seen as no different from those of private enterprise, then why nationalise at all? Mrs Thatcher's de-nationalisation fanaticism seems almost reasonable, if private enterprise criteria apply, and if the profitable parts can be separated from the unprofitable ones. Why, for example, have a BBC if its operational criteria were identical to those of the commercial television and radio network?

The net effect is that nationalisation has been at least partially discredited in the eyes of the users. Comedians can raise a laugh merely by referring to the British nationalised Gas Board's repair service. Many citizens believe that the deplorable unpunctuality of British Rail is due to nationalisation, which is plainly not the whole story, in view of the excellent record of the French, West German, Dutch, Swiss and other nationalised undertakings. Let me make it clear that it is not being argued here that nationalised undertakings must give poor service. The point is that there is much hard thinking to be done about criteria, in the course of which some oversimplified micro-economics needs to be rewritten or disregarded. Where competition is weak, criteria must give sufficient emphasis to function, to quality, to purpose.

So far I have only discussed the operations of nationalised industries from the standpoint of the users of their products, or the evaluation of their operational efficiency. Many socialists consider that of at least equal importance is the position of the workers in these industries. It is certainly of great importance, and a source of much misunderstanding. Let us therefore discuss this question.

Like so many others, the answer is complex and in some respects contradictory. On the one hand, workers in nationalised industries can be excused for feeling that they are not involved, that management is remote and in no way responsible to them. On the other, most workers and their trade unions regard the idea of association with management functions with deep suspicion. The job of managers is to manage, so it is widely held, while the job of trade unions is to demand higher wages, shorter hours and better conditions for their members. Any union official who joins management is widely regarded as having joined 'them'.

What, then, *ought* to be the role of the workforce, of trade unions, in the management of nationalised industries in the transition period, under a government aiming at some species of democratic socialism, and therefore concerned also with not being defeated, either in an election or by less democratic means?

We have seen, in discussing the Yugoslav model, that there exist some serious deficiencies in its kind of self-management. I shall return at length to the issue of the role of workers in management in a model of a functioning socialism later on. At present I shall confine myself to a few propositions of importance in the present context.

One must appreciate that the interests of the producers and the consumers are not identical and can conflict. Just as managers can improve their financial results at the expense of the customer, so can workers. It is, of course, sentimental nonsense to expect them to be less selfish than anyone else in society. Goods are not and should not be produced, or services provided, primarily to suit those who produce and provide. However, British experience over the past decades suggests that we have succeeded in making the worst of both worlds. The labour force and the unions have no responsibility, yet have the power to disrupt operations and insist on overmanning, the power also to demand large increases in pay without the slightest need to concern themselves with the consequences, including the consequences for other workers. Management thus lacks the authority to manage, while trade union power is used negatively as far as output and productivity are concerned, 'positively' to put up costs through wage demands. The Labour government was defeated in 1979 in part because of widespread disgust at union militancy: public opinion polls suggested that those disgusted included many million union members. The most damaging militancy was in the public sector.

Would the sharing of authority with the representatives of the labour force, or some kind of self-management, lead to a constructive and moderate attitude, or on the contrary strengthen the pursuit of narrow sectional interest? Much depends on the answer. Can the trade union movement rise above short-sighted sectional considerations, and support, or even itself initiate, a wages policy instead of a free-for-all? It is clear that in any socialist economy worthy of the name there would have to be regulation of incomes, as a pre-condition for achieving something close to full employment while avoiding continuous conflict and accelerating inflation (with or without physical shortages). Some mature trade unions, for instance, in Scandinavia, have shown that it can be done. In Britain the situation is complicated not only by ingrained 'zero-sum-game' attitudes but also by an antiquated trade union structure and lack of power in the central trade union organs.

Bienkowski puts the problem well in his excellent book:

> To link the prestige of the party with nationalisation, to present it as a panacea for all problems, can easily be the equivalence of placing a noose around one's own neck. After the seizure of power, it gives rise to political pressures for a speed-up of the process; it reveals, within and on the fringes of the party, forces (usually defined as 'ultra-left') pushing for action which contradicts reason and social interest, and may wreck the whole plan of evolution.

The disruption that this would cause can have grave political consequences if democratic institutions exist, since 'the masses do not wish to bear the costs'.[11]

Militant leftists would certainly denounce all this, in the name of an imaginary socialism. If pressed, they would accept that in the transition to the socialism that *they* envisage there would have to be an incomes policy, when purely sectional claims would be regarded as impermissibly selfish. However, the 'socialism' they envisage is some version of Marxist utopia (no vertical division of labour, the end of the 'wages system', a totally undefined workers' control and, of course, abundance; we have been over all this before). The super-dogmatists – I have a particular one in mind – would accept that workers' demands for more should be limited if, and only if, there were no 'elite', that is, no one was in charge, in authority. They do not, however, envisage producing their own periodicals without an editor, nor having the printers vote on their contents! Even if such a society were conceivable in a remote future, it is of course totally inconceivable in any transition period, whether under a democratic or despotic political system (the despotic variant copes with the difficulty by emasculating the unions and arresting strikers).

But let us return to the management of nationalised industries. They must be responsive to the users' needs, operate economically and with technical efficiency, they must reflect government policy where this affects them, they must conform to directives concerning objective, duties and standards and, last but not least, they must associate their employees with the decision-making process, so that they have some real sense of 'belonging', some pride in quality and achievement. More effective representation of the users, the consumers, is vital too, unless their interests are taken care of through competition, which is by no means always feasible. It is no simple matter to reconcile all these objectives. It will require great efforts by all concerned.

It might also require new thoughts about what should be nationalised, and how. These matters will be further discussed in the concluding, 'constructive' part of this book. It is sufficient at present to question the usefulness of the notion that one nationalises a complete industry and puts it under one centrally appointed management, responsible to the government. In some industries this makes perfect sense. For instance, electricity, with its interconnected grid, is recognised as a single system even by marginalists of the most blinkered kind, and not even Mrs Thatcher's anti-nationalisation fanatics have (at least yet) contemplated selling a profitable power station to private enterprise. But there are a great many activities which may be undertaken by separate state or co-operative enterprises, using or responding to local initiative, producing a wide variety of goods and services, in competition with private or state (or other co-operative) enterprises. Their relatively small scale makes meaningful participation much more practicable.

It is hardly necessary to recall that we are in a period of high unemployment, and also that technical progress tends to be labour-saving, that chronic large-scale unemployment contributes to social disorder, and represents waste of human resources, not to speak of its demoralising effects on the persons concerned. Rather than compel or subsidise state or private enterprise to employ labour surplus to its requirements, should there not be systematic encouragement of co-operative enterprise? Small-scale, de-alienating, good for training workers in running their own affairs. These could be based on bankrupt private firms, or started afresh with assistance in the form of low-interest credits, or the state could lease *its* property to a co-operative. Of course, like all solutions, this one does not lack difficulties. What of co-operatives that fail? How much loss, if any, should be borne by the members and how? Might there be difficulties with trade unions, and with private entrepreneurs in similar activities who might complain bitterly of unfair subsidised competition? Could temporary protection be provided against imports, using the infant industry argument? Anyhow, this can be an area of experiment, promising experiment. Do-it-yourself is not only a good alternative to unemployment (i.e. doing nothing), it is good-in-itself, providing opportunities for small groups to show initiative and develop responsibility.

The investment policies of nationalised industries could take effects on employment more directly into account. In Italy there is a kind of nationalised holding company (IRI) whose investment plans for one industry are consciously related to the effects on labour of the plans of other nationalised industries: thus the closure of a steelworks or a shipyard can be timed to coincide with the construction of some new state industry, requiring this kind of labour, in the same area. In Britain it is not clear whose responsibility it is to consider these matters. (Governments have a short time horizon, in Italy as elsewhere, while IRI remains in being, although it has been making heavy losses in recent years.)

One last point must be made, which is only in part concerned with nationalised industries, but has much to do with unemployment and with work-sharing: the question of shorter hours of work. At present, neither employers (state or private) nor unions show the slightest sign of facing up to the issue. The unions, it is true, demand a shorter working week, but insist simultaneously on higher wages, and their members (usually with their organisation's support) strike if lucrative overtime opportunities are withdrawn. Indeed, most demands for 'shorter hours' are consciously directed towards obtaining more and higher overtime pay. Employers also find it convenient to go on in the old way: after all, the cost of paying unemployment benefit does not fall on them.

The need for a new approach is perhaps clearer than the means of effecting the desirable change in attitudes of all concerned. Again, this not by any means easy to achieve, but not (I hope!) wildly utopian either.

It remains to stress that the above pages do not pretend to be a 'recipe' for transition to socialism. It would indeed be presumptuous to pretend that I know the path that leads there. All that *has* been attempted is a discussion of some issues, obstacles and problems which are very likely to be encountered on the way, together with the errors which appear all too likely to be committed, judging from past experience and the resolute refusal of many left-wing socialists to learn from this experience.

Apart from identifying actions likely to be counter-productive, a few positive steps could none the less be indicated – subject to many provisos and reservations, to be sure. A new approach to nationalisation, new both in its endeavours to involve the workforce and, where possible, in providing for competition. This naturally depends on the sector. It would be silly to have several competing electricity-generating networks (though electricity does and should compete with gas, coal and oil for heating). It is far from silly to have a state-owned shipping service competing with a private or a rival state line on routes – such as that across the English Channel – with a sufficient volume of traffic to justify it. Nor is there any overriding need to nationalise an entire industry, rather than specific firms; the latter has been and is the method favoured by French socialists. The advantage of encouraging industrial and service co-operatives has already been mentioned. They too would be operating in a competitive environment, which would or should concentrate their minds on efficient operation and pleasing the customer. As important would be the introduction of elements of workers' participation into the management structures of private corporations. Left-wingers are inclined to turn up their noses at the mention of West German *Mitbestimmung*, yet there is much to be learnt from it.

The role of the state as an investor could become particularly significant, and justifiable on non-political grounds, at a time of recession and mass unemployment. We see pressure in this direction today even from employers' organisations, anxious for some recovery in business. A moderate socialist government could proceed in this direction with a considerable degree of popular consensus behind it, and might retain public support so long as the public sector operated with reasonable efficiency *and* the whole strategy was not wrecked by the refusal of trade unions to co-operate. This co-operation might be conditional upon some restriction on distributed profits (at present the level of profits, seen as a major source of investment finance, is obviously too low), and control over investment abroad. But so much would depend on a whole series of 'unknowns' – the domestic political situation, the extent of recession and unemployment, the state of world trade, relations with trading partners and *their* domestic political situation – that there seems little point in concretising what are no more than broad indications of possible lines of action. Of course all this implies a mixed economy, with the stresses and strains that inevitably accompany it. But stresses and strains we have already!

Transition II: From 'Socialism' to Socialism

It is unnecessary to dwell yet again on the economic defects of the Soviet model. To these must be added important political and social shortcomings: privilege, a despotic relationship between rulers and ruled, the suppression of criticism, recruitment of the ruling oligarchy by co-option, the reduction of democratic processes to plebiscitary unanimity, and so on. The economic mechanism fails to respond to user requirements and generates far too much unintended and avoidable waste. Its centralisation faithfully reflects and reinforces political centralisation.

What could be done to correct all this? There is a vast literature on economic reform in Eastern Europe. It is now being added to by similar discussions in China. Of course, communist-ruled countries vary greatly in size, resources and level of development, and so it would be wrong to imagine that transition of the kind envisaged here should or would take identical paths. None the less, one is struck by similarities rather than differences. The USSR and China might seem to differ very widely, and the bitter political-ideological quarrel might be expected to widen these differences. Yet, when visiting China in 1979, I was struck by the fact that the proposals being discussed by the Chinese for reforming their centralised economy were very much like the proposals which had been debated in the Soviet Union in the previous twenty years. (I said just this in Peking in the presence of a Soviet 'China' specialist, who nodded his head vigorously in agreement!)

The first and major obstacle to overcome is the vested interest of those in power in the continuance of the existing situation. It is one which suits them. They allocate, they decide, 'they never forget themselves', to quote Trotsky. They enjoy power and as many of its fruits as they consider it politic to divert for their own purposes. Any conceivable reform threatens them collectively and (in most cases also) individually. Whether or not one agrees with those who see the ruling stratum as a 'class' collectively owning or controlling the means of production, they are the system's principal beneficiaries, and so a change must seem to them inevitably to transfer some power elsewhere – to other strata, or to some automatically functioning economic mechanism. The one sort of reform which might appear to preserve the centre's authority may be called for short 'computerisation': mathematical programmes would find the best way, the most efficient way, to achieve objectives determined by the top leadership. However, apart from the practical difficulties of implementing this sort of computerisation, discussed earlier, this too could threaten the power structure: it would enhance the role of specialists in programming, and as greatly reduce that of middle-level officials, who now play so large a role in replacing the invisible hand by the visible hand, *their* hand.

If the system suits the needs of the ruling stratum, why, then, should it adopt reforms? In a Western country what Marxists call the ruling class can be expected to resist changes in a socialist direction, but they are not in *direct* control of political institutions; it is therefore possible to discuss what would happen if political power were achieved by those who desire change, and in the resultant conflict it is by no means certain who would win. In a Soviet-type society the top political and economic leadership are one and the same.

Conflicts within the ruling stratum occur, of course, but they would surely close ranks if challenged from below.

Yet change is not excluded: the reason is that the system's malfunctioning, already discussed at length, can create a situation which is intolerable not only for the ordinary unprivileged citizen, but also for the leadership itself. Its own priority objectives become unenforceable, and among these objectives is the necessity to secure popular acquiescence, to satisfy the rising material expectations of the people. Failure to do so is as much a potential threat to stability in the USSR as is mass unemployment in the West. If the system literally cannot deliver the goods, cannot cope with technical progress, cannot catch up with the West, then those responsible for its management must look seriously at remedies, even if these remedies threaten many a vested interest. None the less, we must expect the ruling stratum or class to resist change for as long as possible.

One of the main obstacles to reform lies not only in the negative attitude of those who are able to impose their priorities, but also in lack of commitment to any coherent alternative on the part of other strata of the population. It may be thought that the managerial group favours reform. Managers do write articles which point to inefficiencies, and criticise excessive supervision from above. This may lead to the conclusion that they desire responsibility, and indeed some analysts even suppose that they wish to be capitalists. Unfortunately, or fortunately (according to one's viewpoint), this is not so. A few captains of industry may wish to be more independent, but more typical is the attitude well described by Aron Katsenellenboigen:

> They ask that the state set for them . . . (*a*) a low plan for output and a guarantee of selling any kind of products that they produce; (*b*) high expenditures and guarantee of supply of all necessary resources, including . . . the coercive attachment of the workers to the factories; (*c*) freedom for activities inside the enterprises.[12]

In other words, many managers seek a quiet life, have not the slightest desire, or aptitude, for facing the cold winds of markets or (God forbid!) competition. They do, however, desire more authority over their subordinates, security and, of course, promotion. This last point is overlooked by those analysts who imagine that they wish for ownership. Why should they? They are economic *officials*, within a vast bureaucracy. An official wishes to move up in the hierarchy, not to own the place where he happens to be working. The manager of a small factory wishes to be moved to manage a big one. The manager of a big factory can aspire to become head of an industrial complex, or a deputy minister.

Security in the enjoyment of the privileges due to rank is an understandable aim, no doubt, but hardly one which is consistent with the efficient operation of a reformed economy. So the managers should not be seen as a 'reform lobby'. None the less, some managers do favour economic reforms which enlarge their area of independence, from those above them *and* those below them.

As for the ordinary citizen, the worker in factory and office, he or she is in an ambivalent situation. Obviously they would oppose the management's desire to control them more tightly in the managers' interest. Equally obviously they are the principal victims of the economy's inefficiency: the flow of goods and services, their quality, the responsiveness of the system to the requirements of the customer, give solid ground for dissatisfaction. However, greater efficiency requires realistic prices which balance demand and supply, and in many instances this means higher prices. At the same time, greater mobility of factors of production, including labour, requires workers to move, which conflicts with widespread practices of feather-bedding and overmanning (which the management connives at, since the money comes from the state anyhow, and the extra labour might be needed to deal with unforeseen contingencies). Like his Western brother, the Soviet worker appears to prefer both low prices and the regular availability of the under-priced goods; he would like to keep the advantages of traditional labour practices *and* reap the fruits of (other workers') higher productivity. Therefore, far from there being a workers' 'lobby' favouring necessary reforms, fear of hostile reaction from below may be seen as an additional obstacle to change, though, like those of the managers, the views of the individual workers naturally vary.

This dilemma can be studied in particularly sharp relief in Poland. The workers gained large increases in nominal wages, but with prices frozen there developed a grave shortage of goods, and a catastrophic rise in indebtedness and balance-of-payments deficit. As we have seen, this situation was largely created by a totally unsound 'boom' strategy pursued in the 1970s under Gierek's leadership. But, whoever was to blame, it became necessary to deal with the crisis. The free trade union, 'Solidarity', had an effective veto on any action, which, in the circumstances, had to include painful measures to bring nominal wages into touch with reality, i.e. to lower them in real terms, *and* urgently to stimulate higher productivity. This had to mean a drastic change both in prices and in the clumsy over-bureaucratic planning-and-management system. The ruling stratum which in Poland was reduced in 1980–1 to a state of fear and demoralisation might well have accepted reform. However, Polish workers had rioted and gone on strike several times to compel the government to reverse price rises which, on economic grounds, were not only essential but many years overdue. The logic of a market-type reform encountered grass-roots opposition. It *may* be that the key in Poland will be found in political change: if, instead of an unrepresentative despotic regime, seen as responsible more to Moscow than to its fellow-citizens, the hard decisions were taken and sacrifices imposed by a government seen as national, necessary changes could be implemented. Or they might be forced on the people by the military regime. But it must be added that the market-type flexibility which will be advocated in the succeeding pages is peculiarly difficult to introduce in a situation of acute shortage. There is a dilemma here: unless catastrophe stares one in the face the obstacles to change cannot be overcome, but catastrophe is not the economic climate in which the needed changes can be made. A 'Catch-22' situation, to say the least.

There appear to be two potential 'political' scenarios, diametrically opposed. In one, the central political authority becomes convinced of the need for reform, imposes it upon the middle-level conservative bureaucrats, and the rest of the population accepts it: this was roughly the Hungarian pattern. The other version relies, on the contrary, on the weakness and the disarray of the centre, on effective pressure from public opinion.

The above remarks have concerned political power and the will to act. But to act how? Which way forward from what Bahro called 'real existierender Sozialismus' to some more acceptable version of socialism?

Unfortunately Bahro himself puts forward a programme in which utopian features predominate ('overcoming the division of labour', and the creation of largely self-sufficient communes, etc.), proposals which have little connection with immediate practice. However, he and many other socialist critics (Brus, Szelenyi, Belotserkovsky, even, in his own way, Bettelheim) do stress one factor of unquestionable practical importance: the need to enhance the influence of the ordinary person, as a producer, as a consumer, as a citizen. This contrasts with a very different 'solution', defined by Katsenellenboigen as 'aristocratic', and actually advocated by another *émigré*, Yanov: the reinforcement of hereditary privilege, and the enforcement of social discipline on such a basis. It must be added that such an 'aristocratic' evolution is more probable in the USSR than 'the restoration of capitalism' by the 'elite'. They hold power through rank, and they understandably want secure tenure of office, promotion and the right to pass on privileges to their children. In fact some hold they they have gone a long way already in the achievement of these aims.

Rejecting this, we have only to consider, briefly, one other 'alternative': the democratisation of the planning system *without* the strengthening of market elements. The attentive reader will have a sense of *déjà vu*, or more precisely *déjà lu*. I sought at great length earlier to demonstrate that marketless socialism can only mean *centralised* planning, in which a large and necessarily hierarchical and bureaucratic organisation issues instructions, allocates and co-ordinates. Such a form of organising production can only have as its counterpart the hierarchical and bureaucratic organisation of politics. This is a proposition fully consistent with Marxist analysis which stresses the political and economic consequence of combining political power and economic management. Reform requires steps towards achieving a separation of powers. If a local community, co-operative, factory, or shop were to have the right to act autonomously, it would *have* to have the possibility of acquiring the means of doing so. Unless one assumes an impossible degree of self-sufficiency, two methods, and two methods only, are known by which these means can be obtained. One is by administrative allocation, with conse-quences already discussed; the essential point is that they then cannot obtain the means to act without a decision by a hierarchically superior and remote allocating authority. Whether it is called Gosplan, Gossnab, or a 'people's supply office' matters not at all. No means can be devised to 'democratise' this process, unless it is seriously thought that the allocation of 10 tonnes of metal, 1,000 metres of cloth or electric components should be voted on. (By whom? Where? On the basis of what information?) The sort of abundance, with perfect foresight, which full communism implies, can be excluded: we are referring to a transition which begins in the existing situation, which is evidently one in which not only does scarcity exist, but in which the allocating bodies justify *their* existence by the need to ration resources that are inadequate to meet known requirements. Radoslav Selucky, in his admirable book, puts the point very well:

> If there were exclusive state property in the socialist state, the proletariat would be left property-less, with no direct economic power, with no economic base for its class rule. In this case those that govern would have to be at the same time both the representatives *and* the employers of the ruling class. However, such a situation would be absurd.[13]

If dogmatists reply that 'all should rule', and then quote Marx on the Paris commune, where he speaks of 'self-government of the producers', then we are back to the centralising logic of the marketless economy. It cannot be too strongly emphasised that the dominant position of the apex of the political hierarchy in the Soviet-type system has a very solid economic base: a planning system of this type not only demands hierarchy but concentrates all major decisions at the centre, since only there can the separate producing units be co-ordinated, a coherent plan elaborated. So it is not only logical but in the spirit of Marxist analysis to see in the diminution of the vertically exercised economic functions of the political-economic hierarchy a necessary pre-condition of political and social democratisation (necessary but *not* sufficient, needless to say. The adoption of the type of reform here discussed by no means ensures any genuine democratisation). The only alternative to vertical subordination is horizontal links. But horizontal links, that is, between producers, and between them and consumers (either directly or via whole-saling agencies), equal production for exchange which (again!) is some species of market.

The only method by which means of production can be obtained, other than by hierarchical-administrative allocation, is by purchase, by contract with the producers, or through the intermediacy of wholesalers. As the Russians say, *tret'ego ne dano*, 'there is no third alternative', *tertium non datur*.

There are many reasons why the authorities have not accepted this, some of them bearing only a remote relationship to the economics of the reform model as such (e.g. the diversion of massive resources to the arms race); but one reason, as already stressed, is the very one for which socialists should advocate it: it loosens the grip on society of those in power at the centre.

The most immediate and easiest steps forward (in my view) would be: first, to relax the control of the party and state over agricultural production, and, secondly, to allow the creation of industrial and service co-operatives. Agricultural collectives are co-operatives in law, let them be so in fact, let them genuinely elect their own management and decide what to grow, how to grow it, what animals to keep, how to organise production within the farms, instead of being ordered about. This would require a more flexible, more rational price system, but not an increase in the average prices paid to farms, as these are already very high (owing to the high cost of inefficient production). Not even the most dogmatic neo-Marxists would seriously object to setting the peasant producer collectives free of bureaucratic control. (Or perhaps they would. The word 'market' is, for some, as the red rag to the bull, and deprives them of reason.) As Belotserkovsky correctly observed, producer co-operatives in industry and services achieve two objectives simultaneously. They provide greater freedom of choice for the consumer, and greater freedom of choice for the producer too: he can choose to join a group of his fellow-citizens and undertake productive activities on his and their initiative, or work for a state institution.

This, of course, implies competition: competition for labour, which would have greater freedom to decide for whom to work; competition for customers. The possibility of success will naturally be accompanied by the possibility of failure. As also in the case of co-operatives in transition from capitalism, this will cause problems: how and whom to penalise for failure. There will doubtless have to be trial and error, here as elsewhere. Since competition is seldom popular with those who have to endure it, there would be protests, with appeals to that aspect of the socialist tradition which emphasises co-operation (in the other sense of that word) rather than conflict. Yet it still remains to be shown how choice can exist without competition of some sort. We have already noted that Belotserkovsky sought to distinguish between benign and noxious forms of competition. He had in mind the contrast between, say, manufacturers offering attractive wares to discriminating buyers and million-dollar advertising campaigns to market identical kinds of detergent, or something very noxious indeed, such as efforts to persuade mothers in backward countries to bottle-feed their babies. This distinction may not be easy to define, or to observe in practice, but it is an important and significant one, and we shall return to it.

For the co-operative sector to flourish it would have to be able to purchase inputs. Indeed, the same can (should) be said for the state's own factories. They too should be producing what their customers, whoever they may be, actually require. What else should they do? These customers could be other state enterprises, co-operatives, consumers. In fact, no one, all the way from Brezhnev to the most far-out fanatic, can disagree with the proposition that goods and services are for use, should generally be those the user requires or prefers. *The* question, as has been pointed out at length earlier, is how to achieve this desirable objective. Is democracy the answer? Mihailo Mihajlov thought that it would compel the leadership to satisfy the consumers, for fear of losing the next election.[14] This view is surely mistaken. Were he right, it would be enough for the top leadership to be convinced of the need to produce more for the needs of society. They repeatedly inform us, in speeches and articles, that they *are* so convinced, that they desire nothing better than greater efficiency, technical progress, more consumers' goods and services, production closely attuned to user demand. Democracy is indeed desirable, even essential, for the righting of many abuses, and for determining broad economic priorities too. But, as has been argued at length earlier, the system is now so clumsy that the expressed desires and plans originating with the highest political authority are frequently frustrated, or produce perverse results, including unintended waste of scarce resources, and production for plan fulfilment statistics instead of for the user.

Surely the moral is clear. Whatever else is done, production for use requires a shift of economic 'micropower' towards the consumer. The contracts made, the purchases desired, should form the basis of current production decisions, directly and indirectly; that is, those who produce the needed means of production should also be guided by the requirements of *their* customers. So far I have done no more than paraphrase the relevant paragraphs of several of Brezhnev's speeches. The trouble is that he and his comrades continue to believe in the necessity of subordination of production units to ministries and party officials – a line of responsibility running not to the customer but to one's own hierarchical superior. They still insist on the overriding need to fulfil plans imposed from above. They still consider it necessary to retain the clumsy and complex material allocation bureaucracy. And, finally, they reject a price system which would be essential if any reform were to have a chance of success.

It must be clear that the only way forward is the one attempted in 1968 in Hungary (in broad principle, not necessarily in detail). It can no doubt be modified, lessons can be learnt from the difficulties which were encountered. *There simply is no other way.* A number of intelligent Soviet economists have been saying so for many years. They are aware, too, of the need for caution and for a variety of different organisational forms. Whatever may be appropriate for energy, steel, or heavy chemicals may be totally inappropriate for knitwear, canned tomatoes, electronic components and button-holing machines. Some decisions must clearly remain centralised. Also it must be appreciated that no reform can have a hope of success so long as there is excess demand, which now exists for both producers' goods and consumers' goods, with all its deleterious consequences. It would be important to define carefully the role of the central planners in the field of investment, and its relationship with the decentralised credit-financed investment which would also be necessary. New thinking would also be needed about incomes policy, the use of profits, taxation, differential rent, the avoidance of mass unemployment, the role of trade unions, forms of worker participation in management of nationalised firms, and other predictable and less predictable issues that will doubtless arise. Many of these matters will be discussed again in Part 5.

Sherlock Holmes can be paraphrased as saying that if only one solution of a problem exists, however undesirable and unlikely, then it must be the one chosen. The alternative may be to have no solution. The alternative for Soviet-type systems is to stagger on, in an increasingly ineffective way, with or without political change – or political convulsions.

It appears to me that the creation of small autonomous units, especially co-operatives, would be the most urgent and the most acceptable first step. Most of these would be in the area of consumers' goods and services, and would cover notorious gaps in the sort of 'minor' items Brezhnev recently listed as in short supply: toothbrushes, needles, thread, babies' diapers. Some cafés, a small rural bakery where there may be none, a hairdresser, a holiday home agency, a car repair shop. And if a good cook and his wife wish to open a small restaurant in Tomsk, might not the citizens benefit? Should the cook be treated as a criminal exploiter if he goes so far as to employ a youth to wash the dishes?

Horror, oh horror, will cry the ultra-dogmatists, the market is being brought into being, capitalism is on its way to being restored. Objectively, their refusal to countenance the only workable form of devolution of economic authority downwards can only reinforce the centralisers, the 'bureaucrats', the 'elite', whom the ultra-dogmatists also denounce. A perplexed and honest dogmatist once showed me an unpublished paper entitled 'The two antis'. He had in mind the proposition that one can be both anti-bureaucrat and anti-market at the same time. It occurred to him that this was inconsistent. It occurs to me that he was right!

I will end by again invoking the support of Leon Trotsky. Commenting on Stalin's bureaucratic central planning in the early 1930s, Trotsky argued strongly for the need to combine 'plan, market and Soviet democracy' throughout what he called 'the transitional epoch'. He stoutly defended the need for economic calculation, a sound and stable currency. Far from agreeing that collectivisation of private agriculture provided the means of reducing the area of 'commodity–money relations' (i.e. the market), he thought that, by reducing peasant self-sufficiency, it made possible and desirable 'the great extension' of such relations.[15] True, Trotsky envisaged the ultimate achievement of full communism in which they would cease to exist, and would therefore have strongly disagreed with some of the other propositions which this book contains. But we are dealing here with 'the transitional epoch' and, in the above-cited statements, so was he.

'Developmental Socialism'

It will not be possible here to do full justice to a vast and complex theme. Many of the deformations which threaten, or have accompanied, so-called socialist solutions have in fact been discussed already. Chile was a semi-developed country. But in any case many policies have similar results virtually regardless of the level of development. Thus price control, below market-clearing levels, leads to shortages and black markets in Algeria, Libya, Ghana and Bangladesh and would do so in Great Britain or France. The methods used to cope with the situation may be cruder. Thus in Ghana the military government, having decreed lower prices, proceeded to 'combat inflation' by whipping market women who were alleged to have overcharged. In some cases 'speculators' would even be executed, which had the predictable effect of making shortages worse and putting up the black market price to reflect the higher risk.

An important factor is the relative scarcity of planners, statisticians and organisers of large-scale activities. Far too often there are resolutions about planning, but vagueness about what precisely ought to be planned, how, what *kind* of planning there should be (indicative? Soviet-type 'directive'?), what mix of private, nationalised and collective enterprises should exist, what is to be the role of the market, of foreign investments, how foreign trade should be conducted, by whom, with whom, on what criteria.

Even in Chile, culturally well above the average Third World level, during the Allende administration there was total lack of clarity about planning, no effective power to plan even the so-called *aria social*. Market forces were disrupted, but no substitute for them was introduced, thus making the worst of both worlds. Serious study of the experience of other countries' planning was not undertaken. This seems typical of less developed countries. Also typical was the fact that in Chile a mathematical model was duly developed, by a skilful British expert, though the means to apply its results was lacking. In other countries the statistics upon which to base complex computations are considerably less reliable than in Chile. This, and much else, sets severe limits to the practical application of programming techniques, econometrics and other sophisticated methodologies.

To generalise about the 'Third World', in this or indeed any other context is a highly risky undertaking. Some countries are large, with immense potential, and already partially industrialised: Brazil, for instance. India's social and economic problems, and level of culture and development, are quite different from those of, say, Tanzania or Haiti. So anything that follows is bound to be inapplicable somewhere. None the less, the risk will be taken. So here goes.

A vital first question is: what kind of socialism, what kind of development, is being sought? A country could opt out of the industrialisation rat-race. It might choose instead to follow doctrines made up of a mix of Russian populism and Ivan Illich. Populists (*narodniki*) in Russia were a heterogeneous group, who shared the belief that Russia could follow its own road and avoid capitalism and its evils, finding inspiration in traditional peasant communal institutions. The leading *narodniki* (for instance, Mikhailovsky, Nikolai-on) were well acquainted with Marx's doctrines, and he in turn showed interest in theirs. It will be recalled that Marx had an ambivalent attitude as to the applicability of his doctrines in what would now be called less developed countries, as can be seen from the several drafts of his reply in 1881 to a letter from an early Russian Marxist, Vera Zasulich. Lenin and his followers strongly opposed the *narodniki*, and believed that Russia's path ran inescapably through capitalist industrialisation to a proletarian revolution.

Then there is Ivan Illich, who rejects the bulk of the institutions and way of life of industrial civilisation. Indeed, there is a case to be made for building a society which avoids industrial slums, the alienation that goes with large-scale industry, preserving where they exist communal customs and institutions. Then one avoids creating *favellas* or *bidonvilles* (insanitary overcrowded shacks) which disfigure the overgrown cities of many developing countries, or the urban ghettos of Chicago and places nearer home. What is so good about megalopolis anyhow? Keep out foreign Western ways, limit severely the import of Western technology, discourage or ban Western investment, cultivate the simple life, self-help in the villages, rural co-operation.

In a mild form this sort of policy has been followed by Burma. In a fanatical, extreme and ruthless form it was imposed on the unfortunate people of Kampuchea.

If Mikhailovsky-and-Illich 'socialism' is what the bulk of the citizens desire, and one can abstract from national defence problems, it would be improper for an outsider to raise doctrinal objections. An ideology containing socialist phrases can serve anti-capitalist, anti-landlord purposes. Foreign trade can be kept to the minimum required to obtain essential imports. Without the murderous extremism of the Pol Pot regime, this is a possible variant of the socialist idea.

The trouble is that many developing countries are past the stage at which this is a feasible alternative. Great cities already exist, the taste for the consumable fruits of industrialisation has extended far beyond a small group of landlords and capitalists. The upper part of the working class has already an aspiration for cars and refrigerators, or already has them. The under-employed, the *marginados*, want urban jobs. Who could attempt to 'de-urbanise' Mexico City, São Paulo, Calcutta? Besides, in many countries the rate of population growth makes it impossible to maintain, let alone improve, living standards without the growth of industrial and service sectors, without urbanisation.

However, here is the key to *dependency*. If development means industrialisa-tion, the country taking this road is necessarily engaged in copying the techniques and the products already developed in the USA, Western Europe and Japan. In this sense the USSR too has been dependent. This extends far beyond technology. Millions are attracted by the American way of life, often (it must be admitted) its more garish and materialistic aspects. Some might argue that this is due to Western penetration of mass media and advertising agencies, but this cannot be the whole story, since the same aspirations are extremely strong in the Soviet Union and Eastern Europe, and even in China, although the mass media are under strict control and there is hardly any advertising. Of course there was (sometimes is) also *political* dependency: colonial or semi-colonial status. But Celso Furtado, the eminent Brazilian economist, has correctly noted the dependency-creating effect of aspiring to the Western way of life. Naturally, it then becomes simplest to buy Western products, or, if engaged in import-saving, and industrialising under cover of import restrictions, to buy Western technology and know-how, and/or let Western multinationals in to do the producing.

Socialists, or indeed any serious analysts, must surely reject both the historical analysis and the practical implications contained in the doctrines of Samir Amin. It is simply not the case that the metropolitan countries 'have underdeveloped the Third World' (the phrase is actually Andre Gundar Frank's), unless one defines underdevelopment as a lopsided form of develop-ment which is linked with the world market, in which case the conclusion is in the premisses, as all development has everywhere been lopsided. Can it really be said that foreign investment, foreign-owned subsidiaries, the remittance of profits or their reinvestment, *cause* a country's development to be retarded? Retarded in relation to what? In Chekhov's famous play *The Cherry Orchard*, in the last act, an impecunious landowner enters with a happy smile, and starts repaying his debts. 'Look what happened! Two Englishmen came, and found some sort of white clay under my land and have paid me all this money.' Can it really be argued that the under-development of the then Russian empire was due in any way to these two Englishmen? They may have made a lot of money out of the clay, it would no doubt have been better for the host country if its own entrepreneurs had invested in this clay, but the fact is they did not, and the Englishmen did not prevent them from doing so, but got their opportunity because they were not doing so!

This is not an argument for the unfettered entry of foreign capital, nor do I wish to deny that genuinely excessive profits were made by foreign interests. I will come to these questions in a moment. It is intended only to question the odd way in which history is written (or rather rewritten, because Marx and Lenin both regarded the penetration of Western capital into backward countries as progressive!).

The practical conclusion of Amin's argument can only be: since under-development is due to relations with the world market, since by this route the developed countries siphon off wealth, and since it is due to this transfer of surplus that they *are* wealthy, why, the obvious thing to do is to cut off economic relations with the developed world. Since the West, the multi-nationals, in addition foist 'inappropriate technology' on the hapless Third World, then one should refuse to accept Western capital, assert independence, create one's own R & D base, and so on.[16] Surely this is a recipe for disaster, based upon an incorrect analysis of both past and present.

Of course, the Third World's many countries have had a wide variety of relationships with the developed powers. Who can doubt that colonial subjection delayed and obstructed economic activity in some well-documented instances: thus the British colonial government forbade Kenyan native peasants to grow certain cash crops, compelled them by money taxes to hire themselves out to work for Europeans, and so on. But even in this instance, one can hardly confidently assert that Kenya would have been a developed and prosperous country but for British colonial policy, or that its problems today are caused by links with the world market. Tribute from colonies, sometimes differing little from robbery (for instance, in India), the slave trade, plantations operated brutally with slave labour in the West Indies, these are indeed part of history. But it does not entitle one to argue that Jamaica or India is poor *today* because of their links with the West *today*, or that socialist governments in these countries would improve their people's lives by cutting off these links. Unless, that is, they opt consciously for what I have called the Mikhailovsky-Illich model, which Amin, Gundar Frank and their ilk do not do. *Because* these countries are poor, their intellectuals are not entitled to waste the people's resources on reinventing what has already been invented elsewhere. As Gerschenkron pointed out, it is one of the late-comer's few advantages to be able to utilise the experience and technologies, and learn from the mistakes, of those who came before. Nor, because of past crimes such as enslavement, can one assert that, say, Malaysia, Nigeria, Venezuela, or India, would develop faster, at lower cost, in some better way, by removing themselves from the world market, in which they sell, from which they buy. It is unnecessary to believe in the simple comparative advantage doctrine, or to accept Heckscher-Ohlin, to recognise that evident advantages follow from utilising the international division of labour. Once again, Trotsky can be cited in support, writing at a time when the Soviet Union could trade only with capitalist countries.[17]

But it could be said that now things are different, that developing countries can trade with each other, and with communist-ruled countries. If, as Amin and also Emmanuel argue, resources are transferred from developing to developed countries through 'unequal exchange', this would seem a proper policy for socialists. Yet this view can easily lead to perverse decisions.

Of course, two or more countries with similar governments and aims could and should collaborate, draft joint plans based on mutual specialisation, establish a customs union. Some are simply too small to attempt any serious industrial activity on their own. Few can match the achievements of such city-states as Hongkong and Singapore. But let us return to the odd consequences of accepting the Amin or Emmanuel doctrine on unequal exchange. According to this misinterpretation of the Marxian theory of value, when trade occurs between, say, Tanzania or Bangladesh and the USA or Japan, the latter pair of countries benefit from a transfer of values to them, they 'exploit' Tanzania and Bangladesh through the prices at which trade takes place. This is partly because the more developed countries have a higher organic composition of capital, and partly because they have higher factor incomes, especially higher wages, under conditions in which capital is mobile between countries and labour is not. Note that the argument is not based upon any analysis of the actual prices at which trade in fact takes place, or of any real or imagined adverse movement of terms of trade. It is, of course, the case that the exports of a developed country would, at the world prices ruling, contain fewer hours of labour than are contained in its imports from a poor country. Extremists of the Amin type argue, or imply, that this is indeed a cause (or even *the* cause) of the greater prosperity of the developed country.

Theoretical errors apart, these doctrines produce quite perverse results if used as a basis for trade policy. In the real world, many poor countries export a range of manufactures and import some food and raw materials, while some of the largest exporters of primary products are developed countries, such as the USA and Australia. Suppose that you are the chief planner of Tanzania and wish to acquire tractors and rice, while selling copra. Suppose that tractors and rice can be bought from, and copra sold to, the USA, the USSR and India. Which of these purchases and sales would be most beneficial to Tanzania? Surely, the answer would be in no way affected by the organic composition of capital, or the relative wages or profits, in the countries concerned. In what sense, other than theological, would Tanzania be 'transferring values' if trading with the USA and not transferring them in trading with India, when selling the same product at the same price? If, at the negotiated prices, specifications, delivery dates, trade with India is more profitable, then naturally India is to be preferred (and vice versa). Conversely, if India has a million tonnes of steel to sell, and could sell it either to Tanzania or to Great Britain, would it 'transfer values' to Britain and not to Tanzania, and so 'gain' more by choosing to sell to Tanzania because Tanzania is poorer and has a lower organic composition of capital? If this seems like *reductio ad absurdum*, this is because the argument *is* absurd if applied to an analysis of relative gains from trade. As for the causes of the much greater prosperity of the USA, it is worth trying to calculate what proportion of America's GNP, or profits, arise out of trade with the Third World. The causes of poverty are complex, but I doubt if even Amin would seriously assert that, say, Malaysia would become more prosperous by ceasing to sell rubber, tin and palm-oil in world markets! Or that the poverty of India and China is due to trade with capitalist countries!

Much more to the point are the barriers to migration, without which the very large disparities in incomes could not be long maintained. That, however, raises a host of other issues, social and political as well as economic, which will not be pursued here.

It may be objected that in the preceding pages I have not given sufficient weight to the 'unequal exchange' argument.[18] So let me briefly probe deeper.

I would not wish to deny the obvious fact that the advantages from trade can be unequally distributed. Of course they can. Of course there have been instances where disproportionately large profits accrued to Western capitalist concerns. However, the available statistics do not suggest that Western capitalists always obtained, or now obtain, higher rate of return on their capital in the Third World than they did at home (especially when allowance is made for risk). Had this been the case, then the forecast of Hobson and, following him, Lenin, to the effect that most manufacturing would shift to the Third World, would have long ago come to pass. There is, anyhow, a clear difference between an unequal distribution of advantage and an actual loss from trade, the latter being the implication of Amin's argument. There is also a good case to be made against those Western countries that preach the virtues of free trade, and then erect barriers against imports of Third World goods (to protect their own industries, beet-sugar producers, etc., from competition). This forces the producers to sell cheaply in the restricted markets open to them. However, the logic of this sort of criticism is that the West should live up to its principles, not that free trade is a means of impoverishing the poor and enriching the rich.

More to the point is another and well-founded argument, put by Arthur Lewis, for instance, in his contribution to the symposium held in Glasgow on the bicentenary of *The Wealth of Nations*.[19] Wages are low in most Third World countries primarily because of the low productivity of tropical agriculture, and its effect on the incomes and living standards of the peasant masses. (This is particularly clear in both India and China.) This keeps down the level of incomes in industry, in services, and also in those branches of the economy which export. It is not labour productivity in these sectors which determines the incomes of those working in them, it is opportunity-cost, the low productivity of alternative employment. Thus (the example is my own, the logic is Lewis's) an Indian lorry-driver is not less productive than the American lorry-driver, yet he is paid very much less. The same applies, say, to an Indian teacher. I have seen some highly productive Chinese factory-workers who were paid a miserable wage by Western standards, in no way proportionate to their skill and productivity, yet my Chinese hosts were concerned that this apparently miserable wage is too high relative to the masses of the still-poorer peasantry. The low level of wages affects the profitability of mechanisation, and, because prices are cost-based, also the terms of international exchange. As Lewis puts it, if tea were a temperate crop and wool a tropical product, tea would be dearer and wool cheaper.

This is so, but what can or should be the practical consequences? Emmanuel is surely wrong to ascribe the general relative level of wages to 'institutional factors', as if this level could be substantially raised by government decree or trade union militancy above the limits set by the general level of productivity. It would be surely absurd to treble, say, the wages of Indian tea-workers, to make them a labour aristocracy, paid three times as much as workers in other branches of the Indian economy. The consequences of this, or of an export tax, on revenues from tea exports are problematical. The chances of an effective 'tea OPEC' are not great. It is also important to appreciate that such commodities as tea are only a part of the export trade of the Third World, that many other items (minerals, foodstuffs, manufactures) are sold in competition with similar products made in countries of the developed world. American rice, even American cotton shirts, can be profitably sold in competition with the more labour-intensive rice and shirts of much poorer countries. It is not being argued here that international trade solves all or even most problems of underdevelopment, or that free markets will even out inequalities in factor rewards. Apart from the restrictions on labour migration already mentioned, there are examples of durable regional inequalities within the *same* country (Italy, Yugoslavia and also China),[20] which show us clearly enough that the so-called self-correcting mechanism can fail to function, that government intervention can be essential. This point was made by Myrdal over twenty-five years ago. But this is not an argument against trade; thus no one in Italy, Yugoslavia, or China can seriously argue that the less developed areas should be cut off from the more prosperous regions of their respective countries, even while accepting the case for discriminating in favour of the less developed areas. Similarly, we can and should recognise the special problems of the poor countries of the world, without asserting either that their poverty is due to the rich being rich, or that the remedy lies in autarkic development cut off from the world market.

A Third World country which seeks to develop under socialist auspices will clearly have to face the fact of dependence on foreign trade. In many instances it will be a growing dependence, as its import requirements increase. This has happened in countries under very different economic systems which have attempted import-saving industrialisation. An example perhaps unfamiliar to some readers is Hungary. In its 'Stalinist' period this relatively underdeveloped country launched a very ambitious industrialisation programme, and appeared to some observers to be aiming at autarky. Yet because many of the machines, materials and fuels were unavailable from domestic sources, the effect was greatly to increase the dependence on foreign trade of what had previously been a predominantly agricultural country.

A different example is Cuba. Given the size of the country and of its internal market, the strategy that has been followed relies heavily on one major export crop, sugar, which (because of the US boycott) is bought largely by the USSR and its allies, at a price which is favourable for political reasons, a price which the USSR does not apply to other countries of the Third World, or to its other allies within Comecon. Capital goods and a wide range of manufactures are bought out of the proceeds of these sugar sales.

While overdependence on one export product is risky, and arguments for diversification are strong, one has sympathy with Peter Wiles's remark, that those who on principle are reluctant to export primary products are 'returning the gifts of nature unopened'. If a Bolivian family can become multi-millionaires by selling tin, and Australia derive wealth from exporting iron ore and wool, then a socialist government must try to do at least as well, since it must be aware that its own development plans will call for more foreign currency.

A word on trade with communist countries. So far as prices are concerned, these differ little from world market prices, being, as we have seen, based upon them. Trade is most often conducted on a bilateral barter basis, with or without long-term credits at low interest rates. Advantages and disadvantages are mixed. Sales in the world market for convertible currencies enable one to use the proceeds to buy whatever and from whoever one wants. Bilateral barter ties one to this one supplier. On the other hand, this may provide a market for goods which cannot be sold in Western capitalist countries, either because they are not competitive or because of import restrictions. Low interest rates, if offered, are naturally attractive, as is the prospect of repaying the loan in goods. But one must look also at quality and suitability of machinery, and a whole host of other factors. It is not an accident, surely, that the USSR and its allies had great difficulty in selling their machinery and other manufactures in countries where buyers can choose Western or Japanese goods. The developing country which has, by force of circumstances, been compelled to transfer its dependence on to communist countries is Cuba. There is no doubt that not only the Cubans but also the USSR would be pleased if Cuba could trade with the USA; it is primarily American policy which prevents this.

There are other problems connected with foreign trade: currency convertibility, the desirability of a state monopoly of such trade, various forms of import licensing and tariffs, import priorities (e.g. a ban on luxuries), and so on. Choices have to be made, influenced (in these and in so many other respects) by such considerations as enforceability, smuggling, corruption, black markets, and the like. In many countries at all sorts of levels of development a big gap between official and unofficial exchange rates stimulates massive evasion with large currency holdings held illegally. (A friend in Chile who went into a bank to change a dollar travellers' cheque in 1972 was told by the bank clerk: 'Madam, do not be absurd, come outside and I will give you five times the official rate.') In Yugoslavia it has been found desirable, from the state's point of view, to allow some (limited) convertibility, even allowing foreign earnings and remittances of Yugoslav citizens to be kept in the Yugoslav state bank in foreign currency. (The limits on the right of Yugoslav citizens to purchase foreign currency with dinar are justified by the balance-of-payments crisis. The intention was to allow full convertibility.) This may make sense in other countries too.

The issue of foreign investment is also frequently a source of mental confusion. Indeed, this was rightly pointed out by so 'left' an economist as Emmanuel, he of 'unequal exchange' fame. He drew attention to the fact that virtually all developing countries, and even the Soviet Union itself, actively sought foreign credits of various kinds, so that they cannot be all bad.[21] There is, however, a very important distinction to be made. While the borrowing of capital from abroad, often related to the acquisition of foreign technology, is frequently found to be highly desirable or even indispensable, there are different ways in which it can be done. I could illustrate the distinction by citing examples with negative connotations, all from Latin America. In one, a Mexican economist was indignantly referring to the latest American investment in Mexico: a factory to produce canned dogfood. Orthodox economists might say, if the demand is there, why not? Socialists would be justified in referring to the human needs of the Mexican people, for whom canned dogfood is hardly important. Of course, the demand is a consequence of a highly skewed income distribution, and it is this, as well as (rather than?) policy on foreign investment, that should be the subject of action. Another example is taken from Bolivia, where I was told by local economists that the direction of most foreign investments was determined not by the Bolivians but by the American aid office. In another instance recounted to me (many years ago) American aid officials vetoed a Brazilian road-building project which they were helping to finance, until it was re-routed to avoid crossing a province of whose provincial governor they disapproved. The common denominator: that a government of socialist tendency should have control over the purposes for which foreign investment is undertaken, making it attractive for projects that fit into its development plan, disallowing others (by reason of social priority, import content, export potential, etc.). In some circumstances a state development plan can be set at naught by the decisions of multinationals and other foreign interests. But experience shows that they can be negotiated with, that foreign capital and the know-how it brings is essential.

A word about appropriate and inappropriate technology, a subject about which much nonsense has been written. Thus multinationals, cast always for the role of villains, are said to be responsible for introducing it, yet domestic capitalists also favour labour-saving technology. Partly this is due to the fact that the type of labour the technology saves is costly and (if skilled) scarce. Minimum wage legislation and high social security contributions are another factor. There is also the country's price and exchange rate policy, sometimes designed precisely to favour imports of capital goods. The problem arises because labour-saving technology seems to be the most economically advantageous and profitable. However, this does indeed present a major problem where unemployment or underemployment and large-scale imigration from rural areas call urgently for more employment opportunities. There could be substantial social external diseconomies involved, and so the adoption of technology designed for a quite different context may sometimes need to be discouraged, but imports there must be where the economic advantages are substantial. It is sometimes said that the USSR found the right answer in the 1930s, but I am convinced that this view is based on a mis-understanding: the Soviets bought the latest kind of technology whenever they could, but as they were short of capital (and foreign exchange) they used a great deal of labour-intensive technology alongside it (e.g. for materials-handling) and in non-priority industries.

These things have to be paid for. Evidently, as in all things, one tries to secure the best possible terms, to ensure that the advantage exceeds the expenditures, whether the latter take the form of profit remittances, interest payments, cost of know-how, or whatever. One should not then claim that the poverty of the country is due to this 'extraction of surplus'. Obviously a country would be better off if borrowed capital (and imports of machines and raw materials and food) were supplied free. There are times when some Western countries must feel that *this* is what is meant by a 'new' international economic order!

Such issues as commodity agreements, the desirability or possibility of an 'OPEC' for commodities other than oil, and many other matters of evident current importance would take us far from our subject, and so are left aside.

A socialist development plan – with socialism itself a very distant prospect, however defined – is a subject for several books. So much depends on size, resources and political circumstances. One thing to be learnt from Cuba is the possibility (evidently also the high priority) of a drive for universal literacy where illiteracy is widespread. A development plan mobilising domestic and borrowed foreign resources must in no circumstances become a 'leap forward'; Soviet experience in the early 1930s, China's in the late 1950s, point to the acute dangers of over-enthusiasm, of plunging into unsound projects at the cost of much disorganisation, waste and human suffering. However, conventional microcriteria, linked as they are with incremental decisions, are of only limited use. It is a major challenge to the economics profession to devise dynamic long-term criteria, linked with a 'strategy of economic development', to quote the title of Albert O. Hirschman's book. The strategy recommended by Hirschman includes what he called 'unbalanced growth'. This can be misunderstood. Hirschman himself thought that the Soviet development model was one of *balanced* growth, in the sense of input-output consistency. The implication of his argument is that in a Soviet-type planned economy there is no need for deliberately creating imbalances, as a stimulus for further action. Yet his approach is in fact applicable to the Soviet model too. There were not only extreme imbalances between sectors, with consumers' goods, agriculture and housing neglected, but the Stalin type of plan also contained deliberately unbalanced elements, to act as a goad to action, to mobilise the party and state apparatus to overcome bottlenecks. The potential weakness of this approach is that in practice the pursuit of 'creative' imbalance might justify plans so unbalanced as to cause chaos, of the Chinese great-leap-forward type, or as in Poland in 1971–5. However, the underlying idea is correct. It is unrealistic to assume that the planners, politicians, managers, of any Third World country (other countries too!) will not need prodding and cajoling. One purpose, and not the least, of a long-term plan is its public relations aspect: it has a mobilising function. Enthusiasm is an important element for success; hence the value of ideological appeals and socialist phraseology. It was Gerschenkron who acutely observed that late-comers to industrialisation, where many of its 'natural' pre-conditions are lacking, require a conscious ideology.[22] In some countries this was nationalism, and a pioneer of 'national economics' was List in Germany, 150 years ago.

This is not the place even to begin to discuss planning techniques, let alone the actual content of any plan. Several points, however, are worth making, albeit briefly.

The first is that the word 'planning' may mean several different things: Soviet-type directive planning, with administrative allocation of inputs; or planning confined to the major investment decisions of structural importance;

or some permutation and combination of these. Linked with this question is one on the role of private and co-operative enterprise, in industry, crafts, agriculture, wholesale and retail trade.

Here I must admit to strong personal views. In most developing countries a mixed economy is infinitely preferable, and its logic needs to be carefully studied. By all means let the 'commanding heights' be in the hands of the state, as was the case in the NEP period in Soviet Russia. Large-scale industry, the big mines, the marketing abroad of the principal products, banking, say, but *not* small-scale industry, trade, restaurants, miscellaneous services. (Note that this is the conclusion reached by the Chinese leadership, which has criticised 'the premature transition to a higher stage of ownership' (see above).) The attempt to impose a state monopoly is bound to cause grave discontent and great inefficiency, frustrating grass-roots enterprise and causing a mushrooming growth of petty (and probably corruptible) bureaucracy. If a Marxist dogmatist objects to such arguments, I would repeat and underline the fact that *Marx nowhere said that the petty-bourgeoisie should be liquidated by a 'socialist' police*. The attempt to do so can only lead to a police state, since only by organised terror can a petty-bourgeoisie be prevented from arising when objective circumstances call it into being daily, hourly, every minute (to quote Lenin's words slightly out of context).

Similarly, agricultural co-operation is a desirable aim, but *in no circumstances* should it be enforced upon an unwilling peasantry. This again is a recipe for a police-state. As Engels said a hundred years ago, it is essential to proceed very carefully and patiently. Peasants should be led, encouraged, warned, but not coerced. Great is the cost of such coercion, in human misery and agricultural productivity. It is also a common error in many countries to equate development with industry, with the urban sector, and to adopt policies which have unfavourable effects on agriculture and the peasants. It can have unfortunate results also on the balance of payments: many Third World countries become net importers of food. It also neglects the interest of those who are usually the poorest in the community.

It therefore follows that a typical Third World country which starts to develop in the name of a future socialism should do so with a mixed economy, with some large state enterprises, and a great many private and co-operative ones, in towns and villages. Therefore the market must play a major role, and its logic, especially in the area of price policy, must be taken into account. The state is the major investor, and it may be proper to adopt or adapt the phrase 'state capitalism' to describe this stage, without using it pejoratively. But whatever one calls it, the delicate balance can so easily be wrecked by the wrong kind of price control. The consequences have already been mentioned in discussing the case of semi-developed Chile. Similar actions have been, or are being, taken in large numbers of Third World countries, from Algeria to Sri Lanka, usually for the best of motives. Inflation hits those least able to pay, and it seems simplest to control prices of 'necessities'. A big gap develops between official prices (at which goods can scarcely be obtained) and what becomes the black market. A political campaign is then launched against those petty manufacturers and traders who appear to be the beneficiaries of this, who are denounced as 'speculators', arrested, and so on. Peasants too find it far more remunerative to sell in the 'second economy' than at official prices to official purchasing agencies. This can be seen as a reason for imposing compulsory deliveries on them. Furthermore, in town and country, strict price control of 'necessities' in inflationary times inevitably means that to produce and sell necessities is less remunerative than to produce and sell non-necessities. (I recall that, in one such country, milk was unobtainable, but cream, which was not price-controlled, could be had in plenty.) Protests at this situation may be met by using socialist slogans to impose further limits on private enterprise, to impose production and delivery obligations on urban and rural co-operatives, to extend nationalisation more and more. The negative consequences on everyday living can lead to outbursts by discontented citizens, which can be suppressed if, as in Cuba, the police and army are reliably supporting the government. An election can be fatal, as Jamaica showed in 1980.

But quite apart from elections, which are rare (save in very tightly controlled forms) in most Third World countries, the object of policy of a socialist government must surely be to improve the lot of the masses, to assimilate them more closely in political and economic life, *and* at the same time to accumulate and invest capital. This cannot be done, save at very heavy cost in terms of human welfare, if policies are adopted which disorganise or paralyse the usually very large petty-producer and petty-distributor sectors. Looking at the experience of a great variety of countries, ranging from Cuba and Vietnam through Angola to Algeria, Libya, Ghana, Tanzania and many others, whose actions are influenced in varying degrees by socialist ideology or slogans, one is conscious of a mixture of motives. In some the destruction at the earliest date of the petty-bourgeoisie ('which generates capitalism every day, every hour, every minute', as Lenin said) is a conscious aim. They are tolerated for a short while, and the disequilibria engendered by 'unsound' price policies are viewed as a form of class struggle, the better and the quicker to get rid of noxious social elements. Such a policy has profound political implications, and is associated with Soviet-type despotic institutions and a compulsory vulgar-Marxist ideology, to query which is a sure passport to prison or the local equivalent of Siberia. But there are cases in which this is *not* the objective; the governments in fact favour a mixed economy, being conscious of the economic and political difficulties which would otherwise ensue, but they are driven further and further into measures of control, nationalisation and repression. As indicated at the beginning of Part 4, this is what can happen also in a Western developed country as a result of similar price policies. It cannot be too strongly emphasised that this conflicts not only with the interests of small and medium-scale private enterprise of all sorts, but also with the growth and health of free co-operatives, in town and country alike, since these flourish in a market environment and will wither if subjected to compulsory output plans and administrative allocation of inputs. This would be so in any economy, but, given the shortage of administrators, planners, statisticians, experience, the deleterious effects of centralisation will be multiplied in almost any LDC. For arguments in favour of the spread of self-management, see Horvat's article 'Establishing self-governing socialism in a less developed country'.[23]

If socialism is seen as requiring industrialisation, then obviously the requirements of capital accumulation will occupy a high priority. This must conflict with the aim of an immediate and substantial increase in consumption. From this standpoint the 'demonstration effect', i.e. the example of better living in more prosperous lands, can be a serious obstacle, especially if opposition parties can exploit politically the desire for immediate benefits. Capital accumulation by the *state* presents certain political and economic problems of which one has to be conscious: if there are no big capitalists, and if land reform has removed the big landlords, the state must raise money, and this brings accumulation into the political realm directly and consciously. Savings, sacrifice, become 'visible', felt as such by the people. This too is closely connected with prices: the nationalised sector, state purchasing agencies for agricultural produce, and marketing agencies for export, must provide revenue. (Of course, life is much simpler if one happens to be a member of OPEC and a major recipient of oil revenues!) To take one example of a predictable dilemma in a country where agriculture occupies a large part of the population, pressure from the peasants for higher prices and from the urban population for cheap food can easily result in a very large budgetary subsidy to cover the difference, which is the very opposite of accumulation. (Stalin's method of coping with this dilemma, by forcible collectivisation plus compulsory deliveries at low prices, has a heavy cost in terms of production, not to mention its other disagreeable consequences.) Appeals in the name of national development and socialist aims to defer current consumption would be essential, and would (one hopes) be rendered more acceptable by heavier taxes on high incomes and avoidance of conspicuous consumption. This is not to minimise the difficulties. They are bound to be severe, but not necessarily insuperable. In any event, the alternative, via the extreme inequalities that accompany the kind of route recommended by Milton Friedman and Hayek, can lead to social convulsions, rebellions and repression. The choice is between difficult and perilous paths. There is no easy one. In many if not most Third World countries it is unrealistic to expect to be able to govern effectively while observing democratic procedures. Unlike, say, in Scandinavia, it really can be a case of *kto kogo* (Lenin's 'who beats whom'), with dangers of military *pronunciamentos*, assassination squads and other highly *un*democratic procedures on the part of the opposition. Here again there are wide variations between countries – compare India with Salvador – and it would be quite pointless to generalise, while being aware of the political hazards that attend any advance towards laying socialist foundations.

Notes: Part 4

1 K. Marx; 'The German ideology', in *Collected Works*, Vol. V (London: Lawrence & Wishart, 1976), pp. 48–9; and F. Engels, 'The peasant war in Germany'.

2 *Surviving Failures*, ed. Bo Persson (Stockholm: Almqvist & Wiksell, 1980).

3 A. Nove, 'The political economy of the Allende regime', in *Allende's Chile*, ed. P. O'Brien (New York: Praeger, 1976).

4 Eric Olin Wright, in *New Left Review*, no. 98; see also T. C. Bruneau, F. Parkin and T. F. Sabel, 'Classes under socialism', in *The Future of Socialism in Europe*, ed. A. Liebich (Montreal: Interuniversity Centre for European Studies, 1979), pp. 243–98.

5   *Scottish Journal of Political Economy*, vol. 27, no. 2, June 1980.
6   *Cambridge Journal of Economics*, no. 5, 1981.
7   See S. Griffith-Jones, *The Role of Finance in the Transition to Socialism* (London: Frances Pinter, 1981); the author analyses the experience of Chile and the Soviet Union, as well as that of Czechoslovakia.
8   *Efficiency Criteria for the Nationalised Industries* (London: Allen & Unwin, 1973); also in *Public Enterprise Policy*, ed. P. K. Basu and A. Nove (Kuala Lumpur: APDAC, 1978), partially reprinted in *Acta Oeconomica* (Budapest), vol. 20, 1978, pp. 83–105.
9   NEDO, *Report on Nationalised Industries* (London: HMSO, 1977).
10 *First Report of Select Committee on Nationalised Industries*, Vol. II (London: HMSO, 1968).
11 W. Bienkowski, *Theory and Reality* (London: Allison & Busby, 1981), p. 284.
12 A. Katsenellenboigen, 'Some notes on vertical and horizontal economic mechanisms', unpublished paper kindly supplied by its author.
13 R. Selucky, *Marxism, Socialism and Freedom* (London: Macmillan, 1979), p. 70.
14 M. Mihajlov in his *SSSR i demokraticheskiye alternativy* (Achberg: Achberger Verlag, 1976), p. 46.
15 Trotsky's ideas are discussed, with many quotations, by A. Nove, in *Slavic Review*, Spring 1981, and again in a paper, 'Trotsky on collectivisation and the five-year plans', Fondazione Feltrinelli, 1981.
16 Samir Amin, *Accumulation on a World Scale* (Hassocks: Harvester, 1974) and *Unequal Development* (Hassocks: Harvester, 1976). For a devastating critique from the left, see Sheila Smith, 'The ideas of Samir Amin: theory or tautology?', *Journal of Development Studies*, October 1980. For a different 'radical' interpretation, see A. G. Frank, *Capitalism and Underdevelopment in Latin America* (Harmondsworth: Penguin, 1971).
17 On Trotsky's changing views on foreign trade, see in particular Richard B. Day, *Trotsky and the Politics of Economic Isolation* (Cambridge: Cambridge University Press, 1973).
18 Interested readers should, of course, refer to A. Emmanuel, *Unequal Exchange* (New York: Monthly Review Press, 1972), and *Unequal Exchange Revisited* (Brighton: Institute of Development Studies, 1975).
19 Lewis's paper is in *The Market and the State*, ed. A. S. Skinner and T. Wilson (Oxford: Clarendon Press, 1976).
20 China's regional inequalities are stressed in *Beijing Review*, 10 August 1981.
21 *New Left Review*, no. 73, 1972, pp. 56–7.
22 A. Gerschenkron, *Economic Backwardness in Historical Perspective* (Cambridge, Mass.: Harvard University Press, 1962).
23 *Economic Analysis and Workers' Self-Management*, nos. 1–2, 1978.

Part 5

Feasible Socialism?

Some Social-Political Assumptions

At long last, it seems possible to pass to a picture of a possible socialism. Let me recapitulate: by possible or feasible I mean a state of affairs which could exist in some major part of the developed world within the lifetime of a child already conceived, without our having to make or accept implausible or far-fetched assumptions about society, human beings and the economy. This means, surely, that we exclude abundance (in the sense of supply balancing demand at zero price, the disappearance of opportunity-cost). We naturally assume that the state will exist; indeed it will have major politico-economic functions. The state cannot be run meaningfully by all its citizens, and so there is bound to be a division between governors and governed. Also ships will have captains, newspapers will have editors, factories will have managers, planning offices will have chiefs, and so there is bound to be the possibility of abuse of power, and therefore a necessity to devise institutions that minimise this danger.

In this section I shall abstract from the problems of transition which were discussed earlier. Needless to say, there will be political and social obstacles to overcome and, in the course of overcoming them, many ideas (including my own) would doubtless be substantially modified. In no circumstances should the pages that follow be seen as some sort of blueprint, which would be quite beyond my powers and intentions. They are no more than a sketch, a try-out of a few ideas, related to the previous analysis of both practice and theory. As already indicated, there seems no point in imagining a society without contradictions, or some sort of final golden age of universal freedom, harmony and prosperity. Technology changes rapidly, human needs evolve. It may even be that the elimination of certain tensions creates new conflicts: thus the absence of struggle and strife can lead to boredom, and boredom could be a source of social disorder. (Some fanatics in the USSR in the early 1920s were so consistently opposed to all forms of competition that they campaigned against football, preferring communal gymnastic exercises, but eventually commonsense did prevail.[1] If not even in games can there be winners or losers, some would surely find alternative 'kicks' from drink or drugs.)

Political assumption: a multiparty democracy, with periodic elections to a parliament. The only known way to prevent the formation of parties is to ban them. The notion that several parties are needed only when there are separate social classes is clearly false. On the evils of an imposed one-party system it is hardly necessary to comment. Except in moments of crisis or civil war, parties must not be banned. If parties are not needed or wanted, they will wither away, and individual 'independents' will be elected on personal merit. But this is not likely. The electorate needs to be presented with alternatives, including different economic policies, priorities, strategies, in an organised way. How else, except through parties, with perhaps occasional referendums on issues which lend themselves to this procedure. Should the parliament consist of professional politicians, or part-timers who have normal jobs in factory, office, or farm? The choice depends on what functions the parliament is to perform. Dogmatists unthinkingly opt for the 'worker from the bench', with frequent rotation and recall, and then imagine the elected assembly exercising the tightest control over everyday affairs, which is plainly impossible if its members main occupations are outside the assembly. Or there could be a mixture, with a core of 'professionals' who are members of standing committees who report to plenary sessions.

Enterprises, Markets and Competition

There have been surprisingly few attempts to sketch out a model of the kind that is being attempted here.

Such intelligent Marxists as Rosa Luxemburg devoted considerable skill to discussing aspects of capitalism, and had much to say about the role of the working class in revolution, but she nowhere systematically discussed a socialist economy and how it might operate. Barone's critical remarks, referred to in Part 1, fell on deaf ears. Karl Kautsky, considered in his day *the* orthodox Marxist, did little more than re-state what appeared at the time to be the ideas of Marx and Engels on these questions. His ideas appeared in English in his book *The Class Struggle* (published in Chicago in 1910), and in numerous works in German. There is a succinct and clear exposition of these ideas in Selucky's book, already cited. Kautsky interpreted Marx's not-always-clear statements about socialist productive relations as clearly implying what he called 'a single gigantic industrial concern in which the same principles would have to prevail as in any large industrial establishment', and that production would be for use, not for exchange, i.e. there would be no markets, no commodity production. He duly noted that 'socialist production is irreconcilable with the full freedom of labour, that is, with the freedom of the labourer to work when, where and how he wills'. So he seemed to anticipate the ideas on this subject of Trotsky and Bukharin. However, he believed in political democracy, and strongly opposed Trotsky and Bukharin, and particularly Lenin, when the Bolsheviks seized power. Lenin wrote a furious pamphlet to denounce 'the renegade Kautsky', and Kautsky would doubtless have strongly criticised Stalinist centralised planning had he lived to see it. But all in all it cannot be said that Kautsky developed original ideas of his own on our subject. Another German socialist, Otto Neurath, discussed a socialist economy in a book, *Vollsozialisierung*, but this too took the argument no further. Kautsky's and Neurath's work was known to some at least of the participants in the seminar which discussed models of a non-market, moneyless socialist economy in Petrograd and Moscow in 1919–20. I mentioned these discussions, and the cul-de-sac into which they led, in Part 1 of this book. It is astonishing to note how very few other Marxists tackled these problems, at least until Oskar Lange, and indeed how few have tried to do so subsequently. In the USSR the controversies of the 1920s concentrated understandably on the immediate issues of the time ('primitive socialist accumulation', growth strategy, genetic versus teleological planning), apart from a debate on the law of value under socialism, in which, as we have seen, the majority took the view that it could not exist, without seriously discussing what *would* exist. The triumph of Stalinism snuffed out all serious theoretical discussion, and most of the participants also. I would not wish to denigrate the very interesting work of Dobb and of Dickinson, but they do not seem to me to have produced a coherent model of what a socialist economy might be like. Lerner's *Economics of Control* examined the possibilities of decentralisation and reached conclusions broadly similar to Lange's. Bahro has already been discussed, and so has Šik. Selucky's ideas have had some influence on my presentation, and so have those of Brus.

But let us start, so to speak, from scratch, by asking some elementary and fundamental questions.

How should production be organised? First of all, what *categories of producers* of goods and services should exist, what forms of property in means of production?

Several ideas come together here. The first is the need for variety, and for opportunities for individual and group initiative. We must bear in mind the need to avoid or minimise the feeling of alienation, and take into account *producers' preferences*. As already argued, while consumer preferences, user needs, should certainly predominate in determining what to produce, the preferences of the workforce should play a major role in determining how it should be produced, bearing in mind the need for economy of resources and the technology available. Of course, in the real world 'how' and 'what' can overlap. Thus railwaymen may prefer not to run a late-night train, to the detriment of suburban theatre-goers, and one then needs to reconcile conflicting interests.

An important and highly relevant point was made by André Gorz. This relates to diseconomies of scale, from the standpoint of the producer, the worker. The bigger the unit in which he is working, the more he is likely to feel alienated, remote from management decisions, a minor cog in a big machine. He is surely right that this question of scale, rather than just ownership, can be decisive. From this standpoint, 'small is beautiful' (Gorz, in his French book, quotes these words in English; they come, of course, from Schumacher). He goes a little too far, perhaps influenced by Ivan Illich, in his belief in do-it-yourself as the basis of producers' satisfaction; in his version, the state's industries should aim at providing the means for all kinds of domestic production for use, such as parts for home assembly of radios. No doubt such things are desirable, but many citizens are both unattracted by and incapable of technology in the home, so this can be one of the wide range of possibilities. Gorz is no fanatic, he well realises that economies of scale exist too and cannot, for certain productive activities, be ignored save at prohibitive cost. He therefore accepts that some branches must continue to produce on a large scale: electricity generation, say, heavy chemicals, steel, oil, to name a few. His idea is that workers should take turns to work in such industries as these, and devote to them as few hours as modern technology makes possible, so as to fulfil themselves in small-scale activities. He does not make it clear how the small units are to interrelate. His approach implies a market, but he does not spell this out. (I wrote to him to ask, but he did not reply.)[2]

Human beings vary greatly in the way they like to work. Some seek responsibility and are good organisers, others work better as individuals, still others are happiest in a small team, and so on. Technological economies of scale do indeed differ widely in different activities. Everyone benefits from large-scale generation of electricity, it would be idiotic to decree that every household fetch water from wells, or that pipelines be condemned as inappropriate labour-saving technology, when the only alternative is little men with buckets running across the desert. Gorz is right in his formulation: if large scale offers only a modest saving in costs, one's predisposition should be to opt for small scale, on just the grounds that he advances. Let 'small is beautiful' be an operational guideline in choice of techniques, to be preferred if *ceteris* are almost *paribus*. But be it noted that 'small' means a small number of workers, which may not imply labour-intensive techniques. Sometimes a small number can do the job only if highly labour-saving technology is used. The choice must depend on whether shortage of labour or unemployment is the main problem, and whether the labour that is saved is agreeable or disagreeable, skilled or repetitively boring.

All the above implies the coexistence of a very wide variety of scale, technique and, consequently, of organisation, indeed of production relations.

Radoslav Selucky opts for what he calls 'social ownership', with 'means of production managed by those who make use of them', separated from the state. He does refer to 'the remnants of the yet non-socialised' which would be 'fully compatible with the socialist nature of the model',[3] but this seems to him to be a temporary, transitional arrangement. He appears to envisage an evolution towards one type of producing unit. In my view it is possible and desirable to have several. But, in these and in other respects, it is essential to recall the assumptions of political democracy. The citizens can choose, for example, what sorts of private initiatives to encourage or to tolerate, the desirable forms of co-operatives, the extent of workers' participation in management, and much else besides. They can experiment, learn from experience, commit and correct errors. Successive generations may shift their predominant opinions and objectives. Nothing need be unchanging. Certainly nothing will be. Suppose that we have a legal structure which permits the following species:

1 State enterprises, centrally controlled and administered, hereinafter *centralised state corporations*.
2 State-owned (or socially owned) enterprises with full autonomy and a management responsible to the workforce, hereinafter *socialised enterprises*.
3 *Co-operative enterprises*.
4 *Small-scale private enterprise*, subject to clearly defined limits.
5 *Individuals* (e.g. freelance journalists, plumbers, artists).

The first group would include banks and other credit institutions, and those sectors which by their nature operate in very large, closely interrelated units, or have a monopoly position, or both. The most obvious example is the electricity network: wherever the actual power stations are located, it can only be the centre that knows how much current is needed and which power stations should be feeding kilowatt-hours of electricity into the national grid. Neither the manager of one power station nor its workers should have any decision-making authority over electric power generation. Similarly, a rail network, large integrated steelworks, oil and petrochemical complexes would seem functionally to be large *and* hierarchical. For example, North Sea or Alaskan oil require closely co-ordinated investment and production activities, involving a large number of different units (engaged in drilling, laying pipelines, pumping, maintaining oil-rigs, erecting refineries, operating tankers, etc.). Typically these are activities which, even in a capitalist market economy, are *administered* by large corporations, within which the links are those of subordination-co-ordination, i.e. vertical and not (or as well as) horizontal. In most such instances it must be supposed that organisational and informational economies of scale are of great significance, offsetting the extra cost of corporation bureaucracies. As techniques and computational methods alter rapidly, we cannot be sure whether the sectors which are dominated by large corporations today will necessarily be so tomorrow. Also we must bear in mind that some corporations are large because of the power it gives them over the market and not because of efficiency considerations. They sometimes take over by their financial power smaller units which operate quite efficiently. None the less, it seems clear that in my model of 'feasible socialism' there will be some very large corporations of this sort.

Some of these will have a strong monopoly position. This could be due to the effects of technological economies of scale, or these may be public utilities (electricity, telephones, posts, public transport, and so on) which of their nature tend towards monopoly. In Part 4 I discussed the problems of this kind of nationalised industry, and these must be borne in mind in the present context too. The relative absence of competition opens the possibility of 'improving' the measured performance at the expense of the customer, and this could be achieved just as well within a self-management model as by an 'autocratic' director appointed from above. Selucky, in his book, quite rightly stresses the need for special arrangements in such cases. He recommends tripartite supervision, with management responsible to the state, the users *and* the workforce. This seems an eminently sensible approach. Clearly there would have to be devised criteria of efficiency which take into full account social and economic externalities, and also systemic elements, as well as duty and purpose. Let no one suppose that this will be simple, or can be made simpler by some kind of socialist magic wand. Arguments and conflict there will be, because of both differences of interest *and* the ambiguities of many of the criteria. Cost-benefit analysis will help, but predictably not everyone will agree on the evaluation of cost or (especially) benefit. Thus I am writing these lines on a Hebridean island. The ship which serves the island operates at a loss. The islanders complain bitterly of heavy freight charges, and make the point that for them the ship is the equivalent of a road, or a bridge, on which profit-and-loss accounting should not (or need not) be applied. Those (like myself) who wish to preserve the viability of life in remote islands whole-heartedly concur. However, this implies a much larger transport subsidy, which has an opportunity-cost. Other claimants on limited resources will be less sympathetic. In the end the decision will be political, and will not depend on the 'commercial' judgement of the shipping line or the votes of the seamen who run the ships. Be it noted that shipping to remote small islands is almost inevitably a monopoly, since a ship large enough to brave Atlantic storms cannot be profitably duplicated (whereas the innumerable ferries which cross the English Channel can be separately and competitively operated; there is plenty of traffic to justify it).

But let us return to the list of categories of producers. The big state-owned units could be described as constituting the 'commanding heights' of large-scale industry and public utilities, plus finance. Some will be monopolists in their sphere, but it should not be an imposed monopoly. Thus if for any reason the state electricity grid fails in its duty to supply power at reasonable cost to all users, then it should be open to any group which thinks it can do better to generate its own. But even when there is no monopoly, it is hard to envisage giants of the size of a socialist Du Pont, or Shell, being meaningfully 'self-managed' by the workforce. Perhaps the best way to define a dividing-line between the state-centralised and the autonomous categories is by reference to the range of decisions on production which 'belong' at the level of the production unit, as distinct from the corporation headquarters.

It is worth dwelling on this point, which, at long last, is being seriously tackled in Western theory, for instance by O. Williamson (it is enough to quote the title of his book, *Markets and Hierarchies*), and one should also recall the pioneering work of R. H. Coase and G. B. Richardson.[4] Western orthodox 'theories of the firm' in fact provided no reason for the firm, as an organising entity, to exist at all. To cite again the words of Shubik, there was no difference seen between General Motors and the corner ice-cream store (or indeed between corporations and individuals). Very valuable ideas on this topic can be gleaned also from Kornai's book, *Anti-Equilibrium*, and from the ideas of Shackle and Loasby.[5] There are good solid reasons why certain productive activities are very large scale, and centralised. The manager of one factory within Du Pont, or Imperial Chemical Industries, or Shell, may have little or no more autonomy in decision-making than his equivalent in the Soviet centralised planning system. Why is this so? And how many of the reasons would apply also to a realistically conceived socialist industrial economy? One, applying particularly to investments, may be the huge initial cost, which is only worth paying if there is some assurance that there will be no 'duplicatory' competitive investment. The high cost of R & D is a similar point. In both, the firm is seeking to limit uncertainty, to be able to approach what amounts to *ex ante* planning.

Another reason, related to the above, is informational; to know what investments or output are needed may require the decision-maker to be at the centre. In some instances – oil and chemicals are obvious examples – the large firms are providing the inputs for their own processing and manufacturing, so that vertical integration is the best way to ensure the smooth provision of the necessary supplies. The above points must be distinguished from purely technological economies of scale. Obviously, if Du Pont (for example) owns almost a hundred factories and plants, its size cannot be ascribed to the need to produce its (very varied) output under one roof. To reduce uncertainty, to avoid wasteful duplication, to know in advance the user's requirements, to be confident of obtaining supplies of the needed specification, these are also reasonable objectives for socialist planning. We have seen that to try to include the *whole* economy in an all-embracing disaggregated central plan is impossible, self-defeating, inefficient and also in my view undesirable on social and political grounds, just as it is impossible to internalise *all* externalities. One can only seek to identify sectors and types of decision in which external effects are likely to be substantial, so as to make the task of taking them into account administratively manageable without requiring the creation of a vast bureaucracy. Similarly, analysis of organisational alternatives can show us which are the sectors, the industries, the type of decision, where the cost of centralisation exceeds the benefits (and 'cost' here includes the alienation and frustration caused by remoteness of control), or where the cost of *not* decentralising can be excessive, all this with a built-in preference for small scale. Such a preference, be it noted, is quite contrary to the Marxist tradition, as Gorz has correctly pointed out.

If competition is present, and production decisions 'belong' at the level at which production takes place, then there could be *socialised enterprises* with a major role in management for representatives of the workforce (co-operative property and private property will be considered later). Before discussing the forms this could take, let us consider the role of competition in a model of socialism. The word has undesirable connotations to many a socialist, yet, as has already been stressed, it is inconceivable to imagine choice without competition among suppliers of goods and services. It may help if we examine these matters more closely, recalling the distinction made by Belotserkovsky between benign and undesirable forms of competition.

Let us take an example from culture and education. Only wild-eyed dogmatists (they exist, alas!) can exclude it. Not every competent violinist will succeed in being accepted by the Scottish National Orchestra. It is inconceivable, outside fairy-tales, that every university will be equally prestigious in all subjects, and so there will be competition to get in. Not everyone will win the school 1,500 metres race. Only a few of those who graduate in any subject will be found competent to teach it to students – and students need to be protected from incompetent would-be teachers. A theatre competes for an audience with other theatres, by trying to be a better theatre. A scientific research team will seek to attract funds which might be allocated to rival teams. It seems to me that all this, *within reason*, is benign. But it can become vicious: thus we read of the Japanese children's educational rat-race, which creates misery and drives some to suicide. It was reported that in an American medical school some students deliberately sabotaged experiments by other students, so as to surpass them in the highly competitive examinations. One cannot define the difference in law, but plainly it exists. A football team must strive to win, but to set out to cause serious injury to one's opponents' centre-forward is, to put it mildly, improper. All this has its economic and commercial parallels.

In the Soviet Russian language a distinction is made between 'competition' (*konkurentsiya*), bad, and 'emulation' (*sorevnovaniye*), good. This does not correspond at all to the distinction which I am trying to make. One can cheat and perform vicious acts in the process of 'emulation' as well as in 'competition', and competition for the favour of customers is most definitely *konkurentsiya*.

Suppose that there are sixteen or more firms (socialised and co-operative) engaged in providing some one good or service. Let it be wool cloth, toothpaste, ball-bearings, holiday hotels, or whatever. They base their productive activities on negotiations with their customers. The latter can choose from whom to obtain the goods or services they require. All can obtain from *their* suppliers, whom *they* can choose, the inputs needed to make production possible. They have a built-in interest in satisfying the customer, and so no special measures are required to ensure this (apart from 'normal' regulations about pure food, non-adulteration, correct labelling, etc.). All benefit from this situation as customers (users). As already indicated, few producers actually like to suffer the consequences of competition. Ideally we want people to seek our custom, while we face no obstacles in realising the goods or services we wish to provide, freely choosing our own suppliers. However, having your cake and eating it is excluded by our realistic assumptions. It may be that most citizens will appreciate that others' choice is a pre-condition of the existence of their own.

We would all hope that the *motive* of competitors would not be primarily monetary: they would take pride in being the best, just as in theatre the kind of actors we most admire do not consider that they are in 'show business', and derive satisfaction from being able to play Macbeth with high professional skill (and therefore being chosen to do so in preference to others). Unlike the Soviet Academy, whose members receive immense material advantages, members of the British Academy and of the Royal Society receive precisely nothing, indeed pay a subscription. Shortly after the foundation of the Siberian branch of the Academy of Sciences, I met one of its founder-members and asked him whether there was extra financial reward for those who moved to Novosibirsk. He replied: 'We do not want the kind of people who would go there for that reason.' Schumpeter's words are worth quoting again, in this and many other contexts: 'No social system can work that is based exclusively upon a network of free contracts . . . and in which everyone is supposed to be guided by nothing except his own (short-run) utilitarian ends.' So self-interest alone is not enough. Similar considerations apply to prices: as Kornai correctly remarked, no one takes major decisions on the basis of price information alone. But we cannot assume that the mass of the population will act only for the satisfaction of succeeding, that there will not be a need for material incentives, and disincentives too. This theme we will take up when discussing incomes policies.

What, then, is undesirable, 'wasteful' competition, which socialists would wish to prevent, or at least to minimise? A whole number of examples can be cited. There are certain areas in which competition can have paradoxical, negative results. Thus if there were three TV programmes run by the same public-service-oriented organisation, there would be more choice for the viewer than if there were three competing networks, which tend to put on similar programmes at peak hours. A single integrated service of public transport may make more sense than separate competing units. But what most socialists regard with distaste, and with reason, are massive advertising campaigns, especially for products almost indistinguishable except for name and label, where the advertising costs become a high proportion of the final selling price. What can be done about this? If it is easy to dispose of one's product, advertising is pointless, but then one does not have to bother about the customer either, as in all sellers' markets. Kornai has rightly stressed the desirability of a degree of difficulty in selling. Then the autonomous and competing firms will wish to persuade the customers to buy, to win goodwill by quality and reliability, and to send round brightly produced catalogues suggesting that BLOGGS' WIDGETS are just what is needed. Newspapers would seek to attract readers, by publicly suggesting that *this* one should be read, naturally in the conviction that it is a good newspaper. It seems as impossible to ban this as to prevent a theatre from putting up posters advertising its next play. It can be called 'informational' advertising, and in part it is so. But it can degenerate into the more undesirable and wasteful phenomena: pseudo product innovation and differentiation, excessive expenditure on garish packaging, and so on. Perhaps one could devise a regulation limiting such outlays, on the lines of the limit on election expenses imposed by a number of countries (and perhaps newspapers should be prevented from attracting readers by printing pictures of unclad blondes on page 3; or maybe socialist readers will have no need or desire for such pictures, who knows?). Football teams will compete too, and again we must hope that they will do so without money prizes. We all know players who play their hearts out without expecting financial reward, but Soviet experience shows that football competitiveness which cannot be rewarded by open payment ('there is no professionalism') is rewarded on the side by highly paid part-time 'work'. Finally, there is competition for high political positions. Here again, Soviet 'Stalinist' experience shows that it is possible to 'succeed' by having your rivals executed on false charges, just as at a lower level ordinary citizens would denounce their neighbours to the secret police in the hope of acquiring their housing space. All this shows how the evil side of 'competition' can show itself in all spheres, economic and non-economic, with or without a market. It also reminds us how difficult it is to adopt rules which securely prevent the wrong sort from emerging. It will be necessary to try.

It is worth quoting an example which seems at first sight to be an argument *against* me. What of patents, inventions, technical progress? At least, so it will be said, where there is mutual co-operation there will be no commercial secrecy, all ideas will be freely available for use throughout the economy. If one has a market, with sectional interest prevailing over the general interest, then once again there will be obstacles erected to the diffusion of technology. There are two counter-arguments. One is the familiar one that, without the spur of competition, new technology might simply not be adopted, owing to routine and inertia (and because of the other reasons advanced above in discussing Soviet experience). The other is that to make technological information available is costly; if it is free, this means one is forbidden to charge for it, and so one does not bother to provide it. It turned out, in Hungarian experience, that such information circulated more freely if it *could* command a price! The dogmatist would reply: in a 'real' socialism everyone would pass on useful information for love of his fellows. Again, let us hope so. (The inventor of, say, penicillin would not restrict its use by patent.) But let us not build an economic system on the assumption of high-minded altruism; no more than, in devising a constitutional structure, should we assume that no one would wish to abuse authority. Never let us forget that people have an almost infinite capacity for identifying the (never-too-clearly-defined) general interest with their own.

Socialised and co-operative enterprises would have managers appointed by an elected committee, responsible to this committee – or to a plenary meeting of the workforce if the numbers are small enough to make this possible. The division of functions between professional management, the committee and the plenary sessions can be determined democratically by each unit in the light of its own experience, and its own mistakes.

The principal differences between socialised and co-operative enterprises in a competitive environment would derive from the difference in property relations. In the former the means of production would not belong to the workers, and the state would have a residual responsibility for their use or misuse, or for debts incurred (we will discuss the problem of failures in a moment). Whereas a co-operative could freely dispose of its property, and freely decide to wind itself up. There would also be a difference in income distribution and in liability to tax; of this too more in a moment. In general one would suppose that co-operatives in manufacturing would tend to be relatively small.

Finally we reach *private enterprise*. Presumably even the fanatical dogmatist would accept the existence of freelance writers, painters and dressmakers. My own list would be longer. Indeed, there should be no list. If any activity (not actually a 'social bad' in itself) can be fruitfully and profitably undertaken by any individual, this sets up the presumption of its legitimacy. Perhaps an earlier example could be re-used here to illustrate the point. Water supply is a 'natural' monopoly. If water flows from taps, private water-carriers are an absurdity. So no law is needed to forbid them. But if for some reason the water supply becomes unreliable, this can create a situation in which private water-carriers can make a living. This is indeed far-fetched (the example, not the water!), but innumerable instances of a much more realistic character can be cited. Suppose that there appears to be an unsatisfied demand for a Peking-cuisine restaurant, Fair-isle sweaters, a holiday booking agency, wedding-dresses, car repairs, mushrooms, sailing-dinghies, house-decorating, barley, chocolate-cake, or string quartets. Large state-managed undertakings are otherwise engaged. The smaller socialised or co-operative enterprises may or may not act; after all, it is absurd to assume that all opportunities are always taken, or that lack of enterprise cannot occur even in a competitive environment. (Mistakes can take the form of inaction as well as incorrect action.) Or perhaps an individual has devised some new and economic design or method of production. Why not let him or her go ahead, and produce privately for sale?

So long as it is one individual, there would probably be no objection, except from dogmatists so extreme that they are out of sight, away on the extreme-left. (They may be blandly assuming that under their perfect socialism the 'associated producers' will always provide whatever is needed in whatever are the needed quantities.) But there would be also the possibility of a private entrepreneur actually employing a few people, which makes him an 'exploiter', in so far as he makes a profit out of their work. This is illegal in the USSR today. It is tolerated within defined limits in Hungary and Yugoslavia.

I would suggest that, subject to limits, this should be allowed. Once again it must be stressed that Marx believed that petty producers would become unnecessary in a socialist commonwealth, not that they be compulsorily liquidated by the police. Thus a family farm which may be producing efficiently could employ a few labourers, a restaurant might hire a cook and/or some waiters, a couple of clerks could type letters for the holiday agency, a promoter could hire a hall and a string quartet, a repairman may prefer to work for a private garage, and so on. In each case, the 'entrepreneur' *works*, organises.

Subject to what limits? As already suggested, this could be decided democratically in the light of circumstances and experience. The limit could be on numbers employed, or on the value of capital assets, and could be varied by sector. One possible rule might be that above this limit there be a choice, either to convert into a co-operative or to become a socialised enterprise, with proper compensation for the original entrepreneur. Is this a dangerous loophole for the 'restoration of capitalism'? Not if the limits are observed. Is it a means of illegitimate enrichment? Not if the market and price mechanism are in working order. Obviously, if prices fixed by the state were too low, and shortages were endemic, the private sector could become excessively remunerative. Presumably a wise government would avoid this. But more later on prices, taxes and incomes. Be it noted that there is no provision for any class of capitalists; our small private entrepreneur *works*, even when employing a few others. There is then no *unearned* income, arising simply from *ownership* of capital or land.

Marx justly noted that competition is apt to destroy competition. Adam Smith had observed a century earlier that business men may conspire together for their own benefit. It is by no means excluded that self-managed enterprises can form rings or cartels. Both under modern capitalism *and* in the contemporary Soviet system there is a strong tendency towards mergers. This would have to be resisted, save where the economies of scale are substantial, whereupon the sector might have to be added to the list of those centrally controlled and administered, to prevent misuse of monopoly power.

What, then, of planning? The centre, in this model, would have a number of vital functions. First, major investments would be its responsibility. Secondly, directly or through the banking system, the planners would endeavour to monitor decentralised investments, conscious of the need to avoid duplication and the financing of plainly unsound projects initiated locally. Thirdly, the centre would play a direct and major role in administering such 'naturally' central productive activities as electricity, oil, railways. Fourthly, there would be the vital task of setting the ground-rules for the autonomous and free sectors, with reserve powers of intervention when things got out of balance, or socially undesirable developments were seen to occur. There would plainly also be functions connected with foreign trade. There would be drafts of longer-term plans, incorporating changes and improvements in techniques, working practices, living standards, which would be submitted to the elected assembly. It appears to me that the extent of the necessary planning would be greater than is allowed for by Selucky in his model; the difference is doubtless explained by his experiences in Czechoslovakia, and so by his anxiety to reduce the powers of the state to a minimum.

Another way of defining the functions of the centre would be as follows. In those sectors where externalities are likely to be significant, intervention is essential; it can take the form of regulations (e.g. measures to protect the environment from pollution, ribbon development, ugliness), subsidies (e.g. to public transport, research), the correction of regional imbalances, and so on. Secondly, there will be the quite basic task of determining the share of total GNP to devote to investment, as distinct from current consumption, and this in turn would affect the rules that are made to ensure adequate savings (either by way of taxation or through the use of retained profits of enterprises, or both). There will also be the far-from-easy task of combating inflationary excesses in distribution of personal income and in investments, ensuring as far as possible that the major investments that are made correspond to the expected future pattern of demand, i.e. that the perspective plans are balanced. The centre would have a vital role, too, in ensuring a balance between present and future, where the time horizon of both management and labour is too short, as well it may be: the theory and practice of 'self-management' suggest the danger of overemphasis on short-term gains, which it would be necessary to correct, in the name of the 'time preference of the community'. (Is the term vague and indefinable? Yes, but it makes even less sense today; who could seriously claim that in the present inflation-and-uncertainty-ridden economy the actual rate of savings and investment represents a time preference of any meaningful sort?)

Finally, democratic vote could decide the boundary between the commercial or market sectors and those where goods and services could be provided free. Education, health, social security (including retraining grants for those made redundant by technical change), amenities of various kinds (public parks, museums), the list can be a long one. I suspect the voters of a future socialist society would not wish to make it too long, as they (unlike some people today) would appreciate that free goods and services need to be paid for, and that the longer the list the smaller can be the level of personal disposable income. If people like it that way, they could form latter-day communes, and pay each other just pocket-money. In a less romantic context, when I joined the British army I was issued with uniform, mess-tin, blankets, palliasse, dinners, a tent was provided for me (and seven others) to sleep in, and I received one shilling a day (after deductions). This was 1939, and I would have change from a bag of fish and chips and a half-pint of beer. My French fellow-soldiers thought we were rather scandalously overpaid . . . I know the army is not a commune or a *kibbutz*. A minority, none the less, join it voluntarily in peacetime; they like having virtually all basic consumers' goods and services issued to them free. A minority also joins *kibbutzim* and communes. Let them do so by all means. But it is unrealistic to build a model in which the majority wish to live thus. So it must be supposed that the bulk of goods and services will be bought and sold, and therefore also the inputs they require.

The bulk of current production and distribution would be within the decision-making competence of the producing units, which negotiate contracts with each other. These would naturally have to be enforceable. It cannot be open to a meeting of the workforce to decide by a majority not to observe delivery obligations; there would have to be a penalty.

Mention of penalty leads us into a much-needed discussion of failure. In the Soviet system, one of the many difficulties in the way of enforcing obligations lies in the fact that fines, when levied, are paid out of public funds, penalise no individual, and represent a transfer of state money from one pocket to another. Then there is the equally familiar problem of 'socialist bankruptcy', or lack of it. Suppose investments made on credit from the state bank cannot be repaid because of a change in market conditions, inefficient operation, errors of judgement. Who is to be penalised, and how? In the utopian-Marxist vision all is clear *ex ante*, the plan is faultless through perfect knowledge. In the real world, too, many decisions are meaningfully taken *ex ante*, as when one decides to build additional power stations or signs a long-term contract for the supply of iron ore, based very largely on quantitative, input-output-type calculations. (These may prove mistaken, but infallibility is not a typical human characteristic.) However, the problem is more serious when autonomous units orientate themselves in a market environment. When groups of people are free to respond in a decentralised way to necessarily imperfect market signals, errors must happen quite frequently. Furthermore, competition implies not only winners but also losers. For competition to be possible at all there has to be spare capacity. So the unsuccessful will be unable to ensure full employment of their material and human resources; they will have an excess of expenditure over receipts.

Clearly, this is an inescapable consequence of freedom to act. Equally clearly, the 'punishment' of error (and the reward of risk) will be major problems, major sources of controversy. Inevitably there will be claims for subsidies, sometimes justified. There will have to be devised a procedure for winding up the outright failures, or imposing a change of management as a pre-condition of meeting the debts. Procedures will naturally vary according to the different categories of ownership. Co-operative and private activities must be expected to bear the cost of their own mistakes. At the other end of the scale, the centrally run state sector is plainly the responsibility of government, which would determine the price policy to be followed (which could involve, for instance, large subsidies for deliberately loss-making public transport, or prices far in excess of costs for cigarettes). There is no reason whatever why the workers in these sectors should either gain or suffer from the condition of the profit-and-loss account. Efficiency criteria will not be easy to define, but we have seen that these difficulties exist already. The most awkward problem will arise in the case of those socialised enterprises in which management is responsible to the workforce. Let us consider two likely sets of circumstances. In one, management initiates a production and sales policy which turns out to be a failure; why, the workers may well ask, should they suffer for this, are they not entitled to the rate for the job? Alternatively, management's proposals are rejected by the workforce which votes for an alternative, and *this* is the cause of loss. Should not the workers then shoulder some of this loss? This raises important questions of income distribution and incomes policy, to be discussed in a moment. Yugoslav experience is very much to the point.

Prices, Profits and Theory of Value

The logic of the proposed system naturally requires prices that balance supply and demand, that reflect cost and use-value. This does *not* exclude subsidies whenever these are considered to be socially desirable, or where external economies are significant (public transport, vitamins for nursing mothers, perhaps housing, etc.) and of course some items ought not to be 'priced' at all: education, hospitals, parks, and so on. Just what is to be available free of charge is a matter of democratic political decision. As already suggested, it is likely that a large majority would not wish (for instance) to be fed free, suspecting that this would mean that they will be unable to choose the menu.

Soviet and other experience proves conclusively that comprehensive price control is impossible to administer, that there are too many prices, many millions, as we have seen. To abandon price control altogether could plainly be wrong, given that there will be some industries centrally managed and in a semi-monopoly position. We return to the examples of electricity, oil, telephones, steel, railways, and others in the category of centralised state enterprises. Also some basic agricultural products should be on the list of those prices subject to central control; it is surely no accident that this is the case in virtually every country today, regardless of system. However, the large majority of goods and services can only be effectively priced in the process of negotiation between supplier and customer, the bargain including detailed specifications, delivery dates, quality, and so on. We must naturally expect the producing enterprises to try to 'administer' prices, and wholesale and retail organs would seek to obtain the 'mark-up' they regard as proper, but in the absence of shortages and the presence of choice the buyers can refuse, can go elsewhere, can bargain. In other words, competition should prevent abuse of producers' powers.

The word 'profit' is not always popular in socialist circles. Yet, if prices are economically meaningful, profits at micro level represent the difference between cost and result, between the efforts of the producers and the evaluation of this effort by the users. It is evident that, *ceteris paribus*, this difference should be larger rather than smaller, so long as the profit is not due to monopolistic price-fixing, though of course in no economy is this a perfect measure. It is the appropriation of profits by capitalists which offends, not profit as such. (Similarly, rent as an unearned income of landlords is objectionable, but differential rent must – as we shall see – enter into economic calculations also in a socialist economy.) If profits appear to be 'excessive' where there is no monopoly power, this may well be a reward for enterprise, efficiency and anticipation, and the entry of other producers can force down the price by expanding supply.

The Soviet economist Karagedov examined the role of profits in different systems with intelligence and imagination. He made one point which it is useful for us to take on board. He distinguished, rightly, between profits as a micro criterion and the general level of profits in the economy. With a given level of wages and prices, provided prices correctly reflect supply-and-demand conditions, profitability is an appropriate criterion for efficiency (other things being equal, and abstracting from considerations of quality). If it goes up, then indeed this is a fair measure of the difference between cost (effort) and result. But this ceases to be true at macro level. At that level, incomes (wages) are no longer given, they are a variable.[6] If one imagines a model in which net investments are financed largely out of profits, the magnitude of profits desired would be directly influenced by the level of required savings. In no sense should these be 'maximised'. The balance between consumption and investment (savings) is a political decision, and it would be no evidence of 'inefficiency' if it were decided, by increasing wages, to reduce the level of profits and savings. Of course, if an increase in wages is accompanied by a simultaneous rise in investment and other state expenditures, then the total increase in demand could outrun supply, and the result would be inflation, balance-of-payments crises, shortages and other unpleasant phenomena. One hopes, optimistically, that the democratically expressed desires of the citizens will not take the form of deciding to have the cake and eat it, to distribute more cake than actually exists. Such a danger can no more be eliminated than one can 'abolish' the possibility that power can be abused. Institutional safeguards and political and economic education may – we hope! – reduce the risk of such disagreeable occurrences.

Prices, then, would play an active role in this sort of socialism; this follows from the role within it of market forces. It will be necessary to envisage the division of the economy into a controlled-price sector and a freely-negotiated-price sector, this division more or less corresponding to the degree of centralisation (and monopoly power) of management, with (to repeat) many exceptions for social and cultural reasons.

What theory of value would correspond to this? It must be clear from earlier sections that the idea that 'value' will not exist under socialism makes no sense. Marx's over-emphasis on human effort, his downgrading of use-value, should be corrected. Engels did on one occasion produce what appears to me to be the correct formulation, and this in criticising Ricardo for defining value exclusively in terms of effort: 'value is the relationship of production costs to use-value'.[7] But this was, so to speak, untypical, and most Marxist scholars reject this. But we should accept it. Value is the interaction of cost, of which the principal element is human effort, and the evaluation of this by the user, the consumer, i.e. the use-value of what is produced. The difference between cost and the final selling price is the profit, or surplus. Overstress on marginal utility is as erroneous as its neglect. I know, of course, that for Marx a commodity had to have some use-value, that for him useless goods had no value, but this is too crude a distinction: obviously, some goods are more useful than others. But this has already been dealt with many pages back.

Brus has discussed these matters in a typically stimulating way. One of his subheadings reads 'Why the socialist revolution does not mean the end of political economy as a science'. Obviously, he says, it is important under socialism to obtain 'a maximum effect from a given outlay' or 'a given effect from a minimum outlay'. While Marxian economics was not concerned with rational allocation under capitalism, 'under socialism economics must deal with these problems'. As he says, 'this opens a wide area for the economic application of mathematics, cybernetics and other fields of knowledge'. Unlike some earlier Marxists, Brus can see that 'the overthrow of capitalism' does *not* mean 'the removal of all socio-economic obstacles to and all contradictions in the development of the productive forces'. Of great importance, as he rightly stresses, are organisational matters, choices of instruments. 'Happily the view that there is one, and only one, form of economic mechanism appropriate to a socialist economy is now a thing of the past.'[8]

Very much to the point is a critique of what he calls 'intellectual oligarchs' by Mario Zañartu, a Chilean believer in 'self-governing socialism'.

> For them the only way to achieve [social] solidarity is through an eschato- logical convention. Part of the eschatological attitude of the intellectual oligarchs translates into a blanket rejection not only of capitalism but of many elements found in the economic structures out of which capitalism emerged. They tend to leave capitalism undefined, so it is easy for them to consider it to include such elements as the market and price system, free enterprise by citizens and groups, incentives to productive effort, com- petition to provide the best product, etc. They reject those elements with the same fervour as they reject capitalism, without realising that they are independent of capitalism and are to be found, in different forms, in every economic system. They do not realise that supporting free enterprise [subject to appropriate rules and limitations] . . . means heeding the indica- tions of individuals and groups as to what they perceive their needs to be.[9]

There would be no exploitation, except in so far as a *working* owner-manager may be thought to be deriving additional income from his few employees. (If this is exploitation, then I am 'exploiting' the secretary whom I am employing to type this page!) The disposal of the surplus would be for society to decide, and its scale would be related to the social and other expenditures that needed to be financed through the surplus (as distinct from direct taxes). Another relevant factor would be the level of total investments, and the part which would be financed by the enterprises themselves. The effect of profit on personal incomes I shall discuss in a moment.

Marx in his formulation of the law of value related it to productive labour, and related productive labour to exploitation: that is, anyone exploited by a capitalist is 'productive' (of surplus value). However, he made an exception of the sphere of circulation, buying and selling, which adds nothing to value. These distinctions would plainly be inappropriate for a socialist economy. Surely it would treat all socially useful human effort as productive labour, making an exception perhaps for those items (e.g. public administration, police) which could be regarded as a social cost, albeit a necessary one.

A labour theory of value would be appropriate, in the general sense that, *ceteris paribus*, goods would exchange in rough proportion to the effort required to produce them, with market forces acting to connect use-value, exchange-value and the expenditure of human labour. Physical capital assets would, of course, be seen as contributing to the process of production, but there would be no legitimation of income arising from owning them. The reward of labour would be seen to relate closely to its average productivity, and the degree of income differentiation would be properly regarded as a consequence of several factors: supply and demand for different kinds of labour, social policy, the need for incentives, compensation for heavy or disagreeable work. Someone might remember what Marx, and Mao, said about 'bourgeois right', and one must expect disputes on the subject of what constitutes excessive inequality. More of this in a moment.

The 'transformation problem' (of labour-value into 'prices of production') would disappear, as an unnecessary and pointless detour. Obviously, labour itself would not be paid its 'value', in the sense of the amount necessary to cover the labour-cost of its own production and reproduction. The amount it would be paid would be a function of the general level of productivity, with deductions (decided on by democratic means) for social services, pensions, investments, and so on. Such factors as scarce natural resources, fertile land and land in the centre of cities would be given the valuation appropriate to the process of calculating their most effective use. Whether oil-bearing land has 'value' or is a gift of nature, whether a gift of nature can have 'value', is a point which is more metaphysical than real. Marx was concerned most of all with demonstrating the existence of exploitation, the nature of the surplus and its appropriation by owners of land and capital. Economics in the 'feasible socialism' envisaged here would be much more concerned than was Marx with defining and discussing efficient allocation, calculation and valuation. For purposes of efficient use of resources, it is evident that their relative scarcity is a relevant factor, most obviously so when the resources are non-reproducible – as with oil-bearing land. Time would also have to be taken explicitly into account. Clearly, a project completed in five years is preferable, *ceteris paribus*, to one completed in eight years, even if the direct costs of the two are identical. So there would be interest rates as well as rent, but these would be payments to the state, not to private individuals (with, of course, exceptions, such as renting a room in an apartment, or interest on private savings). The history of economic thought would explain to puzzled citizens that there was a time when the very rich did no work, and that most economists found it quite natural and built their theories on such a basis. It would sound quite irrational to these citizens that the owners of, say, 10 hectares of London's West End could live a life of luxury and ease, and bequeath the same to their children, merely for authorising (i.e. not preventing) others building on these acres. However, the 10 hectares would remain very valuable, and an appropriate rental should enter into any economic calculations involving their use.

Let me give another example. Suppose that the number of people in Scotland wishing to fish for salmon in the rivers grossly exceeds the number of rivers and salmon available. At present (let us say) payment must be made to a duke for permission to fish, and this helps the said duke to be rich. Suppose one eliminates the duke. This makes no difference either to the desire of the citizens to fish or to the number of rivers and salmon in Scotland. So either the numbers who fish will be limited by a permit system (therefore there will be queues, string-pulling, influence, etc.), or a charge will be made. The charge may even be identical to that levied by the duke. Only now it is a rent which is used to cover social expenditures, not an individual's unearned income.

It may be assumed that economic theory will also be concerned with optimal forms of organisational and decision-making structures, recognising (as any sensible theory must) that what appears to be rational and advantageous depends in some degree on the area of responsibility (and knowledge) of the decision-maker. This can be allied with systems theory, and applied to the complex issues of centralisation and decentralisation. Much would need to be said on the role and limitations of the computer; the possibilities of technical progress in this area are vast and unpredictable. Externalities would require to be incorporated in the body of theory, and not treated as exceptions. And since money will exist there will need to be monetary theory, with the possibility of a 'socialist monetarism'; an inevitable consequence of democratic freedom is the existence of pressure groups whose total demands (for higher incomes, social services, investment, etc.) might exceed the resources available: 'the socialist economy is not guaranteed against oversupply of paper money', wrote a Soviet economist.[10] But enough of speculating about the possible content of future socialist economics textbooks!

Division of Labour, Wage Differentials and Self-Management

The utopian nature of Marx's vision of a universal man has been expounded and rejected earlier. However, underlying it are some ideas important for any socialist. No doubt specialisms will persist. The lecturer in Italian is unlikely to be able to teach Spanish, let alone repair teeth, drive heavy lorries, maintain jet engines, be a part-time architect, or milk cows. We must abandon any idea of doing without a horizontal division of labour. However, there must be an attempt to widen opportunities for change of job, changes of specialisation, for those who wish it. Boredom and routine are not social 'goods'. The fullest educational opportunities for youth must be accompanied by generous retraining schemes, including higher education for mature students who have previously repaired teeth, driven heavy lorries, and so on. But of course people vary widely in aptitude, ambition and talents. Activities which I would find boring give others great satisfaction, and vice versa. One can and should encourage changes of job and career, but these are bound to have their limits.

More difficult is the problem of the vertical division of labour. One must first of all identify the functional necessities of subordination, in industry and elsewhere. Why must a ship have a captain, a newspaper an editor, a steelworks a manager? Why must someone be in charge of a building site, of an airport, of a school, of a planning office? Which of these functions require special qualifications and experience? As anyone who has ever worked under inefficient superiors will bear witness, there is such a thing as managerial, controlling *skill*, a knack for personal relationship as well as specialist knowledge, a desire for and ability to carry responsibility. How far is this consistent with rotation? Which should be the elective jobs? On balance, it does seem likely that most human beings will continue to prefer to avoid responsibility and be glad to accept (appoint, elect) others to carry it. (How many university professors wish to be vice-chancellors?) The likelihood of a shorter working week, and the widespread encouragement of technical and cultural hobbies ('do-it-yourself'), may well incline many workers to devote their surplus energy outside the job rather than to 'participate' actively in it, especially if to do so requires hours of 'homework', familiarity with accounts, and so on. So the most likely outcome is a mixture of election and appointment, with the objective necessity of hierarchy duly reflected in the existence of hierarchy. There will be government, there will be managers in charge of electricity, oil, steel and railways, the state planning office will have a chief, who will have deputies, and so on. It will be of vital importance to limit official powers and prevent abuses. The elected assembly would have a key function here, as would a free press.

How much inequality should be tolerated, and how should this be related to hierarchical position? The first point to make is that income differentials (a species of labour market) are the only known alternative to direction of labour. Here it is essential to avoid a mental muddle: some might say that within a commune, or a good *kibbutz*, one can have full equality and rotation in jobs (everyone takes turn at unskilled work such as washing dishes). But this cannot be generalised over the whole of society, partly because it is only workable with small numbers of people who know each other and can meet together daily, and partly because such communes would attract only the enthusiasts who like this sort of life. Trotsky in 1920 envisaged the necessity of direction of labour until such time as people achieved such a high level of social consciousness that they would voluntarily go where society needed them. As argued earlier, this is far-fetched indeed, being based not only on the totally unselfish man, but also on the naive notion that the good of society can be so defined that any citizen can identify it and identify his or her own role within it. A complex, large society with a division of labour makes this impossible.

So we should envisage the degree of inequality which is necessary to elicit the necessary effort by free human beings. Actual wage scales would therefore be influenced by supply of, and demand for, specific kinds of labour. How much differentiation would this require? A great deal must depend on relative scarcities in relation to need, on the general standard of living and on human attitudes. There seems no good reason to make some individuals many times richer than others in order to obtain the necessary incentive effect. In our societies today some pleasant and honourable jobs are, by convention, paid very well. There is no reason why a university professor should necessarily earn more than a garbage collector. Few professors indeed would wish to earn more by turning their efforts into garbage collection! (Adam Smith noted, two hundred years ago, that curates have an expensive education, but earn 'less than a journeyman stonemason'!) One must take into account the belief of most workers on income differentials, and also the almost universal view that a senior officer in any field should earn more than his juniors. Again, we cannot and should not anticipate the extent of the need for differentials or the state of democratic opinion on the subject. What we should anticipate is the require-ment of an incomes policy with appropriate wage and salary scales, and that this will be a thorny and difficult subject, because of the absence of any objective point of reference (other than a labour market). Would a 2:1 or a 3:1 ratio between highest and lowest paid adults be sufficient? In a relatively prosperous society in which the minimum wage assures a reasonable standard of comfort, this does not seem a fantastic prospect. One can also envisage that piece rate payments would be reduced to a minimum: even in today's USA they are largely unnecessary to ensure reasonable effort.

To secure acceptance of an incomes policy, of limits on incomes, has proved to be very difficult, especially where trade unions, pursuing sectional interests, make it their business to demand higher incomes and threaten strike action. Can we hope that the trade unions and government will act together, to devise and help enforce an incomes policy? There would be no large fortunes obtained by those not working. Indeed, there would be no large fortunes at all. A limited bonus scheme linked with profit would be desirable in the socialised (competitive) sector, to provide a material interest for partici-pation in management, despite the probability that this would cause friction. There would, however, be some individuals whose incomes would be in effect uncontrolled: members of co-operatives of all kinds, in town and country, and the small private farmers and other 'entrepreneurs' plus individual craftsmen and professionals. However, the co-operative and small private enterprises take greater risks, can lose as well as win, and in any event it should be possible to limit their take-home pay through the use of the market mechanism, and also by progressive taxation. Would this be sufficient to keep trade union militancy within bounds? It is by no means certain. There would be danger of inflationary wage claims, especially given the commitment to reasonably full employment. There would also be the problem posed by the external world, with comparisons made: some group might find that similar people were better off in another country. However, identification of possible sources of conflict does not imply that they are incapable of resolution.

A question-mark will stand before the role of trade unions. Where virtually everyone is working, where there are no capitalist employers, what task are they to perform? Living standards will not rise through militant wage demands, the distribution of the GNP between individual consumption and various other purposes (investment, social services, etc.) will be for the elected assembly to decide. Yet the freedom to organise, and in the last resort the right to strike, are human freedoms that matter. There would no doubt be some extremists who would be encouraging strikes in the name of an imaginary 'real' socialism, labelling the mixture recommended here as 'state capitalism' or worse. One hopes that good sense will prevail. The right to have *free* trade unions is an indispensable part of the precautions against abuse of power and illegitimate privilege. But in the modern complex world the ruthless use of union power can do very serious damage to their fellow-citizens. Among the important innovations to which they, and the management, will have to adjust is work-sharing, if technical progress is of a massively labour-saving kind.

Reverting to labour's role in managerial decisions in socialised enterprises, one must recall two negative aspects of Yugoslav experience. One is the interest of the workers in not expanding the labour force, at a time of serious unemployment, because to do so could reduce their incomes. The other is the lack of long-term interest of the workers in 'their' enterprise, because it is in fact *not* theirs: they derive no benefit from working for it once they leave it, having no shares to sell. There are possible remedies. One is to have a clearly determined wage rate for the job, this *not* being a function (as it is in Yugoslavia) of the net revenue of the firm. A modest bonus based on profits should then reduce or eliminate the opposition to additions to the labour force. The second problem is more difficult; the word 'shareholder' would cause hackles to rise. Yet some kind of length-of-service bonus, linked with the long-term level of profits or the value of basic assets, could be paid to a worker who retires or transfers elsewhere. (See the example of Mondragon, p. 219 below.) The important point is by trial and error to devise a pattern of personal interest which would incline the workforce to support economically (and socially) efficient decisions. The question then arises (again) of how to penalise those who consciously and democratically take wrong decisions. Several possibilities occur. One is to provide that if the elected committee overrules the management and a loss results, the workforce suffer a (limited) deduction from their pay-packets, proportionate to the (limited) bonus to which they would be entitled in the event of success. How large should *this* be? Would what is called in Russian 'the thirteenth month' be sufficient? Is more needed to overcome risk-aversion? Of course, ideally one wishes to create a model in which the material and moral interest of the sub-unit is always in conformity with the interest of all of society, but in a complex and interrelated economy this must be seen as an *optimum optimorum*, devoutly to be wished but seldom attainable. We know from Soviet (and indeed all other) experience how easy it is inadvertently to create situations in which the pursuit of local interest by labour and management causes conflicts and contradictions.

Co-operatives would, being genuine, be managed by their members. As already indicated, losses or windfall gains would be borne or enjoyed by them, subject to tax or (where socially desirable) a subsidy.

It is worth mentioning that intermediate categories are also possible: for example, in Hungary today small shops and cafés which belong to the state are leased to private operators. Obviously in these instances the revenue of the leaseholder depends on what remains after payment of the lease and other costs, and if this amount proves excessive the charge can be increased.

This is a possible approach to agriculture in a country without an established small peasant class. For example, in Great Britain the large majority of farmers pay rent to landlords. If the land were nationalised, the state would levy a charge (rental, lease) on the family or the co-operative, which would operate the farm. This rental could be differentiated in accordance with the fertility and situation of the land. This would be essential to avoid giving an undeserved bonus to whomsoever happened to be operating in a geographically favourable environment. (Where peasants actually own the land, their expropriation would present acute political problems, and the problem would need to be dealt with by differential taxation.)

There is now a sizeable literature on 'labour-managed' enterprises, to which some reference was made earlier in discussing Yugoslav experience. The interested reader would find particularly useful the Penguin book of readings, *Self-Management*, edited by Jaroslav Vanek. Since a number of serious theorists call into question the rather more positive views of Vanek himself, and since their analyses could apply both to the self-managed socialised enterprises and to co-operatives, we must take note of them, as well as of the actual experiences of Yugoslavia. In the 'feasible socialism' here imagined, a major part of output of goods and services would come from these two kinds of enterprises. So it should be a cause for concern if they are inherently inefficient, or we could identify the specific causes of inefficiency and see if they can be removed without damage to the basic principles of self-management.

It must be recalled that some of the work on the subject is at a high level of abstraction. It is none the worse for that, of course. A certain lack of realism is a legitimate price to pay for theoretical rigour. But one must never forget the extent of the abstraction that has been made from a necessarily complex reality. To give one relevant example, Domar has shown that a change in the assumptions concerning supply of labour to a self-managed co-operative totally alters its (formal, theoretical) response to a rise in price and/or a change in tax. He was referring to Ward's perfectly logical conclusion, on *his* assumptions, that a price rise could lead to the paradoxical effect of making a self-managed enterprise reduce employment and output.[11] There are other reasons too why this outcome is improbable. One is the effect of competition (*real*, not 'perfect' competition!). Imagine ten self-managed enterprises, all producing only widgets, all trying to expand their share of the market – that is, they have the possibility to produce more than they are actually able to sell, a not unrealistic assumption which *must* underlie genuine competition. Suppose the price of widgets rises. While it is possible that in the very short run the 'dividend' for working members could rise if a given firm produced less with fewer workers, is this likely, bearing in mind the following points?

(*a*) There are indivisibilities in processes of production, process specialisation, etc. Labour is not homogeneous.

(*b*) Self-managed units are usually unwilling (sometimes by their rules unable) to dismiss fellow-workers.

(*c*) More important, *what of goodwill?* Customers once lost may never be regained, and, after all, prices which rise today may fall tomorrow. Some at least of the nine assumed competitors will not be so foolish as to miss the opportunity. Some at least, having spare capacity, may be at the stage of increasing returns (falling costs per unit).

(*d*) In the unlikely event of all ten producers deciding to increase net revenue per worker by reducing output when prices rise, what is to prevent new entrants from starting to produce widgets? Of course the existing producers know this and would wish to avoid it, which would affect their actions.

The possibility that existing firms would fail to respond to a price rise, and simply add to their net revenues, cannot be ruled out, even in real capitalism, given the existence of human inertia and informal rings of various kinds. The entry of new firms is an important corrective to such practices, and will be important also in the sort of socialism here envisaged. It would also play a role in reducing the danger of unemployment. Procedures for the setting up of new social and co-operative enterprises must therefore be devised. Bank credits would play a major role in financing these 'starts', and here the state plan can exercise an important influence: regional problems, labour supply, forecast of future requirements, environmental considerations, can and should influence the decisions. But this still leaves unsettled the issue of *who* actually undertakes the task of starting a new firm. For the centralised state sector the picture is clear enough: the central planners, the central body which runs the industry (corresponding to the National Coal Board in Britain, or the Ministry of Electric Power Stations in the Soviet Union), make the calculations, take the initiative, create the enterprise. At the other end, so to speak, the picture is also fairly clear: co-operative enterprises, or petty private businesses, are set up on the initiative of the individuals or groups concerned, with or without direct encouragement from the public authorities. But what of socialised enterprises? One can imagine a range of possibilities. One is 'conversion' of some of the larger co-operative enterprises. Other initiatives should be encouraged. According to the Yugoslav rules, 'any public body, institution, social organisation or group of citizens' may take the initiative. Enterprises can also merge and divide. Central planners might also act, and have the choice of granting credits for the expansion of an existing firm or to set up a new one. Mindful of the need for competition, they might prefer the latter. A manager would have to be appointed *pro tem*, and contracts signed with building firms, suppliers of machinery, and so on. These procedural problems seem unlikely to be insuperable and need not detain us.

More difficult will be the task of devising operational criteria which encourage the efficient use of resources. Though some of the misallocation envisaged by Ward is probably a result of some unreal assumptions, it remains important to study carefully his theoretical analyses, as well as those of Domar, Meade, Bergson and, of course, the work of Jaroslav Vanek (whose own attitude can be seen in the subtitle of his book of readings, 'Economic Liberation of Man'), as well as Yugoslav experience – though bearing in mind how far the practice in Yugoslavia has been inconsistent with its own model.

To discuss all this in full requires another book, not a few paragraphs, so what follows must be seen as no more than a few thoughts, in a constructive spirit, on a difficult subject.

How can one combine self-management with efficient use of resources, while avoiding excesses of inequality? An interesting case is Mondragon, in Spain.[12] This is a very large co-operative 'conglomerate', and worker-members who join must make a sizeable capital contribution, which earns a rate of interest and which is repayable when they leave (subject to a modest deduction, but indexed to the rate of inflation). Management is elected. Income differentials are decided by the workforce (apparently after much argument). Interestingly enough, there are wage and salary scales (i.e. the reward of labour is not a residual); there is, therefore, a profit margin. The wage scales are related to those paid by good private employers in the given sector. The major part of the profits are used for investment and for reserves, but a portion is shared out among the workforce. We cannot concern ourselves here with the detailed history and problems of Mondragon; it may be that it has become too big to be an effective co-operative. However, it suggests certain possibilities. Thus a contribution to capital from each worker-member (in Mondragon a major part of this may be lent to the worker by the co-operative itself, to be repaid out of earnings) makes the member materially interested in the longer-term welfare of the firm; the amount returned to him (her) when he (she) leaves could be varied by length of service and include an extra amount related to the profits made. Equality in this respect is assured at Mondragon by making every worker's contribution equal, i.e. the minimum is also the maximum. (Of course, some capital is raised externally, through credits from the banks.) Such an arrangement best suits co-operative enterprises, but in socialised self-managed enterprises too there could be some scheme which makes reward for long service relate to accumulated profits and/or increase in the value of the enterprise's capital. The essential points seem to me to be the need to link the worker's material incentives with the longer-term health of the enterprise (i.e. to make him or her interested also in investment, to provide a stake in the future), and this is integrally linked with the existence of a wage, i.e. a rate for the job, without which the very concept 'profit' ceases to have a statistical meaning: if the entire net income (after paying for inputs, taxes, etc.) is divided among the workforce, there is no 'profit' as such; yet there ought to be. Which in no way prevents the existence of profit-related bonuses. In Mondragon, according to a friendly but critical survey,

> the combination of participation in decision-making with respect of organis-
> ation of work and the distribution of earnings; narrow differences and fixed
> wages; of an extensive programme of education and on-the-job training; of a
> high degree of security of employment; and of a financial stake in the
> ownership of their own co-operative factory, adds up to a system of collective
> incentives which is not found in private enterprise, which partly explains
> why performance in the co-operatives has achieved such a high degree of
> efficiency.[13]

True, their evidence shows that only a small minority actively participate, but it also shows that the bulk of the workforce appreciate highly their right to participate. Let us be realistic: if everyone wanted to speak at general meetings, there would be no time available for anything else! None the less, we should also heed the warning of Mihajlo Marković: 'one of the greatest dangers for self-management is the formation of a small oligarchic group made up of managers, heads of administration and political functionaries, which tend to assume full control over the workers' council'.[14] It is note-worthy that the large Mondragon complex is divided up for effective manage-ment purposes into smaller units, thus avoiding or reducing the danger of alienation of the workforce through scale and remoteness. The manufacturing units operate in a competitive market environment, and the wage rates are based upon those in existence in analogous private industry in that part of Spain. Evidently, this experience is worth very careful study.

The level of incomes in state, socialised and co-operative enterprises should not vary greatly, to avoid social stress. In Hungary the higher incomes earned in co-operatives did cause friction. It seems reasonable to expect national wage negotiations and a national wage scale for the state and socialised sectors, but co-operatives of their nature must have greater freedom to make their own decisions in this respect. Excessive differentiation could be reduced by a progressive tax (on individuals or on enterprises). There could be rental, lease, or lump-sum payments designed to avoid differentiation due to natural advantages. This could apply particularly to land and minerals. For example, rent or tax levied on farms (whether state, co-operative, or individual) would be varied in accordance with a land valuation survey (cadaster), as indeed is now the case in several countries. The same could apply to shops favourably located in a central area. There would be much room for experiment. The problem, of course, would be to avoid discouraging efficiency and enterprise, as would certainly occur if taxes, leases, rents, were such as to penalise success. But this can hardly be said to be insuperable.

Finally, we must expect any meaningful self-management to alter the worker's frequently passive or negative attitude to work. Textbooks on economics usually ignore this factor. Labour, if not treated as homogeneous, is distinguished only by speciality. Yet men and women can work well or badly, can try consciously to minimise effort or take pride in their work. In arguing that 'the labour-managed system appears . . . to be superior by far, judged on strictly economic criteria, to any other economic system in existence',[15] Jaroslav Vanek makes many points, but the one concerning attitudes, morale and avoidance of conflict, seems to me particularly important. In this connection, it seems necessary again to stress the impor-tance of *scale* ('small is beautiful'). A recent illustration of this from Soviet agricultural experience is the so-called *beznaryadnoye zveno*, or autonomous work-team. It turns out that a group of seven or eight peasants, left to them-selves to organise their own work, can greatly increase productivity, and need not be supervised, in contrast with much larger units. There is a moral here. Of course, I do not suggest that seven or eight is some optimal magic number. But it may well be found that even a good organisational scheme with a cast of thousands would produce disappointing results.

Investments and Growth

Investments would be divided into two parts: those of structural significance, usually involving either the creation of new productive units or the very substantial expansion of existing ones, and those which represent an adjustment to changing demand (or to new techniques). The latter would be the responsibility of management (cleared as required with the elected committee), and the necessary finance would be obtained either from retained profits (and reserves based upon past profits) or from credits from the state banking system. Exceptionally there could be a budgetary grant, where the activity carries with it large external economies or is seen as a social 'must'. It would be the task of the bank, in conjunction with the central planners, to keep a watch on the level of credits and also their destination. One must avoid generating inflationary excess demand for investment goods and building labour, and also avoid a situation in which the same investment opportunity is perceived by many managements: for example, suppose there is clear need for expanding the output of typewriters, there could be wasteful duplication and triplication of this apparently profitable investment, and it might be necessary to grant the credit to the firm which promised to be most efficient and refuse it to the other applicants. As for big, structurally significant investments, these would be the major responsibility of the central planners.

Given that we are discussing an industrialised, developed country, there is no need to assume that *high* growth rates would be a high priority. Since scarcity will be a fact, there will be pressure to provide more material goods, housing, social services, and so on, but that is not the same as a drive to achieve a radical structural transformation in a short space of time. Such a drive may indeed prove inconsistent with reliance on the market mechanism. A large part of investments would therefore be of the 'adjustment-to-demand' sort. It is plainly essential, within a controlled market environment, that firms (state, social, co-operative) have the means to make such adjustments, for otherwise the profits they make would serve no rational purpose. If, for example, demand increases for anything, from micro chips to potato chips, the price would rise and so would profits. The function of this rise in price and profits in a market economy is to stimulate additional production, which, unless there is already spare capacity, requires investments. If this result does not follow, the mechanism would be failing to work, and the existing enterprises would be making excess profits to no social or economic purpose. Indeed, it would be necessary to have a species of socialist anti-trust legislation: in these sectors in which competition is desired and desirable, a watch would have to be kept to prevent the creation of informal rings or cartels, agreements not to expand or not to compete. One way of combating such a tendency is to encourage (by credits on favourable terms, etc.) the creation of new productive units in the sector concerned, another important function of central planners in a 'socialist market'.

Experience points to the danger of investment cycles. A fundamentalist objection to the whole of the conception advanced in the preceding pages would stress this. The absence of comprehensive planning, the role of market forces, would introduce elements of 'anarchy', of uncontrollable zigzags, booms and slumps. Markets provide (imperfect) information about what has already happened. Did not someone use as a parallel a driver who looks out of the rear window at the road behind him?

The criticism has some point. However, imperfect information is a fact also if planning is highly centralised, and the model here put forward places in the centrally planned categories those large investments (in such sectors as energy, steel, heavy chemicals) for which information about future requirements is best collected and analysed at the centre. Besides, as we have seen, investment cycles also occur in centralised, non-market economies. It will indeed be a difficult task for the centre to steer the rest of the economy by remote control, without detailed orders, avoiding mass unemployment and inflation – difficult, but surely not impossible. It will have at its disposal such weapons as credit policy, the setting-up (or the encouragement of setting-up) of production units, control over prices in the centrally managed sectors, the drawing-up and enforcement of ground-rules on profit disposal, income distribution and taxation. True, the greater the freedom allowed to enterprises or to individual citizens, the greater the risk that some undesirable act might be committed. Thus it seems easier to control incomes if the state and only the state employs labour than if the worker can choose to work for a co-operative or for himself. If may also seem easier to avoid duplication, to ensure economies of scale, if there are no separate autonomous production units with the right to decide what they should be producing and how. Yet Soviet experience does not altogether support these assertions. Even if the state is the only employer, different state institutions can compete for labour in a sellers' market and bid away good workers from each other, and uncertainty of supply leads to self-supply, to duplication on a quite massive scale, to the detriment of economies of scale based on specialisation. There is no magic wand. Total control is impossible; the effort to achieve universal planning by an all-knowing centre produces results that no one actually desires (not even the centre). Total de-control is also unworkable, and certainly cannot be seen as a socialist solution.

One must agree with Thomas and Logan when, writing in the context of the Mondragon experiment, they argue that 'at the meso- and macro-levels, a strong planning agency is essential as otherwise a self-managed economy could not function. Phenomena such as the entrance and exit of firms, and the adjustment processes of capital intensity, can only be realised by careful planning and institutional support.'[16] Also correct is the following opinion of Tinbergen: 'It is highly improbable that the proponents of a "laissez-faire theory" of self-management are right. It can be convincingly shown that in an optimum order some tasks must be performed in a centralised way and cannot therefore be left to the lowest levels . . . One should seek the level which "minimises external effects".'[17] So what must be sought is a workable compromise between centralisation, self-management and local initiative. Some Soviet economists, in examining critically their own system, have written intelligently on theories of complex organisations, within which the sub-units are free to take certain categories of decisions. They seem to devise an optimal decision-making structure. Ideally, one wishes to have a situation in which the perceived interest of individuals and groups always conforms to the general interest. For reasons examined already this is an unattainable ideal, just as it is also impossible for some central body to examine every decision in the light of the general interest, i.e. to internalise all externalities. The complications are just too great, the possibilities to consider far too numerous, the perception of interest is inevitably affected by the situation within a complex society of various individuals and groups. The best that can be done, in the field of investment as in others, is to identify in advance the kind of problem or decision which will have significant external effects, that is, effects (positive or negative) beyond the knowledge or responsibility of those directly involved. In those cases in which the cost of internalising (i.e. reference to higher authority) is unlikely to exceed the benefit, freedom to decide on the spot can and should be limited. 'Cost' here includes also frustration and delay.

Foreign Trade

There will, of course, be foreign trade. Either some of the world will not be socialist, or there will be separate socialist countries, though naturally a union of several socialist countries would be both possible and desirable, and/or a socialist 'common market' with close co-operation and perhaps a common currency. One would hope that the clumsy 'state monopoly of foreign trade' of the Soviet type would be unnecessary, but, yet again, the only known alternative is a market, i.e. exchange, and since multilateral trade has evident advantages over bilateral barter, this would seem to imply currency convertibility, and the right of economic units to buy and sell across borders. This in turn means realistic prices and exchange rates. It means also that an individual citizen wishing to travel abroad, or a productive or wholesaling enterprise, will be able to acquire foreign currency without necessarily seeking permission from some government office. Internal and foreign trade prices in tradeable goods would be mutually consistent. Prices would emerge partly as a result of bargaining over specific deals, partly as a result of international price agreements for specific important commodities.

The Marxist tradition is not altogether clear about foreign trade, and it is unfortunate that Marx died before he wrote a promised volume on the subject. Kautsky 'believed that the substitution of production for sale by production for use would require a degree of national self-sufficiency and autarky', for how could market exchange dominate relations between states if it had been eliminated within a national economy?[18] He certainly believed that he was in the orthodox line of Marx and Engels in asserting this. I am here asserting the converse. Given that market exchange will play a major role within socialist states, it must do so also in their foreign trade relations: a major role, but not necessarily a dominant one. Long-term international commodity agreements have been mentioned already. Naturally, as in all forms of exchange, there will be bargaining about prices, with the seller trying to obtain the best possible price. Familiar (and sometimes convincing) arguments will be advanced for protection. Another possible source of conflict would arise if, as is quite possible, some non-reproducible natural resources gradually become physically scarce. We cannot assume that socialist countries will always maintain amicable relations, in circumstances which could give rise to quarrels over access to, say, irrigation water, iron ore, or oilfields. One does not eliminate this danger by substituting any other method for purchase-and-sale. Kautsky's maximisation of autarky is in fact the only alternative to relations based upon exchange. Unfortunately it is simply not the case that capitalism alone is the source of international conflict. One must do one's best to spread the ideology of internationalism, and increase economic and social contacts between peoples, increase interdependence. Autarky is surely a *pis-aller*. The dogmatists' 'alternative' would be either a world socialist common-wealth with production 'directly for use', which implies a degree of centralisa-tion which is surely undesirable as well as impracticable, or perhaps some quite imaginary model of abundance in which the comrades in West Africa freely decide to supply cocoa and bananas in just the right quantities to the comrades in Western Europe for sheer love of humanity, without the require-ment of any *quid pro quo*. No unequal exchange, because no exchange! Not a very likely story, to put it mildly.

The Economic Role of Democratic Politics

It is an essential part of socialist beliefs that there be a real form of economic democracy, that people can influence affairs in their capacities as producers and consumers. It is by this standard, among others, that the Soviet model can be judged and found wanting.

To influence the pattern of production by their behaviour as buyers is surely the most genuinely democratic way to give power to consumers. There is no direct 'political' alternative. There being hundreds of thousands of different kinds of goods and services in infinite permutations and combina-tions, a political voting process is impracticable, a ballot paper incorporating microeconomic consumer choice unthinkable. Majority votes are in any event undesirable as well as unsuitable. What of minority rights in matters of con-sumption? Is it proper for the citizens of a town or a country to vote by a 3–1 majority in favour of *not* providing anything – from string quartets to pumpernickel – which happens to be a minority taste? How can one measure the intensity of desire for anything other than by discovering how much of other things one is prepared to give up to obtain it (i.e. what *price* is one prepared to pay)? With an acceptable distribution of income, and in the absence of large unearned incomes, no better method for arriving at consumer choice is known than that of allowing the consumer to choose, and (save on far-fetched assumptions of 'abundance') this means choosing by using his or her purchasing-power, by buying in shops – what Soviet reformers call 'voting with the rouble'. The shops, in turn, must then have the means of obtaining the goods their customers wish to purchase. There is not and cannot be anything anti-socialist in the notion that the citizens should seek to satisfy their varied needs and tastes to the fullest extent consistent with the productive capacity of society and the welfare of their fellow citizens (i.e. avoiding pollution and other species of external diseconomies). We have surely established by experience as well as by logical analysis the impossibility of incorporating the fully disaggregated needs of millions of people into a comprehensive (and comprehensible) plan.

We have tried to draw the distinction earlier between relative and absolute scarcity. Higher prices and other material stimuli can elicit additional supplies of reproducible goods. However, if what the future holds is an extension of the experience of absolute shortage (as exemplified by fish in the North Sea), then society, by its votes, could opt for a rationing scheme for such products, as a temporary measure at least. This would be a restriction of choice, of course, but might find its justification in the principle of fairness in distribution under conditions when the supply effect of higher prices would be insignificant. One has reasonable hopes that such conditions would not be frequently encountered.

Democratic votes, including referendums, could be utilised to determine (or choose between) broad priorities, to devote more investment resources to, say, retail distribution, public transport, rural clinics, nursery schools, the mass production of deep freezers, or to launch an investigation into the malfunctioning of any branch of the economy. Representatives of users would be given an important function, alongside those of the producers and the state, in the top management echelon of the centralised nationalised industries. These actions are quite different from imagining a 'democratic' vote to reduce (or increase) the output of brown boots or to allocate (or not allocate) sulphuric acid to a given user.

The democratically elected assembly would adopt, amend, choose between, internally consistent perspective plans for the economy as a whole when these were laid before it. Such plans would, of course, be at a high level of aggregation, and would have their primary effect on the pattern of major investments in the next plan period.

Such high-level discussions and decisions would directly touch only a small proportion of the workforce. Participation is most meaningful at a much 'lower' level, i.e. at the workplace. It is useful again to recall Brus's correct argument that workers can effectively hope to participate only at the level at which effective decisions are in fact taken, and that a centralised or marketless planning model leaves little to be decided at the level of the enterprise. 'The larger the group, the more difficult it will be for individuals to identify with distant structures that transcend the horizon of their own work organisation', to quote Thomas and Logan.[19] Vertical subordination must, where possible, be replaced by horizontal links, i.e. by negotiated contracts, agreements, with suppliers and customers. This, it must be insisted, is a pre-condition both of consumer preference and of producers' preference being satisfied, assuming that customers and producers both wish to have some effective influence on their everyday lives. The dogmatist evades this issue by seeking a non-existent species of direct economic-political democracy, in which 'society' decides, in which labour is directly social (i.e. is consciously applied by society for the satisfaction of its wants, without the 'detour' of market and value relations). It will be recalled that Bettelheim criticised the Yugoslav model because the market, not the producers, determines what is produced. However, it is clear that someone (some institution) has to tell the producers about what the users require. If that 'someone' is not the impersonal market mechanism it can only be a hierarchical superior. There are horizontal links (market), there are vertical links (hierarchy). What other dimension is there? Of course, the producers are also consumers, and vice versa, but an inescapable division of labour and of function imply that this is so only at the top of an all-inclusive hierarchical pyramid.

In the competitive socialised ownership sector, and in co-operatives, the workforce would receive encouragement to participate, to attend meetings, to stand for committees, to put forward proposals, to help elect the working management. Not all would be interested, since some would pay greater attention to hobbies outside the work process, and have every right to do so. The smaller the numbers engaged in a given productive unit, the more likely would be the effective feeling of participation, of 'belonging'. Intuitively we surely would all agree that it would be far easier in a group of 50 than in one of 5,000. Individuals would be free to change their jobs, to acquire a different specialisation, to switch from working for the state to working in a co-operative or on their own account. The concept of producers' preferences is a useful one to keep in mind, alongside that of consumers' preferences.

Is It Socialism?

Let me recapitulate. The society outlined in the preceding pages has the following features:

(a) The predominance of state, social and co-operative property, and the absence of any large-scale private ownership of the means of production.

(b) Conscious planning by an authority responsible to an elected assembly of major investments of structural significance.

(c) Central management of current microeconomic affairs confined to sectors (and to type of decision) where informational, technological and organisational economies of scale, and the presence of major externalities, render this indispensable.

(d) A preference for small scale, as a means of maximising participation and a sense of 'belonging'. Outside centralised or monopolised sectors, and the limited area of private enterprise, management should be responsible to the workforce.

(e) Current output and distribution of goods and services should whenever possible be determined by negotiations between the parties concerned. There should be explicit recognition that this implies and requires competition, a pre-condition for choice.

(f) Workers should be free to choose the nature of their employment and given every opportunity to change their specialisation. If they prefer it, they could opt for work in co-operatives, or on their own account (for instance in a family farm, workshop, or service agency).

(g) As an unlimited market mechanism would in due course destroy itself, and create intolerable social inequalities, the state would have vital functions in determining income policies, levying taxes (and differential rents), intervening to restrain monopoly power, and generally setting the ground-rules and limits of a competitive market. Some sectors (education, health, etc.) would naturally be exempt from market-type criteria.

(h) It is recognised that a degree of material inequality is a pre-condition for avoiding administrative direction of labour, but moral incentives would be encouraged and inequalities consciously limited. The duty to provide work would override considerations of micro profitability.

(*i*) The distinction between governors and governed, managers and managed, cannot realistically be eliminated, but great care must be taken to devise barriers to abuse of power and the maximum possible democratic consultation.

The most serious problem, observed Bahro in his writing on socialism, is the reconciliation of partial and general interest.[20] This is correct, and applies also to the model outlined here. It is only in fairy-tales that people live happily ever after, it is only in utopia that all agree (in a pseudo-utopia all are *made* to agree). It is nonsense to assert that fundamental disagreements occur only because of private ownership of the means of production. The assumption of relative scarcity, and thus of opportunity-cost, is enough to ensure the certainty of some conflict. The state, its democratic institutions, will be there to resolve disputes, to settle competing claims on resources, but trade union and other interest groups (regional, or national in a socialist federation of several nations) could make trouble, and in particular cause an overcommitment of resources, excessive incomes, inflation. Some may regard all this, and the presence of markets and competition, as showing that the proposed model is not viable, or not socialist, or both at once. They would doubtless wax sarcastic about 'socialism in one country'. On this last point, I would again stress that a socialist federation, common market, economic community, would be highly desirable (perhaps even essential, certainly for medium-sized, let alone small, countries). But to define 'socialism' as necessarily worldwide, to dismiss any other kind, is to depart from the realm of the feasible within the time scale of the present exercise. In the longer run, 'one world' is a possibility, and it may be that the destructive powers of nuclear weapons are such that the survival into the next century of sovereign states make the survival into the next century of the human race somewhat less than probable. All that is put forward here is the notion that a state or group of states with a legitimate claim to call themselves socialist will be undertaking foreign trade.

Conclusion

I hope that, in presenting a feasible form of socialism, I have nowhere slipped into romantic utopianism, have made no far-fetched economic or psychological assumptions. Is the resulting picture attractive? Is it desirable? This is very much a matter of opinion. For some its lack of romanticism is a serious defect. Socialism is for them a substitute religion, worth dying for. The picture presented here is prosaic, wih an emphasis on practical matters. Outside one of Paris's numerous universities, among the graffiti, was one which read: 'A BAS LA VIE QUOTIDIENNE', which could be translated as 'down with weekdays'. Obviously my doctrines could not satisfy its author. But then nothing practical could! People will still be buying and selling, and 'consumerism' is not excluded; I share with the 'millenarians' a distaste for the excesses of conspicuous consumption (or keeping up with the Joneses), but this is not an attitude that outsiders can impose, either by decree or by assumption. We all hope that thievery and fraud will wither away, but we should realistically assume that locksmiths and auditors will still have functions to perform, and police too. Jealousy is not a noble virtue, but some individuals will probably be jealous of the achievements of others, whether in bed or in the council chamber. Unless one naively supposes that drunkenness is due to private ownership of the means of production and advertising by the liquor trade, some individuals will presumably continue to drink to excess (to mark success or to console themselves for failure), much though I regret this. An imperfect world cannot be rendered perfect because we wish it so, and the assumption of original sin is (alas) a more realistic basis for organising society than, the assumption of a noble savage deformed by the institutions of capitalism and the state.

It is clear that the role of the state will be very great, as owner, as planner, as enforcer of social and economic priorities. The assumption of democracy makes its task more difficult, not easier, since a variety of inconsistent objectives will be reflected in political parties and the propaganda they will undertake. One hopes that an educated and mature electorate will support governments which will keep the economy in balance, avoiding inflationary excess and unemployment, allowing the market to function but not letting it get out of hand. The danger one foresees is not one of a vote to 'restore capitalism'. There was no mass movement of this sort even in countries where the Soviet-type system was intensely unpopular – for instance, Poland or Czechoslovakia. The danger is more one of so 'political' an economy, especially in income and price policy and in investment, that the resultant stresses and strains will lead to economic crisis, which could disrupt both the economic and the political balance. However, both in the economy and in politics there is an inescapable price to pay for freedom to act: people may act wrongly; just as, if there is no censorship, we may be sure that some false, objectionable and misleading matter will get published, and our hope that the citizens will be adult enough to reject rubbish may or may not be disappointed.

Is the 'socialism' here pictured preferable to capitalism, or to the imperfect and mixed 'system' that now exists? Would it attract the opprobrium of critics such as Hayek or Friedman? Is it a stage on the 'road to serfdom'? In my view it would provide better opportunities for more people to influence their own lives and working conditions, reduce the dangers of unemployment and of civil strife, provide sufficient encouragement to enterprise and innovation and give some attention to the quality of life. Of course it *guarantees* none of these things. Nothing can. People can vote for triviality, watch soap-operas on television, leave litter at beauty-spots. Conflicts of interest can go too far and threaten stability. But at least the socialism here presented should minimise class struggle, provide the institutional setting for tolerable and tolerant living, at reasonable material standards, with a feasible degree of consumer sovereignty and a wide choice of activities for the citizens. Would an economic optimum be assured? Of course not! The possibility of economic calculation will be present, but freedom of choice involves both uncertainty and the risk of error. Compared with the inflation, exchange rate fluctuations, zig-zags in interest rates, unemployment, of what passes today for capitalism, decision-makers might well have better means for being right more often.

Mistakes will happen, contradictions will show themselves, rebels will demand change, conservatives will resist, history will neither end nor begin. Economists, philosophers, social scientists of different schools, will be assured of full employment. Unless, of course, a nuclear holocaust puts a stop to it all, and to us all too.

'Permanent revolution' can be a disaster, as China's cultural revolution has shown. It disorganises, impoverishes, confuses. But permanent vigilance, *permanent reform*, will surely be a 'must'.

On this happy(?) note it is appropriate to end this excursion into a feasible, possible future. Many of the propositions put forward here are open to challenge, and I hope they *will* be challenged. This is a kind of long (too long?) discussion paper, intended to provoke both socialists and anti-socialists, provoke them into some hard thinking about the possible, about alternatives. If it succeeds in this, the author will be satisfied.

Notes: Part 5

1   J. Riordan, *Sport in Soviet Society* (Cambridge: Cambridge University Press, 1977).
2   See A. Gorz, Adieux au prolétariat (Paris: Editions du Seuil, 1980).
3   R. Selucky, *Marxism, Socialism and Freedom* (London: Macmillan, 1979), pp. 179, 181.
4   R. H. Coase, 'The nature of the firm', *Economica*, vol. IV, 1937; G. B. Richardson, *Information and Investment* (London: Oxford University Press, 1960).
5   J. Kornai, *Anti-Equilibrium* (Amsterdam: North-Holland, 1971); G. L. S. Shackle, *Decision, Order and Time in Human Affairs* (Cambridge: Cambridge University Press, 1961); B. Loasby, *Choice, Complexity and Ignorance* (Cambridge: Cambridge University Press, 1975).
6   R. Karagedov (see Part 2, n. 27 above) is a talented young economist with a future.
7   The quotation is used by N. Petrakov (*Khozyaistvennaya reforma*, Moscow, 1971, pp. 92–3) to help reconcile his (sensible) reform proposals with orthodox Marxism.
8   W. Brus, *The Economics and Politics of Socialism* (London: Routledge & Kegan Paul, 1973), pp. 80–4.
9   M. Zañartu, in *Self-Governing Socialism: A Reader*. ed. B. Horvat, M. Markovič, R. Supek and H. Kramer (New York: IASP, 1975), pp. 149–50.
10 D. Kazakevich, *Ockerki teorii sotsialisticheskoi ekonomiki* (Novosibirsk, 1980), p. 189.
11 See E. Domar, 'The Soviet collective farm as a producers' cooperative', *American Economic Review*, no. 56, 1966.
12 For a good brief description, see R. Oakeshot, in *Self-Management: Economic Liberation of Man*, ed. J. Vanek (Harmondsworth: Penguin, 1975), pp. 290–8. A valuable longer study is by H. Thomas and C. Logan, *Mondragon* (London: Allen & Unwin, 1982).
13 Thomas and Logan, op. cit. (n. 12), p. 161.
14 M. Markovič, *From Affluence to Praxis* (Ann Arbor, Mich.: University of Michigan Press, 1974).
15 Vanek (ed.), op. cit. (n. 12), p. 364.
16 Thomas and Logan, op. cit. (n. 12), p. 187.
17 J. Tinbergen, in Horvat *et al.* (eds), op. cit. (n. 9), p. 226. The same point about the contradictions 'between the interests of self-managing bodies and the demands of the national economy' is made by W. Bienkowski, *Theory and Reality* (London: Allison & Busby, 1981), p. 269.
18 Cited from Selucky, op. cit. (n. 3), p. 96.
19 Thomas and Logan, op. cit. (n. 12), p. 187.
20 R. Bahro, Die *Alternative* (Cologne. Europäische Verlagsanstalt, 1977), p. 537.

Appendix 1: On Contradiction

Contradictions in 'feasible socialism' are inevitable and will have to be tolerated, indeed are even sometimes to be welcomed, or so I have argued. Some readers of Karl Popper will not agree. Popper of course admits, indeed emphasises, that in a sense contradictions are fruitful, or fertile, or 'productive of progress', but 'only so long as we are determined not to put up with contradictions; in other words never accept a contradiction. If we change this attitude, and decide to put up with contradictions, then contradictions must at once lose any kind of fertility . . . If one were to accept contradictions then one would have to give up any kind of scientific activity.'[1] Am I guilty of an offence, then, by Popperian standards? I do not think so, though perhaps my choice of words (or, dare I say it, *his* choice of words and examples) may not be clear and unambiguous. Popper is perfectly right when the 'contradiction' of which he speaks takes the form of statements such as 'he *was* here on 1 November 1938' and 'he was *not* here on 1 November 1938'. It should be possible to prove that one of these statements is true, or false. Similarly 'phlogiston' either was or was not a valid scientific concept.

The contradictions I have in mind are inherent in institutional arrangements, indeed in the human condition itself. Freedom for me to do what I like can, sometimes does, contradict, is inconsistent with, the freedom of others. My desire to park my car where it suits me best contradicts the desire of others to park there, or to drive unimpeded down that lane, this being a special case of the more general contradiction between individual and social interests. The concentration of decision-making power in the hands of those who have wide-ranging responsibilities facilitates the 'internalising of externalities', the apprehension of wide-ranging consequences, but the lack of vision of micro detail can produce perverse results in practice. Conversely, placing decision-making power at lower levels ensures closer reflection of micro detail, a greater sense of participation, but at the cost of not seeing some possibly important 'external' consequences of one's acts. Popper would, I am sure, agree with all that I have just written, but might attach a different label to these matters. He might well also agree that these are difficulties (conflicts, problems, or whatever) that we must expect to live with in the real world. Of course we will *try* to resolve them, try to find some suitable (or less inconvenient) way of organising car parking, limiting potentially harmful individual actions, devise some approach to an optimum balance between centralisation and decentralisation. But this is not at all the same as unambiguously determining whether X was in some place on 1 November 1938, or the correctness of the theory of relativity, for that matter. As I write these words I see a motor-cyclist passing with the following words on his jacket: 'Helmets Yes, Compulsion No'. He believes that those who wish to risk injury to themselves should be free to do so, while the law says you *must* wear helmets, because injuries impose costs on others. Again this is a contradiction between an individual and society which cannot be resolved as if it were a physical fact or scientific theory. Popper would probably classify these as ethical choices, which in a sense they are. But contradictions can arise out of ideas grounded in durable differences of view or of interest. There is also the important distinction between, so to speak, levels of contradiction. Thus problems arising out of centralisation/decentralisation will probably always be with us, but specific issues *within* this general category – for example, the location of major investment decisions for the oil industry – can be and are decided, resolved. Similarly, one particular car must be parked, even though problems arising from car parking remain, as do contradictions between individual and social desiderata.

In other words, one must indeed try to resolve any specific contradictions, but certain types or species of tension, causes of dispute, will none the less remain in any conceivable form of society.

Popper is more likely in fact to object to the whole notion of attempting to move towards another kind of society. He is a believer in piecemeal reform, in avoiding blueprints of a future world. It is enough, he asserts, to try to resolve the many pressing problems which now face us, one by one. I have a good deal of sympathy for this view. Yet purely empirical reactions to immediate issues, a refusal to have any sort of strategic objectives, surely have considerable limitations in the unsettled and dangerous world of today. Down with utopias, agreed! But if some aspects of a *system* fail to work satisfactorily, surely it is proper at least to consider changing the system.

This is so where partial reform is self-defeating. Consider, for example, centralised planning of the Soviet type. It has an inner logic: the centre acquires information as to needs, issues instructions as to what to produce and for whom, ensures that the means to obey these instructions are provided. As we know, this way of doing things is in many respects ineffective. A cautious piecemeal reformer – let us call him Popperovich – proposes a change: let enterprises in certain industries acquire their inputs by freely purchasing them, instead of having them allocated by the centre. The system rejects this, as a human being might reject an alien implant. The apparently desirable freedom to purchase is in conflict with the rest of the planning system, because the suppliers are not free to purchase *their* inputs, because these suppliers would give priority to those deliveries which are still planned by the centre, because the price system is inappropriate and gives the wrong signals, and so on. As has been pointed out, reform comes in *packages*. An 'economic reform' story relates how the Warsaw traffic control department sent a delegation to London to study London's apparently superior traffic flows. They reported that the only difference in the regulations was that traffic in London, unlike Warsaw, kept on the left. So – believing in *piecemeal* reform – they decreed that, for an experimental period, a third of the traffic in Warsaw should keep to the left.

Note: Appendix 1

1 K. Popper, *Conjectures and Refutations* (London: Routledge & Kegan Paul, 1963), pp. 316–17.

Appendix 2: Two Critiques

Let us now imagine the reaction of a reviewer, writing in an imaginary journal which we will call *The Revolutionary Worker*. (I have never heard of one with that title, and hastily apologise to its editor if by any chance it exists.) Let us further imagine that the reviewer is a serious, committed, intelligent dogmatist, and that he would not be satisfied with mere denunciation: he will not speculate on how much the author was paid by the CIA, or assert that the ideas expressed are indistinguishable from those of the Chicago school. In other words, he proposes to launch a serious attack. Along what lines?

One could be called *definitional*. What is being described here is a possible transitional society, but socialism it is not. I could anticipate that this would be Bettelheim's position, for instance. He was present when I read a paper in Paris putting forward some of the ideas expressed here, and his comment was: 'Yes, indeed, the problems described would certainly arise on the morrow of the seizure of power.' I replied that they would, in my view, be still there after the morrow too.

Did they arise in the USSR, would they arise elsewhere, because of relative backwardness? Or because the class struggle was not waged with sufficient vigour? Surely the answer in both cases must be 'no'. Economic development, industrial growth, lead to a big increase in complexity, in the number of interconnections, in the range of products, in specialisation, in division of labour.

One must anticipate a major criticism: *socialism and the market are incompatible*. This view was that of Marx himself, and of Kautsky, Lenin and Bukharin. It is the opinion of Sweezy, Bettelheim and Mandel. The three last-named are willing to admit that market relations and money cannot just be 'abolished'; that for a time they are needed, but this would be a time of transition.

The disagreement here would centre on the possibility of overcoming the obstacles to the elimination of market relations without creating in the process a large, powerful, economically inefficient and socially dangerous bureaucratic hierarchy. That Soviet-type planning is associated with such a hierarchy, and that it is both inefficient and undesirable, would be accepted, indeed stressed by Sweezy, Bettelheim and Mandel.[1] So my disagreement with their position rests on the view, defended at length in the preceding pages, that no way exists to avoid the dominant role of the 'bureaucracy' unless one reduces the *functions* which give it power. To do so without granting autonomy to productive units and therefore without 'commodity production' and markets, is impossible. Equally impossible is to envisage participation, self-management in any meaningful form, unless this is linked with autonomy of the production units in which people work.

No, my imaginary critic will assert, this shows lack of understanding of industrial democracy. The 'associated producers' will decide. They are the consumers too, so of course they will decide with the needs of fellow-citizens in mind. Soviet experience (he may say) is irrelevant, because of the existence of an 'exploiting' elite, lack of true democracy, and so on. I can only continue to deplore the use of loose slogan-phraseology as a substitute for serious analysis. The real dogmatists would reject this reference to 'serious analysis' as unimaginative empiricism: 'revolutionary praxis' will show the way. What way? They do not know, and seem to have no particular interest in finding out.

The intelligent dogmatist would then direct his fire on weaknesses and inadequacies which certainly do exist in the market mechanism. He would refer to dangers of unemployment, of cyclical fluctuations, of excessive inequalities of income. He would note the growth of large corporations in capitalist countries, within which market relations are replaced by administrative subordination. He might note the advances and great potentialities of computerisation, the micro chip. Markets mean competition, and its negative features are there for all to see. Many effective critical points can be made along this line, without, unfortunately, grappling with the real question, which is: what alternative is there, what is being proposed? In any case, what is here advocated is not an untrammelled free market; a major role exists for planning. That strains and contradictions would arise on the boundary-line between plan and market, between central and local decisions, is indeed predictable, and quite unavoidable – as unavoidable as the fact that the interest and desires of one individual or group might conflict with those of others. If one were to define socialism in such a way that these conflicts and contradictions would not, *could* not, exist, then we are (in my opinion) back to utopia. Such a world appears to me inconceivable even beyond the time scale set here. Inconceivable and undesirable. What boredom, if we never argued!

Yes, the producer is also the consumer. But not (as a rule) of his or her own products. Radoslav Selucky pointed out the dilemma. In the centralised marketless economy, 'since every working man is simultaneously both a producer and a consumer, his economic essence is split in two parts; as a producer he reacts through his material interest in the targets of the plan, while as a consumer he tries to satisfy his material needs and interests through his effective demand'. Because of the many complexities and contradictions inherent in the marketless system, 'if as a producer he meets effective demand expressed by him as a consumer, he would behave against his interest as a producer'.[2] How, in practical terms, can one overcome this contradiction, in the absence of a market?

The dogmatist-critic must also clarify his attitude to autonomous small-scale activities. He may say that they will be uneconomic, and point to the elimination of small corner-shops by supermarkets in the USA, plus other instances of the concentration of capital. I would reply: Yes, it *may* be so, but it is not a matter of legislation, or of extra-economic coercion. Supermarkets did indeed displace the American corner shop, through competition. Socialist supermarkets might do the same. But one should not send the police to arrest the corner shopkeeper for trading, if he were filling gaps in state and socialised trade (and finds this profitable *because* these gaps exist). Of course, it is possible to *assume* that under socialism there will *be* no gaps; *ex ante* planning with perfect information and perfect motivation will take care of all needs. This is no more (and no less) far-fetched than some other asumptions made in orthodox economics. It still remains far-fetched and question-begging. There is indeed no need to consider how to identify and correct error, if error can be removed from the scene by assumption.

The notion of *scarcity* also might be attacked, and the possibility of meaningful abundance defended. That the present world wastes resources, not least on piling up armaments, is undeniable. But can anyone seriously assume the elimination of opportunity-cost, the unrestricted availability of all that people can reasonably want at zero price? Wants do expand, and not only because of advertising. Indeed, the socialists' very proper aim to improve the quality of life sets up additional demands for resources.

The critic may resurrect the notion of a New Man or New Woman, socialised, devoted to the common good. The trouble is that there is a link between this concept and that of abundance. In making choices between mutually exclusive alternatives, an unambiguous common good is operationally undefinable. Nor is there any approach along this line to the question of how to calculate, how to measure cost, how to relate it to result; and no attempt ever seems to be made to consider who is to perform these very necessary tasks, or how a decision once made is to be implemented. Again and again one must stress that three conditions must be met before anything can be done: *information* (what it is best to do, and how best to do it), *motivation* (why bother to do it) and *means*. None of us, however well-meaning and however much we love our fellow-citizens, can have more than a fraction of the vast range of information about economic and technological alternative courses of action. With the best of motives, we cannot act unless the means to do so can be acquired. These could have alternative uses, and in a non-market system they would have to be administratively allocated by some body (somebody) aware of what these might be.

The non-market system advocated by the left-wing critic is *more* hierarchical, more bureaucratic, more dangerous in the power it gives to the state and its high officials, than almost any conceivable alternative. Yet a likely critical line of attack would be to denounce me for imagining a socialism with a continuing distinction between rulers and ruled, that is, a vertical division of labour. There should be, there would have to be, a socialist organisation theory, concerned with the process of decision-making at various levels. The existence of levels, and so of the need for *some* hierarchy, are simple facts of life. Thus while a cargo ship will have within it a division of labour, which includes a captain and a chief engineer, it is evident that neither of these skilled individuals, or the crew, can possibly know where their ship should go. A shipping group, with someone in charge of it, would have the information about cargoes and the movements of other ships. Equally surely some responsible individual (who will not 'rotate' annually) will be in charge of the electricity grid, and someone will have to plan the construction and replacement of power stations, consider alternative locations and generation techniques, and so on. 'The people', or 'the associated workers' can no more do this than I can sing Wotan in Wagner's *Ring*. (Actually, this is a poor parallel. For I *could* sing Wotan, though very badly!) The slogan-statement that they can do so is quite literally meaningless, and this has nothing to do with the intelligence or motives of individuals. What I have tried to set out is a system in which the greatest possible amount of decision-making authority is devolved from the centre, in which hierarchies are multiple and so not all-pervasive, in which individuals or groups can opt out of the nationalised sector if they prefer it, ensuring a reasonable degree of choice for people both as consumers *and* as producers. At all levels the relationship between the organisers and the organised is indeed to be as democratic as the real situation allows. Macro plans would be approved by the elected parliament or assembly, and there would be self-management at micro level, though competition is needed to ensure 'automatic' responsibility to customers, to avoid the otherwise dangerous pursuit of sectional interest by abuse of monopoly power, and to ensure consumer choice. Policy with regard to income differentials, privileges and tax rates would be determined by democratic voting procedures, as would pensions and other social service expenditures. Abuses of power would be publicised by a free press. Political theory would naturally drop the inherently incorrect notion of the 'withering away of the state', and devote attention to the necessary 'separation of powers', checks and balances, countervailing powers, since eternal vigilance would indeed be necessary to minimise abuses that power over others makes possible.

But in the last analysis the intelligent dogmatist reviewer would simply have to rely on faith, faith in the ultimate realisation of Marx's dream of a just, conflict-less, worldwide society of equal citizens, who have conquered scarcity and who build the good life together without money, acquisitiveness, or rivalry. To me this smacks of religion, a kind of sophisticated cargo-cult. I am not by nature a religious man, and interpret 'praxis' as having a great deal to do with practice. Hence my concern with *feasible* socialism, and the constraint of feasibility predetermines one's definition of socialism and leads to a conscious rejection of romantic utopias. My critic will disagree. So be it.

One must also envisage an attack from a quite different quarter. One might see Lord Harris sharpening his sword at the Institute of Economic Affairs. Socialism is to be rejected, and a reasonable-sounding version is to be more vigorously condemned, since (it will be argued) it would surely degenerate into centralised tyranny, would in the end be 'the road to serfdom', as Hayek would certainly say, even though I would be credited with the good intention of avoiding such an outcome. Praise for private enterprise would be accompanied by warnings of dire consequences of an enlargement of the role of the state. Workers' self-management would be seen as ineffective, with references to Yugoslav experience and also to the attitudes and behaviour of trade unions, in Great Britain especially, where their negative attitude to technical progress and productivity is notorious. We might be reminded – and *correctly* reminded – of how the dockers succeeded in wrecking the port of London (and they are well on the way to destroying Liverpool too). Private enterprise would be extolled, its absence deplored. The many difficulties and contradictions which could certainly exist, and have been mentioned in this book, would be strongly emphasised, particularly the problems of risk capital, of reward for success and penalising of failure. There would be little enterprise, innovation would be resisted. Limitations on higher incomes would destroy incentives, discourage initiative, cause talent to emigrate. The mix between plan and market, the limitations on the latter, would not work, would be inconsistent with efficiency. And so on.

My reply would be along the following lines. In an age of giant corporations, the number of individuals who have the opportunity of showing enterprise, of participating in decision-making, is modest and declining. It may well be that, in the scheme here put forward, their number will actually increase. Perhaps a genuine private-enterprise competitive economy does have some advantages over this so-called 'feasible socialism', but what we actually have is very far removed from such an economy, for reasons which lie deep within the nature of the system. The tendency towards mergers, towards huge and potentially irresponsible multinationals, is as strong as ever, anti-trust legislation notwithstanding. Inflation and unemployment are not conducive to efficient resource utilisation. The combination of monetarism, powerful interest groups (among employers *and* unions) *and* modern technology could soon put a quarter of the labour force on the streets. As for the behaviour of the labour force, and of trade unions, this is indeed a vitally important question, but the evidence is not all one way. True, dockers did very seriously damage British ports, to the benefit of Rotterdam and Hamburg, but there were unions also in Rotterdam and Hamburg, proving that not all need be as myopic (and, frankly, stupidly conservative) as the British variety. It is possible that the blind pursuit of sectional interest will wreck a socialist economy, but it could wreck a capitalist economy too. Perhaps demands for higher wages would be less insistent if there were not constantly before the public eye some very rich individuals who did no work, or whose earnings were offensively disproportionate to the work they did do. The danger of some sort of populist tyranny cannot be ruled out, but Hitler rose to power in a capitalist state, and the economic system here proposed is far removed from the one which facilitated the rise of Stalinism. I would then return to the sort of arguments with which this book began.

Is the world of 'feasible socialism', even if feasible, in fact desirable? Opinions are bound to differ on this. Are there some alternatives which are more attractive, and are not utopian? (The Marxist vision is not more utopian than 'perfect competition'.) It may well be so. Critics, forward! You have nothing to lose but the chains that bind you to conventional thinking.

Notes: Appendix 2

1 See Paul Sweezy and Charles Bettelheim's discussion in numerous issues of *Monthly Review* and their other works, and the last chapters of E. Mandel, *Marxist Economic Theory* (London: Ink Links, 1968). Of course, they do not agree in their evaluation of other aspects of Soviet experience.

2 R. Selucky, *Marxism, Socialism and Freedom* (London: Macmillan, 1979), p. 39.

Appendix 3: A Note on Utopia

The terms 'utopia' and 'utopian' have been used pejoratively here, and applied to Marx's vision of socialism and to the ideas of some 'new leftists'. Some readers may be moved to protest, and their protest could be based on a different interpretation of the meaning of the word. It could be argued that all new ideas are 'utopian' when first put forward, because, when first put forward, they could not be applied in practice. Thus, for instance, 'votes for women' could be seen as a utopian notion in 1900. It is utopian (in this sense) to imagine British trade unions modernising their obsolete structures, or the Swiss altering their immigration laws, or the Soviet government today allowing an opposition candidate at an election. So interpreted, a hostile attitude to utopianism equals unimaginative conservatism. As the old academic satire put it: 'Nothing must ever be done for the first time.'

This, however, is not my meaning. Nor was it Marx's. When he contrasted socialism utopian with socialism scientific, he clearly had in mind that the former was some sort of idle dream, not based upon an analysis of realistically envisageable alternatives to an existing situation. Of course, as he said, 'the point . . . is to change it', but man is not free to devise any world of his own imagining. Some things will be impossible. However, even in 1900 women's franchise could not be and was not regarded as 'impossible', though it could not then be introduced. The proposal to make management responsible to an elected committee of workers may be undesirable, may be rejected, but it is not utopian. What *would* be utopian is to assume that such a committee would be concerned only for the common good, or that there would be no conflicts with other groups of citizens. Evidently, opinions can differ as to what should be regarded as impossible. Thus 'the lion shall lie down with the lamb' makes sense only in the context of supernatural religion (or unless one heavily drugs the lion!). But the line between realisable ideals and idle dreams is not always easy to draw.

Agnes Heller, in her interesting book,[1] notes Marx's silence on the rather important question of how 'everyone' (the 'associated producers') can take the necessary economic decisions, and remarks that this is 'no accident', because 'in his opinion the category of interest will be irrelevant to the society of the future, that there will therefore be no group interest or conflict of interest'. She goes on to cite Ernst Bloch's view that there are fertile and infertile utopias. 'There are many respects', she goes on, 'in which Marx's ideas on the society of associated producers are utopian, when measured against our own today and our own possibilities for action; these are none the less *fertile*. He established a norm against which we can measure the reality and value of our ideas.' The Polish thinker Bienkowski wrote: 'let us not reject the utopian Marxist vision: perhaps one day "commodities" and "money" will disappear'[2] (though of course he strongly criticises naive ultra-leftists who desire short cuts). I remain unconvinced. As argued already, while of course recognising the role and desirability of ideals, some of these utopian notions create dangerous illusion, confuse the mind. Let me illustrate with an example. A society without crime is a noble and worthy aim, and we should indeed strive to eliminate crime, and to look at data on murder, rape and burglary as deplorable instances of failure measured against the proper ideal – unattainable but the goal – which is constituted by their absence (and so long as they exist, no one would assert that we can do without police, locksmiths, etc.). However, the notion of society without conflict, in which (to cite Agnes Heller again) 'every individual strives for the same thing . . . every individual expresses the needs of all other individuals and it cannot be otherwise', is impossible (and even undesirable), in my view, and anyone holding such a belief about socialism is bound to be misled, and *dangerously* misled. A belief that crime can be eradicated can lead to action designed to eradicate crime, and such action, though unlikely to be wholly successful, can have positive effects. The belief that under socialism there would be unanimity is not just false; the only action it can give rise to is the *eradication of dissent*, the *imposition* of 'unanimity'. Similarly, the utopian view that power would not be abused, or that there would indeed *be* no power (no state, no need for bodies to mediate between individuals, groups and society, no function for specialists in management of any kind), actively prevents consideration of necessary means to prevent the abuse of (necessary) power, or of the institutional arrangements which could enlarge the area of genuine mass participation in decision-making. Marx's notion that capitalism can and must be replaced by 'a return to "archaic" types of communal ownership' (in one of his draft replies to Vera Zasulich) very properly leads Dora Shturman to exclaim that this represents an 'industrialised primitivism, which is older and simpler than *any* existing forms, including the most backward . . . And this movement *backwards* . . . is presented, in all propaganda-agitational output of Marxism, as a movement *forward!*'[3]

Why did Marx appear to be advocating the 'archaic' (and he even wrote: 'one should not be afraid of the word "archaic"')? Clearly this is because he held that primitive society was united and classless, with of course no division of labour, money, commodity production, or alienation. Marx and Engels considered that 'the main task of mankind is to return to the lost primitive-communist ideals on a new technological basis, not on a communal but on a worldwide scale'.[4] Bienkowski no doubt had the same point in mind when he wrote: 'Nearly all utopias, no matter how scientifically based, in their depiction of the future are unconscious dreams of a return to paradise . . . All of them aim, in one way or the other, to "put an end" to history, to plunge its processes again into an organic fusion of the individual and society.'[5] It is my contention that this kind of utopian thinking must actively mislead, must direct along irrelevant or dangerous roads, anyone who takes it seriously. Many have done so. Many still do so. It is no trivial matter.

Perhaps Bloch could be rephrased: there are harmless and harmful utopias.

Notes: Appendix 3

1   Agnes Heller, *The Theory of Need in Marx* (London: Allison & Busby, 1978), pp. 124–5, 130.
2   W. Bienkowski, *Theory and Reality* (London: Allison & Busby, 1981), p. 177.
3   Dora Shturman, *Nash novyi mir* (Jerusalem: Lexicon, 1981), p. 33. Her ideas and her critique are in many ways similar to those developed in the present work.
4   ibid., p. 23.
5   Bienkowski, op. cit. (n. 2), p. 96.

Name Index

Subject Index

plan targets *see* success indicators
Polish agriculture 141–4
Polish experience 97, 145–8, 179
politics (of reform) 176, 179
pollution 28, 69
  see also environmental protection
price control 102, 125, 160–2, 183, 193, 210
prices in foreign trade 108–9
prices, price mechanism 24, 28, 31, 71, 86,
  93–4, 97–103, 120–5, 131, 143, 179, 210
'prices of production' 25
priorities (of planners) 75
private enterprise (under socialism) 109–10,
  123, 141, 151, 200, 206–7
private plots (in collective farms) 89–90
privilege (in 'existing socialism') 78, 81, 106,
  112, 114, 127, 176–7
producers' preferences 129, 143, 199, 226–7
productive and unproductive labour 3, 35,
  57–8, 158, 212
productivity, relation to real wages 2, 156,
  159, 160, 213
profits, role of 31, 210–11
programming *see* mathematical methods
proletariat, role of (in Marx) 19, 55–8
  see also dictatorship of the proletariat

quality 43, 74, 169
quantitative planning 43, 74

racism 19, 62
'reductionism' 52, 62–3
reform proposals (of Soviet-type systems)
  99–101, 113, 124, 145, 151, 176–83
regional problems *see* planning, regional
religion (socialism as a) 13, 14, 42, 56, 63,
  228, 235
rent 27, 144, 213–14, 217, 221
rent control 161
responsibility 37, 48–9, 69, 95–215, 235
'revisionism' 118, 154
rotation (of leading posts) 50
ruling class 56, 81–2, 106

scale, diseconomies of 1, 19, 33, 70, 73, 77,
  87–8, 121, 142, 145, 199
scarcity 15–20, 44, 60, 225
'second economy' 78, 128–9, 131
selfishness 17
self-management 82, 121, 134–8, 182,
  217–21, 223
sellers' market, *see* shortages
shortages 5, 70–2, 74, 83, 111, 161, 182–3,
  193, 226
simplicity, of economic control under
  socialism 32–9, 59
socialism, definition of 1, 118, 227–8
'socialism in one country' 106, 113, 155
socialism, 'mature' 11, 52

socialist enterprises, proposed varieties of
  200–7
socialist ethics 123
'socially useful effect' 21, 28
social welfare function 28
'solidarity' (Solidarność) 146–7, 178
Soviet system, efficiency of 8, 34, 86
Soviet system, nature of 81–2
state, role of 50, 197, 229
'state capitalism' 81, 216
state, withering away of 10, 118, 235
subsidies 135, 161, 209, 210
'substitutionism' 56, 61
success indicators 73–5, 92
supply of materials 76–8, 179
  see also allocation
surplus, disposal of 212
systems analysis, *see* organization theory

taxation 144, 221
technical progress 15, 76–7, 112–24, 205
tokens, *see* vouchers
'tolkachi' 78
trade, foreign *see* foreign trade
trade, internal 109–10
trade unions, powers and role of 2, 84–5, 114,
  129, 146–7, 160, 172, 182, 216, 236
tradition, role and strength of 6, 112
transformation (of values) 21, 25–6, 213

unemployment 5, 6, 106, 129, 138–9, 159,
  174, 191, 200, 217, 234
unequal exchange 25, 108, 186–9
use-value 20–3, 32, 40, 98, 131, 211
utopia, utopianism 14, 20, 55, 118, 228,
  238–9

value of labour-power 31
value, law of (and socialism) 12–13, 20–32,
  58, 98–9, 199, 211–12
verification, need for 40
vouchers (replacement of money by) 11, 51,
  54

wage scales 83, 215–17, 221
wages system 51, 53, 55, 61, 160
  see also inequality, labour, wage scales
Wars of the Roses 19
wealth tax 158
women 57, 62–3, 84
workers' councils 134, 145
workers' power, *see* dictatorship of the
  proletariat
workers, real attitudes of 56–7
work-sharing 174

Yugoslav agriculture 141–2
Yugoslav experience 82, 133–41
  see also self-management

zero-sum game approach 4, 159, 173